HUMAN RIGHTS, INC.

JOSEPH R. SLAUGHTER

Human

RIGHTS, INC.

The World Novel, Narrative Form,
and International Law

FORDHAM UNIVERSITY PRESS

New York 2007

Library of Congress Cataloging-in-Publication Data

Slaughter, Joseph R.
Human Rights, Inc. : the world novel, narrative form, and
international law / Joseph R. Slaughter.—1st ed.
    p.   cm.
Includes bibliographical references and index.
ISBN 978-0-8232-2817-1 (cloth : alk. paper)—
ISBN 978-0-8232-2818-8 (pbk. : alk. paper)
1. Fiction—History and criticism.   2. Literature and
society.   3. Bildungsromans—History and criticism.
4. Human rights.   I. Title.
PN3491.S58   2007
808.3′93554—dc22

                                    2007039795

Printed in the United States of America
09 08 07   5 4 3 2 1
First edition

CONTENTS

ACKNOWLEDGMENTS

The seeds of this book have been germinating for close to a decade in my research, writing, and teaching on human rights and postcolonial literature, but *Human Rights, Inc.* takes the form it has here in the context of the late emergence of a nascent field that is beginning to sketch the parameters of interdisciplinary study of human rights and the humanities. This means that while the book is of recent origin, I have many intellectual debts to people and institutions who have made formative contributions to the evolution of my thinking on the subject of human rights and the world novel.

The impetus for this project developed from the vibrant intellectual climate of the Ethnic and Third World Literatures program at the University of Texas at Austin. I want to thank my colleagues, teachers, and friends at UT Austin, who challenged me not only with their questions about and commentary on my early work but with their own exemplary scholarship: Ben Lindfors, Mia Carter, César Salgado, Steven Ratner, Gerry Heng, Chris Hudson, Salah Hassan, Fran Buntman, Susan Harris, Zjaleh Hajibashi, Mary Harvan, Aime Ellis, Sandy Soto, Bret Benjamin, Jennifer Wenzel, Bill Holt, David Lapides, and Andy Stracharski. Special words of thanks must be reserved for Barbara Harlow, whose unflagging commitment to rigorous and engaged teaching, reading, and writing consistently pushed me to surpass myself and remains an influential model for my present and future work.

I have benefited immensely from the incisive comments, penetrating questions, trenchant criticisms, and encouragement of my colleagues in the Department of English and Comparative Literature at Columbia University: Gayatri Chakravorty Spivak, Marianne Hirsch, David Damrosch, Gauri Viswanathan, Bruce Robbins, Farah Griffin, Marcellus Blount, Jonathan Arac, Ann Douglas, Ursula Heise, Jean Howard, David Kastan, Julie Peters, Kathy Eden, Karl Kroeber, Ed Mendelson, Maura Spiegel, David Yerkes, Julie

Crawford, Ezra Tawil, and Jenny Davidson. The administrative staff in the department provided daily help: Joy Hayton, Michael Mallick, Maia Bernstein, and Isabel Thomson.

A visiting year at the University of Michigan gave me the opportunity to enter into sustained and stimulating conversation with many people while this book was in the early stages of writing. I especially want to thank Sidonie Smith, Yopie Prins, Patsy Yaeger, Jonathan Freedman, Tobin Siebers, David Halperin, Seanna Oakley, Josh Miller, Maria Cotera, Viv Soni, Miriam Ticktin, and the many other colleagues and students who listened to my public presentations and offered important complications to my ideas.

I have had the good fortune to present draft portions of this project in invited lectures and at numerous conferences (too many to name) where I have learned a great deal about my own book from my co-panelists and audience members. The participants in sessions at MLA, the American Comparative Literature Association, the Cultural Studies Association, and the African Literature Association deserve at least corporate mention. I want especially to thank the organizers of the Law and Humanities Junior Scholar Workshop for the opportunity to present at UCLA an early draft of the first chapter to a large group of smart, interdisciplinary-minded readers and auditors; in particular, I want to thank Katherine Franke, Julie Peters, Brenda Cossman, and Kirstie McClure for their insightful comments. At the ACLA, I was given the chance to present some of my ideas in a plenary session on human rights and comparative literature with Simon Gikandi, Domna Stanton, Gayatri Chakravorty Spivak, and Margaret Higonnet; that experience and the feedback from it have been invaluable. There are, of course, people who don't fall into the obvious groupings of thanks who have been immensely helpful in various ways: Marjorie Agosín, Emily Apter, Greg Mullins, Johannes Morsink, Bert Lockwood, Costas Douzinas, Susan Andrade, the folks at YBC. If I have inevitably missed anyone, I apologize sincerely.

I have to thank en masse (which misrepresents the enormous value of their intellectual stimulation) the many students at Columbia and the universities of Michigan, Montana, and Texas who have taken my courses on human rights and literature over the years and who have consistently pushed me to pursue my questions about the crucial intersections of law, politics, and narrative wherever they may lead; they constantly humble me with their excitement and remind me why ideas and arts matter. I have had excellent research assistance and general moral support from, among others, Melanie Micir, Josh Perlman, Shirley Wong, Amiel Melnick, and Bina Gogineni.

Portions of this book originally appeared as "Enabling Fictions and Novel Subjects: The *Bildungsroman* and International Human Rights Law" in *PMLA*; they are reprinted by permission of the copyright owner, The Modern Language Association of America. I want to thank the anonymous readers, the editorial board, and the editors at *PMLA* for their penetrating criticisms of my submission; in particular, I want to acknowledge Susan Fraiman and Eric Wirth. I also want to thank the anonymous manuscript readers for Fordham University Press, and the production staff who have skillfully shepherded this book into print: Nick Frankovich, Kathleen O'Brien, Margaret Noonan, Loomis Mayer, and Katie Sweeney. I want to thank William Kentridge for permission to reproduce "Blue Head" for the book's cover. I especially want to thank Helen Tartar for her immediate, enthusiastic, and continued belief in this project.

Academic debts are in some ways easy to acknowledge, since it is a relatively straightforward matter of recognizing the work of others; familial debts, because they are broader, deeper, richer, and more enduring, are harder to account for. I've been lucky to have a seemingly bottomless supply of moral, intellectual, and material support as well as inspiration from my family, all of whom have converged lately to find ourselves working, in our own ways and in our own fields, on similar issues of social justice. I can't thank them enough, and I want to let them know how much I love and admire them: Amy Slaughter, Kathleen McKenzie, William Slaughter, David Laffitte, Jeanie Slaughter, Richard and Louise Bell.

Finally, this book would have been impossible without the critical and emotional support of Jenny Wenzel. My constant conspirator and companion, Jenny has been my closest ear and keenest eye, my best reader and my harshest critic. Although there are certainly sentences (perhaps pages) in this book that you would still push me to express better, its quality is a measure not only of your exacting standards but of your sustaining faith in the project and my capacity to see it through; thank you . . .

HUMAN RIGHTS, INC.

The Legibility of Human Rights

Whereas recognition of the inherent dignity and of the equal and inalienable rights of all members of the human family is the foundation
of freedom, justice and peace in the world, . . .

Whereas Member States have pledged themselves to achieve, in cooperation with the United Nations, the promotion of universal respect for and observance of human rights and fundamental freedoms,

Whereas a common understanding of these rights and freedoms is
of the greatest importance for the full realization of this pledge,

Now, Therefore THE GENERAL ASSEMBLY proclaims THIS
UNIVERSAL DECLARATION OF HUMAN RIGHTS as a com-
mon standard of achievement for all peoples and all nations, to the
end that every individual and every organ of society, keeping this
Declaration constantly in mind, shall strive by teaching and education
to promote respect for these rights and freedoms and by progressive
measures, national and international, to secure their universal and effective recognition and observance, both among the peoples of Member States themselves and among the peoples of territories under their
jurisdiction.

—PREAMBLE, Universal Declaration of Human Rights, 1948

All that this document requires therefore is simply that it be rendered
in all the accessible languages of all societies; then let every sentient
member of society weigh its claims against the excuses of dictatorships, intolerance, [and] discrimination.

—WOLE SOYINKA, Nigerian Nobel
Laureate for Literature

I

"Everyone knows, or should know, why human rights are important," writes John Humphrey, Canadian legal scholar and first director of the United Nations Human Rights Division, in a commemorative essay on the fortieth anniversary of the adoption of the Universal Declaration of Human Rights (UDHR) by the UN General Assembly on 10 December 1948.[1] Almost unfailingly, books about international human rights open with one of two seemingly contradictory grandiloquent claims about their importance. The triumphalist version proclaims that human rights law and discourse have at last achieved some form of worldwide normativeness, and that we are now living in the Age of Human Rights. The cautionary version soberly reminds us of the continued poignancy of human rights by noting the global increase of human rights violations over the course of the twentieth century. The difference between the two claims is not a matter of historical accuracy; both reflect facets of the contemporary international condition of human rights. Human rights discourse and law have indeed achieved rhetorical, juridical, and political hegemony in international affairs, but such triumphalist narratives about the virtue of human rights extol legal normalization itself as a sign of humanity's advancement rather than as a probable symptom of its continued benightedness.[2] Human rights thus triumph in their apparent banality, but this progress narrative also tends to disregard the fact that human rights violations—like the international law designed to prevent them—have become increasingly systematic, corporate, and institutional. Even more troubling, the banalization of human rights means that violations are often committed in the Orwellian name of human rights themselves, cloaked in the palliative rhetoric of humanitarian intervention, the chivalric defense of women and children, the liberalization of free markets, the capitalist promise of equal consumerist opportunity, the emancipatory causes of freedom and democracy, etc. Thus the discursive victory of human rights means that ours is at once the Age of Human Rights and the Age of Human Rights Abuse.

Humphrey obliquely invokes both the triumphalist and the monitory versions of such claims in five deceptively simple words: "everyone knows, or should know." His article is not simply a paean to the Universal Declaration; rather, his ironic opening words subtly suggest a number of paradoxes and anxieties about human rights that characterize the articulation of universal principles generally and the legislation of human rights in particular. This referential discrepancy arises from a historical disconnect between the world that the law imagines, or images, in principle and the one that it addresses in fact—between the ideal and the real. Human rights speak the language of universalism and absolutes: "All human beings are born free and equal in dignity and rights" (UDHR Article 1); "Everyone has the right to recognition everywhere as a person before the law" (Article 6); "Everyone has duties to the community in which alone the free and full development of his personality is possible" (Article 29). Human rights are ostensibly inherent and inalienable, deducible, as French philosopher and UNESCO consultant on the UDHR, Jacques Maritain, wrote in 1943, *"from the simple fact that man is man."*[3] Despite the language of simplicity and obviousness that pervades human rights commentary, not every "man" recognizes (or is in a position to recognize) that "simple fact" in a concrete, practicable, or justiciable way. Humphrey's paradox intimates the basic historical and rhetorical condition of contemporary human rights law, which necessarily presupposes the universality of the tautological, commonsense principles it aspires to universalize to make Maritain's man man. This book will argue that the gap between what everyone knows and what everyone should know poses human rights as a question of both literacy and legislation, as much matters of literature as of law.

Human Rights, Inc. is a book about the legibility of human rights; about the literary, political, and juridical effects of transcribing into international legal conventions what the ancient Greeks regarded as unwritten law; about the tensions and gap between what everyone knows and what everyone should know; about how norms of legal obviousness manifest in literary forms; and about how, in an era of intense globalization, those legal and literary forms cooperate to disseminate and legitimate the norms of human rights, to make each other's common sense legible and compelling. More specifically, this book is about the sociocultural, formal, historical, and ideological conjunctions between human rights and the novel, particularly the coming-of-age genre, the *Bildungsroman*, whose plot we could provisionally gloss as the didactic story of an individual who is socialized in the process of learning for oneself what everyone else (including the reader) presumably already knows.

This book elaborates the conceptual vocabulary, deep narrative grammar, and humanist social vision that human rights law shares with the *Bildungsroman* in their cooperative efforts to imagine, normalize, and realize what the Universal Declaration and early theorists of the novel call "the free and full development of the human personality." This goal is part of the UDHR's larger intention to facilitate "the advent of a world in which human beings shall enjoy freedom of speech and belief and freedom from fear and want" (Preamble). Tracking the formula of free and full human personality development in literature and the law—and in literary and legal theory—allows me to excavate a neglected discursive genealogy of human rights that intersects with German idealism and its particular nomination of the bourgeois white male citizen to universal subject. This book traces an ideological confluence between the technologies of the novel and the law that manifests in a common vocabulary and transitive grammar of human personality development, which are themselves related strains of a more general, hegemonic discourse of development. The novel genre and liberal human rights discourse are more than coincidentally, or casually, interconnected. Seen through the figure and formula of human personality development central to both the *Bildungsroman* and human rights, their shared assumptions and imbrications emerge to show clearly their historical, formal, and ideological interdependencies. They are mutually enabling fictions: each projects an image of the human personality that ratifies the other's idealistic visions of the proper relations between the individual and society and the normative career of free and full human personality development.

As sweeping as these claims may seem, this book is in fact rather narrowly focused on the shared image of the human person and its development in the *Bildungsroman* and in human rights legislation. The *Bildungsroman* is not the only cultural form that cooperates with human rights, nor is it the only form through which human rights may be imagined or the literary image of the human rights person might be projected.[4] Other cultural forms certainly interact with, and likely make imaginable alternative visions of, human rights, but the *Bildungsroman* is exemplary in the degree to which its conventions overlap with the image of human personality development articulated by the law. Human rights law and the *Bildungsroman* are consubstantial and mutually reinforcing, but their sociocultural and historical alliance is neither unproblematic nor uncomplicated. Both human rights and the novel have been part of the engine and freight of Western colonialism and (neo)imperialism over the past two centuries. Like "the cultural institution of the novel," human rights law "legitimates particular forms and subjects of history and subjugates or erases others."[5] Thus this book's approach is Janus-faced: Beyond elaborating the sociohistorical cooperation and formal intersections of the *Bildungsroman* and human rights as extensions of the Enlightenment project to modernize, normalize, and civilize (or, perhaps better, civicize) the individual and society, it also examines the problems that such complicity creates, particularly with the *Bildungsroman*'s ambivalent capacity to disseminate and naturalize not only the norms of human rights but also the paradoxical practices, prejudices, and exclusions codified in the law. Some of these complications are forecast in the notion of "enabling fiction" that I adapt from Rita Felski's feminist critique of the Habermasian liberal public sphere—that vaunted realm of democratic group-will formation whose "ideal of a free discursive space that equalizes all participants . . . engenders a sense of collective identity but is achieved only by obscuring actual material inequalities and political antagonisms among its participants."[6]

Human rights' enabling fiction expresses certain laudable aspirations in its projection of an "egalitarian imaginary," but the revolutionary rhetoric of liberty, equality, and fraternity obscures the character of its implementation in "practices and discourses bearing new forms of inequality" as it becomes the hegemonic "common sense" of "liberal-democratic ideology."[7] Yet the discourse of common sense becomes available for appropriation and transformative rearticulation of the egalitarian imaginary by historically marginalized subjects (e.g., women and members of racial, religious, sexual, and class minorities) not comprehended practically within its original enabling fiction. That is, the projection of a normative egalitarian imaginary not only sets the terms and limits of universality's constituency, it makes possible nonhegemonic rearticulations of universality's compass. Thus I am interested not only in the imbrications and normativeness of the forms, institutions, and structures that literature and law project to imagine an international social order of human rights based on the equality and dignity of the human personality, but also in the problems their complicity creates and in the ruptures, paradoxes, impossible figures, and bizarre temporalities that emerge from human rights' enabling (and necessary) fiction that "man (sic) is man (sic)."

Therefore this book does not offer a euphoric celebration of human rights as just the thing that the world needs now; nor a defense of the sentimental power of literature "to make us see the lives of the different with . . . involvement and sympathetic understanding," to "cultivat[e] our humanity" and the civic habits necessary for "world citizenship," as Martha Nussbaum proposes in phrases traceable to the Stoic traditions of cosmopolitanism and the German idealist formulations of *Bildung*—"the free development of the human passions . . . [that] lead[s] to a harmonious personality and to harmonious co-operation between free men."[8] Nonetheless, I share a cautious critical commitment to those humanist ideals and a qualified belief that everyone should know why human rights are important, that we do need a little human rights just now, and that literature does have a capacity to minister to that need. Nobel Prize-winning Nigerian poet, playwright, and social critic, Wole Soyinka, introduced the publication of a 1994 Yoruba translation of the UDHR with the earnest claim that "All that this document requires therefore is simply that it be rendered in all the accessible languages of all societies." In Soyinka's optimistic appraisal, translation alone is all that is needed to release the hegemonizing force of common sense, to transform what everyone should know into what everyone does know. In most of these rhetorical appeals to common sense, both the human and the rights belonging to it are presumed to be known in advance of their articulation in language and their transcription (or translation) into legal conventions. But the legislative history and practice of human rights shows that "to secure their universal and effective recognition and observance" (UDHR) is not just a simple matter of writing down the unwritten ethereal principles of obviousness;[9] rather, it requires the collaboration of writers like Soyinka and the cooperation, or complicity, of literary and cultural forms to make the common sense of human rights norms both legible and legislatable, imaginable and articulable.

Common Assumptions and Crucial Concepts: Reading Across Disciplines

Writing about what everyone already knows presents a challenge, and in many ways my two primary topics—human rights and the

Bildungsroman—could not be better known. Indeed, it seems likely that everyone already knows what human rights, dignity, and personality are, even if few share the dominant technical and institutional vocabulary in which they are articulated by international law. Similarly, every reader of literature surely knows a coming-of-age story when they see it, even if few share the critical and theoretical vocabulary of a *Bildungsroman* specialist. The general conceptual language of human rights and the *Bildungsroman* seem to be ubiquitous in our conversations about society, law, and literature. But there is something peculiar about these two discourses; as I argue throughout this book, both human rights law and the *Bildungsroman* developed as technologies for making common sense commonsensical, for making what is already known effective. This confluence of form and function—and the ubiquity of the two discursive technologies—makes it especially important to question what we presumably already know, to examine how what we know comes to be taken for granted (of how our assumptions become assumable), and to track the operation of the obvious and its manifestation in particular forms and functions.

I am interested in the *Bildungsroman* as the generic name of a kind of literary social work—a function (or practice) that articulates certain social relations—rather than as the name of a typologically consistent literary artifact that is imagined to have remained uniform since its fabled emergence in eighteenth-century Germany. Strict typological studies of the genre claim that, far from being a common and constant literary form—a coherent idealist strain of the realist novel—the *Bildungsroman* was a historical "phantom" of which few "true" examples ever existed, a retrospective invention of nineteenth-century historicist scholars.[10] But if, as Roberto Schwarz has argued, "forms are the abstract of specific social relations," then we might see the *Bildungsroman* genre as a novelistic correlative to the socializing project of human rights law that, nonetheless, has certain generalizable formal manifestations, literary codes, and conventional tendencies that link many eighteenth- and nineteenth-century European novels with their contemporary postcolonial counterparts.[11] Examining the genre's social function helps avoid the pitfalls of speaking about the imbrications of literature and the law as a series of unilateral (or even bilateral) causal relations; from the perspective of their cooperative social work, the correspondences and interdependencies of the *Bildungsroman* and human rights law amount to a network of conceptual, lexical, and grammatical intersections within the larger discourse of human development and emancipation.

I do not assume that all of my readers are familiar with the disciplinary languages and approaches of literary and legal studies that I employ, and so I want to make clear some of the assumptions that underwrite my analysis and critical methodology. I take for granted—although I aim to show how—that law and literature are discursive regimes that constitute and regulate, imagine and test, kinds of subjects, subjectivities, and social formations; that they are "machines for producing [and governing] subjectivity" and social relations (to modify Fredric Jameson's characterization of the *Bildungsroman*).[12] In the fields of legal studies and political science, Wendy Brown formulates this idea as a conclusion about human rights, which, she argues, "produce and regulate the subjects to whom they are assigned."[13] This constitutive thesis—a staple of analysis for Critical Legal Studies, Critical Race Theory, Feminist Jurisprudence, and "Legal Storytelling" practitioners[14]—recognizes that the law is not simply a reactive construct reflecting material conditions and social practices that exist prior to the law; rather, the law is itself an interventionist, positive force that "call[s] into being, and enable[s], particular forms and expressions of personhood"—as well as the social relations in which those forms find expression—that it pretends merely to describe.[15] In the preambular language of the UDHR, "the rule of [international] law" seeks as much to promote as to protect the human rights it enumerates. Beginning with the idea that the law constitutes what it regulates, I explore constitution and regulation as they operate in legal and literary forms and formations to incorporate the kinds of humans that can serve as subjects of rights.

The constitutive thesis is indebted to Michel Foucault's insights about the discursive workings of power and the constitution of the modern individual subject, which he understands to be "an effect of power, and at the same time, or more precisely to the extent to which it is that effect, it is the element of its articulation."[16] Most of Foucault's work attempts to describe the epistemic and social transformation of power during Europe's transition to modernity, when the feudal authority of the sovereign (King, God, Father, etc.)

gave way to a dissemination of personal sovereignty in the individualized, disciplinary routines of self-regulation that are constitutive
of the modern subject itself. Foucault's consistent emphasis on the
creative, rather than the overtly coercive, dynamics of power in
some ways corrects blindnesses in Louis Althusser's work, but it
nonetheless derives its explanatory force from the double meaning
of "subject" that informs Althusser's theory of interpellation: "In
the ordinary use of the term, subject in fact means: (1) a free subjectivity, a centre of initiatives, author of and responsible for its actions; (2) a subjected being, who submits to a higher authority, and
is therefore stripped of all freedom except that of freely accepting
his submission."[17] For Althusser, this double meaning explains and
extends the paradox of the modern civil subject who, as Jean-
Jacques Rousseau provocatively declared, is forced to be free: "The
individual *is interpellated as a (free) subject in order that he shall submit
freely to the commandments of the Subject.*" In terms of human rights
law, as I show explicitly in chapter 3, to become a subject (a freely
and fully developed person) within a particular sociopolitical formation is to be capable of fully exercising the rights enabled by that
formation, which entails, at the same time, a "free" submission to
its norms.

The movement of the subject from pure subjection to self-regulation describes the plot trajectory of the dominant transition narrative of modernization, which both the *Bildungsroman* and human
rights law take for granted and intensify in their progressive visions
of human personality development. This story of modernization is
typically depicted as the course of human emancipation—for humanity in general and repeated in the life of each individual—that
follows the path of Kant's Enlightenment, in which mankind's release "from its self-incurred immaturity . . . is nearly inevitable, if
only it is granted freedom."[18] It has become natural to think of
individual and collective human development in terms of this progress narrative of liberation; even the multiple definitions for the
word "freedom" in the *Oxford English Dictionary* are "plotted" (the
OED's word) teleologically, to track "the development of one
meaning from another," as the individual's progressive liberation
from a malignant regulatory regime and its incorporation into a
benign one:[19]

freedom: 1. a. Exemption or release from slavery or imprisonment; personal liberty. . . . 2. Exemption from arbitrary, despotic, or autocratic control; independence; civil liberty. . . . 4. a. The state of being able to act without hindrance or restraint, liberty of action. . . . 13. The right of participating in the privileges attached to: a. membership *of* a company or trade; b. citizenship *of* a town or city.

Thus, in its definitions for "freedom," the *OED* tells the short story of liberation that both human rights and the *Bildungsroman* amplify, plotting a process of incorporation by which the individual is constituted and regulated as a creature of freedom, emancipated from "the pained and minimally sensate existence of the slave to the burdened individuality of the responsible and encumbered freedperson,"[20] a creature capable of bearing rights and duties—in a word, a person.

The homologue in literary studies to the jurisprudential constitutive thesis underpins most sociological accounts of genre, which this book also offers. Just as the law is not simply a reactive institution that codifies existing social relations, literature is not simply a medium for re-presenting those formations. In his influential essay, "Literature as Equipment for Living" (1938), Kenneth Burke outlined a method for "sociological criticism" that would analyze how a work of art (his literary atom was the proverb, a form and semiotic unit quite similar to the legal tautology) "singles out a pattern of experience that is sufficiently representative of our social structure, that recurs sufficiently often *mutatis mutandis*, for people to 'need a word for it' and to adopt an attitude towards it."[21] Burke suggested that literature provides a shorthand for things that everyone already knows, giving a name to common sense and experience. Raymond Williams complicated the common perception that literature merely reflects life, arguing that cultural forms are not simply derivative from social formations: a "formal innovation is a true and integral element of [social] changes themselves."[22] To be explicit, my general assumption about literary forms is that genres emerge and become conventional (both publicly common and formally regular) to the extent that they make collectively legible—if sometimes distorted—both actual and possible (desirable and undesirable) social formations and relations. In other words, literary and cultural forms (like legal forms) do not simply reflect the social world. They in some ways also constitute and regulate it "when they respond to . . . [and] resolve" what Margaret Cohen (after Pierre Bourdieu) calls "the space of possibles";[23] they help shape how the social order and its subjects are imagined, articulated, and effected. In this sense, my project shares Jameson's disregard for "the convenient working distinction between cultural texts that are social and political and those that are not."[24] Neither does it subscribe to the common distinction between literature and law that understands the former merely to describe what (and while) the latter does. I study human rights and literature as discourses, not as practices per se—although I believe my analysis has implications for human rights practice, if only because discourse is a field of possibilities within which any practice is undertaken. Given their mutual discursive engagements with society, I take it for granted that the social work of literature and the cultural work of law are "interdependent and interrelated,"[25] and elucidating the particular ways contemporary human rights law and the *Bildungsroman* make human rights legible is the aim of this book. My argument that law favors and enables some narrative plots and literary genres over others might be less surprising to some of my readers than my complementary claim that literature has historically favored and enabled some formulations of the law.

Human Rights Paradoxes: The Nonsense in Common Sense

> Human rights have 'only paradoxes to offer'; their energy comes from their aporetic nature.
>
> —COSTAS DOUZINAS, *The End of Human Rights*

If human rights law represents the transcription of precepts about the human personality that everyone already knows, then the act of knowing (like that of legislating) is disappointing in its feeble ability to translate knowledge into outrage, action, or even acknowledgment.[26] We know, as I write this, that the government-sponsored Janjaweed militias are conducting genocide against black African residents in the Darfur region of Sudan, but not only do we do little about it, we—as individuals, nations, and United Nations—mostly refuse to speak its proper name, to convert the knowledge of pogroms into official, and actionable, acknowledgment of genocide.

We knew that the Taliban were a violent and repressive regime, especially toward women, but we did not acknowledge that fact until we needed a humanitarian rationale for prosecuting the so-called War on Terror in Afghanistan. More perversely, we Americans somehow manage collectively *not to know* that we are torturing (or outsourcing the torture of) "enemy combatants"—a pseudo-legal designation that places the individual outside the realm of legal personality and rights—at Guantánamo Bay and elsewhere. Even when everyone knows what they should know, "most people clearly do not react as human rights organizations would like them to. The message . . . moves them—but not necessarily into doing what they 'should.' "[27] The knowledge paradox that Cohen and Seu analyze in their study of the reception and perception of human rights appeals is just one of many to which human rights seem perpetually disposed.

Paradox is the rhetorical form of self-contradiction that challenges received opinion and disturbs the hermeticism of tautological self-evidence to report that, despite appearances, man may not in all cases be man. Paradox publicizes the nonsense in common sense, the unorthodox within orthodoxy. "The whole field of human rights is characterised by paradoxes and aporias,"[28] observes legal scholar Costas Douzinas, but perhaps the most influential and trenchant paradox was identified in Hannah Arendt's study of the condition of statelessness in Europe between the two World Wars:

> If a human being loses his political status, he should, according to the implications of the inborn and inalienable rights of man, come under exactly the situation for which the declarations of such general rights provided. Actually, the opposite is the case. It seems that a man who is nothing but a man has lost the very qualities which make it possible for other people to treat him as a fellow-man.[29]

As Edmund Burke did before her, Arendt concludes that human rights are, in practice if not in principle, not the natural rights of humans *qua* humans but the positive rights of citizens. Karl Marx identified this condition a century earlier as the consequence of the eighteenth-century bourgeois revolutionary declarations of rights and legislated in the very title of the French *Déclaration des Droits de l'Homme et du Citoyen*, which, he argued, bifurcated and "reduc[ed] man, on the one hand, to a member of civil society, to an egoistic, independent individual, and, on the other hand, to a citizen, a juridical person."[30]

In the tradition of Arendt, Marx, and Burke, human rights critics and advocates alike have made an industry of exposing such paradoxes to challenge the legitimacy and egalitarian imaginary of human rights, and to publicize the discrepancy between their universalist rhetoric and actual practice. Such efforts to deploy the "politics of shame" by, and in behalf of, those "suffering the paradoxes of rights" are clearly necessary, but they are also not sufficient or reliable in eliciting their desired ameliorative response.[31] These strategies often underappreciate how inequality has defined the human rights regime and how the regime's discourse, and the *Bildungsroman* form that helps to naturalize it, tends to normalize paradox. As politically strategic as the use of embarrassment may be, such efforts tend to ignore or forget the degree to which the meaning and efficacy of human rights have historically depended upon specific (though changing) paradoxical "exclusions [that] are *constitutive* of the 'neutral' universality of human rights," as Slavoj Žižek has noted.[32] Instead of merely exposing the hypocrisy of rights, our analyses (both literary and sociopolitical) need to go beyond the point at which this revelation is expected to shame governments or embarrass human rights discourse itself; we need to ask, with Wendy Brown,

> How might paradox gain political richness when it is understood as affirming the impossibility of justice in the present and as articulating the conditions and contours of justice in the future? How might attention to paradox help formulate a political struggle for rights in which they are conceived . . . as articulating through their instantiation what equality and freedom might consist in that exceeds them? In other words, how might the paradoxical elements of the struggle for rights in an emancipatory context articulate a field of justice beyond 'that which we cannot not want?'[33]

From the rhetorical force of paradox, Brown's questions distill a future-oriented human rights project that seeks what is beyond the contradictory conditions of (in)justice now. If we recognize paradox's figurative role in human rights instead of treating it as a shameful limitation of human rights discourse and practice, then we can attend to its productive possibilities. Such a project must consider not only the content of human rights law and discourse but also its logical and rhetorical forms—from which, as I show, the content is in fact inseparable—as well as the cultural forms of common sense that cooperate to sustain and substantiate the law's modes of production. Recognizing that forms and formations matter in the human rights project, we can begin to respond to Giorgio Agamben's provocation: "What is the *form of life* . . . that corresponds to the *form of law*?"[34]

Forms of Law: Positivizing Nature

In declaring itself to be a statement of "common understanding" (what everyone knows) that also represents a "common standard of achievement for all peoples and all nations" (what everyone should know), the UDHR formalized Humphrey's paradox in the text of human rights law itself. Rhetorically, human rights are an inventory of axioms about what it means to be human that everyone presumably already knows; practically, it is necessary to admit that, at the very best, they constitute what everyone should know. This tension between a given universality and a sociocultural particularity to be universalized sustains the textual logic of international human rights law, which announces itself simultaneously as a speech act of recognition—simply an acknowledgment of ostensibly natural truths about the human—and as a speech act of declaration that intends to effect the right of everyone "to recognition everywhere as a person before the law" (UDHR). "The rights of man," observes Claude Lefort, "are declared, and they are declared as rights that belong to man; but, at the same time, man appears through his representatives as the being whose essence it is to declare his rights . . . . Rights are not simply the object of a declaration, it is their essence to be declared."[35] Although human rights are presupposed to be self-evident, they must be publicly and officially articulated as such, named as self-evident to be made self-evident. As I elaborate in chapter 1, contemporary human rights law is a generic hybrid: the legislative act of naming what should not be necessary to name positivizes nature, formally positioning international human rights law between natural law (transcendental precepts that presumably go without saying and whose classical literary heroine is Sophocles' Antigone) and positive law (the civil code that obsessively recites its sovereign commandments and whose classical villain is Creon).

The potted history of modern human rights, repeated by the drafters of the UDHR themselves, plots the story of their legislation as an evolutionary process that begins with the revolutionary declarations of the European Enlightenment and culminates in the contemporary international human rights regime. Indeed, the UDHR implicitly evokes this progress narrative in its anticipation of humankind's triumph over "barbarous acts which have outraged the conscience of mankind" with "the promotion of universal respect for and observance of human rights and fundamental freedoms." However, written in the aftermath of World War II, "when faith in the Enlightenment faced its deepest crisis in confidence," the rhetoric of the declaration betrays an anxiety about the confident teleology of civilization.[36] The recent experience of the Holocaust and the two World Wars provided the most spectacular illustration of the failures of the Enlightenment in the very places where it was said to have been achieved. The UDHR is a tacit acknowledgment of those failures, even as it recuperates from the natural law tradition what Costas Douzinas (after Ernst Bloch) calls marvelously its "promise of the 'not yet,'" the promise of an Enlightenment still to come.[37]

The spiritual debt of twentieth-century human rights to the eighteenth-century revolutionary declarations is often converted, however, into a singular line of direct descent. Czech jurist Karel Vasak's influential reading of the history of human rights organizes their development into "three generations" that align with the "three normative themes of the French Revolution": "the first generation of civil and political rights (*liberté*); the second generation of economic, social, and cultural rights (*égalité*); and the third generation of newly called solidarity rights (*fraternité*)."[38] Vasak's heuristic has been mythologized to describe a smooth evolution of human rights legislation from the eighteenth to the twentieth centuries; it has also regularly been invoked to celebrate the UN's legislative activity as a process of consensus-building, and to naturalize, as part of a telos of human progress, the West's prioritization of civil and political rights over social, economic, cultural, environmental, and solidarity rights. Although the generational schema comprehends certain international legislative trends, it is misleading when used to plot a neat, Eurocentric genealogy of contemporary human rights, or to intimate that civil and political rights are (and always have been) divisible from and more fundamental than social, cultural, and economic rights.

As I illustrate in the first two chapters of this book, there are at least as many conceptual, political, historical, and formal differences as there are similarities between eighteenth- and twentieth-century human rights legislation. To keep these differences in view, I maintain Indian legal scholar Upendra Baxi's important distinction between "modern" human rights (those articulated in the language of natural law after the American and French revolutions) and "contemporary" human rights (those positivized in international legal instruments by the UN and regional organizations after World War II).[39] Baxi's critiques offer important correctives to the myopic, Eurocentric "view of [the] authorship of human rights" by appropriately recognizing the "creationist role" that "resistance to power" has historically played in the legislation of human rights—both in Europe in the eighteenth century and after WWII, and in the Third World's struggles against European imperialism.[40] Indeed, while the aspirational tone of the UDHR was penned by a UN that was dominated by imperial and colonial European powers, subsequent international declarations and covenants reflect the crucial contributions and priorities of newly independent states—states that comprised at least a nominal majority at the UN by the early 1960s, soon after the Third World delegations successfully pressed for the adoption of the Declaration on the Granting of Independence to Colonial Countries and Peoples (1960) that formally closed the modern era of high colonialism. When I use the phrase "human rights," I do not imagine that discourse of negative liberty, promoted by Michael Ignatieff, which has been largely unresponsive to alternative visions of rights.[41] Thus, throughout this book, I treat contemporary human rights law neither as a Eurocentric monolith nor as a romanticized jurisprudence of the oppressed; rather, I treat it as a complex of contested—and often contradictory—principles still in formation, whose fissures, discontinuities, and inconsistencies are both the source of its continued emancipatory potential and the evidence for the strong possibility that, when members of the international community contemplated human rights, *everyone* had something else in mind.

Forms of Life: Incorporating the Human Rights Person(ality)

> The declaration would pave the way to a new era of international solidarity, because the basis of rights was neither the State nor the individual, but the social human being, participating in social life, and striving for national and international co-operation.
>
> —LAKSHMI MENON, Indian delegate to the UN, 1948

The drafters of the UDHR took it for granted that their subject of central concern was the human person, and that the law should stipulate the fundamental civil, social, and political protections and privileges necessary for the "free and full development of the human personality." Such a focus may seem unremarkable, commonsensical even, but in a document in which the nuances of every word were debated and revised by the delegations of fifty-eight states over the course of three years of drafting, the formula of personality development remains remarkably stable. I examine the reasons for, as well as the implications and aporias of, this consensus in considerable detail in the first chapter, but I can provisionally note that the language of personality development had a popular and academic cosmopolitan currency among lawyers, literati, and others committed to an international bill of rights in the mid-1940s that perhaps it does not enjoy today. This book elaborates the "image of the person"[42]—the moral creature capable of bearing rights and duties—projected by both law and literature. "Person" is a literary and legal moral category derived from two distinct, though related, Roman traditions: the theatrical (in which *persona* named the mask worn by an actor) and the juridical (where *persona* denoted the capacity of a legal subject to be represented, or to make representations, within the legal system).[43] In the first two chapters, I explain that "personality" is not the thick, multi-faceted differential category of individual identity and self-expression contemplated in psychology and popular culture (although it inevitably has something to do with those). It is not the name of individual, irreducible difference but of sameness, the collection of common modalities of the human being's extension into the civil and social order. "Personality" is a technical term that means the quality of being equal before the law—to put it tautologically, the quality of being a person. It is the basis of the law's symmetrical disposition to each human being. Thus, "person" is the legal vehicle of human dignity, what is common to each of us as social human beings and as theoretically equal subjects—subjects of legal and literary interest like any other, possessing equal capacity to be represented within the law and literature.

Modern eighteenth-century human rights law articulated an image of the person as a natural moral creature, whose insuperable dignity followed from the Kantian supposition that human beings were inherently rational and therefore inherently dignified: "rational beings are called *persons* because their nature already marks them out as an end in itself, that is, as something that may not be used merely as a means."[44] "Person" is the legal category that gives abstract moral dignity its justiciable effect and social consequence.[45] Contemporary human rights law draws upon this tradition when it reaffirms its "faith . . . in the dignity and worth of the human person" (UDHR), but it also implicitly engages the nineteenth-century positivist legal tradition that vested the business corporation with legal personality.[46] Thus, "person" is a "legal abstraction,"[47] an amalgam of civil, moral, social, and political capacities that may mean, as John Dewey complained in 1926, "whatever the law makes it mean; . . . [it] might be used simply as a synonym for a right-and-duty-bearing unit. Any such unit would be a person; such a statement would be truistic, tautological. Hence it would convey no implications, except that the unit has those rights and duties which the courts find it to have."[48] While the person may exist as a legal fiction, an entity "only in contemplation of the law," legislation is not the whole story;[49] "person" also signifies whatever culture makes it signify.

The subtle displacement of the human being by the person in the UDHR all but eliminated "human" as a substantive noun from the text of human rights law, as a proper grammatical subject of universal human rights.[50] Indeed, in the postwar, proto–Cold War debates about the shape and scope of human rights leading to the UDHR, the term "person" became a kind of mask for the human, a rhetorical feint for not naming the human itself as a question. In the 1980s and 90s the legal image of the person resurfaced as the central point of conflict in the cultural relativist–universalist debates, both sides of which proffered, for opposing strategic reasons, an interpretation of the human rights person as a "libertarian . . .

atomized individual . . . possessed of certain inalienable rights by nature" that is foreign to "traditional [communitarian and/or authoritarian] cultures."[51] But as I demonstrate throughout this book, the image of the unitary, monadic, self-possessed individual is a strawman (at least within the *texts* of international law), the product largely of a Eurocentric political and economic agenda (and practice) that reads contemporary human rights law through the conceptual lens of its eighteenth-century predecessors. Certainly there remains an individualist bias in contemporary law that deserves our continued critique, but its image of the person is not merely a rehearsal of its self-sufficient Enlightenment cousin, nor is it fully commensurate or immediately compatible with current Euro-American sociocultural formations. To some degree, the person of human rights law is as foreign to the social orders of the West as it is to any others. The shape and scope of these legal and literary fictions of the person matter nonetheless, because they define both theoretically and in practice who is obviously included and "excluded from the benefits of human rights."[52] The person projected in international law is an over-determined and inconsistent figure, a metonym for multiple and often irreconcilable political discourses and theories of law, history, and the subject.

Like human rights, the *Bildungsroman* has often been read as narrating the emergence of modern egoistic self-reliance by critics who concentrate on the protagonist's (*Bildungsheld*'s) individualism at the expense of "his" sociality.[53] The most extreme examples of this popular reading, which follows Wilhelm Dilthey's early (mis)lead, view the genre as the story of a hero who struggles to "incorporate the latent possibility of emerging as, if not a genius, then at least an exceptional individual."[54] Such readings are generally overdrawn. Both the *Bildungsroman* and human rights law recognize and construct the individual as a social creature and the process of individuation as an incorporative process of socialization, without which individualism itself would be meaningless. By excavating the law's narrative assumptions about (and grammar of) human personality development and reading the law and the *Bildungsroman* in and through each other, we can recognize a social individual that challenges the normativity of the hegemonic interpretations that distort this image of the person. The person that emerges from the law and literature in this analysis is, in every way, a *persona ficta*, an often incoherent, self-contradictory, improbable creature that is neither the atomistic individual of libertarian philosophy nor merely the product of social determinism.

Human rights law (both modern and contemporary) aims to mediate the relation between the individual and the institutions of society and the state, historically both the violator of human rights and the administrative unit that capacitates individuals as subjects of rights and duties, as "person[s] before the law." Indeed, both the law and the *Bildungsroman* (and more especially the German-idealist theory of *Bildung* that it novelizes) take the relations between the individual and society as their primary problematic, and they both posit the human personality as an innate characteristic (or better, a drive) of the human being that seeks its freest and fullest form of expression in publicness, in the figure of the "social human being" described by Lakshmi Menon in her speech to the UN General Assembly at the UDHR's adoption. However, the human personality is also configured as the product of the interaction between the subjective individual and the objective group; thus, it represents the solution (or resolution) to a perceived conflict between the anarchic predispositions of the individual and the conformist demands of society and the state. Both human rights and the idealist *Bildungsroman* posit the individual personality as an instance of a universal human personality, as the social expression of an abstract humanity that theoretically achieves its manifest destiny when the egocentric drives of the individual harmonize with the demands of social organization.

One of the multiple meanings of incorporation comprehended in my title, *Human Rights, Inc.*, is the notion that human personality development is a process of socialization, a process of enfranchisement into "those social practices and rules, constitutional traditions and institutional habits, which bring individuals together to form a functioning political community."[55] But incorporation is also a tropological operation by which the law and literature "personify" the person. The human person is the projection of human rights and the *Bildungsroman*—in the triple sense of a project, a projected image, and a vehicle. Throughout this book, "incorporation" refers to how contemporary human rights law images and produces the human person as a right-and-duty-bearing unit in order to remind us of the figurative activity and hybrid formal character of international law which, as I demonstrate, borrowed content and form from the natural law of modern human rights and the positive law of, among others, colonial corporate charters, to which we can trace some of its "humanitarian" provisions.[56]

The process by which the business corporation fulfilled its own figural manifest destiny over the course of the late nineteenth and early twentieth centuries through the vehicle of the "person" in Western law is instructive here. The corporation initially acquired its "artificial" legal personality by way of analogy to the "natural" human being, which figured it as a metaphorical assemblage of organic body parts and drives, but that analogical operation has since become a dead metaphor in both the law and common parlance.[57] Indeed, the death of the personifying metaphor supplied the revolutionary discursive condition for the corporation's so-called natural life, for its independent existence as a right-and-duty-bearing unit in its own right—for its "emancipation" and "autonomy," in the words of legal scholar Gregory Mark.[58] The corporation enjoys, nearly universally, at least one of the fundamental human rights articulated in the UDHR, since it has already been recognized almost everywhere as a person before the law. I offer this cursory history not merely to remind us that the human rights conception of the human being as a person has a discursive genealogy that is entangled with the corporation and capitalism, nor simply as a concise illustration of law's figurative work—I want to recognize, with Barbara Johnson, the possibility that "what have been claimed to be the essential characteristics of man" may "have in fact been borrowed from the corporation."[59]

Contemporary human rights law has its own enabling analogy embedded in the relation it draws between the inherent, natural human personality it presupposes and the internationalized human rights personality it projects. While the corporation is indeed the product of personification, the human person of human rights is incorporated. Contemporary human rights incorporation is a figurative process of naturalization (both in the civic and epistemological senses) that enfranchises the individual as a "world citizen" within an international system of rights and duties. This tropological configuration of the human person through incorporation—the figural habituation of the individual to the norms and forms of international citizenship—is the project that the law imagines to be the "free and full development of the human personality." The person is the human's legal representation, and, as part of its transformational work, human rights aspires to convince the individual to regard its projected legal image as real rather than artificial. That is, the trope of incorporation endeavors to naturalize the ideological *persona ficta* of the international human rights person so that the legal image of the person might come to be seen as coextensive with the actual human being. Through the human being's incorporation into "universal" rights and duties as a human person, contemporary human rights law tries to rectify the analogical split between the natural human and the artificial person—to repair the rupture between man and citizen that Marx and Arendt critiqued—by elevating the particular (individual) to the universal (humanity), transporting the individual from the confines of the nation-state to the realm of the international. In other words, human rights law aspires to internationalize and naturalize the human person by literalizing it, making it real. The goal of this configurative project is to kill the very metaphor that founds human rights, the enabling analogy that establishes the figural correspondence between—but that also separates—the human and the person. With this generative project, whose "political vocation" *Bildung* theorists usually attribute to culture,[60] human rights become a matter of *technê*, combining the traditional liberal functions of law and literature.

Without personification there is no law, at least as we know it. Similarly, if we credit the work of the Yale School literary critics after the so-called ethical turn, personification is either (or both) "the master trope of poetic discourse" or "the inaugural trope of narration, . . . without [which] there is no storytelling."[61] "To use an anthropomorphism," writes Barbara Johnson, "is to treat as known what the properties of the human are," but although human rights law similarly presumes to know in advance the properties of the human to whom it attributes rights, we can distinguish the trope of incorporation from those of personification and anthropomorphism.[62] In J. Hillis Miller's dissection of literary personification's figurative work, personification is "the ascription to entities that are not really alive first of a *name*, then of a face, and finally, in a return to language, of a voice."[63] Incorporation (legal personification) follows this pattern, configuring the human person with individuality (a name and a face) and sociality (a voice), but incorporation goes beyond literary personification by also ascribing to the person a social mobility and a capacity for liability, including a retroactive responsibility for the figurative process itself.[64] The addition of legal and moral responsibility to literary personification places the burden of incorporation on the incorporated person, who is expected to regard the figurative process as emanating from its own desires, as the consummation of freely and fully expressed predispositions. Although I derive the trope of incorporation from the law, it shows its work most clearly in the extended narrative grammar of the affirmative *Bildungsroman*, as I demonstrate in chapter 2 with readings of Johann Wolfgang von Goethe's seminal novel *Wilhelm Meister's Apprenticeship* and Marjorie Oludhe Macgoye's postcolonial Kenyan novel *Coming to Birth*.

At the risk of seeming excessively academic, I am calling the figurative work of human rights law "incorporation" rather than "legal personification" not only to highlight the similar and curious ways the law works figuratively with people and associated entities (the business corporation, for example) but also to defamiliarize that figurative process by preserving a sense of the perversity of the tropological gamble of human rights, which, despite the rhetoric of obviousness, can only pretend to know the yet unfamiliar properties of the international human that it aspires to effect. Understood in this way, "incorporation" is an inaugural trope of both the *Bildungsroman* and contemporary human rights law, whose implicit narrative of human personality development plots a story of sociocivil incorporation by which the human rights personality becomes legible to the self and others in fiction and in fact. Miller similarly describes literary personification as a transformative act of reading that configures the personified creature as one who can "speak in answer to my speech."[65] If literary personification produces a person who seems capable of responding to my call, incorporation is imagined to configure a person with self-consciousness who can recognize itself as capable of making and answering calls (even its own). That is, as I elaborate in chapter 4, the figurative act of human rights incorporation fulfills itself when the incorporated person acquires human rights literacy: the capacity to read itself and others as human rights persons, as creatures of dignity and bearers of international rights and responsibilities. In extended readings of Zimbabwean Tsitsi Dangarembga's *Nervous Conditions* and South African Christopher Hope's *A Separate Development,* I introduce the term narrative self-sponsorship to theorize this reflexive, retroactive grammatical structure of personal recognition and responsibility as it appears (often in ironized form) in the first-person *Bildungsroman.* As I show, this narrative structure of *Great Expectations,* which is also characteristic of so many contemporary postcolonial *Bildungs-romane,*[66] has a legal correlative in the transformations of international human rights law that have occurred in the decades since the adoption of the UDHR, as rights to social, economic, cultural, and political development and self-determination have been retrofitted to the legal equipment of fundamental human rights and to the qualities of the human personality.

Human Rights Ink: Universalizing the Wuthering Heights *Principle*

> know your rights
>
> —tattoo across the shoulder blades of Angelina Jolie, Goodwill
> Ambassador for the United Nations High Commissioner for Refugees

International human rights is a notoriously feeble legal regime. It comes into being either through formal agreements between sovereign states or as a consequence of state practice; that is, as custom. Although it claims to speak for humanity in general, human rights law consists of principles about the human that state delegations—acting as corporate persons, not as humans—agree to abide in principle. Critics—both those seeking to weaken and those seeking to strengthen the human rights regime—charge that contemporary human rights law lacks the executive, judicial, and regulatory apparatuses that traditionally give domestic civil law the force of law. According to these critiques, human rights law consists of little more than airy platitudes, if not the wholesale "nonsense on stilts" that Jeremy Bentham famously saw in the French Declaration of the Rights of Man and of the Citizen. While perhaps desirable, so the critique goes, human rights are unrealistic, impractical, and impracticable. Such "jurisprudential doubt" about the "very possibility of international law" tends to exaggerate the human rights regime's debility, based on a faulty assumption, as Richard Falk argues, "that law implies government."[67] It nonetheless must be admitted that, from an institutional standpoint, international human rights law has little formal immediacy, lacking administrative formations, social structures, and enforcement instruments comparable to those of the modern nation-state.

But the absence of fully effective administrative and enforcement institutions and the lack of a tangible international community do not mean that contemporary human rights are devoid of regulatory effect or systems of compulsion. If law, like power more generally, operates through a combination of coercion and consent (what Antonio Gramsci theorized as hegemony), then part of its force comes from the cooperation of extrajudicial institutions and discourses. That is, the effective jurisdiction of the law is not restricted to, and its instruments of compliance are not housed solely in, those institutions that bear its name—legislatures, the judiciary, law enforcement, etc. In contrast to the weakness of legal apparatuses, cultural forms like the novel have cooperated with human rights to naturalize their common sense—to give law the Gramscian force of culture. It is in this regard that I consider the *Bildungsroman* to be a particularly dependable ally in human rights law's globalizing designs, a sort of novelistic wing of human rights (to recondition a journalistic cliché about Sinn Fein) that disseminates its norms. The more one reads contemporary postcolonial *Bildungsromane* and works in the fields of law, political science, and sociology, the more the seemingly coincidental linkages between literature and law take on the character of an international and intertextual system. The novels often refer topically, at least obliquely, to the law; likewise, legal, political, and social theory often cite *Bildungsromane* for support. This sociocultural alliance can materialize uncannily. For instance, in his narrative sociology of the 1994 Rwandan genocide, *We Wish to Inform You That Tomorrow We Will Be Killed with Our Families*, Philip Gourevitch recounts a conversation with a man who identifies himself only as a "pygmy." After a cursory reference to *Great Expectations*, Gourevitch's interlocutor expounds his "*Wuthering Heights* principle," a theory of human equality, apparently derived from his reading of Emily Brontë's novel, that "all humanity is one": "The concept is *Homo sapiens*. . . . It is the only hope . . . the only way for peace and reconciliation."[68]

Underneath the thematic similarities between the *Bildungsroman* and human rights stretches a convoluted temporality that manifests itself in a common, peculiar narrative grammar. Human rights law legislates as if its common sense were already commonsensical, thereby transforming its tautological propositions into teleological projections of a time when everyone will know what everyone should know. A similar hypothetical and improbable temporality sustains the *Bildungsroman*; "The as if of the novel," writes the literary critic Frank Kermode, "consists in . . . the establishment of an accepted freedom by magic."[69] The tropological "magic" of literary and legal incorporation presupposes that the person *is* a person in order to effect the person *as* a person. My argument throughout this book charts this complicated, question-begging structure and the transitive grammar of enabling fictions that situates the human personality both before and after the process of incorporation—as both human rights' natural premise and their positive promise. This narrative aspirationalism looks forward to when human rights law's common sense will have become and have been confirmed as universal, cultural common sense—when the human person will have become positively the human person it ostensibly already is by natural right.

Becoming what one already is by right is a serviceable abstract for the plot of the idealist, affirmative *Bildungsroman*, which narrates the normative story of how the natural and the individual might become civil and social—the story of how the individual will partakes of the general will without the recourse to social coercion. In classical *Bildungsroman* (and *Bildung*) theory, the idealist genre imagines a reconciliation of the "conflict between individuality and socialization, autonomy and normality";[70] the human personality is both the product and agent of the perfect harmonization of the individual and society. Many stalwart critics of the *Bildungsroman* maintain with Franco Moretti a historicistic and Eurocentric view of the genre, prematurely eulogizing the loss of its synthetic social vision with the trauma of World War I.[71] But very few nineteenth-century European *Bildungsromane*, or their contemporary postcolonial counterparts, have ever fully invested in the genre's original, idealist vision, and even those three and a half novels that critics seem willing to associate with the idealist impulse are themselves problematical.[72] As part of its social work, the idealist *Bildungsroman* conventionalizes and naturalizes the convoluted temporality of incorporation as the normal process by which historically marginal subjects are to become national citizens, and even those vulgar *Bildungsromane* that do not present a vision of the fruition of the ideal maintain a central concern with the normative process of incorporation.

The idealism of the classical, affirmative *Bildungsroman* seems to have lost much of its social and aesthetic appeal in the ages of modernist irony and postmodern suspicion—except in popular, "subliterary" culture, where its ideological (and rather naive) optimism seems stronger than ever.[73] But the genre retains its historic social function as the predominant formal literary technology in which social outsiders narrate affirmative claims for inclusion in a regime of rights and responsibilities. Thus, although it has allegedly ceased to have viable social work to perform for the Anglo-European white male (the ostensibly already-incorporated and capacitated citizen), the *Bildungsroman* continues to serve—as Marianne Hirsch and others have recognized—as "the most salient genre for the literature of social outsiders, primarily women or minority groups."[74] As we shall see, the historical prominence of the genre—in the globalizing twentieth-, as in the nationalizing eighteenth- and nineteenth-, century versions—corresponds to periods of social crises over the terms and mechanics of enfranchisement, over the meaning and scope of citizenship, over, that is, the process and prospects of incorporation.[75] As Gauri Viswanathan has noted, the demand for the franchise often has a correlative cultural component, "a political demand for readers' rightful inclusion in the social world [literature] portrays."[76] As I elaborate at the end of chapter 2, this novelistic claim to the rights franchise abides by the curious temporal logic I have been describing, laying claim to—as Thomas Keenan explains—"what is proper and essential to me in virtue of what I am . . . and I am, for starters, human, . . . understood here as given or, better, as taken, taken for granted."[77] In this regard, the social work of incorporation the *Bildungsroman* illustrates and performs for its readers and protagonists tends to be conservative of the prevailing egalitarian imaginary, if not of the actually existing sociopolitical institutions in which it is instantiated; the normative genre is tendentially reformist rather than revolutionary.

In calling the *Bildungsroman* and human rights cooperative technologies of subject formation, I mean to suggest neither that the literature is a toady for the law, nor vice-versa. As strains of a more general discourse of human development, the *Bildungsroman* implicitly either endorses or challenges the idealist vision of human personality development projected in the law; more typically, as in the dissensual *Bildungsroman* I describe in chapter 3, it does something of both—cosigning the ideal of the egalitarian imaginary (e.g., democratic citizenship and equal opportunity) while exposing the disparities and paradoxes that emerge when that ideal is practiced in specific institutions and social relations. Any particular *Bildungsroman* may be affirmative or critical (or both) of dominant social formations and the discourse of development, but in this engagement it is never indifferent to matters of human rights. As the dominant literary technology of human rights incorporation, the *Bildungsroman* can both articulate narrative claims for inclusion in the normative rights regime and criticize those norms and their inegalitarian implementation by demonstrating the discrepancy between their universalist rhetoric and reality.

Like the novels of Dickens, Flaubert, Austen, and other nineteenth-century social critics, many contemporary postcolonial *Bildungsromane* vivify the marginality of the narrator-protagonist (sometimes that of the author as well) to the rights franchise of the nation-state, but they also expand this frame by foregrounding the dislocation of the *Bildungsheld* from an ostensible global order of human rights. In addition, these contemporary examples share with their classical precursors a vision of *Bildung* as both a writing and reading practice, even as they radically displace the scene of novelistic activity from a room of one's own to modernity's disavowed spaces: an Islamic *zenana*, a prison cell, a secret torture chamber, a paralegal military encampment, an ad hoc forensic laboratory, etc. Literally written in the margins of the dominant social text, these novels make the excentric scene of narration a topos of the *Bildungsroman*. The eponymous protagonist of Guadeloupean novelist Myriam Warner-Vieyra's *Juletane*, for instance, writes her story—a tale of personal and social dispossession resulting from an unwanted polygamous marriage—in the margins of a school girl's discarded exercise book that is rediscovered by a social worker after Juletane's death. While he was a political prisoner, Kenyan author Ngũgĩ wa Thiong'o famously penned one of his *Bildungsromane, Devil on the Cross*, on toilet paper—an event that serves as the beginning and end points of his own prison memoir, *Detained*. This topos is doubled in Argentine writer and journalist Omar Rivabella's *Requiem for a Woman's Soul*, in which a priest reconstructs the shredded waste-paper diary of a political prisoner and, in the process, intercalates his own story of historical and political consciencization as an incorporative act of simultaneously reading and writing the text of the tortured other and the self. In Mario Roberto Morales's *Face of the Earth, Heart of the Sky*, Toribio, a young Maya peasant forced into the Guatemalan counterinsurgency campaign of the 1980s, subversively pencils (and erases) his own stunted developmental narrative between the lines of an army training manual supplied by covert American military "technical advisors." In these novels, as in Tununa Mercado's *In a State of Memory* and Michael Ondaatje's *Anil's Ghost*, which I analyze in chapter 3, the corruption of the *Bildungsroman* form represents a corruption of the norms of human rights; this generic perversion formally indicts the antidemocratic state and rejects its authoritarian claims, even as the novels perform the traditional social function of the *Bildungsroman* genre. That is, they insist on the abstract legitimacy of human rights principles while still challenging—in their formal struggles with the genre's normative conventions—some of their practical racial, ethnic, gender, religious, and class biases.

Suspicious Vehicles: After-marketing the Genres of Nationalism

Human rights are a law and culture whose effects depend upon processes of personal and global incorporation to sustain their modes of production and consumption, and to extend the conditions necessary to patronize their franchise. The *Bildungsroman* has acted as a cultural surrogate for the missing executive authority of international human rights law, expanding its purview by projecting the social and cultural conditions out of which human rights might be recognized as commonsensical. This claim has important consequences for our understanding of the history and sociology of the

novel, but it also involves a crucial critique of the status of contemporary human rights law as law. Although I suggest that the
Bildungsroman has been doing some of the sociocultural work that
the law cannot do for itself, the limitations and contradictions of
the literary genre, the law, and their ideological alliance, should also
be recognized.

Barbara Harlow has provocatively suggested that the

> thirty articles [of the UDHR] translated the standard literary paradigm of indi-
> vidual versus society and the narrative conventions of emplotment and closure
> by mapping an identification of the individual within a specifically international
> construction of rights and responsibilities. The Declaration, that is, can be read
> as recharting the trajectory and peripeties of the classic *bildungsroman*.[78]

But such a radical translation presses the historically nationalizing
Bildungsroman into the service of an international order largely in
advance of the administrative institutions and social formations
necessary to sustain such an order. Even as the UN projected its
vision of an international domain based on the universal "dignity
and worth of the human person" and on "the equal rights of men
and women," they grounded that new world order in the traditional
Westphalian model of state sovereignty, on "the equal rights . . . of
nations large and small" (UDHR). Thus, universal human rights,
like their modern predecessors, are channeled primarily through
the nation-state, so the individual must still be nationalized before
being internationalized—patriated before being expatriated. It may
be "that the forms of global feeling are continuous with forms of
national feeling,"[79] but human rights have largely failed to prefix
"inter" to the nation or to append the international to their teleology of personality development. If contemporary human rights
have failed to deliver fully on their transformative promises—to internationalize the individual and to procure their effective universal
recognition and observance—it is partly a consequence of the residual nationalism and historically narrow universalism comprehended
by the legal and literary forms that the UN implicitly conscripted
to imagine and realize an international order of rights—an international community of freely and fully developed persons.

Benedict Anderson famously argued that the modern nation-
state depended upon print capitalism—particularly the novel and
newspaper—to give it affective imaginative communal form;[80] it

also relied upon a public sphere that, for Jürgen Habermas, took the "specific form" of a "bourgeois reading public" to make its sociality palpable and to foster national common sense.[81] Those institutions, along with modern human rights law, not only served to make the emergent nation-state formation legible and sensible— they legitimated its democratic integrity, formal unity, and egalitarian imaginary by introducing the popular media of enfranchisement into a national society of readers and by naturalizing the sociopolitical terms of disenfranchisement. Abiding what we might call the Westphalian narrative unities of nation-time and -space, the traditional *Bildungsroman* provided the dominant novelistic form for depicting and acquiring this new national and historical consciousness, which it emblematized in the individual's emergence in the public sphere as a right-and-duty-bearing citizen—as a person before the law. In articulating human rights as a project for the protection and promotion of the free and full development of human personality, the UN retasked the literary form to work beyond its historically nationalist boundaries to transport the individual to the realm of the international.

"The trouble with borrowing a rhetoric of fellow feeling from the nation," recognizes Anthony Appiah, "is that the national story is so much a story of a nation among [and against] nations, an *international narrative*."[82] In raising the *Bildungsroman*'s traditional nationalism as a question, I do not mean to suggest that a literary genre is forever bound by its historical social service or that it cannot be retooled for new purposes. Indeed, the nineteenth-century history of the European *Bildungsroman* reveals that both the idealism so often attributed to the genre and the conventions critics identify as constitutive of the type are themselves more honored in the breach than in the observance. That said, I do mean to recognize that the transportation of the *Bildungsroman* from the national to the international is not a simple matter of translation—of merely replacing the nationalist codes and conventions with still largely unknown (or vaguely defined) international ones. One place to observe the work and problematics of generic translation is through a topos of the *Bildungsroman* that remains remarkably consistent from the eighteenth century to the present, from Germany to Ghana (and back): a scene of reading, in which we read of the *Bildungsheld*'s reading of other *Bildungsromane*. Anderson took this novelistic image to be the quintessence of national imagining, in which "the imagined community is confirmed by the doubleness of our reading about our young man reading."[83] But many contemporary postcolonial *Bildungsromane* (like few of their European predecessors) translate these *mise en abyme* scenes of reading to construct literary genealogies that situate readers (both the novels' protagonists and its real readers) in an international imaginary, a translinguistic, intertextual order of *Bildungsromane* that places pressure on the parochial nation-statism of the traditional genre. For example, along with the revolutionary theory of Frantz Fanon, Che Guevara, Régis Debray, and pan-Arabic Baathists, the Saudi novelist Turki al-Hamad's Hisham (*Adama*) reads classic European *Bildungsromane* and is particularly affected by the novels of Dickens and Maxim Gorky's *Mother*; Zimbabwean author Tsitsi Dangarembga's Tambu (*Nervous Conditions*) responds to, and is ultimately deluded by, the novels of the Brontës, Louisa May Alcott, and Enid Blyton; Nigerian writer 'Biyi Bandele-Thomas' Rayo (*The Sympathetic Undertaker*) measures himself against Camara Laye's *The Dark Child*, itself modeled on Flaubert's *Sentimental Education*;[84] Guatemalan Arturo Arias' Máximo (*After the Bombs*) mixes Mayan stories of humankind's emergence from the *Popol Vuh* with his passion for Flaubert and Thomas Mann; Martiniquan Joseph Zobel's José (*Black Shack Alley*) syncretizes local oral forms with *lycée* prescriptions of French classics and extracurricular reading of René Maran's *Batouala* and Claude McKay's *Banjo*.

This topos of contemporary *Bildungsromane* imagines a geocultural and geopolitical alternative to the Westphalian model of the nation-state and of national citizenship as the ultimate expression of human sociality and personality. What emerges from this reading is not merely a transnational matrix of postcolonial *Bildungsromane* whose contemporary protagonists read classical *Bildungsromane* (which, along with the Jamesonian "national allegory," is how the Western literary industry has typically marketed the phenomenon); more important, the imaginary topography of an inchoate international literary public sphere begins to take shape, for which a reconditioned *Bildungsroman* retains its privileged function as the genre of incorporation. In this sense, as I argue in chapter 5, each of these books functions—for its author and protagonist alike—as what I call a *Clef à Roman*: a generic key to the lettered city (the international literary public sphere) that comes with an almost obligatory novel about an individual's attempts to gain access to a public sphere.[85] The *Bildungsroman* serves as the primary enabling fiction for an international literary public that is emerging (we like to think) in advance of the administrative structures and social formations that such a sphere ordinarily serves—for imagining the contours and terms of participation in a projective international order still to come.

Of course an international literary public sphere is not the same as an international community, nor is it the international as such; but, as Habermas's reading public prefigured and then shadowed the nation-state, perhaps it foreshadows human rights' imagined inter-nation. That is, perhaps the topoi, grammar, and forms of the contemporary *Bildungsroman*, in the various transformations and reformations the traditional genre has undergone in its globalization, intimates the institutions, and prepares the imagination, of a future international human rights domain. As I examine in detail in chapter 3, the public sphere provides the ultimate setting of *Bildungsromane*; it is also the location of their publication, circulation, and consumption—activities that on a global scale remain differentially inflected by North–South power relations that belie the egalitarian self-image of the cosmopolitan reading public as a "world republic of letters."[86] Given these disparities, we should approach both hegemonic international human rights and the *Bildungsroman* as necessary but suspicious vehicles, not because they naturalize a monadic, self-sufficient Enlightenment individualism (which is more sociable than most critiques admit) but because of the historically narrow, generic universalism and the residual nationalism of the forms they conscript to project a new universal, international citizen-subjectivity. Furthermore, we must be wary of the constitutive exclusions and prejudices canonized with any genre's institutionalization as the dominant form of incorporation into an international literary public sphere. This is the formal narrative gambit of both contemporary human rights and a still largely NATO-centric "world literature" that eagerly consumes and canonizes—to the likely exclusion of alternative generic forms and constructions of human rights—stories of the historically marginalized when they come in the familiar national dress of the *Bildungsroman*, narratives that intensify the dominant enabling fictions that human rights and the *Bildungsroman* are intrinsically universal and fundamentally egalitarian. In this regard, the racialist lesson that Gourevitch's pygmy draws from his reading of British *Bildungsromane* should be cautionary; he concludes—perhaps for reasons not unlike ·"dark-skinned" Heathcliff's—that his opportunities for free and full personality development, and thus for his incorporation as a human rights person, depend on marrying a "white woman," since "only [she] can understand my universal principle of *Homo sapiens*."[87]

Human Rights, Incorporated: The Commodification of Human Rights and the Bildungsroman

In his 1979 epidemiological assessment of the postmodern condition, which is in many ways a eulogy for *Bildung*, Jean-François Lyotard pronounced the death of "the Enlightenment narrative, in which the hero of knowledge works toward a good ethico-political end—universal peace."[88] Lyotard infamously predicted the obsolescence of the "old principle that the acquisition of knowledge is indissociable from the training (*Bildung*) of minds, or even of individuals."[89] The passing of those Enlightenment principles was to bring an end to the traditional social work of narration as a mode of transmitting "positive and negative apprenticeships (*Bildungen*)."[90] The announcement of the death of Enlightenment master narratives was, of course, greatly exaggerated, as attested dramatically by their resurgence after 9/11 in stories of a universal Manichean struggle between good and evil—between civilization and barbarism. Nonetheless, although both human rights and *Bildung* (and their narrative instantiation in the *Bildungsroman*) remain active, they have been commodified and marketized— incorporated—in the era of multinational capitalist globalization.

The incorporation of my book title, *Human Rights, Inc.*, has multiple valences: With its economic sense, I mean to go further than Upendra Baxi's controversial (and to my mind persuasive) argument that "human rights movements organize themselves in the image of markets," inevitably merchandizing "human suffering and human rights."[91] I also intend something more than the kind of cynical economy of international human exchange astutely surmised by Rey Chow: "In exiling its political dissidents in single file [to the West], while others continue to be arrested and imprisoned, the mainland Chinese government is, de facto, setting itself up as a business enterprise that deals in politicized human persons as precious commodities."[92] In this economic system, the West is corporatized as a human-rights-concerned consumer, whose demand for politicized human beings from the non-West creates both an international human rights market and a Chinese business opportunity. As I examine in chapter 5, this economy of Western-consumer demand and non-Western supply has an analogue in the metropolitan literary industry's appetite for Third World *Bildungsromane* that turns multicultural, postcolonial reading into a kind of humanitarian intervention—a market-forced imposition of certain literary norms that are almost compulsory.

With my book title I mean also to evoke the fact that the discourse (and politics) of human rights have been incorporated by many multinational companies as part of their corporate culture and part of their publicity and investment-portfolio literature. With personalities that are almost human, these "Frankenstein monsters" (as U.S. Supreme Court Justice Louis Brandeis characterized corporations in 1933) have in recent decades again assumed the mantle of "the public good"—now as voluntary marketing strategy—that was once mandated in their charters.[93] The social welfare consideration that provided the primary rationale for making corporations legal and moral persons like everyone else is recast as "strategic philanthropy," as humanitarian initiative and goodwill.[94] Corporations brand liberty, equality, and fraternity for sale. Korean war–era military machines carry the name "Liberty"; a sneaker company accused of sweating child labor offers an annual human rights prize; in 1995, Royal Dutch Shell PLC converted into a public relations opportunity the short-lived, international outrage at its association with the Nigerian government's hanging of nine tribal and human rights activists—including author and publisher Ken Saro-Wiwa—who sought to end the company's environmental, social, and cultural degradation of their land and people. Shell's bland corporate website—which previously published dry quarterly financial reports—suddenly became a place to promote its global "commitments" to human rights and social responsibility. More recently—to further emphasize its heightened humanitarian and

cultural sensitivity—the site offers an overview of Nigerian literature, complete with a venal, unabashed appropriation of Saro-
Wiwa's story as a kind of literary human rights martyrdom:

> Nigerian society has always placed the writer in the role of watchdog of the
> community and social commentator, perhaps the best known being playwright
> and environmental activist, Ken Saro-Wiwa. . . . Nigerian writers explore the
> realities of social conditions such as justice, morality, trust, accountability, gov-
> ernance and law and order. Until very recently, many lost their freedom, and
> Saro-Wiwa, even his life, as a result of doing so.[95]

This brazen corporate branding of human rights is not new: In
1959, Theodor Adorno complained about the perversions of consumerist culture, which were reducing classical humanist principles
to *Halbbildung*. What were once seen as natural rights are now after-
marketed to those with enough money to buy their "liberty" from
underregulated companies who often deprive others of their liberty
and who often sacrifice the principles of equality and fraternity in
its manufacture. Like their nineteenth-century predecessors, the
colonial charter companies, but without the sovereign oversight
that a charter entailed, these emancipated corporations outfit the
profit motive in the dominant, sonorous humanitarian rhetoric of
progress, rights, development, and responsibility for "underdeveloped" peoples. In other words, they claim to be the new global
engines of *Bildung*, making equal opportunity and social mobility
available not only to their advantaged consumers but to the disad-
vantaged producers of their goods in the economic, social, and political "backwaters" of globalization.

Human rights have also been commodified by the nation-state as
the discourse of choice for various repressive domestic practices and
(neo)imperial foreign policies. So, for instance, a Hollywood-ac-
tion-hero-turned-California-governor can solemnly declare at the
2004 Republican National Convention—referring obliquely to the
war in Iraq—that "we're the America that fights not for imperialism
but for human rights and democracy." Imperialism and the rhetoric
of human rights have never been mutually exclusive; in fact, as I
show throughout this book, the discourses of both human rights
and *Bildung* have, since their eighteenth-century European articulation, provided some of the spirit and humanitarian rhetorical cover
for colonialism and the civilizing mission. The Western news media

(Anderson's newspaper) and the literary industry (Anderson's novel) participate in this banalization of rights. In late 2001, for instance, CNN ran a BBC exposé of the Taliban's treatment of women, "Behind the Veil," in preparation for the war in Afghanistan, although the documentary had sat in its can for two years while women's rights groups and other human rights activists urged the media to broadcast it. In 2003, Norma Khouri published *Honor Lost* (*Forbidden Love*), a fabricated story about the honor killing of a young woman by her father and brothers in Jordan that was initially passed off as a memoir. Insensate to Jordanian women's groups' warnings that the book's misrepresentations damaged their credibility and causes, Western media and readers made the fraudulent biography a bestseller; even more disturbing, some reviewers conscripted the book to bolster support for the U.S. war in Iraq, citing it as evidence of the humanitarian imperative of invading Jordan's *neighbor*.

A more general commodification of the *Bildungsroman* has occurred in recent decades in the surge of Euro-American publication of works by historically marginalized peoples (e.g., postcolonials, indigenous peoples, diasporic and immigrant populations, as well as metropolitan racial, ethnic, religious, gender, and sexual minorities) who perhaps "for the first time find themselves in a world increasingly responsive to their needs."[96] Part of the legacy of multiculturalism and a larger transnational "memoir boom,"[97] the "rise . . . of published life narratives" corresponds—as Kay Schaffer and Sidonie Smith have observed—to the period in which human rights became the *lingua franca* of international affairs.[98] Although the linkage between the proliferation of the *Bildungsroman* and the globalization of human rights discourse is not incidental, it is also not simply a reflection of social transformations that are supposed to be taking place in the global South. That is, it is not merely a symptom of some natural telos of literary, humanist globalization, whereby authors and cultures suddenly recognize the innate appeal of the *Bildungsroman* and adopt or adapt it to their particular circumstances. Thus, rather than assume—with Jameson and others—that these novels simply reflect current sociological and cultural facts of life in the Third World, we must recognize the impact that the highly centralized Western markets (both popular and academic) have on global literary production.[99] The largest audience for postcolonial *Bildungsromane* from the global South still resides largely in the literary industrial centers of the North, where the novels are typically published, distributed, taught, and consumed, and whose readers seem to have an insatiable appetite for the stories of Third Worlders coming of age.

The force of Western-market demand for *Bildungsromane* can be quite strong. Witness *Hotel Rwanda*, a film that not only manages to capitalize on the Rwandan genocide that was largely ignored by the film's viewers ten years earlier but does so by mobilizing the *Bildungsroman* formula within a Hollywood idiom. It transforms the corporate story of genocide from Gourevitch's sociological study into the individualist story of a hotelier who finds his ultimate purpose in the social order through his over-identification with multinational tourism capital and its purported indifference to colonial history and ethnic difference. In fact, this *Bildungsfilm* has a second hero, which also discovers its own historical and social consciousness—Sabena SA, operators of the Hôtel des Milles Collines and Belgium's now bankrupt national airline that in the 1920s replaced Joseph Conrad's steamships in serving "Belgium's interests" in the Congo and its colonial League of Nations mandate territory of Ruanda-Urundi.[100] Or, consider Afghan writer Khaled Hosseini's bestselling novel, *The Kite Runner* (2003). Riverhead Books, an imprint of Penguin Group (USA), Inc., carefully calculated, crafted, edited, and packaged Hosseini's debut *Bildungsroman* to satisfy a sudden, war-induced American taste for success stories from Afghanistan.[101] The novel none-too-subtly endorses as humanitarian intervention the U.S.-Allied invasion of Afghanistan and the "War on Terror" by reifying the United States as the land of perpetual opportunity and freedom while hypervilifying the Taliban as a gang of Nazi-loving, heroin-using, homosexual pedophiles intent on repressing the free and full development of the human personality. Mine are cynical readings of a popular film and a hit novel, but my title, *Human Rights, Inc.*, means to acknowledge this dark side of literary and legal humanitarian virtue (as the title of David Kennedy's study has it): the commodification and banalization of the alliance between human rights and the *Bildungsroman*.

The globalization of both human rights and the *Bildungsroman* is propelled, I suggest, at least as much by a consumer-driven commodity economy as it is by the translation into "the accessible languages of all societies" of their appealing humanist common sense.[102] As I argue in my reading of Calixthe Beyala's *Loukoum: The 'Little Prince' of Belleville* in chapter 5, some of the social relations abstracted as form in contemporary postcolonial *Bildungsromane* are the international market dynamics that have helped canonize the genre as the dominant global novel of human rights incorporation—as a *Clef à Roman*. As human rights claims, many contemporary postcolonial *Bildungsromane*—like many of their nineteenth-century European counterparts—make legible the inequities of an egalitarian imaginary; however, most of the novels I analyze also reveal some of the disparities enacted both when the *Bildungsroman* becomes the institutional genre of incorporation into an international community of rights holders and when its paradigm of human rights personality development is projected as the apogee of human sociality. Consequentially, some of the not-yet-hegemonic norms of universal human rights begin to become internationally legible in the appropriations and transformations of the *Bildungsroman*'s normative generic conventions. Thus, such novels are not unmitigated evidence of some irrepressible march of freedom and human rights; rather, part of the social forces and formations that these *Bildungsromane* make legible are the global power dynamics and market relations in which both their publication and human rights are implicated. They demonstrate not the "universal application and full triumph" of human rights but the hegemony of their emancipatory discourse and the current state of their still-unfulfilled promise, of their "tradition of what has not yet become."[103]

Literature and the Law: Some Limits of a Novel Approach to Human Rights

In his 1992 Oxford Amnesty Lecture, literary critic Wayne Booth proposed that human rights be understood as protections of an individual's "freedom to pursue a story line, a life plot."[104] His narratological vision—which, not incidentally, he presents as a corrective to John Stuart Mill's citation in *On Liberty* of Wilhelm von Humboldt's influential theory of *Bildung*—comprehends a human right to plot, what I have elsewhere called a "right to narration."[105] For Booth, this freedom to plot is a pre-social (natural) right that is

exercised socially (positively); thus, the freedom to pursue a story-
line amounts not to libertarian, individualistic, poetic license, but
to a freedom to "carve . . . out" a plot from "all the possibilities
every society provides," from the options enabled and regulated by
particular social relations.[106] My study suggests that human rights
law does indeed recognize an implicit freedom to plot a life story,
and the species of person that the law describes is, in effect, *homo
narrans*. However, although the law—like Lyotard and Emmanuel
Levinas in their analyses of human rights—presumes that the individual's narrative capacity and predisposition are innate and equally
shared by all human beings everywhere, the particular forms in
which the will to narrate finds expression are inflected and normalized by the social and cultural frameworks in which the individual
participates—as I argue in chapter 3—precisely through the incorporative process of freely and fully developing the human personality.[107] This book proposes a narratological understanding of human
rights law and discourse, but it also attempts to elaborate the problems with, and limitations of, such an understanding. Thus, my narratological, structural, sociological, and tropological analyses may
shed light on the cooperative cultural work of the law and the social
work of literature, but shifting the disciplinary terrain (or into an
interdisciplinary terrain) in no way dispenses with the problematics
of prejudicial normativity, exclusivity, and injustice conventionalized within either the law or the literature. The problems of equality and social justice do not end when we recognize the importance
of narrativity to human rights; indeed, many problems may only
begin when we consider "the question of narration" in human
rights.[108]

    I am arguing that the *Bildungsroman* is the novelistic genre that
most fully corresponds to—and, indeed, is implicitly invoked by—
the norms and narrative assumptions that underwrite the vision of
free and full human personality development projected in international human rights law. But I want to be clear about what I understand to be the limits of my claims about the historical and
sociocultural alliance of the *Bildungsroman* and human rights. I am
writing about the dominant international legal construction of
human rights and about the predominant literary genre in which
individual claims to those rights are novelized, although my readings of the literary and legal forms are not themselves dominant. In

other words, the ideological and formal intersections that I identify in this book are hegemonic linkages between the institutionalized international form of human rights law and the largely Western-canonized novelistic form and story function of socialization. My study of those intersections in no way exhausts the consubstantial relations between literature and the law, or even between the novel and human rights; but clarifying the hegemonic complicity of the *Bildungsroman* and international law might offer a methodology for thinking the formal, historical, sociological, and ideological human rights implications of other, nonhegemonic literary genres. My focus on prose narrative—rather than on poetry or drama, for example—reflects Hayden White's critical insight "that narrative in general . . . has to do with the topics of law, legality, legitimacy, or, more generally, authority," but it is also shaped by the figure of the person and the developmental grammar of its figuration that the *Bildungsroman* shares with human rights law.[109] Other novelistic forms have other relations to human rights, engage other aspects of the law, feature other figures, and perform other sociocultural functions.

I venture here some tentative hypotheses about some of those probable relations. In its mode of composition and "its extraliterary elements," the *testimonio* genre bridges a fairly rigid social (and usually geopolitical) divide, binding—not unproblematically—the subaltern with the intellectual, activist elite to challenge the hierarchical power structures that tend to naturalize disenfranchisement and trivialize systemic violations of the subaltern's human rights.[110] Recent international epistolary fiction, like Janette Turner Hospital's "Dear Amnesty" (1990) and Sindiwe Magona's *Mother to Mother* (1998), breaks down the ordinary social, racial, and geopolitical boundaries to sympathy and solidarity by connecting geographically dispersed letter writers in an imaginary collective—the material and moral weight of which cannot be measured by the usual demographic metrics for freedom of association and assembly, but only by the freight of airmail sacks.[111] The chivalric romance seems intimately linked to the story of the human rights worker, whose well-intentioned idealism, often coupled with a misunderstanding of local social relations and cultural traditions, exacerbates the problems they intend to rectify. *Don Quixote* emerges as the parodic prototype that presents a rather pessimistic view of the prospects in the modern world for "humanitarian intervention," for a *desfacedor de agravios* (righter of wrongs) to achieve something more than tilting at windmills.[112] Cain, Postlewait, and Thomson's *Emergency Sex and Other Desperate Measures* and, to some degree, Michael Ondaatje's *Anil's Ghost* rewrite that venerable tradition, critiquing, while holding onto, the idealist fantasy of an effective international community. The *picaresque* novel narrates the story of a perpetual social outcast, whose eternal exclusion from the rights franchise vivifies the hypocrisy of society's universalist rhetoric. The *picaro*, who seems to have unbounded physical mobility but no real upward mobility, is buffeted about by social forces beyond his control—a subject who cannot become a citizen from a lack of necessary personal agency and an improper polity that has failed to activate egalitarian means of incorporation. Cristina Peri Rossi's *The Ship of Fools* and Arturo Arias' *After the Bombs* update the genre to engage specifically with human rights.[113]

As a number of critics have recently argued, in mid-eighteenth-century Europe, the sentimental novel helped forge the first modern transnational "imagined community" on a "sentimental model of reading" that "enabled individuals to grasp the abstract form of an appeal to universality upon which a document like the Declaration of the Rights of Man and the Citizen was based."[114] In this reading, the communitarian ethos and popularity of sentimental novels in eighteenth-century France anticipated the sociopolitical logic of the French revolution itself, but literary sentimentalism was displaced after the revolution in what Margaret Cohen calls "a hostile takeover" by the emergent "codes" of realism.[115] The *Bildungsroman* has generic debts to both *picaresque* and sentimental novels;[116] it narrates the story of a social outsider who acquires the personal agency to convert the *picaro*'s unbounded physical mobility into social mobility, and it posits the cultivation of a democratic, humanitarian sensibility as the culmination of modern subjectivation. I argue in chapters 4 and 5 that contemporary human rights imagine the freest and fullest expression of the human personality to be the development of a profound feeling for human rights themselves—a fellow-feeling for the equal humanity and fundamental dignity of the human personality, both in oneself and others.

By definition, both literary genre and law are normative. Although the idealist *Bildungsroman* and international human rights law respond to issues of rightlessness, they do not begin by imagining in what the rightless (the victims of human rights and undemocratic social formations) consist; they begin by imagining the normative, rights-holding citizen-subject—an abstract "universal" human personality that "presumes particular forms of embodiment and excludes or marginalizes others" and that has been historically defined as "always already [white, propertied, and] male."[117] Out of this enabling fiction, the rightless and marginal emerge as creatures who lack (either innately or practically, depending on the rhetorical politics of the praxis) what the incorporated citizen-subject enjoys. Thus, the literary and legal collusion I am describing projects a normative process of human personality development. From the perspective of international human rights law, *"Bildungsroman"* becomes the generic name for the conventional novelistic form of the story of the rights claimant, for the literary articulation of an individual's claim to have normative rights. From the perspective of the *Bildungsroman*, human rights are the primary modern democratic social ideology that sustains its transitive narrative grammar and its egalitarian ideal.

In emphasizing the cooperation of the *Bildungsroman* and human rights, I do not propose a unified narrative theory that resolves or dispenses with the scandalous inconsistencies and contradictions of human rights discourse and practice, the temporal and logical paradoxes of the law, the paralogical aporias, or the improbable rhetorical figures and practically impossible subjects of human rights. Neither does a narratological understanding of contemporary human rights remove them from political, cultural, social, and economic systems, or shield them from cynical governmental or corporate manipulation or cooptation in the service of domination. On the contrary, the complicity of human rights and the novel means that the field of literature is itself implicated in the discursive regime of human rights, so that it too must be recognized as an arena for the political, cultural, social, and economic manipulation of— and struggles for—human rights, as the use of Khouri's *Honor Lost* to legitimate war and Royal Dutch Shell PLC's repugnant appropriation of Saro-Wiwa's life's work and death story for its own economic self-interest should remind us. The virtue that literature is traditionally understood to hold over law is its capacity to represent contradiction and paradox without a professional disciplinary obligation to offer a logical resolution—without a compulsion to decide in favor of one or another party. This capacity to sustain ambiguity and complexity makes the *Bildungsroman* a powerful ally in naturalizing the law's paradoxes and exclusions—that is, in normalizing the law's intolerable (in its own juridical terms) ambiguity and ambivalence and in making its contradictions commonsensical. However, this same ambivalence makes the generic form an especially important medium for challenging and rearticulating human rights assumptions and practices. Thus, recognizing the concordant sociocultural work that the *Bildungsroman* and international law perform permits us to think about how literary technologies of representation cooperate to make the impossible (and exclusionary) figures of human rights compelling and to challenge the legitimacy of that compulsion.

Finally, I do not pretend that this narratological understanding of human rights resolves the practical and ethical questions we must continue to confront in advocating for human rights or in reading world literature—imperatives that today more than ever seem necessarily linked. What it does do is clarify some of the narrative assumptions that underwrite, and historically have underwritten, human rights law and practice, as well as some of the human rights legal assumptions that sustain, and are sustained by, the modern novel and the *Bildungsroman* in particular. In this, a narratological approach opens for analysis the ways in which the globalization of literature and the law are mutually implicated. This mutual implication suggests that writing and reading entail a model of juridical ethics as much as law-making and law-abiding involve a model of narrative ethics. Articulating the narrative subtexts and implications of legal form(s) enables us to recognize some of the ways that law functions as culture: The law projects and depends upon cultural narratives for its effective operation, legitimation, and social compulsion; and, in turn, legal norms favor and disfavor the literary forms in which those cultural narratives find social and conventional expression. Likewise, recognizing some of the human rights implications of literary form(s) means also becoming attentive to the often-unpredictable ways in which our reading practices are themselves implicated in the possibility and project of realizing a world based on human rights.

Novel Subjects and Enabling Fictions: The Formal Articulation of International Human Rights Law

Personality essentially involves the capacity for rights and constitutes the concept and the basis (itself abstract) of the system of abstract and therefore formal right. Hence the imperative of right is: 'Be a person and respect others as persons.'

—HEGEL, *Philosophy of Right*

In modern times, the fundamental right [is] the [social] right of the individual fully to develop his personality, which implie[s] the right to all the factors essential to that development.

—KARIM AZKOUL, Lebanese United
Nations delegate, 1948

Everyone has the right to recognition everywhere as a person before the law.

—Universal Declaration of Human Rights (Article 6)

Literary Subtexts of the Law: Robinson Crusoe *and the Universal Declaration of Human Rights*

Like mythical twins separated at birth by the geographical accidents of British imperialism, two Watts—Ian and Alan—found themselves grappling with the battered legacy of the Enlightenment's

45

emancipatory promise in the aftermath of World War II, converging on *Robinson Crusoe* as a signal literary marker of the historical emergence of rationalized individualism. The apprentice literary critic Ian Watt, studying the "relation between the growth of the reading public and the emergence of the novel," was writing at St. John's College, Cambridge, what was to become his seminal work, *The Rise of the Novel,* in which *Crusoe* features as both the coming-of-age story of *homo economicus* and "a monitory image of the ultimate consequences of absolute individualism."[1] Meanwhile, across the English Channel, Alan Watt, Australian delegate to the Third Social and Humanitarian Committee of the United Nations, was at the Palais du Chaillot in Paris, revising the text of the Universal Declaration of Human Rights (UDHR), which would be adopted by the General Assembly on 10 December 1948.

During consideration of the UDHR's Article 29, the lone statement of human obligations (as opposed to human rights) to remain in the Declaration after three years of drafting, Alan Watt proposed an amendment that would fundamentally reconfigure the international legal character of the relation between the individual and society. As drafted, the article declared that "Everyone has duties to the community *which enables* him freely to develop his personality" (emphasis added); Watt's amendment construed a more integral relation between the human personality and society: "Everyone has duties to the community *in which alone* the free and full development of his personality is possible" (emphasis added).[2] Debate on this emendation revolved around several key problematics: its image of the human person; the terms of the individual's debt to the community for having developed what the UDHR generally refers to as "the human personality"; the shape and scope of the community to which such obligations are entailed; and the extent to which a "community" can take responsibility for the development of human personality.[3]

Alan Watt's proposal, greeted by the Latin American delegations that had consistently lobbied for a pairing of rights and responsibilities, intended to moderate what many delegates perceived as the Declaration's individualist excesses. Thus, the delegate from Cuba spoke for a number of states parties when he cited the precedent of the Bogotá Declaration (American Declaration of the Rights and

Duties of Man), concluded only months earlier, to argue that Watt's proposed article made the social contract character of human rights explicit by reminding the individual "that he was a member of society, and that he must affirm his right *to be deemed a human being* by clearly recognizing the duties which were corollaries of his rights" (emphasis added).[4] From the earliest days of the UDHR's inception in 1946, some drafters had expressed reservations about the document's individualistic bias and the danger that a statement of rights without correlative obligations might be construed as personal license. As often as these questions were raised, they were deferred for the sake of consensus, as René Cassin— French delegate and chair of the Third Committee—wrote, in order not "to delve into the nature of man and of society and to confront the metaphysical controversies, notably the conflicts between spiritual, rationalist, and materialist doctrines on the origins of human rights."[5] But the Third Committee was the last stop for the draft declaration before its final consideration by the UN General Assembly, and such controversies that had been generally suppressed for three years threatened to disrupt the legislative project. It was to settle these questions that the delegates invoked *Robinson Crusoe*, and Daniel Defoe took his official place among the unacknowledged legislators of the world.

Wary of the image of the person emerging from the Australian amendment and concerned that it endorsed a kind of social determinism, Belgium's delegate, Fernand Dehousse, raised the first substantial objection to what he called Watt's "inaccurate statement, for while there was no doubt that society contributed to the development of the individual's personality, it was no less true that the development was conditioned on other factors."[6] Concurring with the Belgian delegate were China, the U.S., and Lebanon, each of which (along with France) was represented on the original "Nuclear Commission" of drafters in the persons of P. C. Chang, Eleanor Roosevelt, Charles Malik, and Cassin. Worried about what Watt's amendment "might give rise to," Dehousse buttressed his objection with an *explication du Crusoe*: "It might . . . be asserted that the individual could only develop his personality within the framework of society; it was, however, only necessary to recall the famous book by Daniel Defoe, *Robinson Crusoe*, to find proof of the contrary."

Mistaking Crusoe for the Enlightenment heuristic fiction of "natural man," Dehousse found in the novel sociological "proof" that contradicted what he regarded as an erroneous emphasis on the community over and against the individual. Watt's amendment, he portended, might lead some people to conclude "that it was the duty of society to develop the human being's personality; that principle, might, perhaps, be in harmony with the philosophy of certain countries, but it might equally well run counter to that of other peoples." Playing Defoe as his literary universalist trump, Dehousse defended the ahistorical, natural figure of a self-sufficient individual human personality, ironically, in the proto-language of cultural relativism.

Apparently persuaded by this interpretation of *Crusoe*, Alan Watt withdrew his proposal, at which point the Soviets sponsored it in their name. Praising Watt's amendment for "rightly stress[ing] the fact that the individual could *not fully* develop his personality outside society," Alexei Pavlov contested Belgium's reading: "The example of *Robinson Crusoe*, far from being convincing, had, on the contrary, shown that man could not live and develop his personality *without* the aid of society" (emphasis added). In fact, Pavlov noted, "Robinson had . . . at his disposal the products of human industry and culture, namely, the tools and books he had found on the wreck of his ship."[7] Defoe's novel served the legislators similarly as an enabling fiction—a shared cultural product of human industry and society, salvaged from the shipwreck of Western civilization, enlisted in their own efforts to found a new world on universal recognition of "the [inherent] dignity and worth of the human person" and "of the equal and inalienable rights of all members of the human family" (UDHR). Although the delegates drew contradictory lessons from *Robinson Crusoe*, the literary dispute brought the UDHR to resolution; debate on the nature of the relation between the individual and society ended swiftly, alternative amendments were withdrawn, and, if a vote can be taken as evidence of such things, Pavlov's reading proved the more compelling to the interpretive community of the UN. Thus, with no objections and six abstentions, human personality entered international law as both the product and medium of social relations in Article 29: "Everyone has duties to the community in which alone the free and full development of his personality is possible."

Beyond the adoption of the UDHR, 1948 was a watershed year in the reconfiguration of the international order, which saw the establishment of the Organization of American States, the declaration of the state of Israel and the appointment of the perennial "Palestine Question" on the UN agenda, the electoral victory of South Africa's National Party and its consequent legislation of apartheid, and the Berlin Blockade that demarcated emergent geopolitical lines of Cold War conflicts. In the previous year, the General Agreement on Tariffs and Trade (GATT) was signed and the Marshall Plan for the reconstruction of Europe proposed; the era of decolonization began inauspiciously with the partition of India and Pakistan, followed in 1948 by the independence of Ceylon and Burma. This decolonization process would accelerate over the course of the next two decades as the imperial powers of the nineteenth century were forced to retreat from formal empire. By 1966, when the UN completed what is sometimes called the International Bill of Rights with the passage of the legally binding International Covenant on Civil and Political Rights (ICCPR) and the International Covenant on Economic, Social, and Cultural Rights (ICESCR), the voting rolls of the General Assembly had more than doubled from the fifty-eight constituent members who adopted the UDHR.

In the summer and fall of 1948, some of these historical forces were palpable in the deliberations of the Third Committee, its attention split primarily between consideration of the text of the UDHR and discussion of the perpetual crisis of displaced persons and refugees from Palestine. If the Cold War implications of recent events were not yet fully apparent on a global scale, an ideological chill was perceptible at the UN. Writing in 1972 at the height of the First World–Second World standoff, René Cassin would recall that, with the growing geopolitical tensions in committee, the declaration emerged at the last possible moment of international consensus.[8] Thus, the 1947 decision to separate the International Bill of Rights into the nonbinding Universal Declaration and the two justiciable Covenants was an act of desperate pragmatism to ensure that something of the unwritten law, even if only a statement of aspirations, was committed to parchment.

Into this interbelline atmosphere, Defoe's *Crusoe* was cast. Given the geopolitical context, the fate of one fictionalized Englishman cast away on a seventeenth-century island in the Orinoco effluence may seem rather beside the point. Indeed, the invocation of this "first novel"—a designation Ian Watt commends by arguing that "it is the first fictional narrative in which an ordinary person's daily activities are the centre of continuous literary attention"—is rather unusual among the Third Committee's more predictable, if scattered, allusions to Locke and Rousseau, Lenin and Marx.[9] Although it adds little nuance to the classical disputation over the constitutive roles of nature and nurture in the development of the individual, the contest over Defoe's novel intimates the general terms of debate about the human personality and its sociality that have always attended the articulation of human rights. Pavlov's social-materialist reading, in which "full" personality develops from the dialectical interaction of individual and society, rebuts Dehousse's libertarian reading of "possessive individualism," in which "free" personality development requires protection from society. This controversy is as much about private property as it is about personality.[10] Dehousse subscribes to a Lockean view, in which the right to private property is foundational and the primary proprietorship is to hold property in one's own person; Pavlov, by contrast, suggests that the human personality is a product of the collective labor of society, to which are due in return certain obligations as part of a social compact. Despite their differences, both extrapolated from *Crusoe* transcendent literary proof to substantiate their ideal of human personality development, an ideal that in the Committee's deliberations had so far proved incapable of substantiating itself.

Dehousse's reading of *Crusoe* backfired when its supposed common sense encountered an equally obvious reading with more momentum. But, to some degree, this literary conflict of common senses substituted for full-blown philosophical debates about "the nature of man and of society" that seemed destined for endless deferral. The Third Committee generally followed the precedent established in the Human Rights Committee (HRC) that drafted the UDHR, adopting what French philosopher and UNESCO consultant on the UDHR, Jacques Maritain, mildly reproved as "a practical viewpoint."[11] Thus, they concerned themselves not "with seeking the basis and philosophic significance of human rights but only their statement and enumeration." Having strategically chosen to beg obtuse and contentious questions about a philosophy, sociology, and anthropology (let alone a psychology) of the human rights subject, the committees construed their charge as the expedient "assembly of the rights and faculties indispensable, in our epoch, to the blossoming [*épanouissement*] of the human person [*personne humaine*]."[12] If this sonorous mandate made it possible to bypass most "metaphysical controversies" about the origins and theoretical legitimacy of human rights, those conflicting philosophies nonetheless found other forms of expression. Surprising though it may be that the ludicrous Robinson Crusoe acted as a serious literary surrogate for those controversies, even more surprising is the efficiency with which the novel's invocation dispatched the perpetually nagging problematics of man and society by supplying an iconic literary shorthand for entire canons of intricate theoretical arguments. Specifically, the novel facilitated a conflicted consensus by making it possible to recognize the human personality as both the primary agent and component of human society, as both a product and tool of human social industry and culture (in Pavlov's words)—the proper end to which social formations should be directed.

The turn to literature, and to the "first novel" specifically, has more than an incidental logic. Although literary criticism may intuit an intimate relation between the novel's rise and human rights (as Erich Auerbach did in 1946 when he attributed the emergence of "modern tragic realism" to the "convulsions" of the French Revolution), rarely are those linkages named explicitly, except in passing (as Roberto Schwarz did when he suggestively identified a "combination of individualism and the Declaration of Human Rights" as the sociopolitical stipend of nineteenth-century novelistic realism).[13] If literary critics can be trusted in matters of self-interested, disciplinary claim-staking, the project of human personality development legislated in contemporary human rights might properly be described as novelistic. Indeed, literary theorists writing contemporaneously with the UDHR tended to describe the novel's primary virtue as its capacity to represent "particular individuals in the contemporary social environment."[14] Northrop Frye, for example, asserted that the genre's distinguishing mark and "chief interest" is the "human character as it manifests itself in society."[15] Thus, a literary critical consensus in the mid-twentieth century seems to have defined the proper subject matter of the modern novel as the problematics of social personality, of "characters wearing their *personae* or social masks."[16] In this regard, Ian Watt's proposal that the rise of the novel required certain epistemic and economic changes in the conception and social organization of humanity—changes corresponding to the European emergence of the bourgeoisie as a political class and of the bourgeois white male citizen as the universal subject—might equally well describe the rise of liberal human rights legislation. This homology becomes clear if we replace the words "novel" and "literature" with "law" and "jurisprudence" in Watt's famous observation: "The novel's serious concern with the daily lives of ordinary people seems to depend upon two important conditions: the society must value every individual highly enough to consider him the proper subject of its serious literature; and there must be enough variety of belief and action among ordinary people for a detailed account of them to be of interest to other ordinary people."[17]

In fact, human rights and the novel—especially its idealist *Bildungsroman* variant that takes as its explicit thematic what Georg Lukács described a year before the adoption of the UDHR as "the fulfillment of the fully developed personality as a *real growth* of actual people in concrete [social] circumstances"[18]—are more than merely homologous; they are mutually ratifying. As related strains of a more general discourse of modern development, each supplies the other's enabling fiction in their idealist projections of the blossoming of free and full human personality. But if "the development of . . . characters in the course of time" and within a social order is a properly novelistic problematic, then human rights legislation—as the articulation of a novelistic project—is part of those other developmental projects of civilization that are historically "connected with the growth of the bourgeoisie in a modern capitalist system":[19] urbanization, modernization, industrialization, mercantilism, nationalism, colonialism, and imperialism. Edward Said has proposed that "without empire . . . there is no European novel as we know it," and a similar codependency becomes evident when we examine the sociohistorical and formal correspondences between international human rights law and the idealist *Bildungsroman*, whose hegemonic norms and forms are themselves "unthinkable without each other."[20] In this regard, it is worth noting Friday's absence from the *Crusoe* debates. Although it would be a mistake to read the delegates' concern for Crusoe rather his "man Friday" as an endorsement of imperialism, the imperialist underpinnings of both the novel and human rights allow them to rearticulate Defoe's narrow, colonialist imaginary of the social and civil order of Robinson's island, in which Friday may be a man, but he is never granted personality in the technical sense of the term that I discuss in this chapter. The delegates' focus on the role of cultural and human industrial artifacts—rather than on relations with Friday, for example—in Crusoe's socialization (or personalization) allowed them to disregard Friday as a potential novelistic protagonist of human rights. Such blindness suggests something of the exclusions entailed and enacted in contemporary human rights law that, presumably, would aspire to promote the free and full personality development (and *Bildungsromane*) of so many Fridays.

In the UN committee's reading of Defoe's novel, books and other instruments of culture supplied Crusoe with an archival substitute for society, an alternative literary means for developing his human personality. For the drafters of the UDHR, these books functioned as surrogates for society because the alliance between the novel and imperialism is more than discursive and epistemic. Thanks to transnational cultural exchange across the "literary channel"[21] and to the material circulatory systems of imperialism, *Robinson Crusoe* represented for the delegates a common universal culture (a "world heritage"), in which reposed the collective wisdom of centuries of social history, practice, and theory necessary to rearticulate the proper relations between individual and society as international human rights law. Despite their conflicting interpretations of Crusoe's story, the delegates read it as an allegory of subject formation and of the endurance and legitimacy of Enlightenment principles of (European) civilization. These principles were imagined to remain latent in even the isolated human personality—from which they are theoretically derived—and in the artifacts of civilization, awaiting activation in the reestablishment of social relations, enacted by Crusoe's daily reading in his salvaged library. Thus, the delegates valorized not the novel's fantasy of Crusoe's industrious personal prosperity on an island colony outside history and society—a time and space that Defoe describes in legal terms as "civil death"—but rather its delicate literary solution to the temporary disruption of civilization's progress, allegorized in Crusoe's biography of shipwreck and the re-creation of a little European (read human and universal) society that he deliberately quit in his youth.[22]

In this reading, the force that Crusoe calls "Providence" materializes not in divine injunctions or in an essentialist human nature, but
in the fortuitous delivery of the flotsam of European culture and
society—the traces that make it possible to plot his island isolation
not as desertion but as an experiment in sustaining minimal social
and civil continuity. As the books are to Crusoe, so *Robinson Crusoe*
is to the UN delegates in their articulation of an international legal
Robinsonade for a new world order.[23] Forming the novelistic subtext of Article 29, Crusoe's novel underwrites the law, warranting
the human rights personality's legal image, sociality, and role as
the medium through which the reconciliation of the individual and
society is to be effected and expressed. Despite appearing to settle
the metaphysical questions, the literary ambivalences of the novel—
whether it is individualist or socialist, whether the Providence of
God and Nature or human industry and culture sustain Crusoe—
have a related formal ambivalence in the text of the law; that is, as I
will show in this chapter, the novel's thematic ambivalence has an
objective correlative in the hybrid form of international human
rights law itself.

The UN delegates' encryption of *Robinson Crusoe* within the text
of Article 29 illustrates something of the historical cooperation between the novel and human rights—between what is typically regarded as the sociocultural work of literature and the civil and
political work of law. I return to questions about this alliance and
its relation to power throughout the book, but in this chapter I
focus on the formal, historical, rhetorical, and institutional conditions of international human rights law that make it especially dependent upon cultural forms to give its precepts moral force. In
particular, I describe what happens to the forms, norms, and force
of the law when "the imprescriptible rights of man" are indeed
scribed by man. Thus, this chapter is about the textuality of human
rights law, about the forms, figures, codes, and conventions that the
unwritten law takes in writing. I begin by analyzing the image of
the human person (and the development of its personality) that the
law both takes for granted and articulates, situating this figure at
the intersection of natural and positive law approaches to personhood. The bulk of this chapter considers the temporal and narrative
implications that emerge from the rhetorical disjuncture in international human rights law between taking something for granted and

projecting something as an aspiration to be realized. I examine the formal properties of this imaginative texture of enabling fictions (which recurs throughout the text of human rights law) to show how the gap between natural and positive law, between what everyone knows and what everyone should know, is largely a cultural gap—a gap that is ordinarily bridged not by the coercive force of law but by the "consensual" work of culture. I read the literary properties of the law in order not only to isolate some of the narrative assumptions behind—and constructions of—human rights, but to disrupt both the parochial Euro-American claim to human rights as its unique patrimony of universalism and the too-easy dismissal of human rights for its Eurocentrism. Thus, my analysis of legal narrativity stresses the formal, conceptual, and effective discontinuities between contemporary human rights law and its eighteenth-century counterparts in order to isolate some of the basic rhetorical devices of the law and some of the grammatical and temporal structures that it shares with the modern novel. Just as *Robinson Crusoe* (in some ways) made the principles behind Article 29 articulable, the sometimes convoluted, improbable, abstract rhetorical structures of the law that I identify in this chapter will become most technically refined and commonly legible in the literary conventions of the *Bildungsroman*.

Generic Engineering: Forms and Creatures of the Legal Imagination

> In each of us there dwells a mystery, and that mystery is the human personality. We know that an essential characteristic of any civilization worthy of the name is respect and feeling for the dignity of the human person.
>
> —JACQUES MARITAIN, *The Rights of Man and Natural Law*

The abstract equality of the inalienable human personality and its inherent dignity is the theoretical foundation of contemporary international human rights law, which comprises "the ensemble of things to do and not to do" that follow "in *necessary* fashion, . . . *from the simple fact that man is man*, nothing else being taken into account," according to natural law advocate Jacques Maritain.[24] These unwritten principles are theoretically articulable when

human beings reflect upon the requirements of the existential tautology that "man is man," applying their reason to discover what
Maritain calls "the highest exigencies of the personality."[25] Little
critical energy is expended today on this figure of the human personality (and the formula of its development) which founds contemporary international human rights law, and although the language
of personality persists in the legal conventions that have followed
the Universal Declaration, it has to some degree faded into the
background of the law; most analysts seem to take it for granted,
treating the "human person" of the UDHR as a simple synonym
for the human being or individual. But, while the UDHR might
appear "simply [to] take . . . rights for granted" as part of "a studied
attempt to reinvent the European natural law tradition," that view
of the law is enabled partly by the same conceptual ambiguities
within the term "human person" that made this figure available to
uphold the UDHR drafters' conflicted consensus over Article 29.[26]

In the first half of the twentieth century, the term "human personality" had a hold on both the popular and academic international imagination that it seems not to have at the beginning of the
twenty-first. It appears, for instance, in proposals for international
declarations of rights drafted independently by renowned international jurist Hersch Lauterpacht and British novelist H. G. Wells,
both of whose "private" efforts were singled out for commendation
on the floor of the UN General Assembly at the adoption of the
UDHR.[27] Lauterpacht makes "the sanctity of human personality
and its right and duty to develop in freedom to all attainable perfection" the ultimate rationale for his "International Bill of the Rights
of Man."[28] Wells, on the other hand, with characteristic acerbic wit,
situates it as part of the first right that follows from the preambular
fact that "man comes into the world through no fault of his own."[29]
The idea of the sacred inviolability of the human personality was
popularized in the socioreligious doctrinal vocabulary of Personalism,[30] but it was also current in the discourse of political science[31]
and in the literary and social thought of writers like John Middleton
Murry, who in 1932 declared "the sovereignty of the human personality" to be in desperate need of civil and political restoration.[32]
Similarly, when, in anticipation of the UDHR, UNESCO's Committee on the Philosophical Principles of Human Rights undertook
an unauthorized inquiry into the possibility of a cross-cultural

metaphysical consensus on the source and content of human rights, the term "human personality" emerged from the thirty-one opinions returned by leading intellectuals from various UN member states as a common (if polysemic) denominator for what Pierre Teilhard de Chardin called a "new charter for humanity."[33]

The ubiquity of the human personality in mid-twentieth-century political theory, humanistic and social sciences, religion, literature, and popular culture granted it a certain commonsensical status that allowed the UDHR drafters to avoid metaphysical controversies by not looking too directly at the figure of the human rights person nor asking too pointedly after its origins and character. The "human person" became a kind of synecdoche for often-contradictory political theories of law, history, and the subject—a stenograph for complex philosophies of human nature. In other words, the abstraction of "human personality" arbitrated between competing ideologies, sustaining a synecdochical theoretical consensus not on the basis of a shared understanding of its contents or origins, but on a practical agreement that was possible because the term was already so deeply embedded in the conceptual vocabulary of the various political and social philosophies held by the UN delegates. "Human personality" was not a floating or empty signifier; or, rather, it had the kind of emptiness that comes from being overloaded. In the "human person," the natural law advocate could find the work of God and Nature, the positivist could recognize the effect of social and historical contingency, the spiritualist could hear an entire neo-Kantian doctrine of Personalism, and the materialist might foresee "the creation of those material conditions of production which alone can form the real basis" of Marx's prophesied "higher form of society, a society in which the full and free development of every individual forms the ruling principle."[34] My sense is that the person the delegates imagined when they discussed human personality was not always (or perhaps ever) the same thing—each of them had some other person in mind.

To comprehend the image of the person that international human rights law articulates, we must understand the juridical meaning of the word "person" and the work that "person" does that "human" does not. Human rights law is something of a misnomer; in fact, just as what we call humanitarian law is the law not of peace but the law that "seeks to 'humanise war,'" the technical name for the body of international law that we commonly refer to as human rights is *jus gentium*, the "law of peoples" or the "law of nations."[35] The "human" cited in the title of the UDHR is not a human as such; it is a person as a member of a people or nation—a particular kind of human activated as a legal and moral unit with "rights . . . [that] are formulated *in* society."[36] Similarly, although in popular speech we tend to use "person" and "individual" inter-changeably, they are not the same thing; person "is not so much a trope for 'individual man' as it is a trope for a position in certain contexts."[37] "The person of abstract right is a formal-universal person," writes Robert Williams, glossing Hegel; "When human beings think of themselves in this way, the result is a formal individualization that all share."[38] From the point of view of the law, "person" is a technical term designating "a right-and-duty-bearing unit";[39] it has no necessary relation to the human being since it merely names something that has been endowed with the capacity to "enjoy . . . the protections of the law and of the forces of the law."[40] This act of endowment charters a creature that can function as "a foundation for legal predicates," as "a [grammatical] subject of rights"; as—tautologically—a person before the law.[41] In the case of human rights, "person" is the rhetorical vehicle through which the law personifies (or incorporates) the human as a creature capable of bearing its rights. It is the legal mask (*persona*) for the human's figural projection in the law—in the sense of both an image and a task still to be completed. As its legal representative and representation in human rights law, the person's figurative correspondence with the human cannot itself be taken for granted because it is the figure through which international, universal humanity is to be attached to the individual human.

Just as person is not the same as the human or the individual, personality is not individuality. As it appears throughout human rights law, "personality" does not have the popular psychological meaning of the complex of characteristics that are unique to an individual; rather, it is imagined to be an individual instance of the abstract, universal human personality. Technically, "personality" names the condition of being a person—the legal capacity to act like every other person before the law or "to be someone for all practical purposes."[42] Thus, personality is "a social achievement," the expression of "what one *has*—a property that one may acquire" within a particular juridicosocial formation.[43] Personality is not the emblem or expression of individual psychological differences. It is the basis of the symmetrical relations that the individual shares with all others before the law. In fact, the supposed predisposition of every individual to be recognized as a person is the fundamental condition of similarity of human beings with respect to the law— the quality that theoretically disposes the law in a democratic formation to treat all individuals as equals. In his gloss of the UDHR, child-developmental psychologist Jean Piaget made this distinction between personality and individuality (or, "the ego centred in itself"): "The personality . . . is the individual freely accepting discipline, or contributing to its development, and voluntarily submitting to a system of reciprocal [social] standards which subordinate his own liberty to a respect for that of others."[44] Thus, personality is the collection of modalities of extension and expression that the person takes in relation to the social, cultural, economic, civil, and political formations within which the individual human, or any other entity, is capacitated to act as a subject of rights and duties. In this sense, each of the UDHR's articles can be understood to address a particular facet of human personality.

These technical matters of personality are legible in the text and context of *Robinson Crusoe*, which was written at a time when the modern legal meanings of "person" were being conventionalized in European law. Defoe rarely uses the word "person," and only in two senses: in its older meaning, to identify the physical individual; and in a newer one, to name a creature capable of entering into social and legal contracts, of enjoying rights and assuming responsibilities. The novel's denial of personality to Friday has a telling contrast with Crusoe's characterization of his menagerie of "subjects," which includes mostly domesticated animals: "I had the lives of all my subjects at my absolute command. I could hang, draw, give liberty, and take it away; . . . Poll, as if he had been my favorite, was the only person permitted to talk to me."[45] Even before the subject Friday, Crusoe's talking parrot qualifies as a person with attendant civil rights ("freedom" of speech) and duties, primary among which is to speak Crusoe's name incessantly and thereby to affirm both of their dialogic social personalities.

Defoe's comic take on personality has a serious historical subtext: At the time of *Crusoe*'s publication in 1719, the legal personality of the "business form" had recently become "a popular vehicle for financing [both] colonial enterprises" and private ventures.[46] Defoe himself advocated British commercial expansion in South America and supported the South Sea Company's application for a monopoly grant to trade on the Orinoco.[47] After receiving its Royal Charter of incorporation, the company was discovered to have artificially inflated its worth by greatly exaggerating its capacity to conduct business in the Americas; the "South Sea Bubble" broke, devastating British financial markets and public confidence in the corporate form of legal personality. In response, Parliament passed the Bubble Act of 1720, which reserved chartering authority to the Monarch and retarded the development of the legal machinery necessary to govern the joint-stock company and its personality for a century.[48] Nonetheless, legal personality has a tendency to evolve, and, by the early twentieth century, in the Western democratic legal regimes, "the business corporation had become the quintessential economic man"—a Robinson Crusoe in its own right.[49]

I cite this historical context for Defoe's novel to recognize the contingency and elasticity of legal personality (and perceptions of it); the contents and scope of personality change over time, expanding and contracting the rights and duties it confers as well as incorporating entities other than human beings as persons before the law. The discursive history of corporate personality over the course of the nineteenth century suggests that even those things that may begin as purely legal fictions tend to become social realities over time—that is, the artificial legal personality tends to come to be perceived (and to be treated) as natural, at least in the ways we speak about it.[50] Indeed, as I demonstrate throughout this book, positive rights have a general tendency to become natural. If Poll's personality strikes us as comically and obviously artificial, in the context of Crusoe's island universe it makes some sense to speak of the parrot as a person "granted" the natural right of speech. "The evolution of generic international legal personality for humans"[51] has followed a similar pattern, and one of the discursive gambles of contemporary human rights law is its articulation of a fictional international human rights personality that it aspires to bring to life; in other words, contemporary human rights law projects an artificial international legal personality for the human being as a goal to be achieved through the recognition and enjoyment of the rights and duties that the law ascribes to it.

The human personality as articulated in the UDHR is a syncretic construct of a hybrid legal regime; it could be said—as the Saudi delegate to the UN Third Committee Jamil Baroody did—that the declaration is, paradoxically, "based largely on Western patterns of culture" even though it might not run counter to "the patterns of culture of Eastern States."[52] Although the human person stands at the discursive intersection of Western and Eastern political formations and cultural patterns, liberalism and Marxism, and natural law and positivism, it looks rather different from each of these conceptual perspectives.[53] The human person in the Universal Declaration is a legal figure and social creature more fragile and tenuous than its Enlightenment cousin. Synthesizing (not always coherently) various strands of philosophical, social, and political thought, the UDHR projects a human person that is not quite "natural man" (the deposit "of Nature and of Nature's God," in Thomas Jefferson's phrasing in the American Declaration of Independence) and not quite "positive man"—a creature fully interpellated by society, its institutions, and its laws.

Beyond mediating between the individual and society in Article 29, the formulaic "free and full development of the human personality" supplies the goal toward which compulsory, technical, and professional education are to be directed, and through which "the strengthening of respect for human rights and fundamental freedoms" and the promotion of "understanding, tolerance and friendship among all nations, racial or religious groups" are to be fostered (Article 26). A broadly construed right to "social security" and to the realization "of the [indispensable] economic, social and cultural rights" (Article 22) are intended to secure (along with human dignity) the full development of the human personality.[54] The Universal Declaration recognizes the "dignity and worth of the human person" in its preamble (an act of recognition that it characterizes as the "foundation of freedom, justice and peace in the world"), and it subsequently grants to "everyone" their own "right to recognition everywhere as a person before the law" (Article 6). The preamble initially treats the human personality as if it were an innate aspect of the human being, but the articles describe it as an effect of human rights—the product of contingent civil, political, social, cultural, and economic formations and relations; on the whole, the

Declaration images the human person as an improbable composite of a pre-social, natural human personality and a positive project of personality development.

In his introduction to UNESCO's inquiry into the philosophical foundations of human rights, Jacques Maritain described an epistemic battle at the UN between "two antagonistic groups: those who to a greater or lesser extent explicitly accept, and those who to a greater or lesser extent explicitly reject, 'Natural Law' as the basis of [human] rights."[55] His own spiritual predilections and political humanism favor natural law, which he characterizes as an endowment of "man with certain fundamental and inalienable rights antecedent in nature, and superior, to society." He contrasts this vision to the positivist view which holds that "man's rights are relative to the historical development of society, and are themselves constantly variable and in a state of flux." Natural rights are pre-social and prehistorical—imprescriptible, if by that word we recognize both a temporal and a textual aspect so that they are, at least theoretically, outside the influence of the time and text of society and civil law. Modern eighteenth-century human rights are deduced from, and constitute, the Enlightenment philosophical experiment called "natural man," the fictitious pre-social creature from which derives the classic social contract itself. Thus, natural law is, necessarily, *la loi non écrit* (the unwritten law)—as Maritain revives its ancient name—the law prior to inscription. This does not mean, however, that it has no literary textual existence, only that it resists transcription, losing something in its translation into legal codes. According to natural law, the personality that animates the person of human rights is a mysterious force that exists prior to the individual's incorporation into society; it is an instantiation of Nature and Nature's God, directed to its freest and fullest expression in the transcendental and universal human personality—a personality that the UDHR aspires to realize as an international human personality.

Positive legal theory, on the other hand, views the human personality as the product of a legal fiction: "All [persons] are artificial and man-made. . . . As the subjects of legal attributes, they do not exist in the outside world but get this character only through the attribution of the legal system."[56] Positive law is statutory law—what John Austin, the nineteenth-century theorist of legal positivism, defined as "law set by political superiors to political inferiors."[57] For this reason, Ernst Bloch regarded positive law as a "transparent ideology of domination" allied with naked power against its "subtly abstract enemy"—natural law.[58] Speaking purely theoretically, natural law and positive law differ primarily in the source of their authority and the degree to which they respond to historical circumstance. Nature and Nature's God underwrite natural law; positive law is guaranteed by the sovereign's sanction—what Austin glosses vividly as "an evil [visited] in case I comply not."[59] Whereas natural law's compulsions are conceived to be moral and rational—the expression of self-evident truths warranted by a transcendent authority—positive law expresses "a signification of desire" backed by the executive sanction of a superior invested with the will and means to enforce its rules, to impose its obligatory aspect. In other words, positive law derives its force from the institution of political sovereignty—the power "to issue decisions in the imperative."[60] Whereas natural law comes clothed rhetorically as timeless common sense and self-evidence, positive law presses to become common sense through the force of the commandment—a sociohistorically contingent precept, the legitimacy of which depends upon the threat of violence.

In their reinvention of natural law, the drafters of the UDHR took the skeleton of its eighteenth-century form, but they transposed it into international law without either the full body of social institutions or the metaphysics that had historically buttressed modern human rights law. In so doing, they articulated an image of the human person that is neither fully natural nor fully artificial—a figure that is, like international law itself, an "intermediary between natural law and positive law."[61] This hybrid image is a symptom of the generic condition of contemporary human rights law; that is, the split personality is replicated in and intensified by the textual form of the law itself, which aspires to make "the sovereignty of the human personality" sovereign.

Autogenic Incorporation: Therefore, "the [Good] People" Is Its Own Subject

> It would take gods to give men laws.
>
> ROUSSEAU, *The Social Contract*

The textual life of contemporary human rights law began in 1948 with a technically invalid syllogism in the preamble to the Universal

Declaration. Simplified, that syllogism reads: (major premise:) The "recognition" of inherent human rights "is the foundation of freedom, justice and peace in the world"; (minor premise:) "A common understanding of these rights and freedoms is of the greatest importance" to realize that recognition; (conclusion:) "*Therefore*, the General Assembly proclaims this *Universal Declaration of Human Rights* as a common standard of achievement for all peoples and all nations." The UN concludes from its premises not an existential fact about the relationship between a common understanding and the foundation of human freedom; rather, it deduces the need for a speech act of recognition that publicly identifies human rights as inherent and inalienable, and it declares *this* declaration to be *that* speech act of common recognition and understanding.

There are competing canonical stories about the genesis and genealogy of the UDHR. The first plots the UDHR within a narrative that traces the "starting point of human rights in the modern sense" to the French Declaration of the Rights of Man and of the Citizen (DRMC) and the American Declaration of Independence, so that, at least with respect to human rights, the European eighteenth-century age of revolutions "date[s] the beginning of the modern era" as such.[62] The other story stresses the multiculturalism (or multitraditionalism) of the declaration and is generally framed in agonistic, Cold War terms: "The Communist rights tradition—which put primacy on economic and social rights—kept the capitalist rights tradition—emphasizing political and civil rights—from overreaching itself."[63] The lines of demarcation between a Marxist-Leninist tradition and a liberal-individualist tradition were not actually so formal or predictable as this narrative suggests. Nor do these traditions represent some substantive international cultural diversity, since they share at least as many assumptions as they contest. Neither of these stories is inaccurate; nor, however, do they represent adequately the figure of the human personality that emerges from international human rights or the law's formal hybridity. These two narratives are sometimes oddly intermingled by apologists for a parochial, Western-rights universalism, who argue that human rights are simultaneously the unique patrimony *and* universalist contribution to humankind of the Greco-Judeo-Christian tradition. Ironically, cultural relativists repeat this story to demonstrate that international human rights are "a Western construct with limited applicability" and to argue that authentic human rights are "local," contingent upon particular cultural and social traditions and conditions.[64] This canonical narrative (consolidated, like all canons, through mantric repetition) caricatures twentieth-century international human rights law and its particular brand of normative personalism in terms of the analytical expectations created by their modern eighteenth-century counterparts. Recitation of this genealogy intensifies the liberal arrogance of a West that views itself as the foremost champion of human rights, and it over-emphasizes the continuities and coherence of human rights and its image of the person at the expense of the productive discontinuities, inconsistencies, and disjunctions that I believe are the sources of contemporary human rights' greatest promise.

The syllogistic preamble to contemporary human rights law captures part of the paradoxical incoherence of human rights; formally, international law is a generic hybrid, articulated in delicate tension between the description and prescription of human rights— between constatation (the confirmation of "simple facts," or common sense) and declaration (the enactment, or calling into being, of those existential facts—the rights that the UDHR aspires to make common).[65] Despite its theoretical irreducibility to transcription, natural law emerges with certain characteristic formal conventions when humans venture to put the unwritten law into writing. To ascertain those conventions, it is important to see how some of the tensions between natural law and positive law (between constatation and declaration) manifest themselves textually. Thus, in this section, I examine some of the important formal and conceptual discontinuities between contemporary human rights law and its modern eighteenth-century counterparts, since these differences not only challenge the European patrimonial arguments about international law; they also inflect its grammar of human personality development. I deliberately cite from portions of the documents typically invoked to confirm the UDHR's lexical and ideological debt to the Enlightenment declarations to better highlight the distinctions of the two rights regimes.

The 1789 French declaration begins with a rehearsal of its necessity and objectives:

The representatives of the French people, organized as a National Assembly, believing that the ignorance, neglect, or contempt of the rights of man are the sole cause of public calamities and of the corruption of governments, have determined to set forth in a solemn declaration the natural, unalienable, and sacred rights of man, in order that this declaration, being constantly before all the members of the Social body, shall remind them continually of their rights and duties.

Despite its title, the French declaration disavows the declarative activity of its speech act, presenting its enumeration of the "natural, unalienable, and sacred rights of man" as merely an act of constatation, of *putting before* "all members of the social body" the rights that are supposed to preexist the incorporation of that body, the election of its representatives, and the declaration itself. From this pre-social, unwritten natural law, the declaration presumably derives its first solemnly declarative right that "men are born and remain free and equal in rights" and, therefore, that "social distinctions may be founded only upon the general good" (Article 1). In locating human freedom and equality in nature, the DRMC makes political society not only subsequent but also subservient to nature, such that society's only legitimate purpose becomes "the preservation of the natural and imprescriptible rights of man" (Article 2).

The French declaration's preambular statements of self-justification echo in the preamble of the UDHR:

Whereas disregard and contempt for human rights have resulted in barbarous acts which have outraged the conscience of mankind, and the advent of a world in which human beings shall enjoy freedom of speech and belief and freedom from fear and want has been proclaimed as the highest aspiration of the common people . . .

Like the "representatives of the French people" in the DRMC, the "conscience of mankind," incorporated in the body of the UN itself, is a reactive formation, an embodiment constituted through the supposedly common experience of outrage at—and in response to—the recent and spectacular disregard for the rights on which both the French and the Universal declarations elaborate; both documents construe a kind of negative commonality from the disregard for natural rights. Thus, although (hu)mankind already exists as a corporate entity (according to natural law), that collectivity is discovered in the negative—through the recognition of a communalizing sense of outrage at what the always already-incorporated *corps social* has done to itself.

In theory, the rights exposited in both legal documents, like the social body to whom they attach, preexist their declaration, even if in the UDHR their enjoyment is deferred into an adventist future. In modern human rights law, rights are imprescriptible because they cannot be prescribed—they can only be recognized and re-stated. In contrast, contemporary international human rights law dispenses with the fiction of imprescriptibility. The UDHR combines the intentions of the French Declaration's first two articles in Article 1, but with an important difference—the preamble no longer supplies an antecedent transcendental authority (or a suprahuman vantage from which) to certify the passive construction of its claim: "All human beings are born free and equal in dignity and rights. They are endowed with reason and conscience and should act towards one another in a spirit of brotherhood." The natural-law language of inalienability remains in the UDHR—stipulated in the preamble as "inalienable rights of all members of the human family"—but the natural-law guarantee of their consecration has disappeared from the UN declaration. Instead, the preordained "sacred rights of man" (DRMC) are replaced by the UDHR's future-oriented "common understanding of these rights and freedoms" that serves to justify the rhetorical turn from the preamble to the text:

> *Now, Therefore,* The General Assembly *proclaims This universal declaration of human rights* as a common standard of achievement for all peoples and all nations, to the end that every individual and every organ of society, keeping this Declaration constantly in mind, shall strive by teaching and education to promote respect for these rights and freedoms and by progressive measures, national and international, to secure their universal and effective recognition and observance . . .

The "therefore" that simultaneously separates and conjoins the preamble and the text of the UDHR does similar rhetorical work, albeit with different metaphysical and political force, as the "*en conséquence*" that signals the legislative turn in the French Declaration: "*Therefore,* the National Assembly recognizes and proclaims, in the

presence and under the auspices of the Supreme Being, the following rights of man and of the citizen." "Therefore" signals the transition from unwritten to written law, but more than marking the
turn from prologue to decalogue (from pre-text to text), the
DRMC's "therefore" also announces what Seyla Benhabib has
called "an act of self-constitution; 'we, the people' who agree to
bind ourselves by these laws, are also defining ourselves as a 'we' in
the very act of self-legislation."[66] "Therefore" is constitutive of the
social body in much the same way that the Cartesian "*ergo*" is constitutive of individual being—a sort of *ergo*nomics, the law-giving
and humanizing, of "therefore." This point is perhaps clearer in
the compact formula in the American Declaration of Independence:

> We, therefore, the Representatives of the united States of America, in General
> Congress, Assembled, appealing to the Supreme Judge of the world for the
> rectitude of our intentions, do, in the Name, and by the Authority of the good
> People of these Colonies, solemnly publish and declare, That these United
> Colonies are, and of Right ought to be Free and Independent States . . .

"We, therefore": we, representatives already acting in the name of
the "good People" whose incorporation we are about to declare,
are constituted collectively by and in the "therefore," both by consequence of a common sufferance of colonial indignities and for the
purpose of making public the rightness of our common independence.[67] "Therefore" becomes a trope, the transitive figure that
turns natural law positive and the philosophical pretext of human
nature into legal text. "Therefore" is a performative figure that positivizes nature, prescribing the inherent rights rehearsed in the
preamble to articulate a second nature, both a secondary reclamation of natural rights and a proclamation in which the nature of the
human personality becomes an intentional and socially contingent
project of (re)naturalization.[68]

In the eighteenth-century declarations, The People—as a corporate entity capable (at least in a strict legal sense) of making such
declarations, although presumably existing prior to the declarations
by common suffering and the "Laws of Nature and of Nature's
God" (American Declaration)—is rhetorically positioned as the effect of the declarations themselves. Jacques Derrida observes of
declarations of independence—particularly of the American declaration—that if The People "gives birth to itself, as free and independent subject, as possible signer, this can hold only in the act of

the signature. The signature invents the signer."[69] Derrida calls this autogenic structure, in which "fabulous retroactivity" produces The People as themselves responsible for and to the law, an "unheard-of thing" that is also "an everyday occurrence."[70] The autonomy and sovereignty necessary for making a legal representation of independence are legible (for Derrida) only in the self-assignation of a signature that depends upon a textual ambiguity—an "undecidability between . . . a performative structure and constative structure."[71] But rhetorically, the moment when the constative transforms into the declarative—the moment, in fact, when the two most fully (and undecidably) overlap in the performative—occurs in the "therefore" that marks the shift from a statement of natural and experiential terms of *commonality* to the positive autogenic incorporation of a civil and political *commonalty*. This tropological turn about a "therefore" is characteristic of the unwritten law's transcription—it both disconnects and connects the preambular, constative rehearsal of rights taken for granted (whose immanence is presumably guaranteed by the extratextual, eternal authority of Nature) with the articles' declarative statements of rights that imminently follow (logically, causally, and temporally) from the preamble.

The discursive process of civil and political autogenesis simultaneously signs over responsibility for the law (that is, signs for the law) to this corporate mass now to be known as "The People," and produces it as both lawmaker and law-abider—both author and *dramatis persona* of the law. If the revolutionary declarations wrested "divinely authored royal sovereignty" from the monarchy to relocate it in The People (and, individually, in the citizen),[72] this refraction of authority and responsibility begins to situate sovereignty within the figurative operations (the rule) of the law itself, which is construed to be the expression of The People's autonomy and to be coextensive with its general will. Nonetheless, the guarantors of this figurative displacement in the modern revolutionary declarations remain Nature and Nature's God, whose sponsorship is invoked to certify the transaction and transcription of the new law. The DRMC is contracted "under the auspices of the Supreme Being" and in the name of The People ("the good People" in the American declaration). These are autonomic acts, in the literal and reflexive sense in which autonomy names the condition of giving the law to oneself. The self-sovereignizing act incorporates The People as state—the administrative medium through which The People distribute human rights to themselves. The modern declarations are, as Seyla Benhabib notes, "performative act[s] of republican self-founding."[73] Thus, the "experiment of the modern nation" is not merely a political, civil, or social one; it is also rhetorical, transubstantiating The People's sovereignty on the transcendental sovereignty of Nature.

Autogenesis operates according to a figural logic of incorporation that both corporatizes (gives body to—makes a legal person of) and capacitates (gives rights and duties to—attributes a legal personality to) the subject. The incorporative figure of "therefore" is a foundational trope of enabling fictions that project the imaginary conditions they intend to realize. In the case of the modern declarations, The People is incorporated with the capacity to frame its own articles of incorporation. The People in the French and the American declarations is self-producing, self-incorporating, and self-personifying; but it is not self-substantiating, since the major premise in the syllogistic formulation of modern popular sovereignty remains nature's imprescriptible, pre-textual patronage. In other words, Derrida's analysis notwithstanding, The People is not yet autonomous; its self-declared sovereignty is transacted vicariously under the benefaction of Nature, whose apparent self-substantiation is drawn upon to ground the rhetorical act of self-founding—the figurative legal work of The People's autoincorporation.

If gods were needed to give modern human rights law to men, no such "unheard-of thing[s]" stand surety for the figurative conjurations of the UDHR; the secularized, tropological "therefore" comes to occupy the offices vacated by gods. Today we have the vestigial, rhetorical form of natural law in a rather soft positive legal regime that appeals to "every organ of society . . . to promote respect for these rights and freedoms and by progressive measures, national and international, to secure their universal and effective recognition and observance." Similarly, all that's left in the UDHR of nature's patronage is a discursive trace in the imperative to "act towards one another in a spirit of brotherhood," which can only be spirit after the national representatives of the international "common people" unnamed the symbolic function of Lacan's Name-of-the-Father. Neither does the UDHR have an autoconstitutive effect—it does not produce either the UN or the common people as the double subject of its jurisprudence in the same ways that the eighteenth-century declarations produced The People as legislators and adherents of its own laws.[74] The "position of the guarantor of the completeness of the law" remains open in contemporary human rights law—an opening, as I will show, that literary and other cultural forms are sized to fill in order to install the human personality (and its putative sovereignty) in the place vacated by Nature and Nature's God.[75]

There is no pre-text to positive law—no preamble to the commandment. Positive law does what it says it does because it always pronounces itself in the prescriptive (or imperative) mode, backed by executive sanction that may constitute a threat but is not a pretext. Positive law has no figurative turn about a "therefore." The UDHR preamble emerges without citing the traditional natural-law pretext (the extratextual warrants of Nature and Nature's God), but it also comes without any executive force other than its appeal to common, "brotherly" sense. Contemporary human rights law is hybrid because it appropriates formal aspects of both eighteenth-century natural and nineteenth-century positive law without conscripting their substantiating metaphysics or institutionalizing the social, civil, and political force that underwrote those legal regimes. As such, the UDHR exposes the fundamental tautological condition of all law. Without warrant or sanction, without the premise of Nature or the dictum of an executor, contemporary human rights law is enthymematic, requiring that what is taken for granted be—therefore and thereafter—obsessively recited and rearticulated, as the past sixty years of "frenetic legislative activity" at the UN seems to confirm.[76]

International human rights law operates discursively without the traditional guarantees for its figurative work of incorporation—without a rhetorical net, as it were. This is not merely a speculative, poststructural insight but the actual political and juridical condition of international human rights law; historically, the legal authority to substantiate law's tautologies arrives only as a retrofitting of its conventions. For instance, when provided at all, rights of petition—introduced in the English Bill of Rights (1689) and fundamental in eighteenth-century declarations[77]—and instruments of enforcement are appended as "Optional Protocols" to international treaties.[78] Thus, states may ratify legal conventions without submitting themselves to international scrutiny or exercising the option to extend to their citizens the right to claim their rights. The recent establishment of the International Criminal Court (ICC) represents a similarly belated attempt to retrofit human rights with coercive force, with the sanction to execute its weak, positivized natural law. Although conceived early in the creation of contemporary human rights as a mechanism for prosecuting crimes of genocide, the ICC was only formally established after sixty states had deposited their ratifications on 11 April 2002; it remains to be seen what force it may have. My point is that the extratextual guarantee of contemporary human rights only arrives after their tautological declaration. If these efforts cannot rename the transcendental Father, they do attempt to revive his sovereign function—to give international law the force of law.

Taking Rights for Granted: The Revolution Will Be (Tautologically) Formalized

> God may have died . . . but at least we have international law.
>
> —COSTAS DOUZINAS, *The End of Human Rights*

Despite his misgivings about the suspension of metaphysical questions in drafting the UDHR, Jacques Maritain welcomed the moral (if not the weak legal) force of the declaration, which, he wrote, "pending something better," would "be a great thing in itself, a word of promise for the downcast and oppressed throughout all lands, the beginning of changes which the world requires, the first condition precedent for the later drafting of a universal Charter of civilised life."[79] Having dispensed with the project of producing a legally binding treaty, the Human Rights Committee took up the seemingly impossible task of transposing "a word of promise" into a law that might become a "thing in itself"—a self-substantiating legal and moral discourse of human rights. Perhaps more acutely than in the wake of World War I—when Lukács wrote that "the immanence of meaning in life had become a problem"—after World War II the UDHR architects chose not to "think . . . in terms of totality," but in the received *forms* of totality, even as they dispensed with the figures historically invoked to certify that total-ity:[80] God and Nature—the Sovereign and the Patriarch. In articu-lating a positivized natural law without nature, the UDHR drafters took from the Enlightenment declarations not so much their formal premise as the rhetorical form of their emancipatory promise.

"Forms," wrote Brazilian literary and social critic Roberto Schwarz, "are the abstract of specific social relations" that "retain . . . and reproduce" at least some "of the more or less contingent body of conditions in which a form is born."[81] Frederic Jameson calls these structures "cultural patterns," which must have once been "vital responses to infrastructural realities . . . attempts to re-solve more fundamental contradictions—attempts which then out-live the situations for which they were devised, and survive, in reified forms . . . [to] become part of the objective situation con-fronted by later generations."[82] The contingent body of conditions that produce forms seems to leave certain structural traces and exi-gencies that survive even in a form's afterlife; many UN delegates sensed something improper about a human rights law that con-tained no reference to a transcendental authority. Eleanor Roose-velt—chair of the UDHR drafting committee—lamented over this condition in her nationally syndicated "My Day" column the morning after the declaration's adoption:

> Paris, December 10—I would have been delighted to see in the preamble a paragraph alluding to the Supreme Power. I knew very well, however, there were many men around the table who would violently be opposed to naming God, and I did not want it put to a [roll call] because I thought for those of us who are Christians it would be rather difficult to have God defeated in a vote.[83]

Roosevelt detects the spirit, if not the proper name, of God en-crypted in the preamble,[84] and although her elegy reflects the atti-tudes of many of her UN colleagues, they begrudgingly conceded to P. C. Chang's persuasive argument against cultural parochialism to delete "the words 'by nature'" in draft Article 1: "Those who believed in God could still find in the strong opening assertion of the Article *the idea of God,* and at the same time others with different concepts would be able to accept the text" (emphasis added).[85]

Perhaps Gayatri Chakravorty Spivak has some of this history in mind when she suggests that it was necessary for contemporary human rights "that the question of nature . . . be begged (assumed

when it needs to be demonstrated), in order to use it historically"
and, furthermore, that this logical begging "has been forgotten."[86]
But in our forgetful era of crisis-driven human rights practice, we
might remember that the UDHR was itself composed under the
sign of emergency, when questions of nature were not so much
begged as they were understood to be beggared by historical circumstance and the outrages of fascism. The emergence of the legal
form of contemporary human rights without its train of traditional
benefactors does not mean that the law somehow dispensed with
the formal necessity of a guarantor. In fact, the history of contemporary human rights law might be written as a quest narrative for
universally acceptable candidates to occupy the vacated position of
law's underwriter—a quest to unbeg the begged questions.

Begged questions—like the figure of paradox discussed in the
introduction—are generally understood to be logical fallacies, but I
want to consider their productive capacities and their formal and
rhetorical properties. Begged questions are brands of tautologies
structured around premises that either remain unstated or are repeated as conclusions. In either case, calling something a "begged
question" draws attention to what is written out of the tautological
formulation, suggesting that there is a certain rhetorical (perhaps
strategic) exclusion in the form's hermetic autoreferentiality. Having unnamed the Name-of-the-Father, international law conventionalized the paralogic and rhetorical figure of the begged question
(*petitio principii*) as the armature of human rights. That is, contemporary human rights law not only suspends questions of (human)
nature; the rights supposedly derived from that nature are themselves articulated across the impossible span—signaled by the law's
"therefore"—of a now-unsecured and positivized natural law, the
form of which is the begged question itself, repeating the natural,
preambular premises in the positive promises of its articles. The
tautological structure of contemporary human rights law is the formal symptom of this metaphysical begging, but it is not a simple
sign of the law's debility.

Roosevelt bemoaned the secularization of natural law, but we
could recognize the process (in formal terms) as its positive tauto-
logization—the juridical effect of a "rhetorical revolution," after
which "it was no longer felt necessary to derive rights from a god,

especially a Christian God, or reason, or innate moral sense or nature."[87] Recognizing that this rhetorical revolution severed the form of natural law from its substantiating metaphysics should make it possible to counter the genealogical fallacy that regards contemporary human rights as simply the reincarnation of modern European rights. This recognition also allows us to avoid the positivist fallacy that dismisses its partial formal inheritance of natural law as archaic Enlightenment residualism. For many analysts of human rights law, the discovery of its tautological structure announces the limits of both the law and the analysis. It arises, for instance, as a parenthetic interruption in the work of Talal Asad: "the *Universal Declaration* does not define 'the human' in 'human rights' other than (tautologically) as the subject of human rights that were once theorized as natural rights."[88] But instead of surrendering before the apparent impasse of tautology, Asad admirably circumvents the theoretical blockage by returning with a slightly different inquiry: "But what kind of human does human rights recognize *in practice?*"

I do not want to be too cavalier about the meaningful differences between human rights discourse and practice, but neither do I want to help reify an analytical separation of the two. The complicated formal condition of contemporary human rights law is, at least partially, constitutive of (and constituted by) both discourse and practice; we can therefore insist upon the importance of the legal form itself—upon the sociopolitical implications of its purposive formal abstraction. We can also confront the theoretical blockage by returning with another question: What kind of human does human rights recognize in tautology? What, that is, emerges from the formal structure of the legal tautology itself? What kind of person, with what form of sociality, does tautology describe and prescribe? As a matter of rhetoric (and, as we shall see, of narrative) these are questions of culture as much as of law. (As I explain in the next chapter, the development of novelistic plot emerges from just such a begged structure, and this legal form has a correlative narrative possibility made legible in the *Bildungsroman*.) In this line of questioning, begged structures and tautologies are more than just symptoms of the logical and juridical infirmity of human rights law. Untethered from the sociopolitical conditions of their "birth," these now-improper forms represent not only part of the objective conditions we must confront but also the formal conditions of future possibility. That is, despite its apparent formal debility, there remains a certain productivity to the tautological form of contemporary human rights law—what work, then, does this improper form now perform?

"The Promise of the 'Not Yet' ": Discursive Aspiration and the Cultural Magic of Tautology

> The primary purpose of the Declaration [is] not simply to achieve moral success, but to enable man, all over the world, to develop his rights and, in consequence, his personality.
>
> —MELCHOR AQUINO, Philippine UN Delegate,
> in the UN *Yearbook*, 1948

"Human rights are literally the rights one has simply because one is a human being," both common sense and the international legal scholar Jack Donnelly tell us.[89, 90] Contemporary human rights law conventionalizes this tautological articulation of common sense generally, and the UDHR does so specifically, around the formula of "the free and full development of the human personality." Commemorating the UDHR's fortieth anniversary, John Humphrey intimated this tautological form of legal common sense in his assertion that "everyone knows, or should know, why human rights are important. They are important because without them there could be no human dignity. Life without them, many people think, would not be worth living."[91] Humphrey's encomium advertises the tautological, rhetorical architecture of enabling fictions, which, in the case of human rights, presuppose the human dignity and personality that they legislatively enable. Humphrey suggests that human rights not only protect but effect human dignity. Indeed, the UDHR repeats its preambular "recognition of the inherent dignity and of the equal and inalienable rights of all members of the human family" in a positive declaration in Article 1: "All human beings are born free and equal in dignity and rights." Located on both sides of the law's transitive "therefore," human dignity both precedes and derives from human rights, warranting their recognition and emerging from their declaration; thus, rhetorically, dignity (the Kantian quality definitive of the category "person") is both a founding natural rationale for, and the positive product of, human rights legislation.

Humphrey valorizes contemporary human rights law's tautologies as confirmations of common sense, and, in many ways, the UDHR drafters understood their legislative task to be precisely the articulation of common sense—the consensual "sense that founds community."[92] Since at least 1789, when the Marquis de Lafayette proposed to the French National Assembly a *déclaration des droits* that would "*'dire ce que tout le monde sait, ce que tout le monde sent'* (say what everyone knows, what everyone feels)," legislation of the obvious has been the rhetorical mode of the transcription of hitherto-unwritten human rights law.[93] The paradox of the obvious is, obviously, that it can be as logically uncompelling and as practically and politically unpersuasive as it is comforting and familiar. The Canadian delegation to the UN, for example, registered its indifference to the inclusion in the UDHR of Article 6—"Everyone has the right to recognition everywhere as a person before the law"—by announcing that it "could not attach much importance to the statement of so obvious a principle."[94] Nonetheless, "so obvious a principle" entered the UDHR in its characteristic tautological form; the preamble already recognizes the inherent "dignity and worth of the human person" that Article 6 prescribes to every person as a right.

Tautology is the basic rhetorical and legislative form of obviousness—of truths held to be self-evident, as the American declaration has it. The legal tautologies of contemporary human rights are the rhetorical and formal remainders of Jefferson's Nature and Nature's God, structural traces of transcendence remaining after the UDHR drafters wrote out the traditional underwriters of natural law. As such, tautology is the positive rhetorical and logical form that the natural-law categories of inalienability and inherency take as the names of capacities for something to be the same as itself, or to persist as itself. Tautology is the emphatic form of saying what everyone already knows and feels—of common sense, or the formal manifestation of a hegemonic will to common sense. It indeed marks a boundary of knowledge, though not where the semiotician of modern mythology, Roland Barthes, posts it at the limit of reason, but where international legal scholar Walter Weyrauch locates it, at "the periphery of one's [intellectual] culture."[95] This cultural inflection is important because tautology delimits the margins of a culturally situated logos, signaling the site where culture-bound knowledge confronts its own limits and turns back on itself to produce the most concise and chiastic formulation of communally constitutive common sense: Human rights are the rights of humans, inalienability is inalienable, imprescriptibility cannot be prescribed, a person is a person. Tautology's hermetic self-containment and self-referentiality may make it "an empty, or vacuous, proposition" that reveals "nothing about how things are in the world," since its "truth-value" depends not on its content but on its form.[96] But, if tautology's content matters little to its truth value, then we must pay attention to the structure, motivations, operations, and effects of its formal properties as well as to the sociocultural conditions and contexts that make its truth-value compelling—that make these "unheard-of thing[s] . . . everyday occurrence[s]."[97]

The fortified redundancy of tautology rejects the burden of logical proof to stake its claim in the formalism of common sense, which, "since it is magical," writes Barthes, "can only take refuge behind the argument of authority."[98] The rhetorical form of self-evidence and immanence, tautology mystifies the foundation of its authority to assume the cultural positivity of a proverb: "Man is man."[99] Tautology is culturally conditioned and contingent; its pretense of self-sufficiency protests too much about its commonsensical status, obfuscating the depth of its dependence upon the work of adjunct discursive technologies. We might therefore recognize tautology as the formal expression of a discursive and legislative will to self-sufficiency (or sovereignty) rather than as the presumptive announcement of its achievement—the expression of an imminence that aspires to be immanent. To say that the commonsensical formulation is culturally contingent is not only to recognize tautology's reliance upon culture to make it meaningful, it is also to recognize that tautology is culturally constitutive—the corporate "everyone," who already knows what it has to say, is to some degree incorporated by that knowledge, by the extent to which a tautology is (or comes to be) compelling cultural common sense.

Paradoxically, contemporary human rights law articulates the free and full development of the human personality as a tautology. Humphrey suggests that the UDHR pre-positions dignity and the human personality as inalienable and inherent qualities of the pre-social human being in its preamble, but, in rearticulating those as prescriptible rights, the declaration also recognizes that both society and human rights violations impinge upon the development of human personality and its dignity. Expression of the ostensibly innate universal human personality is therefore contingent upon the particular social, economic, cultural, civil, and political relations of which the human person is a part and an effect. Thus, a tautologized contemporary human rights law posits the primary existence of what it seeks to articulate, claiming as *a priori* what is simultaneously, impossibly, and necessarily *a posteriori*—both before and after the law. That is, the human rights personality preexists society and law *and* comes into being through social interaction and the collective declaration of human rights. Ultimately, of course, these personalities are one and the same; underwriting and underwritten by human rights, the human personality is both natural and positive, pre-social and social, premise and promise. This double positioning, which occurs in the rhetorical modes of constatation (confirmed as pre-text in the preamble) and declaration (affirmed as text in the articles) gives the legal tautology a temporal dimension and a plot trajectory. With the introduction of time, tautology becomes teleological (or entelechial), which also transforms the human personality into the means by which human rights themselves are to come into being.[100] The tautological structure of this teleology formally animates the human person and the natural-law categories of inherency and inalienability, establishing the legal armature for international human rights law's story of personality development in the transitive, narrative grammar of enabling fictions, by which nature is to become a second nature and the human person is to become (and to be recognized as) the freely and fully developed and dignified international human rights person. From this transformation, the human rights plot of personality development emerges as a plot of incorporation—a plot of the development of a human person and personality capable of occupying the place of the "human" in international human rights. Articulating human personality as the engine and product of development, contemporary international law positivizes the inalienable, self-substantiating categories of natural-law endowment as transitive and reflexive projects of attaching human dignity to human dignity, the person to the person,

"man" to "man"—in effect, as teleological projects of tautologiza-
tion. As we shall see in the following chapters, the *Bildungsroman*
makes legible this esoteric, improbable plot structure of human
rights subjectivation and its narrative grammar for becoming positively what one already is by natural right.

The rhetorical form of the law makes "the full development of
the human personality and the sense of its dignity" matters of culture and cultivation, situating the human being capable of bearing
rights and duties as their product in the mode of a subject yet to
come—a subject not-yet-fully capable of recognizing the inherent
dignity of the human personality or itself as a person before human
rights law (ICESCR).[101] While the eventual adoption of the UDHR
was still in doubt, Eleanor Roosevelt defended the document
against fears about its potential threat to U.S. sovereignty by elo-
quently summarizing this improbable, figurative temporality in *Foreign Affairs*: "If the Declaration is accepted by the Assembly, it will
mean that all the nations accepting hope that *the day will come* when
these rights *are considered inherent* rights belonging to every human
being" (emphasis added).[102] Roosevelt reconciled the seemingly in-
congruous time frames of human rights by animating the natural-
law category of inherency as an inherency-in-becoming that anticipates the day when human rights law's common sense will become
the public culture of an international human rights order, when
formal tautologies will become, in practice and effect, redundantly
tautological—when the natural human being will become the international human rights person. The legal tautology of inherency assumes the activity of a transitive verb, converting the human
personality and its dignity from a condition or quality into a project.
This proleptic vision of inherency-in-becoming anticipates a future
anterior perspective from which a projected inalienability of human
rights will have been recognized as inalienable, an imaginary perspective from which the "project of becoming a person"—a project,
as Drucilla Cornell notes, "that can never be fulfilled, once and for
all"—may yet be viewed as the consummation of free and full
human personality development.[103] In other words, Roosevelt's inherency-in-becoming describes a human rights (and by implication
a human personality) to come, a human rights that will be human
rights when it is recognized as human rights, not by the force of

executive authority or transcendental source but by its cultural enforcement—its coming into common moral, material, and customary force. Human rights law is therefore not precisely tautological
because it is *not yet* tautological, because it is *not yet* socially and
culturally redundant, because the human person is *not yet* the
human person of international human rights.

not yet

The tautological-teleological complex of Roosevelt's promissory
note for an inherency-in-becoming captures the improbable temporality of contemporary human rights (and its projection of human
personality development) that in many ways remains, practically
and institutionally, what the UDHR describes as humankind's
"highest aspiration" and a "standard of achievement for all peoples
and all nations." The drafters of the UDHR articulated a rhetorical
solution to the problem of the law's substantiation by positing the
human personality as sovereign—as self-substantiating in its own
right. The tautological form of the law therefore appears to be
merely a formal reflection of a proleptic human personality that is
itself imagined to be tautological (self-same). But, of course, historically, as the horrors of the Holocaust demonstrated to the UDHR's
drafters, the human personality has rarely proven to be self-substantiating in practice. Thus, the beginnings of the modern novel
and the founding legal texts of the Enlightenment served the UN
delegates in 1948 as reference points, not for the restoration of
some prelapsarian sociohistorical moment (and its fiction of natural
man) but for the resurrection of a failed promise—as the preamble
to the UDHR envisions it, for "the advent of a world in which
human beings shall enjoy freedom of speech and belief and freedom
from fear and want" and the "realization" of the inherent "dignity
and worth of the human person." If the UDHR is epoch-making
(as many of its advocates heralded at the time) the epoch of human
rights is situated proleptically as a world to be achieved in a future
that will be in effect, as Costas Douzinas' book eponymously calls
it, "the end of human rights"—the achievement of its telos and
obsolescence. The logic of advent articulated in the UDHR remembers forward from the eighteenth century not to relocate some
pristine Enlightenment tradition of liberty, equality, and fraternity,
but to take possession of its tradition of the future—a formal precedent for the formally unprecedented, the revolutionary "stipend of

human rights" that, as Ernst Bloch says, is "so anticipatory of humanity."[104]

If international human rights law has been relatively injusticiable as law, equipped with a historically feeble enforcement regime, it has had somewhat more success in its observance as custom—that is, as a culture. Richard Falk refutes the common Hobbesian skepticism about "whether international law is really law at all" by arguing that such critique is based on a misleading comparison to an "empirically questionable . . . idealization of domestic legal order," suggesting that if "the existence of an order of legality depends on rates of compliance, then international law seems rather solid as a legal order."[105] Falk's assessment assumes that a lack of human rights violations constitutes, *ipso facto*, compliance, and therefore that the international human rights legal conventions have achieved some compulsory, customary status. Historically, however, the compulsions of law's tautologies have depended upon extrajuridical modes of substantiation. In other words, historically it has been sociocultural forms and relations more than administrative institutions and legal appliances that have given international human rights law whatever force of custom it enjoys—that have cooperated to make its tautological brand of common sense functionally commonsensical.[106]

Daniel Defoe's novel yielded to the delegates of the UN's Third Committee the sociocultural "common sense" that made it possible to articulate the dialectical relations between the individual and society in the legal language of Article 29. The invocation of *Crusoe* and the facility with which the delegates debated its meaning demonstrate the extent to which the (European) UN in 1948, speaking in the assumed name of the world's "common people," already shared a set of common, if ambivalent, cultural narratives that in many ways constituted the body as an interpretive international community. Indeed, the novel's dissemination and globalization—in part the effect of colonialism and a cosmopolitanism whose prestigious institutions of higher education most of the UDHR drafters shared as alma maters—positioned it as a cultural candidate to underwrite a legal principle that had so far proved imprescriptible. Perhaps it is saying too much to suggest that *Robinson Crusoe* acted in the capacity of God, but it seems only marginally less heretical to admit that, structurally, it stood surrogate for Nature, or the idea of God. Crusoe is, the drafters argue, self-sovereign, but that nominal self-sufficiency is contingent upon (in their reading) his reading, and upon the social relations he enters with (European) human industry and culture through its tools and books. In other words, his self-sufficiency is contingent upon his literary socialization, through which Crusoe discovers for himself the necessity of the social contract and the civic institutions that ultimately manifest themselves on his island domain as complete extensions and expressions of his universal human personality. The Crusoe fantasy depicts problems that face human rights law: of how responsibility for socialization and incorporation might be located with the individual personality itself; of how "the law [might be] seen to be freely accepted [by the individual] and to derive from his or her own will";[107] of how the fabled sovereignty of the human personality might become again sovereign; of how positivized nature might come once again to be read (at least affectively) as natural. The UN delegates collectively read *Crusoe* not as the story of monadic self-sufficiency but as the novelistic expression of a will to self-sovereignty—a will that similarly inclines international human rights law to its aspirational international domain and the UDHR's abstract, universal human personality to its manifest destiny in an individually practicable international human rights personality.

Given their dual commitments to the welfare of the individual and the Westphalian institution of state sovereignty, it is not surprising that UN delegates turned to the novel as the supple cultural form most often implicated in modern problematics of both individualism (Watt) and nation-state formation (Anderson); nor, for that matter, that they turned to the literary technical means created with the beginnings of the modern novel to substantiate and inaugurate the legal vision of their own new, self-creative beginning. Although Crusoe cuts a rather ludicrous figure as a bookkeeper of both self and state, he resolves the conflict between individual and society through his meticulous narrative invoicing[108]; in a fabulous fusion of multiple personalities (King, Governor, and individual subject), personal sovereignty (autarky) becomes miraculously coextensive with the administrative geography (autarchy) of an island "state" cast outside ordinary civil time. The fantasy of Crusoe's accidental civilizing mission becomes an exercise in "narrative. . . . *self*-government"—a narrative self-civicizing mission.[109] Ironically, this seemingly antisocial, isolationist fantasy of complete congruity between human personality and political subjectivity provided the enabling fiction to underwrite the UDHR's ideal of sociality.

Without universally effective warrant or sanction, without a substantiating metaphysics or compelling institutional immediacy, international human rights law remains largely an aspirational discourse—a discourse in waiting. That is, contemporary human rights is largely a proleptic discourse and law governing a future universalism, awaiting actualization in the Foucaultian institutions and Althusserian apparatuses of its projected international domain. Therefore, from a legal and institutional point of view, international human rights continues to have a weak civil and political form, with no unitary existence comparable to that of the modern nation-state. To renew the Enlightenment's emancipatory promise, the UN borrowed from the repository of institutional forms that developed with the Westphalian nation-state—itself incorporated partly as an effect of modern human rights legislation—for its projection of a Dumbarton Oaksian international formation proleptically constituted on international human rights still to come.[110] In its articulation of an international imaginary that is based on nation-statist forms, the UN deferred to what it understood to be the *de facto* geopolitical relations of state sovereignty and reserved the adjudication of so-called international human rights to its member states. Thus, the projected human rights-based international order has little in the way of forms of its own. I do not mean that it has no material immediacy or sensible existence; rather, its institutional and administrative structures remain weak, and it has little in the way of cultural forms that are not proper to the nation-state to provide symbolic legitimation for its projected social formations. What civil and political palpability it does have is sustained (or intimated) not by its own autonomy or self-substantiation, but by the cooperation of ulterior social, cultural, and economic forms and formations that circumstantiate the norms of the law and an imaginary domain called the international.[111]

The UN's use of *Robinson Crusoe* to substantiate the legal principle of the social development of the human personality dramatizes one of the roles that cultural forms sometimes perform as enabling fictions—as subtexts of the law. I suggest that, for better or worse, the novel form had been doing for more than two centuries some of the incorporative, transitive, sociocultural work that the UN delegates aspired to rearticulate and transpose as international human rights law after the devastation of World War II and the outrages of crimes against humanity. The *Bildungsroman* is one of the primary carriers of this globalizing and normalizing human rights culture, acting—if rarely so immediately as *Crusoe* did for the UDHR—as a cultural surrogate for the missing warrant and executive sanction of human rights law, supplying (in both content and form) a culturally symbolic legitimacy for the authority of human rights law and the imagination of an international human rights order. But the genre does not emerge from the international domain as such; rather, it internationalizes, both in its generic formal conventions and in its global circulation. As I show throughout the remaining chapters of this book, the *Bildungsroman* has been an especially important ally in naturalizing the positive norms of human rights, in resolving the conceptual incongruity of teleology and tautology, and in imagining an international, intertextual order. As a legal discourse without its ordinary formal institutions, international human rights law depends on such cultural positivism to underwrite its denatured legal tautologies—to make their common sense compelling.

Becoming Plots: Human Rights, the *Bildungsroman*, and the Novelization of Citizenship

To raise the question of the nature of narrative is to invite reflection on the very nature of culture and, possibly, even on the nature of humanity itself. . . . [The] growth and development of narrative capability . . . has something to do with . . . the status of the legal system, which is the form in which the subject encounters most immediately the social system in which he is enjoined to achieve full humanity.

—HAYDEN WHITE, *The Content of the Form*

To undergo *Bildung* is to identify with humanity: a humanity that is itself an ongoing process of self-realization or becoming.

—MARC REDFIELD, "The *Bildungsroman*"

Broken Promises and Lost Plots

In her first major speech as United Nations High Commissioner for Human Rights in 1997, Ireland's former president Mary Robinson admonished the international body for having abandoned its historical mission of "realising human rights": "Somewhere along the way many in the United Nations have lost the plot and allowed their work to answer to other imperatives."[1] Recalling the purposes for which the UN incorporated itself in 1945, Robinson insisted that "almost by definition and certainly according to its Charter, the United Nations exists to promote human rights." Indeed, the Charter's preamble rehearses the organization's statement of purpose, enumerating the common principles and goals of a plot for "building up a culture of human rights"[2] that united the nations as a corporate international body endowed with "the conscience of mankind" (UDHR): "To save succeeding generations from the scourge of war, . . . to reaffirm faith in fundamental human rights, in the dignity and worth of the human person, in the equal rights of men and women and of nations large and small, and . . . to promote social progress and better standards of life in larger freedom" (UN Charter). In reminding the UN of its originary promise to realize human rights, Robinson cautions the "international community" against instrumentalizing the spirit of human rights and transforming its humanist plot into the clinical language of "macroeconomics," with its econometricized "surrogate" objectives of "human wellbeing," "human security," "basic needs," and "good governance." With the increasing influence of developmental economics and "human capabilities" approaches to human rights, these terms have come to monopolize the bureaucratic language, if not the law, of human rights;[3] Robinson affirms her preference for the holistic, "empower[ing]" words of the Universal Declaration of Human Rights (1948) and other international legal treaties. In the High Commissioner's exhortation to the UN to rediscover its purpose and to "take hold of it boldly and duly,"[4] "losing the plot" could mean not only that the UN had lost its way but that, because the delegates had been answering to "other imperatives," the humanist discourse of human rights risked being overrun by seemingly plotless accounting methods for representing and imagining the contemporary social world and human development.

Admittedly, I am perhaps drawing heavy implications from what is, finally, a rather ordinary use of an English colloquialism: "to lose the plot." However, I exploit this fortuitous formulation because it exemplifies a more general intersection of the conceptual vocabularies of human rights and narrative theory that I explore at length in this chapter. When Robinson reproached the UN for straying from its historical plot and losing the thread of the human rights plot to other imperatives, she suggested that state and other interests have corrupted the basic humanist vision of free and full human personality development—that the professionalization and institutionalization of human rights have effectively turned it "from a discourse of rebellion and dissent into that of state legitimacy," as international legal scholar Costas Douzinas has suggested.[5] But, in fact, lamentations over a degraded human rights plot—and the blunting of its counteractive force—draw too neat a distinction between a rebellious spirit of human rights and their current crass instrumentalization by states and other international actors. As I show in this chapter, with regard to rebellion and legitimation, both human rights and the *Bildungsroman* equivocate as a matter of form.

Although the language of rights helped prepare the European revolutions of the eighteenth century, the modern legal regime of human rights emerged not in those revolutions but in their wake, as a postrevolutionary reaction to the excesses of the *ancien régime* and as a legislative program to consolidate the sovereignty and legitimacy of the new bourgeois state. Thus, the state is both the "target and raison d'être" of human rights.[6] Like those declarations of state legitimacy, twentieth-century human rights law sought to legitimate the UN and its vision of a postwar new world order. It was, after all, state actors working in congress through their national representatives at the UN (under the assumed name of the world's "common people") who declared international human rights law and who situated themselves as an international body mediating between the individual and the institutions of the sovereign nation-state. Like its eighteenth-century counterparts, the Universal Declaration enlists the human person in its legitimating activity with the exhortation that

> every individual and every organ of society, keeping this Declaration constantly in mind, shall strive . . . to promote respect for these rights and freedoms and by progressive measures, national and international, to secure their universal and effective recognition and observance, both among the peoples of Member States themselves and among the peoples of territories under their jurisdiction.

Given that the self-interest of states is built into international law, the language and legislation of human rights have historically been ambivalent, constituting both a discourse of rebellion and of state legitimacy.

International human rights law consists of principles by which states parties agree to abide for the promotion and protection of the rights of their own citizens, calibrating the limits of legitimate state power by the abstract (moral) anthropometrics of the "inherent dignity" and "worth of the human person" and its capacity for "free and full development" (UDHR). In other words, despite the lofty humanist language, the UN is incorporated as an international body on the principle of symmetrical obligations that individual sovereign states mutually, but severally, agree to assume in relation to their own citizens—rather than to an international or universal humanity as such. In this regard, a primary novelty of contemporary human rights law is the internationalization of a legal regime of state legitimacy—internationalized, nonetheless, through the old Westphalian model of state sovereignty. Consequently, the legitimacy of the UN, and therefore also of its individual member states, depends in principle upon honoring their reciprocal obligations to protect and promote what Mary Robinson called the plot of human rights.

Contemporary human rights law proposes to regulate the relations between the individual and the state most conducive to the free and full development of the human personality. It takes two persons as its subjects: the individual human being and the state, which is imaged both as "a predator that must be contained"[7] and as the democratic institutional manifestation of The People's will that administers legal personality to human beings—"a necessary power for the enabling and flourishing of personhood."[8] Although the nonbinding UDHR appears concerned primarily with the human individual, this double subject is explicit in the two justiciable international covenants of 1966—the International Covenant on Civil and Political Rights (ICCPR) and the International Covenant on Economic, Social, and Cultural Rights (ICESCR)—in which "States Parties" alternate with the human person as the grammatical and legal subject of rights. Thus, while "*Everyone* shall have the right to recognition everywhere as a person before the law" (ICCPR Article 16), it is "*The States Parties* . . . [who] agree that education shall be directed to the full development of the human personality and [of] the sense of its dignity" (ICESCR Article 13). The alternation of these grammatical subjects in contemporary human rights law vivifies one of the paradoxes that I have already noted: Human rights are not yet the rights of humanity in general; they are the rights of incorporated citizens—the rights of persons acting in their corporate capacity *as state*.

Contemporary human rights law attempts to reconcile the continued historical primacy of the state and its institutional needs with what the UDHR takes to be the aspiration of the human personality: to consummate its manifest destiny in internationalized citizenship. The UDHR's solution to this perennial Enlightenment problematic is to pair the individual and society in a dialectical relation in which the human personality is both the product and engine of their interaction that brings the modern state and the modern citizen-subject into mutual, simultaneous being in an international context. Like its eighteenth-century counterparts, international human rights law imagines an idealistic reconciliation of its two primary subjects in which individual and social demands become fully congruent through the mechanics (or aesthetics) of the democratic state—a reconciliation that Robinson Crusoe ironically and haplessly stumbled upon with his shipwreck. The UDHR's articulation of the ideal social relations between the individual and the state intimates the formal rudiments of human rights' undeclared narrative. The generic elements of this narrative consist of two primary actors (the human person and the state), a probable conflict between them, a means of remediation in the human personality, and a temporal trajectory that emplots a transition narrative of the human being's sociopolitical incorporation into the regime of rights and citizenship. This is the story that the Universal Declaration plots as the free and full development of human personality, an idealist plot to repair the division of civil "man" from its juridical abstraction, which Eleanor Roosevelt intimated in the idea of a coming inherency and Karl Marx anticipated as the "re-absor[ption]" of "the abstract citizen" by the "real, individual . . . human being."[9] The UDHR sets the mark of narrative closure—of "full development"—at the human person's retrospective recognition of this plot as the expression and consummation of its own proclivities. This projected closure to the plot of human rights incorporation aligns it with "the project of the Enlightenment" more generally, which "aspired to create persons who would, after the fact, have wished to have become modern,"[10] which itself entails a project that aspires to accustom the human being to regard this personalizing plot as the natural pattern of human personality development.

As I will show over the course of this chapter, in abstraction, human rights and the modern *Bildungsroman* share this basic plot structure that manages the pressures of both human rebellion and state legitimation; moreover, human rights discourse and narrative theory draw upon much of the same conceptual vocabulary of plot, character, and setting in their respective analyses of the sociology of human development. To some degree, the Gordian knot of rebellion and legitimation can be unraveled through the concept of plot and its otherwise-seemingly distinct literary and political connotations. On the one hand, "plot" is the name of the narrativization of causality and consequence—"the principle of interconnectedness and intention" that emerges from, and models, the cultural "syntax of a certain way of speaking our understanding of the world."[11] On the other hand, "plot" names a concerted effort to subvert entrenched power, authority, and institutions—an effort to disrupt the conventional chains of connection and causality, to rebel against what Peter Brooks calls the "dominant legalities of the fictional world."[12] Brooks suggests "that in modern literature this sense of plot [gunpowder plot] nearly always attaches itself to the other: the organizing line of plot is more often than not some scheme or machination." A similar ambivalence in the contemporary human rights plot of incorporation engenders a tension between revolution and evolution. In other words, human rights law aspires to domesticate the impulse of the revolutionary plot of rebellion into the less-spectacular, reformatory plot of human personality development as the progressive harmonization of the individual and the state. As part of its institutional conservatism, human rights law aspires to normalize, publicize, and disseminate both its plot of human personality development and responsibility for it, so that rebellion—as an act of collective self-assertion—might be trans-plotted into socially acceptable modes of narrative protest that make individual claims on the state. In fact, by the logic of human rights, the state's institutional legitimacy depends upon, and is intensified by, the normative modes for expression of consent and dissent that it conventionalizes and makes available to what Georg Lukács called "the problematic individual."[13]

   In the previous chapter I characterized this international human rights plot as novelistic, partly because the rise of the novel has been consistently implicated in the rise of human rights' two primary persons: the individual and the state. Indeed, narrative theory written contemporaneously with the UDHR tended to hail the novel as the literary genre most intensely concerned with the problematics of socialization—with the encounter between the "contingent [social] world and the problematic [but ordinary] individual" as "realities which mutually determine one another."[14] Accordingly, the novel is seen as the paramount medium for representing the socioaesthetic construction of modern, bourgeois individualism, and the paramount model for imagining the modern nation-state as a social community. In this regard, the novel can be described as a technology for making the institutional abstractions of both the human person and the nation-state formation (individually and collectively) sensible. Historically, narrative individualism and narrative nationalism are interdependent, and the modern novel has naturalized their inter-formation within what I have called the Westphalian unities of nation-time and nation-space—the "time space" (chronotope) through which human rights law also plots its favored story of human personality development.[15]

The human rights plot is also novelistic in a more narrow generic sense. Part of my interest in this chapter is in the transformative effects of plot and in the ways in which novels attribute the agency for that narrative transformation to persons within the novels themselves. The *Bildungsroman* is ideally designed to effect such a transfer of narratorial agency. The implicit *Bildungsroman* narrative of personality development codified in international law unfolds the plot for transforming personal rebellion into social legitimation with the individual's progressive incorporation into the regime of universal human rights—a plot for keeping the broken promise of the Enlightenment with the individual's reabsorption into universal humanity through the "natural" medium of the nation-state. Although contemporary human rights law appropriated much of its form from the eighteenth-century revolutionary declarations in order to rearticulate their emancipatory promise, it filters that spirit of enlightenment through the antirevolutionary conceptual vocabulary of German idealism; the philosophy of *Bildung* (and its novelization in the idealist *Bildungsroman*) articulated a transitive grammar for the elevation of the bourgeois male citizen to the universal class. A notoriously untranslatable word that denotes simultaneously image and image making, culture and cultivation, form and formation, *Bildung* names an achieved state as well as a process of humanistic socialization that cultivates a universal force of human personality (*Bildungstrieb*) that is naturally inclined to express itself through the social media of the nation-state and citizenship.[16] It represents the eighteenth-century German-idealist solution to the perceived conflict between individual and society—a project for "the integration of a particular 'I' into the general subjectivity of a community, and thus, finally, into the universal subjectivity of humanity," as Marc Redfield has described the plot of the *Bildungsroman*.[17] Contemporary human rights law plots its normative story of human personality development in the mode of the idealist *Bildungsroman*, which, as Wilhelm Dilthey suggested a century ago, obeys a kind of postivized natural law: "A *lawlike development* is discerned in the individual's life; . . . Life's dissonances and [social] conflicts appear as necessary transitions to be withstood by the individual on his way towards maturity and harmony" (emphasis added).[18]

The narrative homology between human rights and the *Bildungsroman* is not merely fortuitous; both articulate a larger discourse of development that is imagined to be governed by natural laws and that is historically bound to the modern institutions and technics of state legitimacy. As I discussed in the previous chapter, international law has proved largely incapable of keeping its emancipatory promise to realize human rights—to procure their effective universal recognition and observance everywhere. Consequently, it depends on vicarious sociocultural modes of substantiation to legitimate its formal tautologies. The idealist *Bildungsroman* is a particularly cooperative ally in this respect, acting as a positivistic cultural surrogate for the missing metaphysical warrant and executive force of human rights law. In both its thematic content and its literary social work, the traditional idealist *Bildungsroman* anticipated the Universal Declaration's plot of human personality development, naturalizing the normative syntax of the UDHR's way of declaring its understanding of the world in advance of that declaration.

This chapter shows the rhetorical and narrative structures that I identified in the previous chapter at work in the normative conventions of the idealist (or affirmative) *Bildungsroman*, which I distinguish from more ordinary, vulgar versions of the genre (that are the subjects of the remaining chapters) on the basis of its optimistic representation of "the education of an individual . . . [who] finds his place in the world and his sphere of activity by morally submitting himself to the community represented by the State."[19] The following sections examine the generic conventions of the idealist *Bildungsroman* as well as its historical social role: incorporating the problematic individual into the rights and responsibilities of citizenship, and thereby legitimating the democratic institutions of the emergent rights-based nation-state. The affirmative *Bildungsroman* normalizes the idealist vision of what Dipesh Chakrabarty calls the dominant transition narrative of development and modernization, which not only patterns the novel, biography, historiography, and human rights law, but also "underwrote, and was in turn underpinned by," the institutions of the modern European nation-state.[20] This enlightenment-progress narrative centers the individual within a "state/citizen bind as the ultimate construction of sociality."[21] Indeed, both human rights law and the *Bildungsroman* posit the nation-state as the highest form of expression of human sociality and the citizen as the highest form of expression of human personality. With the "state/citizen bind" posited as the ultimate horizon of human personality development, the nation-state consistently emerges as a problem for the abstract universalism under which both human rights and *Bildung* are theorized.

This chapter assembles the conceptual vocabulary that contemporary human rights law and the theoretical formulations of *Bildung* share in their comparable idealist articulations of free and full human personality development as the working-out of the state/citizen bind. This common vocabulary is indicative of an underlying transitive narrative grammar that the human rights plot of incorporation shares with the affirmative *Bildungsroman*. To demonstrate this confluence, I tease out some of the normative generic conventions of this grammar from the novel that most theorists of narrative and *Bildung* take to be the norm and ideal of the genre: Goethe's *Wilhelm Meister's Apprenticeship* (1795). I also examine a less-well-known example, Marjorie Oludhe Macgoye's novel, *Coming to Birth* (1986), which imports to Kenya—almost wholesale— the idealist vision of classical *Bildung*. While most postcolonial *Bildungsromane* trouble the narrow universalism of the genre (as all of my examples in subsequent chapters do), Macgoye's novel rearticulates the fiction of the *Bildungsroman*'s egalitarian imaginary to normalize the social formations and relations of a rights-based nation-state and its institutions of citizenship. Macgoye's novel demonstrates some of the ways in which the plot of the idealist *Bildungsroman* has historically supported not only the sociocultural forces of nationalization but also those of imperialism and the "civilizing mission." Indeed, nineteenth-century European colonialism and its international legal agreements represent their own kind of projective internationalism, which, ironically, are direct precursors to contemporary human rights law and its vision of an egalitarian international order. I examine therefore the complicity of *Bildung* theory in rationalizing colonialism to historicize the rebellion-legitimation ambivalence found in both the affirmative *Bildungsroman* and contemporary human rights law. The chapter closes with a discussion of this ambivalence in the idealist *Bildungsroman*'s social role as the normative novelistic form of an affirmative human rights claim—a narrative petition for incorporation in the franchise of human rights—that symbolically legitimates the dominant sociopolitical formations even as it challenges the narrow scope and exclusionary terms of their current deployment.

Fate and the State: Guarantees of Human Personality Development in Goethe's Wilhelm Meister's Apprenticeship

> The cultivation of my individual self, here as I am, has from my youth upwards been constantly though dimly my wish and my purpose. . . . Now this *harmonious cultivation of my nature*, which has been denied me by birth, is exactly what I most long for.
>
> —Wilhelm Meister writing to a friend

By a cosmopolitan epistemic coincidence, the literary and social critic Georg Lukács anticipated the UN's formula of human personality development in an essay on Goethe's *Wilhelm Meister's Apprenticeship* published one year before adoption of the UDHR. Citing *Wilhelm Meister* as the prototype and rule of the *Bildungsroman* genre, Lukács considered the social causes and implications of Wilhelm's driving desire to play the role of Hamlet in a production staged by a band of traveling actors. Lukács attributes Wilhelm's decision to leave home and join the troupe to "his insight that only the theatre will enable him fully to develop his human capacities under the given social conditions. Hence theatre and dramatic poetry are only *means* here to the free and complete development of the personality."[22] Although Lukács ultimately sees Wilhelm's quest for the "harmonious cultivation of my nature" (*Bildung*) as unfulfillable outside the theatrical world, he nonetheless endorses the social impulse of its idealist vision of "the free development of the human passions—under proper guidance, which does no violence to them—[that] must lead to a harmonious personality and to harmonious co-operation between free men."[23] Compared to his more famous study of *Wilhelm Meister* in *The Theory of the Novel* (1920), in which he praised its romantic image of the problematic individual who "find[s] responses to the innermost demands of his soul in the structures of society,"[24] Lukács' later reading is cynical about the prospects for holistic socialization in a capitalist world where the division of labor has debased social relations and "ossifie[d]" the human personality "to the point of caricature."[25] While "harmonious personality" may no longer be possible in a mundane modern-capitalist legal order, Lukács turns his focus to that other classical realm where personality has historical purchase, emphasizing in Goethe's novel the edifying function of literature and the emancipatory possibilities of theater as social simulacrum—where the human personality expresses itself through the mask of a *dramatis persona*.

Lukács ultimately reads Goethe's novel as monitory of a practical incompatibility of idealist humanism with an emergent capitalism, which he characterizes in Hegelian terms as a "struggle between poetry and prose"—between the poetry of the spirit and prose of everyday social life.[26] The many variants of the formulaic "free and full development of the human personality" that appear throughout Lukács' later study (like those that stipple contemporary human rights law) represent attempts to reanimate the spirit of poetry in a disaffected world, like Goethe's, where "the victory of prose" seems "already decided." The idealist *Bildungsroman* is a genre in which the conflict between poetry and prose is converted into the condition of possibility for human personality development. Accordingly, *Wilhelm Meister's Apprenticeship* ends not in the lofty realms of the spirit nor in Wilhelm's theatrical triumph, but with his return to the now spiritualized prosaic business of life: the management of estates and capital, the responsibilities of fatherhood, an arranged marriage that he accepts as the fulfillment of his own desire, and his initiation into the masonic Society of the Tower—a private socio-economic association with civic, political, and cultural pretensions. At the close of the novel, the Society of the Tower claims to have secretly orchestrated the social interactions that develop Wilhelm's personality and lead to his incorporation.

While much theory of the novel shares the conceptual vocabulary of contemporary human rights law, the idealist *Bildungsroman* shares its narrative logic and grammar. Goethe's *Bildungsroman* is often credited by literary critics with inaugurating the "teleological character of the genre"[27]—the first novel in which modern historical time makes its mature appearance, as Bakhtin wrote, in the evolutionary "image of *man in the process of becoming*."[28] However, Goethe's novelization of the humanist ideal of free and full human personality development patterns a more convoluted plot than this linear understanding recognizes, modeling not a straightforward transition narrative but rather imbricating "the principles of circularity and progress."[29] The interlinking of these time frames is most clearly and succinctly formulated in Wilhelm's letter to his childhood friend, Werner, in which he protests against the social disadvantages of his birth and justifies quitting his father's household and business: "The cultivation of my individual self, *here as I am*, has from my youth upwards been constantly though dimly my wish and purpose" (emphasis added).[30] There is a temporal (and even a dramatic) irony in the counterweight of Wilhelm's declared longing for development and change—"the cultivation of my individual self"—and his deictic insistence on personal integrity and permanence: "Here as I am." Indeed, the two forces combine in the novel, and the chronological plot returns Wilhelm to objective, material conditions of life at the end of his apprenticeship, approximating those from which he departed. The novel offers multiple emblems of this Hegelian arc of alienation and return[31]—the restoration of his grandfather's valuable art collection, the return to estate administration, his family name, etc.—but this wishful pattern of development is best exemplified in the story of Wilhelm's fatherhood: Before leaving his childhood home, Wilhelm impregnates his first love, who, unbeknown to him or the novel's reader, gives birth to a son before conveniently dying. These events are revealed only at the conclusion of his social apprenticeship, when, during his seemingly impromptu initiation ceremony, the Society of the Tower confirms Wilhelm's growing suspicion that the orphan boy whom he has been raising as a son for a number of years is, in fact, his biological son, Felix. Having played the social role of Felix's adoptive father, Wilhelm's voluntary fatherhood is legitimated by the social recognition of his biological paternity; he has freely chosen to become the civil father that he already was by nature.

The emplotment of Wilhelm's story as an extended narrative paternity test obeys the basic narrative grammar of subjectivation that I characterized in the previous chapter as the process of becoming positively what one already is by natural right. This grammar of personality development is both transitive and reflexive, and it patterns the narrative structure for representing the idealist modern process of "convincing the subject that what he must do is also symbolically right."[32] Wilhelm's voluntary affirmation of fatherhood is the symbolic confirmation of the end of his apprenticeship—the emblem of his social maturity and mastery. Somewhat stupefied when the secret Society of the Tower reveals its existence to him, Wilhelm's only vocal response to the unexpected ceremonial presentation of his "articles" of apprenticeship is to ask the Abbé "whether Felix is in truth my son."[33] In confirmation, the magisterial Abbé ventriloquizes nature: "Thy Apprenticeship is done; Nature has pronounced thee free." Read through the motif of fatherhood, the ideal of socialization in Goethe is the achievement of voluntarism and conviction—the willingness to risk the Freudian hypothesis of paternity, as Marc Redfield has suggested,[34] and so to act in all things as if one were the natural father of (foster) sons.

At the bottom of modern democratic civil society sits a similar hypothetical imperative: to live with others as if they were brothers (in the historical gendering of the citizen) or, in the language of the UDHR, to "act towards one another in a spirit of brotherhood." In fact, Goethe imbricates the paternal and fraternal hypotheses when he links Wilhelm's social mastery with his voluntary assumption of fatherly responsibility, an affirmation replete with civic implications: "In this sense his apprenticeship was ended," observes the narrator, confirming the Tower's proclamation, "with the feeling of a father, he had acquired all the virtues of a citizen [*eines Bürgers*]."[35] In Goethe's novel, citizenship names the categorical distinction between ignorant subjection (the father as hapless sperm donor) and the conscious affirmation of social relations (the father as willing foster to his own child). In other words, socially responsible fatherhood supplies the novel's model of civic virtue, the model by which one joins the brotherhood of the Tower. The cultivation of "the feeling of a father" toward minors and of a brother toward others marks the symbolic promotion of the subject to citizen—to a person before the law.

If choosing one's friends and family is a hallmark of modernity, then Goethe's novel sits on the transitional cusp between archaic residual social formations based on binding filial structures (e.g., family, religion, estate, divine–feudal chains of being) and emergent modern affiliative structures of bonding based, in principle, on volition (e.g., surrogate families, social clubs, class, democratic fraternity).[36] The convoluted temporality of human development in Goethe's novel is partly the consequence of a hybrid plot structure that awkwardly combines the principles of natural filiation and positive affiliation. The novel celebrates Wilhelm's acquisition of modern civic virtue, but it does so, ironically, by renaturalizing the social institution of fatherhood—by making his voluntary civic fatherly disposition coincident with his natural position as Felix's father.[37] The confluence of natural and civic biology offers an ironic consummation of the contorted temporal logic of his desire to become "my individual self, here as I am." Wilhelm's habituation, after the fact, to what could not, in the end, have been otherwise configures a developmental plot that is simultaneously tautological (confirmative of the same: Wilhelm a biological and social father) and teleological (productive of difference: Wilhelm the *convinced and voluntary* biological and social father). The teleology of "the cultivation of my individual self" becomes a tautology ("here as I am") expressed in time, which has neither the full unpredictability of real evolutionary time nor the timeless formal certainty of tautological truisms. This tautology–teleology dyad patterns the grammar of Wilhelm's journeyman plot that finally proves him worthy of his patronymic: *Meister* (Master).

This is the improbable grammar and hypothetical plot structure of the story of modern socialization (or personalization), which obeys the generic laws that rule all enabling narratives of subject-ivation, whose "temporality [can]not be true," as Judith Butler observes, because its representation is, "inevitably, circular, presupposing the very subject for which it seeks to give an ac-count."[38] In *Bildungsroman* criticism, the common names for this "lawlike" process of subjectivation are: assimilation, acculturation, accommodation, apprenticeship, and socialization (generic labels that, in the case of *Wilhelm Meister*, are overdetermined by his in-corporation in the Society of the Tower). These terms share a pro-gressive temporality in which the presumably cross-purposive compulsions of individualism and socialization, self-determination and social-determinism, unfold and enfold in the development of the protagonist's (*Bildungsheld*'s) human personality. Like human rights law, then, the *Bildungsroman* has its own double subjects—the individual and society—that need to be reconciled in the plot through dialectical interaction. German idealism envisions this process as the entelechical unfolding of a natural predilection of the individual human personality (*Bildungstrieb*) toward its self-expres-sion in the social and universal human personality; it imagines a relational individualism—a harmonious concordance of the per-son's universalist predispositions and the interpellative force of so-cial formations and relations, of which the human personality is a part and an effect. In his early writing, Lukács extracted this ideal from Goethe's novel:

> an ideal of free humanity which comprehends and affirms the structures of
> social life as necessary forms of human community, yet, at the same time, only
> sees them as an occasion for the active expression of the essential life sub-
> stance—in other words, which takes possession of these structures, not in their
> rigid political and legal being-for-themselves, but as the necessary instruments
> of aims which go far beyond them.[39]

In this vision of modern subjectivation, the human personality is socially contingent—it is both the effect and impetus of the inter-activity between the subjective individual and the objective forms of the social world. In other words, as in the UDHR, the human personality is simultaneously the medium, means, and manifesta-tion of the reconciliation of society with the individual, whose de-sires for self-realization can only properly find synthetic fulfillment in public forms of social expression—in the "world of convention."[40] The texture and institutions of the social world of convention (including legal conventions, which are the forms "in which the subject encounters most immediately the social system in which he is enjoined to achieve full humanity"[41]) are imagined ideally to represent social manifestations of an abstract universal human personality; that is, the institutional world of convention offers formal objective correlatives to the private individual personality that is itself a personal instantiation and institution of the social order. Thus, German idealism conceives of harmonious human personality development (*Bildung*) simultaneously as an *unfolding* of an individual's latent humanity in its encounter with the structures of the social world and as an *enfolding* of the individual within and by those structures. The theorists of *Bildung* code this double movement of incorporation as enlightenment—as the emancipation of the human being (and humankind more generally) from Kant's self-incurred tutelage. These are the forces that are magically reconciled in the fortuitous coordination of Wilhelm's biological paternity with the social institution of fatherhood. The transitive and reflexive grammar of Wilhelm's development brings him to the point of public acceptance—translated into personal will—of what he must otherwise have been by the conventions of society, biology, sponsorship, family inheritance, the law, and his family name: the father of Felix and a *meister Bürger*, a fully incorporated and capacitated citizen of the Society of the Tower, itself a corporate surrogate for a proto-German bourgeois state.[42]

Goethe's *Bildungsroman* shares its improbable plot structure with contemporary international human rights law, but it also shares the modern metastructural dilemma of how to imagine this transitive, narrative grammar functioning without the transcendental assistance of a suprahuman force capable of guaranteeing its figurative work. Goethe did not leave the ultimate working-out of Wilhelm's development plot to the full forces of either nature or history. Structurally, the contrived plot (or plotting) device of the Society of the Tower embodies both forces, coordinating the seemingly aimless events of Wilhelm's meanderings into a rectilinear (intentional and consequential) meaningful series of necessary biographical stages in a social apprenticeship. One of the novel's many "guarantees of development,"[43] the Tower acts as a narrative insurance firm, straitening the vagaries and risks of a modern secular chronological plot into the inevitability of an older "sacred masterplot that organizes and explains the world."[44] Goethe underwrites the contingencies of personality development with the social security of the Tower, which pronounces Wilhelm "free" in the assumed name of Nature, all the while orchestrating the social conditions that enable his incorporation. As a *deus ex machina*, the Tower usurps the authorizing function of Nature and Nature's God, converting contingency into fatality, and thereby acting as a surrogate for fate.[45] But the Tower (and its corporate sponsorship of Wilhelm's story) is also a surrogate for an emergent nation-state, and in that capacity it acts as a *socius ex machina*, whose invisible machinating hand bends the teleological drift of Wilhelm's social career into a tautological confirmation of what he already was from the first pages of the novel: the father of Felix. In this process of self-saming, which is akin to the self-identification effect of what Paul Ricoeur describes as "keeping one's word," the Tower keeps Wilhelm's promise to develop himself "here as I am" for him.[46] The social patronage of the Tower becomes a form of narrative sponsorship that guarantees that the apparently disordered events of Wilhelm's life in fact have inherent meaning because they can be given meaning in a well-ordered life story—they can be plotted, naturally, as a *Bildungsroman*. Indeed, Wilhelm accepts the articles of apprenticeship prepared by the Tower as the narrative of development that he would have plotted for himself if he had possessed the personal mastery that he supposedly acquires through socialization—through his incorporation into the society of the plotting brotherhood.

"The novel," Lukács famously declared just after World War I, "is the epic of a world that has been abandoned by God."[47] The *Bildungsroman*, like international human rights law, which is the postivized natural law of a world without God, articulates a quest narrative of "the problematic individual's journeying towards himself, . . . towards clear self-recognition."[48] In both law and literature, the human individual is made problematic and novelistic by the loss of the transcendental authorities that guaranteed the plot of classical epic—God(s), the sovereign, the patriarch, nature. Like the rhetorical device of the "therefore" in contemporary human rights law, which transposed eighteenth-century natural law without its sustaining metaphysics, the literary device of Goethe's Tower effectively positivizes nature, simultaneously incorporating it into the very structures of society and displacing it into a second civic nature. Historically, this displacement of transcendental guarantees of development corresponded with, if it did not initiate, "the emergence of narrative plot as a dominant mode" for the "plotting of the individual or social or institutional life story."[49] The loss of the traditional underwriters of epic and law had similar consequences for the modern novel as it had for contemporary human rights law. Personality supplants nature as the base of both narrative plot and human rights; the certain tautology of being is supplanted by the uncertain project of becoming, even of becoming what one already is by natural right. In other words, becoming "my individual self, here as I am" becomes a problem.[50]

Human rights law and the *Bildungsroman* are legal and literary regimes that imagine an idealistic scenario for the human personality to become the sovereign guarantor of its own development. But Goethe's *Bildungsroman* represents a generic transition to the realist novel; here the epic guarantees of gods and nature are not-yet-fully replaceable by the uncertain sovereignty of the human personality. Instead, the Society of the Tower occupies the authoritative and regulative offices vacated by Nature and Nature's God as well as those of the rejected patriarch (Wilhelm's father) and the petty feudal princes, giving Wilhelm's story the secular equivalent of the epic guarantee of the individual's ultimate—even if much delayed and deferred—arrival. As I will elaborate in the following sections, the idealist *Bildungsroman* is not a generic homage to the centered subject or the autonomous human personality; rather, it is the novelistic symptom of a social anxiety about the perpetual vassalage of the human personality. In this respect, the Tower acts as a guarantor of biographical progress—a surrogate for both vestigial fate and the emergent modern state. Its secret sponsorship ensures Wilhelm's development as a virtuous father and citizen, although Wilhelm himself only becomes aware of the civic implications of father-feeling after he has already acquired the sensibilities and fellow-feeling of the citizen.

The logical and temporal twisting of the developmental pattern in Goethe's novel emplots the citizen-subjectivating story of "responsibilization" (in Charles Taylor's term): the narrative process by which the *Bildungsheld* retroactively becomes responsible for its plot of personality development.[51] The transitive and reflexive grammar of personality development patterns a narrative of incorporation in which the subject being incorporated becomes responsible retroactively for the figurative act of incorporation itself, and thereby for both fate and the state. In strictly novelistic terms, the *Bildungsheld* is retroactively "armed for existence, ready to live his novel" as the protagonist of his *Bildungsroman* that he nevertheless always already was by literary convention.[52] This tautological–teleological structure is particularly clear in first-person *Bildungsromane* like *Great Expectations*, in which the protagonist becomes its own narrator (as we shall see in chapter 4). However, Goethe's novel also represents Wilhelm's retroactive assumption of personal responsibility for the plot of his responsibilization in the scene of the Tower's dramatic presentation of his articles of apprenticeship. In taking possession of his indenture, Wilhelm effectively endorses (or better, signs for) its contents, and the Tower effectively transfers to Wilhelm the responsibility for the plot of personality development that he always imagined himself responsible for anyway.

Given the idealist *Bildungsroman*'s generic thrust toward social responsibilization and modern democratic citizenship, Wilhelm's fascination with Hamlet might appear anachronistic. In the person of noble Hamlet—as with Robinson Crusoe on his island—the personal and political fully converge; Hamlet bears the patriarchal imperative to avenge the murder of his father, who, as the sovereign, is the embodiment of both divine and human law—the singular incarnation of all the names of Lacan's symbolic Name-of-the-Father. Wilhelm imagines his effort at "harmonious cultivation" as a project to restore the "nature, which has been denied by my birth," and thereby, like Hamlet, to restore the "proper" order of things. The accident of his bourgeois birth, as he complains in his letter to Werner, denied him the privileges and opportunities enjoyed by the nobility that are necessary for the cultivation of his personality. In this sense, playing the theatrical role of Hamlet offers Wilhelm vicarious enjoyment of the possibility of harmonious personality that he claims is his by right—if not by birth, then by nature. Wilhelm's claim to a natural right of personality development (*Bildung*) is a political appeal for the rights of the bourgeoisie to enjoy the historical privileges of the nobility. Notwithstanding

Wilhelm's conflicted plot impulses (to become and to be), his incorporation into the Society of the Tower constitutes neither a revolution nor a restoration; it is a novelistic reformation that rearticulates aristocratic privileges and dignity as bourgeois rights. It reforms the constitutional terms of the social order not by overturning the historical privileges of the aristocracy but by expanding the possible enjoyment of those privileges. The affirmative action of the Society of the Tower (and of the idealist *Bildungsroman* genre generally) problematically fulfills Wilhelm's "wish" and "purpose"; even as it enables Wilhelm to rebel against the demands of his father, it reaffirms many of those social expectations that he imagined himself to reject. Wilhelm's incorporation into the Tower rearticulates the egalitarian imaginary, but it does so by restoring Wilhelm's lost aristocratic birth rights and recoding that restoration as the activation of natural rights.

Keeping Broken Promises: Plotting Modernization and the Historical Consciousness

> These peoples (the underdeveloped, the unaligned, the neutral) are in a hurry to "modernize"; so let us carry the banner of modernization for them and help them to modernize fast. . . . Here, then, is a field in which we can excel—*the modernizing of the world.*
>
> —CHARLES MALIK, Lebanese representative to the UDHR drafting
> committee, *Man in the Struggle for Peace*

The cultivation of Wilhelm's personality in Goethe's novel has a progressivist and, thanks to the Tower's interventions, an apparently inevitable *telos*. This is the linear temporality that Robert Scholes and Robert Kellogg considered the central technical innovation enabling the modern novel. Published the same year that the UN completed the two Human Rights Covenants, Scholes and Kellogg's *The Nature of Narrative* (1966) echoes the human rights formula of personality development in describing a sublimation of Aristotelian plot to character in "modern narrative": "The movement toward chronological plot . . . is part of the general movement to emphasize character . . . its episodic pattern allows for *free and full character development* without interference from the requirements of a tightly knit plot."[53] For Scholes and Kellogg, the novelistic virtue of chronological emplotment is its capacity to represent what E. M. Forster dubbed "round characters," making the rounding of character itself the plot of the modern novel.[54] Linear plot, which gives narrative importance to the element and passage of routine time, is supposed to add dimension to the image of the characters that form in the reader's mind over the course of the story—a dimensional complexity usually recognized as personality (in the psychological rather than the legal sense). Thus, modern novelistic plot is understood to be constitutive, rather than derivative, of character.

In the technical sense of personality as I have been examining it, the human rights plot of incorporation also entails a rounding of character; however, the complexity of the human rights personality is figured not in psychological terms but in terms of the rights and responsibilities that the person is enabled to enjoy within a particular social formation. If the sovereignty of the human personality is not yet certain enough to ground chronological plot in Goethe's novel, neither is the emergent technology of modern linear plot yet sufficient to round off Wilhelm's personality. Goethe doesn't leave the final outcome of Wilhelm's socialization to the ordinary retroactive mechanics and retrospective properties of novelistic linear plot, which "impose . . . a meaning on the events that make up [the narrative's] story level by revealing at the end a structure that was immanent in the events all along."[55] In a heavy-handed way, the Tower instructs Wilhelm and the reader in the operations of modern chronological plot, showing how to divine the hidden consequence within life's seemingly random sequence of events; but it does so, ironically, by plotting against it, contriving to twist the loose linear plot of personalization into a "tightly knit plot." The revelation of the Tower is a revelation of the meaningfulness of linear time that gives retrospective purpose and direction to the events of Wilhelm's biography—indeed, that gives *biographical* meaning to the banal biological and social events of daily life.[56] The Tower, not the plot, ensures that Wilhelm's personality is rounded with the social rights that he claims were unduly rescinded by his birth.

The generic sociological name for Scholes and Kellogg's plot is "modernization," presumably the narrative pattern of European civilization's collective transition to modernity that "repeat[s] itself in each life" as the progressive manifestation of the human person-ality in time.[57] It patterns the dominant realist narrative modes not only of the modern novel (most especially the *Bildungsroman*) but also of biography and historiography more generally—the life sto-ries of human beings both individually and collectively. For in-stance, the plot-logic of linear development is essential for the corporate-progress narrative that the UN tells itself about its for-mation (UN Charter), but it is also fundamental for human rights and the personalizing narratives of modernization that the UN as-pires to enable "common people" to tell for themselves (UDHR). In fact, in the writings of the early UN delegates, the founding of the organization and the act of declaring human rights are routinely figured as evidence of humankind's coming of age—the *Bildung* of the species. In this story, the recent crimes against humanity be-come, retrospectively, temporary crises that make humanity's even-tual maturity (in the objective form of the UN) not only necessary but inevitable in a progress narrative still unfolding. Charles Malik, Chair of the Human Rights Commission in the 1950s and one of the primary drafters of the UDHR, is perhaps the most insistent upon this narrative of modernization; he characterizes human rights as a plot for "*the modernizing of the world*," and he advocates this project, in blustery, Cold War terms, as the moral advantage that "Western, Christian civilization" has over the material, develop-mental promises of communism in a Manichean struggle for the hearts and minds of the "underdeveloped" Third World.[58]

The plots to modernize the world and the individual are inter-connected; the story that human rights projects for the individual is "itself subsumed in the larger narrative of the civilizing process, the passage from savagery to civility, which is the master narrative of modernity."[59] Modernization is the dominant theme of a more-general discourse of development that consists in the "mass of [ready-made] notions" about human evolution and social progress that prefigures our narrative ways of articulating the relation of in-dividual human beings "to the social formations in which they are indentured to live out their lives and realize their destinies as social subjects."[60] The abstract idea of modernization encompasses and links the principles of what Hayden White calls "historicality" and "narrativity": the modern common sense that real social events have an eventual coherency of meaning and importance that can be made legible in narrative, that human experience "can be both lived and realistically comprehended as a story."[61] Thus, the term "modernization" encompasses not only the historical processes by which modern social formations and relations take shape; it refers also to the emergence of modern chronological historical time, by which those processes of shaping are given form and plotted as progress narratives; and it names the process of the individual's emergence into that "real historical time."[62] In Bakhtin's time-sensitive reading of *Wilhelm Meister*, the imbrication of these three processes is precisely what is novel about the Goethean idealist *Bildungsroman*; they concur in the dynamic figure of the *Bildungsheld*, who "emerges *along with the world* and he reflects the historical emergence of the world," an emergence that births both an "unprecedented type of human being" and modernity itself, "accomplished in him and through him."[63] In the legal context, modernization becomes the dominant theme and plot pattern for narrating the emergence of both the modern world of law and that "unprecedented," well-rounded modern character: the person. The modernizing plot enables all sorts of creatures—human beings, corporate institutions (societies of the Tower), states, etc.—to "fashion their personal stories as *Bildungsromane*"; as stories of becoming persons before the law.[64]

As Raymond Williams has argued of cultural forms generally, the *Bildungsroman* emerges as "an integral element" of the changes that it narrates; its "formal innovation" makes legible "changes in consciousness which are themselves forms of consciousness of change."[65] The *Bildungsroman* narrates the formation of the *Bildungsheld*'s modern consciousness of change—a historical consciousness "obtained in the course of history and determined by history, and the very consciousness of this gaining and determining," as Hans Gadamer described the process and effect of *Bildung*.[66] In the *Bildungsroman*, acquisition of a historical (plot) consciousness (symbolized in Goethe as father-feeling) means not only that "changes in the hero himself acquire *plot* significance" but also that the "hero" becomes capable of retrospectively finding for himself progressive continuity in the radically discontinuous.[67] Development of this modern historical sensibility, which permits persons to think of themselves as benefactors and agents of progress, "is conceivable only in terms of its interest in law, legality, and legitimacy," writes

Hayden White after Hegel; indeed, it seems that the narrative imagination only takes shape when the prevailing social formations in which the individual participates begin to be perceived as problems—that is, when "the legal system functions as a subject of concern."[68] More specifically, modern historical consciousness—particularly in the *Bildungsroman*—is concerned with the legality and legitimacy of the nation-state formation, its democratic integrity, and the possibilities of *"man growing* in *national-historical time."*[69] In other words, in the context of the emergent modern nation-state, historical consciousness is better understood as national-historical consciousness; this awareness of living one's life within the Westphalian unities of nation-space and nation-time, which Goethe's narrator praised as a primary virtue of the bourgeois citizen, is a sort of civic sixth sense that gives personal texture to the abstraction of the nation-state and citizenship. Cultivated within the constraints of the state/citizen bind (whose "naturalness" it reinforces), modern historical consciousness fosters an awareness of being subject to the law—of being a subject of legal rights and responsibilities, like anyone else.

Most of the literary and social theorists that I have quoted esteem Goethe's *Bildungsroman* as the epitome of the transition narrative of modernization for its rendition of both modern historical time and Wilhelm's conscious affirmation of the state/citizen bind. Of course, the principles of historicality and narrativity that sustain the plot of modernization are as historically contingent as the notion of a multidimensional (well-rounded) human personality, whose representation they appear to make possible. The idealist *Bildungsroman* is a literary artifact from that historical period of social evolution that sociologists of modern Europe describe, "in many idioms," as the "Great Transition": "the transition from feudalism to capitalism, the emergence of market society, the emancipation of civil society from the state, the increasing division of labor, and the rationalization of the modern world."[70] Positioned "at the transition point from one [epoch] to the other," the plot and form of the classical *Bildungsroman* bridges the transition from ritual, feudal, agricultural, and cyclical time to modern, secular, historical time, when evolution itself becomes the dominant hermeneutic for plotting human social events and establishes the syntactical patterns by which similarity and difference may be identified across time.[71] The conceptual Enlightenment revolution that birthed modernity and inaugurated the Westphalian chronotope made it possible (even necessary) to imagine human civilization (and individual life stories) in terms of the emancipatory plot-logic of progressive linear improvement. This vision of "continuous history," which secures the modern transition narrative, is, as Foucault wrote, "the indispensable correlative of the founding function of the subject: the guarantee . . . [and] promise that one day the subject—in the form of historical consciousness—will once again be able to appropriate . . . everything that has eluded him."[72] The classical *Bildungsroman* emerges with the "Great Transition" as a form—a symptom and novelistic abstract—of the consciousness of this modernizing change that promised to replace the social "world of subjection" with "the world of right and discipline."[73]

Enlightened modernity promised to liberate "man" by recognizing what Giorgio Agamben calls his "bare life" as the substance of the citizen, as the foundation of constitutional law. This process of recognition is enacted officially in the modern declarations of human rights that brought the democratic nation-state into being and symbolically in the transition narrative of the idealist *Bildungsroman*. It is contingent upon the Enlightenment notion that the natural human personality itself has an innate predisposition to become a civic person—that is, that man telegraphs the citizen. However, along with the institution of popular sovereignty (through which the people give themselves the law), modern human rights effectively cut short the transformational project that it claimed to affirm by legalizing an operative distinction between man and citizen, as is evident in the title of the French Declaration of the Rights of Man and of the Citizen (1789). The result is a paradoxical "historical figure" of Enlightenment civil subjectivity that is neither man nor citizen, but is what Étienne Balibar calls the "Citizen Subject."[74] The effect of an interrupted teleology and a broken emancipatory promise in the French declaration, the citizen-subject is suspended between the titular natural rights of man and the positive rights of the citizen, a "figure that is no longer the *subjectus*"—the individual subjected to the authority of another—"and not yet the *subjectum*," the individual as sovereign in its own right. In the context of postrevolutionary France, franchise qualifications for this modern citizen-subjectivity included property ownership and education; in Germany, where there was as yet no formally centralized nation-state, the qualifying criterion was *Bildung*.[75]

Reproducing Citizens: Bildung *and the T(r)opology of the Nation-State*

> [Man] seeks to grasp as much world as possible and bind it as tightly
> as he can to himself. . . . It is the ultimate task of our existence to
> achieve as much substance as possible for the concept of humanity in
> our person.
>
> —WILHELM VON HUMBOLDT, "Theory of *Bildung*"

The tension between poetic universalism and prosaic nationalism is present within the earliest Enlightenment formulations of *Bildung* that were given conventional story form in the *Bildungsroman*.[76] *Bildung* is the German idealist name for the achievement of the process and product of what German philosopher, linguist, diplomat, and pedagogical theorist, Wilhelm von Humboldt, characterized in 1794 as "the ultimate task of our existence." It is a philosophy for bridging the gap between concept and substance—between the spiritual universe and the concrete social world. It imagines a humanist process of transubstantiation by which the individual concretizes its abstract species image and realizes the intellectual enabling fiction of a harmonious, natural human personality through self-contemplation and self-cultivation of "a universal sense"—a transcendental sense of identification with humanity in general.[77] In this regard, *Bildung* is a philosophy for positivizing human nature. Denoting both a process of image-making and the resultant image, *Bildung* is the name of a trope, a figurative idea that turns the "concrete" individual into an instantiation of humanity's totality.[78] Originally signifying the human face (*persona*), in German mysticism *Bildung* is the spiritual process of personification by which God's image manifested itself in the purified human personality.[79] Over the course of the "Great Transition" the term acquired its secular inflection, sparked by the 1738 German translation of Shaftesbury's *Characteristics*, in which it signified the process of the aristocratic "formation of a genteel character."[80] The eighteenth-century philosophical effort to reconcile the subjective condition of the human being with the objective social world gave *Bildung* its bourgeois humanist valence as a studious effort to live life as an art—an effort of individuals to "develop their own innate potential through interaction with their environment."[81]

As with human rights, *Bildung* is formulated in the metaphysical language of abstract universalism, but it is practiced in the concrete social context of the emergent liberal nation-state, the "objective," as Friedrich Schiller wrote, and "canonical form in which all the diversity of individual subjects strive to unite."[82] That is, while it imagines a restoration of a transcendental wholeness supposedly lost in the social transition to modern prosaic civilization, *Bildung*'s more pedestrian work is to reconcile the perceived conflict between the natural inclinations of the human individual and the normalizing regulatory demands of society and the nation-state. Indeed, with one eye on the intellectual universe of conceptual humanity and the other on the mundane object world of states and citizens, early theorists of *Bildung*—including Herder, Fichte, Schiller, Hegel, Schlegel, Goethe, and Humboldt—extolled its service to the nation: articulating a socio-aesthetic process for producing (and reproducing) good citizens that demarginalizes and incorporates the human person into the dominant social, civil, and political body of The People.[83] Like languages (in the Herderian model), *Bildung* has "the power of alienating and incorporating, and by its own force it proclaims the national character."[84] Thus, *Bildung* is among those other universal forces (or entelechies)—e.g., history, culture, and abstract humanity—that Enlightenment philosophers imagined to be working out naturally, through the state/citizen bind, to manifest themselves in the ideal forms of nations and national subjects.

In Humboldt's polymathic theoretical writings, the "ultimate task" (*Bildung*) supplies the abstract moral benchmark for his liberal reformation of the modern German university, and for establishing the proper limits of governmental power in a well-ordered democratic state—a model that John Stuart and Harriet Taylor Mill famously imported to England in *On Liberty*. For Humboldt, the purpose of the state is to preserve (but not to administer) the freedom and "variety of situations" necessary for "the true end of Man"—for the citizen's *Bildung*—"the highest and most harmonious development of his powers to a complete and consistent whole."[85] Thus, properly constituted and restricted, "the State is not in itself an end, but is only a means towards human development," and its legitimacy is determined by the extent to which its social formations and relations harmonize with the predispositions of the individual, whose highest development they ensure.[86] Finding in the social institutions of the state the objective expression of its own humanity, the individual who has achieved *Bildung* will voluntarily "attach himself to the State; and the State should test itself by his measure."[87] In such an ideal state, the "roles of man and citizen coincide as far as possible."[88]

Through *Bildung*, German idealism assigns to culture the "political vocation" of achieving these ultimate tasks: turning man into citizen, "articulat[ing] society into an organic community," and "transform[ing] the masses into a dynamic and self-generating whole that approximates or actualizes the ideal of freedom."[89] Thus, Humboldtian *Bildung* describes a civic course of acculturation by which the individual's impulses for self-expression and fulfillment are rationalized, modernized, conventionalized, and normalized within the social parameters, cultural patterns, and public institutions of the modern nation-state. In this idealized model of socio-aesthetic modernization and enfranchisement, culture conducts a civilizing (or civicizing) mission that has two complementary centripetal effects: centralizing the nation-state and centering its citizen-subjects. In Humboldt's idealist philosophy, the nation-state represents the highest and most natural form of human sociality, and the citizen is the most fully developed form of the human personality. In other words, it is here that the classical society/individual dyad becomes the modern Chakrabartian state/citizen bind, and the story of the emergent proto-nation-state becomes fully congruent with the stories of the national-historical emergence of its proto-citizens. If this account of *Bildung* evokes Fredric Jameson's infamous "national allegory," by which "all third-world texts are necessarily . . . *to be read as . . . the story of the private individual destiny* [that] *is always an allegory of the embattled situation of the public third-world culture and society*,"[90] this is partly because "Western" readers have tended to interpret contemporary postcolonial *Bildungsromane* through the lens of that allegory and because the "first meager shelf of 'Third World classics'" that Jameson proposed to read as national allegories "consisted almost exclusively of bildungsromane."[91] In other words, Jameson's national allegory is a prescription for reading *Bildungsromane* according to the synecdochical, ethno-nationalist logic of *Bildung* itself.

Enlightenment philosophers of human rights and *Bildung* elaborated their solutions to the perceived conflict between individual and state in the name of the universal and in the service of nationalization. Their histories and contents are implicated in the cultural nationalist projects that sought to establish continuity between individual birth, the nation, and the universal.[92] The Declaration of the Rights of Man and of the Citizen was instrumental in the "Francification" of France;[93] its modernizing, domestic civicizing mission was aimed to centralize the nation-state and its citizen-subjects. Despite the egalitarian pretensions of the Rights of Man, postrevolutionary bourgeois France effectively nationalized those "imprescriptible and natural" rights as "uniquely [its] own, concerned with French values and culture," conscripting them (as I discuss in the next section) to rationalize the colonial *mission civilisatrice*—the universalization of French civilization.[94] Similarly, over the nineteenth century, *Bildung* and the *Bildungsroman* were retroactively enshrined as the unique national expressions of German values and culture—as "the German national genre" that was "not for export."[95] We might recognize these French and German sentimental identitarian attachments to the Rights of Man and *Bildung* as effects of the implicit national bearing of their ostensibly universalizing designs. Historically, what French *civilisation* and German *Kultur* cultivated were not primarily universalist sensibilities about the inherent and inalienable equality of man but chauvinistic senses of national particularity—of what it means to be, and how to become, freely and fully developed French or German citizens.

Bildung and modern human rights were both technologies of incorporation whose historical social work was to patriate the once politically marginal bourgeois subject as national citizen. As such, they articulated nationalizing projects intended to consolidate and legitimate the emergent bourgeois nation-state and its institutions of citizenship. Franco Moretti has famously declared that the *Bildungsroman* "narrates 'how the French Revolution could have been avoided'"—an appraisal that Swiss educational reformer Johann Pestalozzi issued before the revolution, warning in his "Education for Citizenship" (1780) of the potential for violent revolt if the ruling classes continued to deny the advantages of *Bildung* to the masses.[96] As an idealist trope of evolution, *Bildung* emerges as an analogue to modern state formation—a cultural correlative of the revolutionary impulses that were restrained by the Weimar Classicists who "oppose[d] the violence of the French Revolution with the concept of steady, organic growth."[97] Viewed from this international perspective, the *Bildungsroman*'s progress narrative represents a German cultural nationalist counternarrative to the violent eruption of the modern French nation-state and its institutions of rights-based citizenship.

If *Bildung* comprises a reactionary alternative to revolution, it shares this pacific spirit with modern human rights law. The French declaration of rights similarly articulated, after the event, how the revolution could have been avoided, and how future revolutions might be avoided through the reproductive mechanics of popular sovereignty. Although they emerged from the context of revolution, both human rights law and the *Bildungsroman* are reformist, rather than revolutionary; their social preservationist impulses conjoin in the Universal Declaration of Human Rights, where safeguarding the free and full development of human personality intends to obviate violence as a legitimate mode of collective self-determination: "It is essential, if man is not to be compelled to have recourse, as a last resort, to rebellion against tyranny and oppression, that human rights should be protected by the rule of law."[98] Both human rights law and the *Bildungsroman* project individualized narratives of self-determination as cultural alternatives to the eruptive political act of mass revolt. They are discursive regimes of reformation that attempt to universalize the historical opportunities for personality development and "dignity that feudal society offered only to the aristocracy";[99] in this way, they aspire to replace revolution with evolution—fighting with narrative plotting. In this sense, *Bildung* and human rights are tropes of amplification and expansion rather than of substitution, and the convoluted teleological–tautological plot logic of their narrative forms synthesizes the temporal dialectic of evolution and revolution into the improbable time frame for the arrival of a second human nature.

Although the idealist *Bildungsroman* imagines socialization to be a mutually beneficial encounter between the individual and a dynamic world of conventional forms that is, at least, "partially open to penetration by living meaning," the genre is tendentially conservative of the world of convention.[100] In particular, it endorses the egalitarian imaginary of the democratic nation-state by valorizing the responsiveness of its forms to the individual and by demonstrating the variety of situations that the state makes available for the individual's particular (but generic) plot of personality development. In other words, the *Bildungsroman* is as concerned with conserving democratic formations and social relations as it is with the conformation to those arrangements of the individual, through whom we see them operating. From this perspective, the classical *Bildungsroman* is only superficially interested in the exemplary individual whose story it narrates. The genre is more broadly concerned with the legitimacy of social institutions—with their propriety, preservation, and promotion—and with the institutional formation of the type of socialized individualism upon which their perpetuity depends.

The individualism imagined in the idealist *Bildungsroman* is not an atomistic, self-sovereign subjectivity (notwithstanding Wilhelm Dilthey's influential misreading of the genre, which he claimed "gave expression to the individualism of a [German] culture whose sphere of interest was limited to private life"—a judgment that tends to quarantine *Bildung* from historical questions of social power).[101] What the novels demonstrate is not the formation of "an apolitical subjectivism," as Pheng Cheah has rightly noted, but "the process of incarnation, objectivation, or actualization of universal ethical and political ideals as a second nature."[102] *Bildung*'s enabling fiction (which does not mean that it is unreal, but that it remains to be realized) posits the individual's desire for self-expression as presocial but inclining toward the world of convention, where it is actualized through socialization. Like the human person imaged in human rights law, the idealized individual in the classical *Bildungsroman* is socially and narratively contingent—an incomplete figure (like Wilhelm Meister) whose uncertain personal sovereignty depends upon society to give its individualism effect and meaning. The individual of *Bildung* and human rights is a social institution that would make no sense on its own; nonetheless, their image of the individual is normative—the incarnation of an institutional individualism necessary to animate the social formations and relations of the modern nation-state.

In 1819, little more than two decades after the appearance of Goethe's novel, Professor of Eloquence Karl Morgenstern proposed to call the literary genre the *Bildungsroman* "because of its content" but also "because precisely through this presentation [of the hero's *Bildung*] it encourages the cultivation [*Bildung*] of the reader more fully than any other type of novel."[103] Like *Bildung* itself, which names both a cultural mode of production and its cultured product, the novelization of *Bildung* is thought to perform what it thematizes—to effect in the reader the civilizing process of personality development that it narrates for the protagonist.[104] In other words, the *Bildungsroman* not only takes the social modernization of the individual protagonist as its subject matter; the novels also presumably have a social tutorial effect, performing transitive work as literary "machines for producing subjectivity, machines designed to construct 'centered subjects.'"[105] Tasked with this mission, the *Bildungsroman* represents and reproduces the socially acceptable form for the story of the human personality's coming to historical and autobiographical consciousness—for both the novel's protagonist and its reader, as potential civil subjects. In this sense, the genre itself becomes part of the objective world, a cultural form and social institution with which the individual's untutored impulses for self-expression must be reconciled to acculturate to the modern social order.

In its educative social mode, the idealist *Bildungsroman* imagines an optimistic resolution to the "conflict between the ideal of *self-determination* and the equally imperious demands of *socialization*" through which both the protagonist and the reader are urged to learn to "perceive . . . the social norms as *one's own*."[106] The *Bildungsroman* naturalizes the trope and plot hermeneutic of *Bildung*. In its production of an idealistic image of mutual accommodation between individual and society, the classical *Bildungsroman* aspires to reproduce in the social world the accommodationist norms that it elaborates in the world of fiction. That is, the self-reflexive genre of the *Bildungsroman* is not only thought to work on its own to produce the kinds of modern social subjects whose formation it fictionalizes, but, in doing so, it also normalizes the dominant conceptual language and story grammar for narrating one's own accommodation to society as a story of citizen-subjectivation. As with any language, in which the individual encounters "customs and institutions of his people [as] a pre-given body of material which, as in learning to speak, he has to make his own,"[107] the *Bildungsroman* is part of an already-saturated world of conventions—a world in which the genres of human sociality predate (and will, in one form or another, outlive) the individual human being. Human personality development becomes a delicate business of adapting sociocultural forms for oneself and adapting to their established formal constraints. Thus, *Bildung* comprehends a cultural reproductive process by which the social forms and formations of the nation and national-historical consciousness are made "self-generating."

Grounded in the tenets of natural law and articulated according to its enabling fictions about "man," both human rights and the *Bildungsroman* elaborate aspirational, hegemonizing projects for the individual to "be . . . raised to the universal."[108] They are both culture-bound because they project a culturally inflected story of incorporation that is directed toward a particular kind of cultural binding that has universalist pretensions. (As we shall see in the following section, this hegemonizing tendency, repeated as both the form and content of human rights and the *Bildungsroman*, carries within it the impulse of imperialism.) In their didactic social function, they are conceived to have a self-generating capacity not only to naturalize the universalist common sense of human rights and *Bildung*, but to constitute the normative subjects they pretend merely to regulate—to realize in the concrete social world of convention the persons they imagine to populate the abstract universe. As part of their civilizing work, they conventionalize an idealistic transition narrative for free and full human personality development that is oriented to the social formations and relations of the modern nation-state, endorsing its egalitarian imaginary and democratic mechanics by plotting a story of how individual will becomes congruent with group will and of how the individual's natural impulse for self-expression finds itself already manifest in the socially acceptable genre of the *Bildungsroman*.

The North Atlantic theoretical models of modern democratic constitutional nation-statism have a formalist obsession with these sorts of reflexive structures and reciprocating institutions of the civil industry of rights-based popular sovereignty—the public sphere, elective representation, parliamentary debate, the social contract, the general will, etc. Human rights and the idealist *Bildungsroman* share this democratic fetishization, which regards popular sovereignty's institutional forms as having invisible hands with quasimagical powers to transfigure their own subjects. Humboldt's plan for the modern citizen sketches a theoretical blueprint for what will become, with the consolidation of the modern state and its sovereignty, a kind of democratic formalism. By democratic formalism, I mean a hypothetical (and necessary) faith in the alchemistry of liberal state institutions to produce and reproduce the particular human personality upon which their machinery depends: a human capable of occupying the place of the human in human rights; of playing the role of the *Bildungsheld* in the *Bildungsroman*; of acting as both author and *dramatis persona* of the democratic rule of law. What I am calling democratic formalism ascribes to the institutions of the modern nation-state the power to realize the kinds of subjects that were posited in the enabling fictions about human sociality and personality that made institutions of popular sovereignty imaginable in the first place. From this idealist perspective, the social world of convention consists of institutions that are objectified forms of human nature, founded on, and charged with realizing, their own enabling egalitarian fictions in the form of persons.

The hypothesis of democratic formalism proposes that state institutions and structures, theoretically derived from the vicissitudes of the human personality to facilitate its harmonious development, establish the patterns and rules of their operation in anticipation of the very subjects required to animate and occupy them. This hypothesis remains largely an unspoken assumption about democratic forms, but in times of perceived social crisis it is typically verbalized as common sense (and contested as such) in public debates over the effectiveness of institutions in interpellating proper democratic citizen-subjects.[109] The democratic formalist proposition is bolstered by the humanistic ideology of *Bildung* that "invok[es] a concept of man in general as a producer of form, and as a producer, in particular, of the forms of himself."[110] While the idealist theories of *Bildung* and human rights articulate projects of socioaesthetic formation by which the individual comes to recognize itself within sociocivic forms, the formalist hypothesis attributes to these democratic institutional "forms of himself" a self-perpetuating, personifying capability that it characterizes as emancipatory.

Democratic institutions, then, take on a Foucaultian figurative life of their own, deemed capable of forming their own occupants, stamping their own subjects, and inscribing the psychical and physical dispositions, reflexes, and habits necessary for their institutional existence. That is, these engines of second nature ostensibly conduct their own civilizing mission by producing and reproducing a national culture of human rights and participatory citizenship that, theoretically, automates democracy. In this automated model, forms are (trans)formative, institutions are tropological, and culture is cultivating; in its tutorial function, the *Bildungsroman* form cooperates with these nation-statist institutions of democratic reproduction in an attempt "to achieve as much substance as possible for the concept of humanity in our person."

Filling Out Forms: (Post)Colonialism and the Limits of Democratic Formalism in Marjorie Oludhe Macgoye's Coming to Birth

> Of all forms of apprenticeship that of democracy is the most time consuming, expensive and nerve racking. It also requires a good deal of patience when the people let one down. . . . Africa, which is so malleable in many ways, throws out a challenge to modern physical and biological science, as well as to the town planner and social engineer, to examine the extent to which these changes are to be guided by human intelligence. Planning is the conscious application of intelligence to national and local evolution. It is a determination not to meet circumstances as they arise but to master them with foresight.
>
> —LEONARD WILLIAM THORNTON WHITE ET AL.,
> *Nairobi: Master Plan for a Colonial Capital* (1948)

If the Enlightenment philosophers of *Bildung* saw in the nation-state and citizenship the highest worldly forms of expression of an abstract universalism, the universalist impulse does not just get absorbed into the chauvinism of cultural nationalism; it also underpins the imperialist project, which is bolstered by an exaggerated, formalist faith in the institutions of democratic modernity. Indeed, the thesis of democratic formalism tends to go without saying in the domestic national context, but it surfaces explicitly in the figures of imperialist speech, when, for example, the militaristic, economic project of European colonialism is rationalized as a humanitarian civilizing mission—as Ngũgĩ wa Thiong'o famously described it, when "the night of the sword and the bullet [is] followed by the morning of the chalk and the blackboard."[111] Or, in the contemporary context of the "War on Terror" in Afghanistan and Iraq, when the trigger finger of military invasion is justified by the projective human rights ink of the "purple finger" of popular democratic elections.[112] The rhetoric, if not the practice, of these projects is imbued with the spirit of *Bildung.* While it may be well known that the "Rights of Man" were enlisted to rationalize the French *mission civilisatrice*—a mission to bring "universality" to those that the universalist rhetoric paradoxically left out of the universal imaginary— less familiar is the rhetorical assistance that *Bildung* provided to nineteenth-century colonialism.

In his posthumous 1836 tome on linguistics, Humboldt characterized the transformative work of *Bildung* as a project of humanization, whose intellectual fruits consisted in "the idea of merely respecting a person as a human being" and the "sentiments of the resultant human rights and duties."[113] Humboldt regarded the refinement of *Bildung* as the crowning achievement of German (and more generally of European) humanist civilization, distinguishing the moral gravity and imperial magnanimity of modern Europe from its "ultra-nationalistic" classical predecessors. Thus, for Humboldt, the sentimental education of *Bildung* that attunes the human to its own humanity devolves upon its universalized (that is, already nationalized) subjects a global missionary responsibility:

> It is an admirable prerogative of our most recent era to transport civilization to the remotest parts of the earth, to associate this effort with every enterprise, using every means at our disposal. The governing principle of universal humanity at work here denotes a level of progress to which only our age has ascended. . . . The Greeks and Romans were far less effective in their colonies in this respect.

Such an ethnocentric conception of the principle of universal humanity rationalizes here, in the early years of the modern human rights era, colonialism and imperialism as legitimate vehicles of a globalizing *Bildung* humanism that is obliged to universalize the idea of the universal and inherent "dignity and worth of the human

person," as the UDHR has it a century later. Like the UN's imagination of an international human rights order, Humboldt derives
from his ideal of "universal good breeding [*Bildung*]" an intimation
of universal humanity not as natural fact but as a project that remains to be realized through "every means at our disposal," and
he gives this humanitarian brief to the mercantile, missionary, and
military agents of imperialism: their mission is to globalize *Bildung*,
to universalize the ostensibly universal ethos and attendant sociocultural conditions of modern Europe—in short, to spread the good
news of human rights by any means necessary.[114]

Like the ambivalence of contemporary human rights law, this
rights-man's burden (to trope on Kipling) emerges from a fissure
within the idea of *Bildung* that puts natural law's logic of being
in tension with the positivistic logic of becoming: an immanent,
tautological universal*ism* in tension with an imminent, teleological
universal*ization*. This equivocation of universalism underpins the
transitive, narrative grammar of both the *Bildungsroman* and human
rights, and it resonates in mid-nineteenth-century arguments for
British imperialism—in John Stuart Mill's *On Liberty* (1859), for
example, which is in many ways an extended gloss on Humboldt's
The Limits of State Action (1854) that argues for "the absolute and
essential importance of human development in its richest diversity
[*Bildung*]" (in the translation that provides Mill's epigraph).[115] In a
caveat on the colonial applicability of his libertarian philosophy,
Mill describes the developmental conditions, deliberative habits,
and social dispositions deemed necessary for the *practice* of liberty:

> this doctrine is meant to apply only to human beings in the maturity of their
> faculties. We are not speaking of children. . . . [And] we may leave out of
> consideration those backward states of society in which the race itself may be
> considered as in its nonage. . . . Despotism is a legitimate mode of government
> in dealing with barbarians, provided the end be their improvement, and the
> means justified by actually effecting that end. Liberty, as a principle, has no
> application to any state of things anterior to the time when mankind have be-
> come capable of being improved by free and equal discussion.[116]

For Mill, the right to liberty attaches to human beings only upon
their completion of a successful sociocivil apprenticeship, when
people quit barbarism and become capable of proper participation
in public discourse, and thereby of being further improved by civic

and political institutions. Thus, liberty is conceived not as the natural condition of the human being but as a right (with duties) acquired with social and civil maturity, and colonial despotism becomes a "muscular" humanitarianism. Indeed, both the civilizing mission and human rights—at least as we have known them—seem practically unthinkable without a formalist faith in the capacity of institutions to cultivate their proper subjects, and without the organic, teleological plot of human personality development—the enabling *story* that the humanistic notion of *Bildung* prefigures as the *history* of human liberation.

At least since the Atlantic movement for the abolition of the slave trade, the *Bildungsroman* and human rights discourse have been part of the freight of globalization as the West has prosecuted it through colonialism, (neo)imperialisms, international humanitarianism, and multinational consumer capitalism. One of the primary carriers of human rights culture, the *Bildungsroman* has been a conspicuous literary companion on those itineraries, traveling with missionaries, merchants, militaries, colonial administrators, and technical advisors—as the numerous allusions (both explicit and oblique) to *Great Expectations, Jane Eyre, Sentimental Education*, and *Wilhelm Meister's Apprenticeship* in contemporary postcolonial *Bildungsromane* attest. In the colonial context, the genre provides novelistic accompaniment to Ngũgĩ's "morning of the chalk and blackboard"— circumstances that provide the backdrop to his own early *Bildungsroman, Weep Not, Child* (1964). The *Bildungsroman* is enlisted by colonial authorities to transmit "humanist ideals of enlightenment": "the shaping of character or the development of the aesthetic sense or the disciplines of ethical thinking."[117] However, as Gauri Viswanathan has shown in the case of India, colonial literary education enabled those ideals "to coexist with and indeed even support education for social and political control."[118] The differential application by the colonial power of universalist principles in the colony and at home has led a number of critics to conclude that the official modes of importation of the *Bildungsroman* to the "periphery" deployed the genre "as an intensely conservative discourse of socialization, viz.; one which aims to achieve the symbolic legitimation of authority" not by producing citizens (as it had in Europe) but by reproducing subjects.[119] In other words, the foreign service of the *Bildungsroman* tended to consolidate a split between citizen and subject that, in Europe, the genre aimed to reconcile. European "civilizing" colonialism persisted on the technical difference between citizens and subjects—with a moral correlative in the difference between the putative civic virtue of the colonizer's father-feeling and the "childish" incivility of the colonized[120]— even as it justified itself in the conventions of progress narratives as a necessary humanitarian intervention to tutor the colonized peoples in the discipline of liberty, the practices of self-government, and the habits of citizenship. While the conservatism of the discourse of socialization theorized in *Bildung* and novelized in the *Bildungsroman* may seem especially blatant in the colonial context, in its historical social function as a novel of demarginalization, the affirmative *Bildungsroman* has traditionally served to legitimate authority by normalizing the dominant sociopolitical practices and patterns of nation-statist modernity and by affirming the capacity of those systems to distinguish good citizens from bad subjects.

Decolonization puts the thesis of democratic formalism in crisis when the colonial power begins to worry publicly that all that it leaves to the postcolonial nation are empty governmental forms too feeble to produce their required subjects. The generic positions taken in imperial departure debates are predictable, and those pertaining to Ngũgĩ's native Kenya are typical. Just weeks before formal Kenyan Independence on 12 December 1963, both houses of the British Parliament reviewed the prospective text of the postcolonial constitution, prepared under the auspices of the British Secretary of State by representatives of Kenya's major political parties and British colonial administrators. The Peers not only questioned the preparedness of Kenyans for self-governance and the robustness of the institutional infrastructure being legated; they also scrutinized the validity of the democratic formalist thesis itself—the very logic of the civilizing mission. Those MPs calling for a calming of the wind speed of change argued that Kenyan political autonomy "must be conditioned by [Kenyans'] capacity to conduct their own affairs, after our departure, on a basis of what may be comprehensively termed 'free institutions.' "[121] The dominant conceit of the debates construes decolonization as a problem of filling British legal and civil forms with African content. Even those Lords most openly cynical about the "assum[ption] that parliamentary government is a kind of fool-proof mechanism, completely automatic, with built-in stabilisers which guarantee freedom with order" (367) ultimately acceded to the confident institutional vision of decolonization proffered by the Minister of State for Colonial Affairs: "We can help set the pattern; we can lay down the rules. But theirs is the game and theirs its carrying out."[122]

Personal and national development as matters of filling out forms is the theme of Marjorie Oludhe Macgoye's novel *Coming to Birth* (1986), which narrates the transition from British colonialism to Kenyan post-colonialism through the personal experiences of Paulina, a socially and politically disenfranchised ethnic Luo woman from the provinces who "finds herself" in the postcolonial Kenyan capital, Nairobi. Paulina's emergent national-historical consciousness is coded as a triple *uhuru*, simultaneously the liberation of a woman, of the Kenyan nation, and of black Africa more generally. The novel subscribes to the democratic formalist thesis and adheres rather strictly to the generic conventions of the traditional *Bildungsroman*, even as it takes for its protagonist an unconventional and multiply marginal figure. The course of Paulina's demarginalization spans three decades, from the Mau Mau insurgency in the waning days of British colonial rule in the 1950s to the eve of the death of independent Kenya's first president, Jomo Kenyatta, in 1978. This proleptic narrative closure is figured as the political condition of possibility for the birth of a more democratic post-colonial-state formation—a birth that is prefigured in Paulina's own long-awaited pregnancy, whose term corresponds to the anticipated death of "the father of the nation."

The novel is about the birth pains of both postcolonial statehood and democratic citizen-subjectivity, or personality. In *Coming to Birth*, the relations between individual and state are allegorical—rather than dialectical, as in the classical idealist *Bildungsroman*—and the novel imbricates personal, racial, and national *Bildung* in terms of Paulina's trials with motherhood and her physical and spiritual movement from the "trivial intimacy of time spent at home" to her debut in an emergent modern democratic public sphere.[123] The major events of Paulina's biography—relocation from a small village to Nairobi, marriage to an initially abusive husband and the violent death of their only son, matriculation in Homecraft schools and her success as a teacher, reconciliation with her husband that leads to her final pregnancy—intersect with national and international events: the lifting of colonial Emergency regulations, Kenya's formal independence, the retrenchment of authoritarianism (signaled partly with Ngũgĩ's imprisonment) and its foreshadowed relief in Kenyatta's projected death, etc. Thus, the story of Paulina's coming motherhood (like Goethe's symbolic use of fatherhood) comprises both a *Bildungsroman* and a conventional national allegory that "becomes a narrative of the becoming of the nation and the struggle for dignity. . . . Her story become[s] all our story," as Ngũgĩ writes in a blurb on the novel's cover.

The novel's revolutionary focus on a marginal ethnic Luo woman is to some degree tempered by the conservatism of its *Bildungsroman* form and its confidence in the legitimacy and efficacy of the public institutions of nation-statism legated by British colonialism. Although the novel acknowledges some of the obstacles to postcolonial state formation, it nonetheless accepts the nation-state and the state/citizen bind as inevitable and natural forms of the human personality's self-expression—as the ultimate horizon of individual and collective emancipation. Macgoye's novel presents an optimistic vision of the commensurability of the personal and the political, narrating the progressive absorption of the postcolonial citizen by the once-colonial subject through the harmonization of individual desire and institutional state design. However, unlike the dialectical ideal imaged in the classical *Bildungsroman*, Paulina's encounter with concrete social reality results not in reconciliation but assimilation; modernity's statist structures all preexist Paulina and remain largely unaffected by her presence within them. Yet the novel narrates the transitive process of citizen-subjectivation along many of the conventional axes and topoi of the traditional *Bildungsroman* plot: the physical and psychical displacements of the country by the city, orality by literacy, filiation by affiliation, the "obsessive requirements of [tribal] ritual" by "tak[ing] what comes and mak[-ing] the best of it."[124]

Macgoye's narrative is especially attentive to the contours and rhythms of Westphalian modernity, and Paulina's physical and spiritual journey attunes her to what Bakhtin called a "completely new, *spatial* sphere of historical existence."[125] In Bakhtin's account, the "time space" of nation-statist modernity emerged in eighteenth-century Europe along with the new democratic sociopolitical forms and formations, including the *Bildungsroman*, which narrates and normalizes the acquisition of this novel national-historical consciousness. In contrast, the chronotopographical groundwork for modernity's institutions in Africa was overlaid on the continent at two international conferences during the European winter of 1884–85. Meeting in Germany, the European colonial powers negotiated consensual terms for scrambling Africa into spheres of influence. The resultant treaty, the General Act of the Conference of Berlin, constitutes an international law of imperialism by articulating the rights and duties that European nations agreed, jointly and severally, to assume in relation to the continent and its peoples. An immediate precursor to contemporary international human rights law, the General Act established the statutory legitimacy of colonialism, charging Humboldt's "every enterprise" with "the development of trade and civilization in certain regions of Africa." Some of the provisions of this early international law survive in contemporary human rights: "Freedom of conscience and religious toleration are expressly guaranteed to the natives, no less than to subjects and to foreigners" (Article 6). However, the treaty is primarily concerned with the economic, social, and cultural rights of the European powers and their agents (particularly the colonial charter companies) rather than with the civil and political rights of the natives—e.g., "The trade of all nations shall enjoy complete freedom" (Article 1); "Foreigners, without distinction, shall enjoy protection of their persons and property" (Article 5).[126] Meanwhile, in Washington, DC, the International Meridian Conference established the "universal day" and ran its zero degree through Greenwich, England, which, by a longitudinal irony of geography, also bisected West Africa "and thus doomed them together to the same time of day."[127] The international chronotopography—with its latitudes and longitudes of nation-statist "time space"—coordinated all at once the Westphalian parametrics for Africa's projected modernity. In Africa, the scientist matrix of modernity formally preceded (and anticipated) the rights-based nation-state, the structures of citizen-subjectivity, and the teleological story-form of their emergence: the *Bildungsroman*.

Macgoye's novel accepts Westphalian modernity's institutions as immutable and inevitable; it posits that "nationalism is a necessary thing" for the "long-deferred" identity of peoples "just emerging from marginality"—"the only thing that will give us [colonial peoples] an international dimension."[128] The novel graphs Paulina's transformation across the colonial divide of subject and citizen on the predetermined grid of nation-statist time and space; Paulina's life story thus becomes temporally synchronous and spatially contiguous with that of modern Kenya itself. Venturing into Nairobi for the first time, Paulina loses herself in the tightly regulated, racialized space of the colonial capital:

> The side-road opened into a massive highway full of traffic, with barbed wire in some parts and residential buildings between tall trees. She remembered having come uphill to the hospital—but . . . perhaps simply she remembered from Kisumu and from the conversation of many house servants on home leave that the official quarter is always up and the labouring down. To call them west and east would only be confusing but it still applied.[129]

If Paulina is disoriented by urban colonial space—as the free indirect narrator asks patronizingly, "How could she understand that Nairobi was a city?"—she nonetheless has an intimation (experienced as a vague memory or habit) of her "place" in the social, political, and racial topography of the city, with its class implications of up and down and its Orientalist overtones of West and East.[130] By the second chapter, however, Paulina's emerging cognitive compass begins to comprehend the urban design and its regulations; entering the modern institutional spaces of the City Park and museum, Paulina encounters an array of "tribal culture," duly registered and ordered: "real leopards and giraffes . . . and implements from different tribes. She enjoyed it and begged to go again."[131] In this carefully orchestrated space, Paulina confronts not an ethnographic version of some tribal past preserved, catalogued, and historicized as cultural heritage, but a museumized, proleptic, egalitarian imaginary of a postcolonial democracy—a vision of a multiethnic, detribalized future that serves as a cartographic legend for her subsequent negotiations of the modern time-space of independent Kenya.

Paulina is mostly reactive to the urban imperatives of Nairobi and the institutional demands of the state, impelled by the compulsions of their forms to become the kind of (gendered) subject they require. The novel invests the city of Nairobi and the ready-made structures of the colonial (and later the postcolonial) state with transformative capacities. This humanitarian-structuralist vision also inspired the urban planners who, in 1948, sketched the "Master

Plan for a Colonial Capital" that they hoped would become *"the Plan of the Citizen of Nairobi."*[132] Macgoye's *Bildungsroman* narrates a similarly optimistic scenario in which the institutional arrangements of modern space "kindle the imagination, canalise social energies and thereby 'civilise'" Nairobi's African population.[133] Paulina becomes the personal effect of governmental institutions, which operate as perfect tropes and leave no remainder of human substance (or personality) in their figuration of modern citizens—in their habituation of the mutable individual to the modern demands of urban geography and the biorhythms of nationalism.

The initially unimaginable scale and canalizing force of the capital city becomes progressively personal; by the novel's close, Paulina no longer wanders with "no fixed address" but moves with purpose, "every inch the city dweller."[134] A few years after Kenya's independence, Paulina leads her sister on a tour of Nairobi that demonstrates her transformation: "She managed to show her Parliament Building, the Post Office, the park. . . . And out of her private memories she showed her the museum too, and . . . the milliary stone."[135] Nairobi's urban *geo*graphy becomes Paulina's personal *bio*graphy—the public inscription of her personal desires and private memories; this sociocivil transformation has a political correlative in her sudden awareness of "pieces of legislation [that] controlled her life without her ever knowing it."[136] The narrative rewards her blossoming modern sensibilities with a job as a "general factotum" to a couple engaged in national politics—he's an MP and she's a women's organizer—which accelerates her assimilation into modern Kenyan bureaucracy: the national bank, parliament, and the passport and post offices in particular. After the political imprisonment of a prominent woman MP, Chelagat Mutai, Paulina proclaims the quintessential affirmation of democratic historical consciousness: "We must do something. . . . *we* are the government."[137] Her free and full identification with state institutions manifests itself in the novel's closing scene, when she voluntarily fills out the necessary forms to register her long-awaited pregnancy at the public family-planning clinic.[138] Unlike in Goethe's novel—where voluntary fatherhood brought with it the virtues of the citizen—in Macgoye's *Bildungsroman* the virtuous female citizen is rewarded with motherhood.

While the commencement of Paulina's journey to historical consciousness is figured as losing herself in the city, her arrival is recorded as finding herself in the newspapers as a kind of foster mother to postcolonial Kenya's dispossessed street children. If the novel and newspaper facilitated the individual's imagination of belonging to a national community, they did so partly by synchronizing their readers in what Walter Benjamin called "homogeneous, empty time"—the time of the modern nation-state.[139] In *Coming to Birth*, the public media keep this time, displacing seasons of planting and harvesting with national (and eventually international) news cycles. The metrical rhythms of the radio and newspapers counterpoint the "trivial intimacy of time" in the village, where "there was always something to talk about . . . and yet rarely anything to think about."[140] In contrast, in Nairobi "people died on the radio or in the newspapers every day." The tempo and tenor of the news initially alienates Paulina because "it was not like anyone you really knew or had a duty to," but as she learns to imagine herself knowing, and having duties to, the nation's dead, the pulse of national history progressively becomes as familiar as "whispers," until her own biography intersects with the public sphere.[141] When she intervenes to "discipline by kindness," as the newspaper headlines announce, a group of feuding street children, Paulina "found herself briefly in the news."[142] Macgoye's *Bildungsroman* performs the genre's historical incorporative work of nationalizing the marginal subject to such effect that Paulina comes to regard the capital city and the national public sphere as the natural chronotopia of her own biography of citizen-subjectivation.

Along with assuming the emergent virtues and sensibilities of Kenyan citizenship, Paulina begins to imagine herself in international time and space through the medium of the nation. In *Coming to Birth*, the formalist thesis bears fruit; the modern state institutions accomplish all of the incorporative goals of *Bildung* and human rights: nationalizing and internationalizing the individual as well as civicizing and universalizing the human personality. Indeed, although "Kenya was a hard enough idea to get hold of," when Paulina hears reports of the 1969 assassination of Mozambique Liberation Front leader Eduardo Mondlane by the Portuguese, Africa itself becomes more than "a name on a map."[143] While Kenya, as an independent state, acquires historical meaning within an international statist system of geopolitical distinctions and conventionalized sociocultural differences, Paulina's newly acquired civic habits and sociopolitical sensibilities also incorporate her into an imaginary international order. The pregnancy that is to fulfill her expectations for self-determination (and, by allegorical extension, those of Kenya) fixes Paulina's global position at the symbolic center of the postcolonial state, with the "the milliary stone where you could measure your distance [and difference] from Bahoya in Australia, or the Pyramids of Egypt or the Pope in Rome."[144]

The novel celebrates Paulina's historical emergence, but its real protagonist and hero is modernity itself, which comes to birth in the forms of postcolonial state institutions and democratic social formations and relations. The novel imagines these forms as immutable, inevitable, and efficient machines for producing modern subjects; Paulina's story of civic activation ultimately cosigns the legitimacy of the abstract (if not the concrete) nation-statist institutions and fortifies the democratic fiction of their egalitarian incorporative mechanics. Ironically, although they educe Paulina's historical consciousness, modernity's institutions are themselves treated in the novel as ahistorical and unproblematic legations to Kenya by the British at independence. Despite the fact that Kenya's institutional structures are largely the formal residue of "the attitudes and objectives of the former colonial power," and "therefore, frequently proved to be dysfunctional to the goals of the independent government of Kenya," Macgoye reanimates these abstracts of colonial power relations for service in the production of the postcolonial nation-state and the reproduction of its citizens, as if decolonization were merely a matter of transferring ownership of automated, acultural technologies of statecraft.[145]

The novel's Eurocentric, formalist view of modernity ultimately proposes that the *Bildungsroman* form is part of the ostensibly disinterested, neutral technologies of statist modernity. Given the novel's underlying faith in democratic formalism, there is a generic inevitability to Macgoye's reconditioned *Bildungsroman* and to Paulina's activation as a Kenyan citizen. This inevitability is replicated at the narratological level of composition, in which the novel's free indirect narrative voice acts as a Society-of-the-Tower-like guarantor of Paulina's development. Identified in the text with benevolent Europeans (including Macgoye herself[146]), the free indirect narrator effectively governs the emergence of Paulina's autobiographical and historical consciousness, administering the necessary sociocivil information,

modern dispositions, and habits until the generic prescriptions become her own—until her historical self-consciousness begins to work
all by itself. The stylistic blurring of the line between Paulina's un-
formed consciousness and a modern narrative consciousness foreshadows the ultimate correspondence of her personal desires and
society's designs—the full canalization of her untutored impulses for
public expression into the conventions of the *Bildungsroman*.

Macgoye molds Paulina's story to the most traditional conventions of the affirmative *Bildungsroman* to frame identitarian and
gendered claims for inclusion in the franchise of modern citizenship, as well as to claim the right to write Paulina's story in the
dominant transition narrative of modernization. Like the governmental institutions that seem unchanged by Paulina's occupation of
them, the classical *Bildungsroman* seems largely unaffected by her
placement in the role of its protagonist. However, if Macgoye's
novel conforms too perfectly to the genre's conventional form, and
accredits too optimistically both a postcolonial, egalitarian imaginary and the formal automation of democracy, it nonetheless challenges the racist and sexist assumptions behind the law and the
literature. For example, it refutes the racialist pessimism of some
British parliamentarians who warned before decolonization that the
institutions of Westminster democracy become mere "costumes for
the men . . . . [whose] sober shapes can be seen performing the
strangest antics, unless the people inside them have a real grasp on
the civil ideas which they are designed to express."[147] Likewise, in
narrating the conformability of a black, African woman to the forms
of modern society, Macgoye's novel counters the historical gender
discriminations of colonial and postcolonial Kenya—as well as of
the *Bildungsroman* genre itself—by demonstrating the equal (even
superior, in Paulina's case) capacity of African women to be brought
to birth by—and, in turn, through democratic participation, to give
birth to—the institutions of modern nation-statism.

In affirming the literary and statist forms as universal, even scientific (in the Althusserian sense), Macgoye's novel blurs the distinction between colonial civilizing missions and domestic civicizing
missions, treating them both as efficient engines of modernization.
This scientist view endorses the idea that modern and modernizing machinery (including the *Bildungsroman*) are not culture-bound
in the ordinary sense; rather, it suggests that the social institutions

that developed with the state/citizen bind belong to the culture and irrepressible force of modernity itself—a force that theoretically derives from the natural impulses of the human personality. Just as the novel treats colonial and postcolonial state institutions (in their abstraction) as legitimate and continuous, Macgoye's use of the *Bildungsroman* is continuous with the social function that Goethe imagined for the form. Macgoye conscripts the genre to reperform for the black, African woman the historical social work of demarginalization that it did for the eighteenth-century bourgeoisie— reclaiming it from its colonial employment to once again reconcile, rather than police, the citizen–subject divide. The social use of the form makes an implicit claim that the black, African woman is as probable (or almost) a subject of serious literature as any other; or, more specifically, as that historically universal subject: the white, European, bourgeois male. This is an ambivalent act of appropriation, narrating a protest against the marginalization of the African woman in the novelistic form whose affirmative action tends to reinforce the legitimacy of the institutions responsible for her historical exclusion. Writing in the dominant novelistic form of demarginalization is a rebellious act that challenges the historical gender and racial exclusions of the state and the lettered city, but it is also a legitimating act that attests to the fundamental elasticity of the forms themselves; it intensifies the enabling fiction that the nation-state and the *Bildungsroman* are neutral and natural technologies—that modernization is simply a bureaucratic matter of filling universal democratic forms with local content.

Affirmative Bildungsromane: *Novelized Claims of "A Right to Have Rights"*

> The question of the creation of a right and the question of the creation of a subject of rights are therefore only two aspects of the very same process.
>
> —ALEXANDER NÉKÁM, *The Personality*
> *Conception of the Legal Entity*

Like contemporary international human rights law, the affirmative *Bildungsroman* offers a narrative model for enfranchising the disenfranchised, for unproblematizing the problematic individual, for keeping the broken emancipatory promise of the Enlightenment by repairing the citizen–subject divide. Its coordinated plot of modernization, with its confident temporality and guarantee of development, narrates the story of the human personality's transition into modern citizenship and validates the constraints of the state/citizen bind as the condition of modern freedom. Goethe's idealistic vision of harmony between man and society and Macgoye's version of postcolonial assimilation configure this transition as a narrative of demarginalization—a process by which the historically marginal subject is progressively incorporated into the social forms and formations of democratic modernity. In this sense, the genre provides the dominant literary technology by which historically marginalized subjects claim the normative rights and responsibilities (legally round personality) that are commensurate with the emergent modern historical consciousness of national belonging (psychologically round personality) that the novel narrates. The affirmative *Bildungsroman* has consistently served as a genre of demarginalization, even if in the early examples the gap between who counted as demarginalizable and central subjects appears infinitesimal—marked principally by the nonage and minimal class disadvantage of its protagonist, something that, all other things being equal, would likely be transcended by time and patience.[148] Both human rights and the *Bildungsroman* are social technologies of demarginalization that project the generic terms not only of incorporation but also of how such incorporation might come to be recognized as the consummation of personal will and purpose—as the freest and fullest expression of the proclivities of the human personality. The *Bildungsheld* must be convinced not only that "what he must do is also symbolically right," but that the conventional novelistic form for that story of convincement (the *Bildungsroman*) is the symbolically right form for narrating potentially disruptive complaints against the inequities of the social order as claims for inclusion in its franchise. In this sense, *"Bildungsroman"* becomes the generic name of a certain transitive, human rights social work that, through its narrative heuristic of human personality development, tends to reinforce the dominant structures of the state and to legitimate the normative logic and grammar of human and social development generally.

Both Goethe's *Wilhelm Meister's Apprenticeship* and Macgoye's *Coming to Birth* present hopeful visions of the harmonization (*Bildung*) of the personal impulses of the individual with the social formations and relations of an inchoate state. The idealist project of *Bildung* and the *Bildungsroman* emerged as imaginative formal technologies along with the new incorporative mechanics of the rights-based nation-state to reconcile the forces of rebellion and legitimation—to plot the possibility of creating harmonious consent; their "great achievement," according to Moretti, was to supply a narrative "legitimation *of* the social system inside the mind of individuals."[149] Few contemporary *Bildungsromane* sustain the earnest optimism found in the novels of Goethe and Macgoye, which narrate affirmative claims to enfranchisement on behalf of their protagonists; but, as we shall see in the following chapters, there is a continuity in the genre's social function even in those first-person postcolonial novels that narrate the failure of incorporation and the corruption of the democratic egalitarian imaginary. If the particular idealism of the Goethean solution to the problematics of modern socialization was fully imaginable only from within "the transitional crisis of a very brief age of transition," the social function of its promising novelistic form nonetheless seems to become salient wherever there are similar sociopolitical crises over the constituency of the state and of the historical universal.[150] The genre of demarginalization tends to emerge as a particularly vital form when the terms, mechanics, and scope of the rights franchise are under contest. In other words, it tends to become a vital literary form within a particular identitarian group when the public sphere is susceptible to reform; however, as we shall see in the following chapters, the social work of the *Bildungsroman* also brings up for public review both the egalitarian imaginary and the practical terms of the people's constitution. In this regard, the genre tends both to shadow the historical condition of the public sphere and the state and to foreshadow their reform.

The idealist *Bildungsroman* narrates a politically ambivalent story of incorporation into the advantages and virtues of bourgeois citizenship that transforms personal rebellion into social legitimation. Both human rights and the *Bildungsroman* are tendentially conservative of prevailing social formations. Plotting novelistic and social evolution as an alternative to civil and political revolution, the ideal-ist *Bildungsroman* narrates the normative constitution of the modern rights subject—the story of the (re)absorption of the citizen by man; of how human nature might harmoniously become the socially practicable human personality; of how "man" and "citizen" might come to codesignate the human person. What emerges from the process is a socially contingent personality imagined to prevent cer-tain antiestablishment collective and collectivizing revolutionary actions.[151] Part of the tension between rebellion and legitimation (which analysts like Mary Robinson and Costas Douzinas identify in the contemporary condition of human rights) is the foreseeable outcome of the international legal regime's appropriation of its principal forms and formations (including the *Bildungsroman*) from the Westphalian model of nation-statism, in which human rights historically functioned as both a discourse of popular rebellion and a law of state legitimation.

That tension, however, sustains the plot of the affirmative *Bil-dungsroman*. In part, the democratic legitimacy of any social system is determined by its capacity to respond with recognition to claims against it; in this regard, both human rights and the *Bildungsroman* are important discursive instruments for making what might other-wise appear to be "radical alternatives" to "social norms and prac-tices . . . seem acceptable," as Eve Tavor Bannet has written of early-feminist uses of the genre.[152] In fact, it is this institutional complicity with the modern systems of the nation-state that gives the genre of demarginalization its reformative potential by making it the socially acceptable novelistic mode for the narration of suf-fragist claims on the rights-based state; such claims, like those in Goethe's and Macgoye's novels, aspire to broaden the scope (if not to revolutionize the basic principles and mechanics) of the state's rights franchise.

Both the *Bildungsroman* and human rights are calibrated to the parametrics of the nation-state, sharing not only the state/citizen bind but also the temporally awkward inherency-in-becoming plot of incorporation oriented toward the horizon of Westphalian soci-ality. The idealist *Bildungsroman* provides symbolic legitimation for human rights' narrative of becoming what one already is by right, and in that cooperative role it gives generic novelistic form to the affirmative human rights claim—the positive declaration of a right that must be made to be activated. As a matter of practice, even those rights that are construed as natural, inalienable, and imprescriptible come into effect only when people claim them.[153] A "constative declaration," the rights claim transacts the rhetorically obvious "in order to make," in Thomas Keenan's marvelous phrase, "what's already so manifest manifest."[154] Like the declarations of rights that I studied in the previous chapter—by which people incorporate themselves as The People—individual speech acts of rights-claiming abide an improbable temporal logic: "The rights claimed cannot simply pre-exist the claim that is made for them . . . and the 'I' that claims them for itself cannot be given either." In other words, a rights claim requires a subject who is prepositioned to claim rights who will, in principle, only have acquired such capacity through a successful claim. Both the grammatical subject of rights—the subject capable of taking rights as predicates—and the rights it claims come into effective being through the act of claiming. The affirmative, de-marginalizing *Bildungsroman* makes just such a claim for recognition and inclusion in the human rights franchise, plotting the teleology of human personality development as the narrative expression of tautological obviousness—becoming what one is by right; a narrator (among the already-incorporated) oversees a story of the development of a protagonist's autobiographical consciousness until the character becomes capable of recounting the acquisition of the capacities, habits, and dispositions necessary to narrate the story of their acquisition after the fact, and to plot it from the position of the incorporated citizen-subject as the consummation of personal will. These novelistic declarations of rights assert to their protagonists the positive rights of the citizen that ostensibly already belong to them by natural right; that is, the *Bildungsroman*, explicitly or implicitly, narrates "a right to have rights."[155]

The *Bildungsroman* narrates its demand for sociopolitical recognition by reasserting the essential tautology of human rights (that the human is a human) and by insisting that the universal predicate ("a human") has been misused or misunderstood—that this particular human is by right a member of that universal human class. In this sense, the affirmative *Bildungsroman* declares a right to have rights by implicitly demonstrating that its protagonist is as plausible and inherently proper a citizen-subject as anyone else. This individualized rights claim treats freedom as something to be "seized rather than accorded as a founding human right," but the socially affirmative action of the genre is larger than the individual whose incorporation it narrates;[156] through what Margaret Cohen has called "the realist [narrative] contract between reader and text," the novelistic exemplarity of the socially marginal protagonist—his or her status as a "representative member of society," or of a portion of society—makes a claim on behalf of a class of historically marginal subjects.[157] From an institutional perspective, the idealist *Bildungsroman*'s insistence on the validity of the abstract moral logic of human rights endorses not so much the rectitude of its particular protagonist's claim to incorporation as it does the fundamental rightness of rights themselves. That is, although a rights claim speaks to historical exclusion from the regime of rights and to the hypocrisy of their actual practice, it tends to reify the legitimacy of the very principles that had institutionalized the acceptability (the "rightness") of the claimant's prior exclusion. Paradoxically, then, each successive and successful claim for enfranchisement in the human rights regime makes the regime less supple by expanding its effective discursive authority—normalizing more people within its "transcendent inclusiveness" and affirming the apparent universal legitimacy of its legal and literary conventions and institutions.[158]

In these respects, the idealist *Bildungsroman* is a socially conservative and politically ambivalent literary gesture; it accredits the democratic formalist thesis that the social formations and relations of the well-ordered nation-state are legitimate and appropriate to educe their proper subjects *and* it amplifies the enabling fiction that human rights and the *Bildungsroman* genre itself are intrinsically universal and fundamentally egalitarian. As part of the modern nation-state's technologies of reproduction (of self-constitution and self-regulation) the idealist *Bildungsroman* and human rights law provide "model ideolog[ies] that can be deployed wherever or whenever differences and identities need to be naturalized."[159] The affirmative *Bildungsroman* gives positive narrative form to this naturalizing process by reifying the norms and forms of participatory democracy that incorporate people as The People and human beings as right-and-duty-bearing citizens. But in conventionalizing the normative forms of the citizen-subject and its story of citizen-subjectivation, the law and literature naturalize the sociopolitical terms of both inclusion and exclusion that are constitutive of The People. In other words, as we shall see in the following chapters, these reflexive, reproductive technologies configure both the citizen-subjects who count as The People and the naturalized exclusionary terms and practices that keep some people from counting in the democratic universal census. All the same, this ambivalence can be constructive, since it is the normativity and social acceptability of the literary form that makes it a useful vehicle for carrying the human rights claims of the marginalized; such appropriations of the form begin to rearticulate the democratic imaginary (in Laclau and Mouffe's sense) and to widen the effective compass of the sociohistorical universal. Although a rights claim is an essentially conservative expression of discontent with the social system, it remains a necessary act, inasmuch as the nation-state continues to figure as the ultimate sociopolitical expression of a universal human personality in our international legal agreements, and inasmuch as human rights continue to constitute our best projection for keeping the broken promise of a world of universal human equality and dignity—that is, inasmuch as human rights continue to represent "that which we cannot not want."[160]

Normalizing Narrative Forms of Human Rights: The (Dys)Function of the Public Sphere

A law may claim legitimacy only if all those possibly affected could consent to it after participating in rational discourses.

—JÜRGEN HABERMAS, "On Legitimation Through Human Rights"

Fragile, tentative democracies time and again hurl themselves toward an abyss, struggling over this issue of truth. It's a mysteriously powerful, almost magical notion, because everyone already knows the truth—everyone knows who the torturers were and what they did, the torturers know that everyone knows, and everyone knows they know. Why, then, this need to risk everything to render this knowledge explicit? . . . 'It's the difference . . . between knowledge and *ac*knowledgment'.

—LAWRENCE WESCHLER, *A Miracle, A Universe*

When Victims Become Citizens: Storytelling as Incorporation

"When the police came to mamCatherine's house in 1976, they said: . . . Let's search the bedroom."[1] The scene of this domestic invasion by the state is Catherine Mlangeni's South African township home, to which apartheid police had come looking for her son Bheki, who was then a student but would later become a prominent human rights lawyer. That night, mamCatherine succeeded in saving her sons, but fifteen years later Bheki Mlangeni would be decapitated at home by a bomb the police had planted in a walkman. The scene of the account of these state visits to the Mlangeni hoι. established by the narrator in *The Story I Am About to Tell*, a pι produced in the late 1990s by members of the Khulumani Supporι Group, which formed in 1995 to help apartheid victims to speak out about their experiences and to facilitate their personal and civic rehabilitation. After Catherine Mlangeni recounts the night of the police raid in her own isiZulu words, the narrator introduces the play's full *dramatis personae*—"three actors and three real people"— explaining in English that "these are real stories about their lives. Stories that they want to tell. . . . The true stories about our lives are what make our *history*. . . . Tonight we are going to hear *her* story, *her* story and *his* story. Stories that you, and us, have to share and bear a common responsibility for, if we want to heal our souls and the soul of the nation."[2] Set in a shared taxi, the play explores the possibilities and problematics of reconciliation in postapartheid South Africa through the publication (in the broadest sense) of personal stories by three apartheid victims. To underscore the intersections of private life and public art, the narrator announces that the home invasion "is where Catherine Mlangeni's story starts. You may have heard how it ends, at the Truth and Reconciliation Commission."

At the end of the twentieth century, the confluence of the vocabulary and concerns of human rights and literature was perhaps nowhere more apparent than in the phenomena of truth commissions. If, as the *Truth and Reconciliation Commission of South Africa Report* suggests, the work of the TRC "seized the imagination of many South Africans" and spawned "creative approaches to reparation and healing," no other human rights issue, topic, or scenario seemed to capture the international literary imagination like the human and social drama of truth commissions.[3] The narrative problematics of truth and reconciliation became material for both creative and academic work.[4] Literary and legal concerns—the creative and juridical arts—intersected in the sociopolitical work of truth commissions. These intersections are legible in the citational relationship between the Khulumani play and the TRC; *The Story I Am About to Tell* names the TRC as the endpoint of Mlangeni's story and cites TRC transcripts in her repeated performances of the testimony she previously presented to the Human Rights Violations Committee, and, in turn, volume six of the TRC's seven-volume final report cites the play—which ran concurrently with the TRC hearings—as exemplary of many creative efforts that extended the work of reconciliation and reparation into "civil society."[5] The play and the TRC are mutual intertexts, and both make space for Catherine Mlangeni to publicize her personal story as part of "the broader national process of 'building a bridge' between a deeply divided past of *'untold suffering and injustice'* and a future 'founded on the recognition of human rights, democracy, peaceful co-existence, and development opportunities for all.'"[6] (emphasis added).

Like most of the nearly two dozen truth commissions around the globe that preceded South Africa's, the TRC's mandate was to assemble "as complete a picture as possible" of the human rights atrocities committed against the population by the state (and other groups contesting its legitimacy) under the previous political regime. But the TRC was unique in a number of ways: its ability to identify by name both victims and perpetrators of violence; its fully public hearings, which were broadcast in near-real time through various media in and outside of South Africa; its capacity to trade amnesty for truth; its theorization of the relationship between truth and narrative; and its emphasis on the "healing potential of telling stories" for the survivors of human rights abuse.[7] Thus, the TRC understood public storytelling, especially by those disenfranchised and disbarred under the legal regime of apartheid, to be essential both for "recover[ing] parts of the national memory" and for "restoring the human and civil dignity of . . . [the] victims by granting them an opportunity to relate *their own accounts* of the violations of which they are the victims," as stipulated by the Promotion of National Unity and Reconciliation Act (1995). Through the act of telling their personal stories in public, individuals were to regain the human and civil personality and dignity lost under apartheid. Storytelling was thought to have an incorporative effect, "helping the *victims* to become more visible and more valuable *citizens* through the public recognition and official acknowledgement of their experiences."[8]

The Story I Am About to Tell underscores the TRC's faith in the restorative powers of storytelling by tracking the emergence of Catherine Mlangeni's story from the private bedroom to the public sphere. If a knock on the door in 1976 is the beginning of a story of "untold suffering and injustice" that needs to be told and heard, its telling in 1996 is the end of the story—that is, public delivery of the story marks the conclusion of its plot even as it signals the beginning of its public life as story, when it becomes available for dramatic reperformance. Catherine Mlangeni's story is therefore as much about a fundamental need to tell untold stories in a forum that "validat[es] . . . the individual subjective experiences of people who had previously been silenced or voiceless" as it is about communicating the particular facts of her son's silencing.[9] In both the play and the TRC report, personal stories have an inherent force of their own; stories have a will to be told, and part of the work of the TRC—like that of the Khulumani Support Group—becomes "providing an environment in which victims could tell their own stories in their own languages" so that the public can "share and bear a common responsibility" for *her* story, *his* story, and national *history*.

The TRC undertook its historic civicizing mission of turning knowledge into acknowledgment with an awareness that it involved more than the collation of an official history of apartheid. The commission was as concerned with its formal, performative procedures and its mode of producing a shared national memory as it was with the final publishable findings of fact that were destined for the National Archives. In other words, the commission was as interested in the social norms and "the *process* whereby the truth was reached" as in the product of its dialogical excavations of forensic and social truth—"the truth of experience that is established through interaction, discussion and debate."[10] It sought to provide a public space in which the personal "narrative truth" of dispossession, disenfranchisement, and human rights abuse (that had been "officially ignored" and strategically suppressed under the previous regime) could be told, heard, acknowledged, discussed, compared, and combined into a common story—a new democratic national imaginary in which apartheid's victims and beneficiaries could participate as coactors.[11] It is the communalizing story space of public spheres—like those made manifest in the hearing sites of the TRC and the shared taxi of *The Story I Am About to Tell*—that interests me in this chapter.

A public sphere is a story space that not only enables but also shapes and constrains narrative; moreover, it is not simply a clearinghouse for the publication of personal narrative truth but a kind of story factory in which the norms of public discourse become legible both in the social interactivity of storytelling and in the story forms that it disseminates, conventionalizes, and canonizes as "socially acceptable narrative[s]."[12] In the case of the TRC, the commission acted both as a surrogate for a distrusted and narrow apartheid public sphere and as a transitional, self-contained precursor for an emergent democratic national public sphere. As it toured the country, staging its hearings in the presence of local audiences, the TRC's promotion of dialogue and respect represented a self-conscious attempt to rectify and revitalize the forms and norms of an egalitarian public sphere. Thus, its public hearings were intended to assist "the restoration of the dignity of the victims" by "giving the voiceless a chance to speak, giving the excluded a chance to be centred and giving the powerless an opportunity to empower themselves" while "promoting transparency, democracy and participation in society . . . as the basis for affirming human dignity and integrity" more generally.[13] In this regard, the TRC was a traveling civics lesson that sought both to realize the enabling egalitarian fiction of a national public sphere open to all voices, and to normalize the deliberative habits and democratic practices of citizenship. If the test of the egalitarian ideal of a public sphere is the degree to which its formerly disabled, disenfranchised victims are enabled to participate as citizens, then citizenship is a matter of having not just the vote—which was extended with the democratic elections of 1994—but also a civil, public voice. Of course, the dialogic dynamics of the TRC produced generic conventions for testimony and narrative truth that, like all public spheres, excluded certain kinds of stories and personal experiences even as the commission promoted an ideal of an all-inclusive community of speech.[14] But, by the TRC's own logic, participation in the discursive public sphere becomes the hallmark of citizenship—the highest form of the human personality's self-expression in traditional human rights discourse—that is exercised through storytelling and story-listening.

My discussion of the TRC forecasts some of this chapter's arguments about the role of the public sphere in normalizing and naturalizing common sense—the incorporative sense that sustains the social imaginary and hegemon. As a showcase for the civic habits that the TRC hoped to see realized in a national public sphere, the work of the commission was as performative as informative. Like knowledge, democratic practices are cultivated through rehearsal and repetition; in this sense, the hearings of the TRC have something in common with their restaging in *The Story I Am About to Tell*. As South African artist and social critic William Kentridge has emphasized, "what the 'real people' [in the play] give is not evidence itself, but performances of evidence";[15] the audience, as the play's narrator suggests, likely already knows how Catherine Mlangeni's story ends, because they have heard it before at the TRC. A similar dynamic of *déjà entendu* operates with truth commissions. "Often the basic facts about what happened are already known," notes the TRC report; "what is critical is that these facts be fully and publicly acknowledged"—placed "on public, national record."[16] In other words, part of the work of truth commissions is to provide a space for the official acknowledgement of the untold suffering that everyone presumably already knows and thereby also to (re)activate, as a second (civic) nature, the dialogical processes and discursive practices of an emergent modern democratic state's anticipated "more visible and more valuable citizens."[17]

The TRC was an exceptional form of a public sphere in a state of transition and transitional justice that sought to make legible what everyone already knows, to normalize a new common sense, and to transform victims into citizens; similarly, the dramatic restaging of this discursive process in *The Story I Am About to Tell* is an extraordinary literary form for the story of incorporation. As I argued in the previous chapter, the *Bildungsroman* is the more ordinary story form of incorporation for a democratic social order that either is already established (and generally perceived as legitimate) or is coming to birth in a timeframe somewhat longer than that of a new South Africa. Theoretically, the liberal public sphere is a sociocivic story space that connects personal biography and nation-statist historiography—that constructs figural relations between *her* story and *history*. Historically, the affirmative *Bildungsroman* is the liberal public sphere's most favored novelistic form for plotting human personality development and the acquisition of civil and human dignity as the normative story of modern socialization, liberation, and emancipation. This generic privilege might be partly accounted for by the fact that the idealist *Bildungsroman*'s plot naturalizes the discursive operations of hegemony as Gramsci described them; it plots the course of the individual's socialization, tracing the path by which, in modern democracy, the particular comes to partake in, or to become itself an instance of, the sociohistorical "universal."[18] In this sense, the genre validates both the discursive mechanics of the liberal public sphere, by which individual will becomes congruent with group will, and the logic by which the *Bildungsroman* becomes the dominant story form of human rights incorporation.

Human rights, as law and discourse, comprise what Makau Mutua describes as a "cultural package . . . of basic assumptions about the individual and his relationship to society" that "present[s] political democracy, and its institutions of governance, as the sine qua non for a victimless society."[19] This chapter considers the role of the public sphere in disseminating, conventionalizing, and naturalizing the basic assumptions about the human personality and sociality that sustain the human rights package and its implied "legal, political, social, and cultural" institutions of governance, of which the public sphere is itself a part.[20] The liberal public sphere is the primary dialogic engine of hegemony in a democratic formation; it is the place and space in which, as Jürgen Habermas idealized it in his classic study, "private people come together" and, through the "public use of their reason," amalgamate their individual opinions into a consensual "public opinion," a hegemonic general will.[21] Historically, the modern public sphere emerged with the democratic nation-state, human rights, and the *Bildungsroman* as part of the institutions of popular sovereignty that set the Chakrabartian state/citizen bind as the ultimate horizon of human personality development. As with the TRC, the public sphere is a regulatory institution that, in its ideal formulation, not only converts personal opinion into common sense but also gives personal stories their socially acceptable and conventional generic forms. Thus, although the liberal public sphere is idealized in its enabling fiction as "a free discursive space that equalizes all participants,"[22] its regulatory function makes it a crucial location for democratic struggles over the hegemonic conceptions of the individual and its relation to society. Accordingly, the public sphere is the primary domain of social contest over the narrative "system of discursive meaning production by which individuals can be taught to live . . . an unreal but meaningful relation to the social formation in which they are indentured to live out their lives and realize their destinies as social subjects."[23] Given this ideological assignment, one of the key discursive, democratic functions of the public sphere is to ensure that the tautologies of human rights are institutionally, socially, and culturally compelling.

This chapter considers the centrality of the liberal, national public sphere to the human rights package of social, cultural, and political institutions that include the *Bildungsroman* and constitutional democracy. That centrality is apparent in both the norms of human rights law and the form of the affirmative *Bildungsroman*. Thus, one of my goals is to demonstrate how the normative human rights assumptions about the individual and its relations to society and the state that are novelized in the idealist *Bildungsroman* are predicated upon the existence of an operative, national public sphere. The affirmative *Bildungsroman*, like human rights law, is practically unthinkable without at least a vision of a liberal public sphere—a point that Habermas implicitly reinforces when, at the beginning of his seminal study, he reads Goethe's *Wilhelm Meister's Apprenticeship* as symptomatic of the transition to modernity of an "economically and politically backward Germany."[24] As I examined in chapter 2, both Goethe's novel and Macgoye's *Coming to Birth* narrate the public debut of a "properly" socialized individual, and they set the dominant national (or proto-national) public sphere as the *Bildungsheld*'s final destination—the realm "where the hero . . . must prove himself."[25] More importantly, as the title of Todd Kontje's study of the genre, *Private Lives in the Public Sphere*, perhaps suggests, the public sphere represents more than the ultimate setting for *Bildungsromane*; it is also the world of the publication, circulation, and consumption of the protagonist's personal story—the ultimate destination for the *Bildungsheld*'s *Bildungsroman*. Thus, the *Bildungsroman* naturalizes in the public sphere not only its own narrative conventions for plotting the story of socialization but also the norms and forms of proper participation in the democratic state, along with, as we shall see in this chapter, the dominant political and social terms of inclusion and exclusion that it abstracts from the actual historical relations and conditions of participatory, deliberative democracy.

This duplication of the plot and theme of the *Bildungsroman* in the social life of the physical artifact of the novel leads to my second set of analytical concerns with the role of the public sphere in the human rights package. The public sphere is not just a space that processes, regulates, and circulates stories and their generic narrative forms; it mediates between the realms of political governance and private life, fixing the terms of separation and interaction between the state's administrative institutions and the social world of the people. Indeed, in human rights law (both modern and contemporary) and democratic theory, the liberal public sphere is charged with vigilating the state and its observance of human rights. In this regulatory capacity, it is neither fully antagonistic to nor fully complicit with the administrative institutions of the state.[26] By the logic of popular sovereignty, it becomes the primary site for the defense of the group from itself, of people from The People. In its hypothesized ideal form, the public collectively ensures that the structures of the state correspond to—indeed, in the idealist theory of *Bildung*, are institutional expressions of—public will, itself a conventionalized, objective expression of the individual's subjective personal will.

Human rights law and discourse valorize the public sphere as a primary location of the enjoyment and protection of an individual's human rights; however, historical assumptions about the civic virtue and emancipatory character of publicness also make it a primary site of human rights violation—a place where citizens are exposed to each other and to the repressive potential of the state.[27] Thus, the public sphere is also a place of discrimination, disadvantage, and vulnerability. Recognizing the ambivalence of the public sphere as an engine of incorporation and disincorporation, this chapter elaborates one of the two complementary rhetorical operations by which human rights configure the human individual as a person before the law—as a subject of rights and duties. As we saw in chapter 2, human rights law incorporates the human person as a synecdoche for human "capacities for achievement"; it also makes the human person a synecdoche for human "weaknesses and needs."[28] In other words, the human rights person is both incorporated as an instantiation of a group's developmental potential and as an incarnation of its vulnerability. These two figural models of incorporation operate simultaneously but for the sake of analysis, I have separated them in this study. I will return again to the developmental model in chapter 4 with my discussion of contemporary postcolonial *Bildungsromane* and the mid-twentieth-century rise of development discourse in the international arena. Here I consider the vulnerability model of incorporation through the mechanics of the public sphere—a discursive space of both enfranchisement and disenfranchisement that has the capacity to make citizens of victims as well as victims of citizens.

The liberal public sphere's centrality to both human rights and the *Bildungsroman* will be demonstrated in this chapter by an examination of its role as a discursive machine for producing, conventionalizing, endorsing, and disseminating collective common sense. If, as I am suggesting, the *Bildungsroman*, the public sphere and the democratic state are interdependent elements in the human rights package, then the degree and form of their interdependency is perhaps best legible not in the idealist *Bildungsroman*, where those relations are taken for granted, but in examples where those relations have ruptured. Thus, I analyze two decidedly nonaffirmative *Bildungsromane* in which those interconnections short-circuit: Argentine writer Tununa Mercado's *In a State of Memory* (*En estado de memoria*, 1990), which is set during the military repression of Argentina's "Dirty War," and Sri Lankan-Canadian Michael Ondaatje's *Anil's Ghost* (2000), which is set during one of the declared states of emergency in Sri Lanka's protracted civil war. Neither text would be classified as a *Bildungsroman* according to strict typological criteria. Nonetheless, both novels are engaged with the normative conventions and readerly expectations of the genre, taking what Pierre Bourdieu calls "positions" within "the finite universe of potentialities" and conventional "constraints" that circumscribe the *Bildungsroman* genre.[29] Both of these novels have an obsession with the public sphere and are concerned with its place and function in the narrativization of individual biography. Indeed, the positions taken by these novels within the field of generic *Bildungsroman* possibilities are partially determined by their treatment of the public sphere, the state, and the egalitarian imaginary that sustains both. *In a State of Memory* and *Anil's Ghost* narrate the foreclosure of the idealist *Bildungsroman*'s story of free and full human personality development when the Habermasian public sphere is under siege by the state and when citizenship obverts to disenfranchisement. Thematically and formally, Mercado's and Ondaatje's novels are interested in the narrative consequences of political repression—the generic deformation of the idealist *Bildungsroman*'s conventions in a state whose public sphere has been disarticulated. They ask a generic question: What happens to the story form of human personality development when the modern institutional guarantors of social order and meaning—the democratic state and public sphere that replaced Nature and Nature's God—have been perverted? These *Bildungsromane* are novels of a world abandoned by the democratic state, to trope on Georg Lukács's famous description of the novel as "the epic of a world that has been abandoned by God."[30] That is, as we shall see, the deformation of the *Bildungsroman* genre in these novels is a symptom not of Lukáscian "transcendental homelessness" but of Arendtian statelessness. The centrality of a national public sphere to the complex of democratic institutions prescribed in the human rights package is demonstrated in these novels by the perversion of the idealist *Bildungsroman*'s generic conventions, reflecting the political and social distortion of democratic norms. Thus, even as there is a discontinuity in the generic conventions of the *Bildungsroman*, continuity remains in its social function as a human rights claim; the corruption of the literary form represents a corruption of the legal norms of human rights and acts as a formal indictment of the antidemocratic state and a rejection of its authoritarian claims.

Between People and The People: The Public Sphere and Conventions of Citizenship

> The social order is a sacred right which is the basis of all other rights. Nevertheless, this right does not come from nature, and must therefore be founded on conventions. . . . A people, says Grotius, can give itself to a king. Then, according to Grotius, a people is a people before it gives itself. The gift is itself a civil act, and implies public deliberation. It would be better, before examining the act by which a people gives itself to a king, to examine that by which it has become a people; for this act, being necessarily prior to the other, is the true foundation of society.
>
> —JEAN-JACQUES ROUSSEAU, *The Social Contract*

In Jürgen Habermas' classic account of the rise and decline of the liberal public sphere, this formal institution of public-will formation coalesced during the eighteenth century alongside—or in the civic shadow of—the modern rights-based nation-state. Habermas describes the spontaneous generation of this democratic space of debate in quasi-religious terms, as conjured wherever two or more individuals gather in its name: "A portion of the public sphere comes into being in every conversation in which private individuals assemble to form a public body."[31] Such a public is autoincorporative, generated merely by mutual, deliberative acts in which matters of public interest are discussed. This court of public opinion is the place where The People most immediately exercises its popular sovereignty and where, in the absence of any absolute or transcendental guarantee of its rights, The People gives itself the law at the moment that it comes into being. In other words, through the discursive activity of the public sphere, The People nominates itself to stand surrogate for Nature and Nature's God as the guarantor of rights. As we shall see, the public sphere is a space where The People functionally produces and reproduces not only public opinion but also itself—as both author (lawgiver) and *dramatis persona* (lawabider) of rights and responsibilities.

The modern declarations of human rights, which articulated the constitutional principles that founded the democratic state, conceived of the public sphere both as the location of the civil exercise of human equality and as a zone of defense between people and the state. Thus, the eighteenth-century declarations sought to promote and protect this alchemistic space of group-will formation with guarantees of a right to petition and freedoms of assembly and expression. Contemporary international law retains and reinforces an idealized version of the liberal public sphere as part of its prescribed cultural package of democratic institutions, reaffirming not only the emancipatory assumptions about publicness that underpinned modern human rights (and the idealist *Bildungsroman*) but also the democratic faith in the regulatory capacity of public discourse and debate to keep the state from overreaching itself.

Positioned between people acting as private individuals and The People acting in their corporate capacity as state, the public sphere plays an ambivalent role in mediating between them; it both regulates the state through the formation of public opinion and it manufactures consent for the state's legitimacy. In principle, the liberal public sphere maintains a healthy democratic suspicion of the state, which is constitutionally Janus-faced, both the administrator and violator of human rights—the sociopolitical unit through which the human being is capacitated and incapacitated as a subject of human rights. But the Habermasian public sphere ultimately cosigns the state's democratic legitimacy, even (perhaps especially) when it contradicts and counteracts the state. Similarly, human rights law and discourse reify the public sphere both as the primary site of free expression and assembly and also as the primary discursive institution that safeguards those freedoms from the state. In fact, the drafters of the UDHR believed a functional public sphere to be such a powerful antidote to fascism, totalitarianism, and racism, that they took the rare step of establishing a Sub-Commission on the Freedom of Information, which advised expanding the traditional protections for opinion and expression to include the freedom "to seek, receive and impart information and ideas through any media and regardless of frontiers" (Article 19).[32] Article 19 bolsters the public sphere's capacity to act in defense of human rights by complementing freedom of speech with a right of reception, a right of hearing that was dramatically implemented in the story space of the TRC's exceptional public hearings. It also purposes to make national borders permeable to the exchange of information, laying the communications groundwork for the supplementation of a Habermasian national public sphere with, as we shall see in Michael Ondaatje's *Anil's Ghost*, a transnational public—an international court of world opinion, of which the UN itself might act as an important forum.

The international legal formulation of the right to public expression is premised on a liberal faith in the capacity of free speech to facilitate the realization of a collective, or communal, rationalism that is nonfascist, nonracist, and nonsexist. The idea that open dialogue strategically forecloses some forms of speech—incitive or hate speech in the International Covenant on Civil and Political Rights (Article 20)—underscores a basic ambivalence within the liberal public sphere's charge to convert individual expression (what the TRC called personal "narrative truth") into socialized speech ("dialogic truth").[33] As the condition of possibility for a democratic public sphere, freedom of speech would seem to imply "a myriad and chaotic world of unique and free linguistic agents, all equally possessed of the power to join the anarchy of speech."[34] Yet, as human rights law's use of a freedom of speech to inhibit fascist expression suggests, the liberal public sphere is not generally a site of either anarchic speech or eccentric, individualist expression; rather, one of its idealized functions is to discipline linguistic and narrative anarchy—to transform socially disruptive speech into socially acceptable forms by burnishing the sharp, individualist edges off the human personality.

Human rights and the liberal public sphere are symbiotic; the former supplies the "constitutive and regulative institutional norms of [public] debate in democratic societies," while the latter negotiates the effective scope of human rights themselves: "their meaning, their extent and their jurisdiction."[35] If, as Habermas has recently suggested, human rights "institutionalize the communicative conditions for a reasonable political will-formation,"[36] then the public sphere can be understood to be constituted by and around particular systems of rights and duties whose norms, I will argue, become legible in the forms of communicative activity that a public conventionalizes. Those norms of discourse abstract and sustain patterns of sociality that constitute "proper" public forms for the exercise of citizenship, which tend, in turn, to naturalize the official conditions and scope of political participation in the state. In human rights law, freedom of speech is not license, and the public sphere that it enables is a world of convention—a space of mutually regulated and regulatory speech that produces a public culture of organized diversity through its normalization of the grammar, syntax, lexicon, and themes of proper public speech, of what counts as speech, of how speech counts, and of who counts as a speaker.

Habermas' liberal public sphere, and the version rearticulated in international human rights law, presupposes an ahistorical, pre-social human equality that consists, at minimum, of a universal human capacity to produce "communicative speech actions" and an inclination to participate in the social community of speech.[37] Indeed, Habermas idealizes this politicized national speech community as a democratic space of debate over the public text, and he accredits its own enabling, egalitarian fiction that "access is guaranteed to all citizens."[38] But in the context of the emergence of the modern nation-state, the democratic "capacity to speak to others," which

Jean-François Lyotard regards as "perhaps the most fundamental human right," is exercised within a historical public sphere whose social texture took the "specific form," Habermas writes, of "the bourgeois reading public"—a "world of letters . . . [that] assumed political functions."[39] The specific, historical form of a bourgeois "reading society" belies the enabling fiction of an egalitarian public sphere open to all, and the practical differences between the two suggest that enfranchisement into the idealized national and international world of letters projected by human rights law depends upon more than some innocent, pre-social capacity to speak to others or a predisposition to participate in public debate.[40] That is, the right to join the community of public speech cannot be protected merely by the negative civil and political "rights of communication and participation" that presumably guarantee access to all and have an immediate impact on the condition and possibility of deliberative democracy;[41] rather, it is also promoted with (and dependent upon) positive rights that enable individuals to acquire the minimum social, cultural, economic, discursive, and other resources of personality that, in practice if not in principle, are necessary to participate in the community of speech as full citizens, "whose right to address others is recognized by those others."[42] Indeed, many of those rights typically understood as quintessentially positive rights—e.g., to employment, health care, and social security—have profound implications for the constitution and vitality of the public sphere and the possibility of participating in the community of speech. In other words, all human beings may be *naturally* poised to join the democratic community of speech as "possible interlocutor[s],"[43] but only some are *positively* enabled to do so.

Speech, as Stanley Fish has repeatedly insisted, "only occurs in communities," and the discursive relations of a public sphere incorporate The People as a political, social, cultural, and sentimental reading and debating society, which is to say that a public speech community is "both sociological and textual."[44] The public sphere binds its citizens together in a complex of interlocking, communicative social relations that are both actual (practiced among real, intimate "historical readers" through participation in interactive conversation and public debate) and imaginary (conducted across distances of time and space "by the figures of speech and thought found in cultural artifacts," as Margaret Cohen has explained of the formation of "imagined communities of sentimentality" more generally).[45] If in the modern nation-state "nationals are bound together . . . [by] language, law, and literature,"[46] it is the public sphere that conventionalizes and canonizes the shared linguistic, legal, and literary texts through which we interact as coparticipants in the political community of speech. Community membership is predicated on meeting a discursive qualification, on accepting (or appearing to accept) a public's conventional "limitations on speech"—its dominant discursive norms and its prevailing forms of expression.[47] In other words, incorporation into the rights and duties of public citizenship is functionally contingent not only upon a capacity to participate as a proper linguistic subject but also upon some form of consent—a demonstrable willingness to play by (or better, with) its rules of speech, since such participation likely bends or reshapes the rules. From the perspective of speech, we might recognize citizenship as the name of a minimal mastery of, or a functional literacy in, the dominant discursive conventions operating within any given sphere—e.g., its socially acceptable story patterns, symbology, lexicon, thematic predilections, and principles of emplotment.[48]

The democratic public sphere constitutes and regulates a (re)-public's legal and literary common sense—the public culture. Publics are convention-making bodies that tend to codify common sense and the generic forms for its expression. In contemporary international law, the public sphere is the primary engine for the production and normalization of the common sense of human rights, naturalizing the law's tautologies and expanding the sociocultural commons (the *res publica*) within which they may be effectively taken for granted. Historically, the predominant narrative form that abstracts and regulates the communicative social relations of the national public sphere is the realist novel. While the novel form, along with the newspaper, may have facilitated the imagination of national community and made the Westphalian unities of nation-time and nation-space palpable, it belongs not to the nation-state as such but to its deliberative correlative: the bourgeois reading public, where it is traditionally set, consumed, and discussed and whose sociality it makes legible. The realist novel is symbiotic with the national public sphere, which supplies not only its favorite imaginative settings and reservoir of themes but also its ordinary consumers. In this sense, the modern novel is more than an object of public discourse, it is also a technology of projection that gives the bourgeois reading public a literary image of itself (even if distorted) that illustrates historically, as Edward Said argued, "the limits of what they can aspire to, where they can go, what they can become."[49] Speaking generally, the novel emerged with modern human rights, and it publicizes in imaginative terms the emergent social possibilities and boundaries of the emancipation of the individual in the new political formation of the rights-bound nation-state. The realist novel's narrative conventions (e.g., its teleological temporality, its egocentric logic of causality, and its supposedly democratic aesthetic) re-present and reinforce the dominant discursive parameters for participation in the liberal public sphere and the prosaic shape of acceptable narratives about publicness—the generic principles by which stories about human sociality and personality development are to be plotted.

Often heralded as the most democratic of modern literary forms, the novel's techniques of representation repeat the egalitarian fiction of the bourgeois public sphere: that they are both socially inclusive and open to everyone. However, if the public sphere normalizes its conditions of incorporation partly through the story forms that it favors, those forms also tend to naturalize the public's terms of disenfranchisement. Despite its egalitarian fiction, the historical institution of the Habermasian public sphere entailed certain systemic exclusions—epitomized in the eighteenth-century revolutionary fixation of white, male, property-owning citizens as the universal class—that are often reproduced, reenacted, and reinforced in novels themselves. That is, the realist novel has historically acted as a literary agent for the reproduction, conventionalization, circulation, and conservation of the liberal public sphere's social norms and communicative forms; in that service, it tends to normalize the racial, gender, ethnic, religious, and class discriminations prevailing in both the public sphere and the state by making its selection of representative individuals and plots, as well as its depiction of modern social relations, appear neutral and natural. "The capacity to represent, portray, characterize, and depict," wrote Said of the social contingency of the novel, "is not easily available to just any member of just any society; moreover, the 'what' and 'how' in the representation of 'things,' while allowing for considerable individual freedom, are circumscribed and socially regulated."[50] We could tighten Said's sociological thesis about the novel to say that full membership in a society is, to a great degree, contingent on abiding by the social regulations for the "what" and "how" of representation. In its social-tutorial role, the realist novel form not only naturalizes its own narrative conventions for the representation of "things" but also the social conditions, abstracted from the actual relations of participatory democracy, that enable and disable some members of society to represent themselves in the public sphere and the state. In other words, the novel form naturalizes the constituency of the public sphere and the rights-based nation-state, as well as the terms of their franchise that determine who counts as The People and that keep some people from counting at all.

The *Bildungsroman* is a unique and vital variant of the modern novel because it is especially equipped to normalize the conditions of inclusion in and exclusion from the public sphere. As the favored novelistic form for the modern rights-based nation-state's story of socialization (or incorporation), the *Bildungsroman* purposes to bridge the gap between exclusion and inclusion; what it normalizes is the process and story form for enfranchisement. That is, the *Bildungsroman* does not simply reconfirm the centeredness of the already-centered subject; as a human rights claim, it is a narrative instrument for historically marginalized people to assert their right to be included in the franchise of the public sphere and to participate in the deliberative systems that shape social normativity itself by setting the limits between the enfranchised and the disenfranchised. In this sense, the democratic social work of the *Bildungsroman* is to demarginalize the historically marginal individual—to make the socially unrepresentative figure representative. Thus, the exemplarity of the affirmative *Bildungsroman*'s protagonist lies in its relatively modest marginality, a model marginality that is capable of being transcended or transformed by proper training in the socially acceptable forms of speech and the social norms of the bourgeois reading public. Thematically and sociologically, the viability of a candidate for the affirmative *Bildungsroman*'s incorporative work appears largely pegged to the historical condition of the public sphere itself—to the actual or imminent expansions and contractions of the franchise, which the novels both reflect and catalyze.

The didactic mode of the modern novel is especially apparent with the *Bildungsroman,* in which the "education of the protagonist is simultaneously that of the reader";[51] the genre "elicits the reader's identification with the *bildung* narrative of ethical formation, itself a narrative of the individual's relinquishing of particularity and difference through identification with an idealized 'national' form of subjectivity."[52] This process of identification constitutes an education not in individuality but in personality, the capacity to participate within the national public sphere—the sociopolitical community of speech—as a full right-and-duty-bearing citizen.

As socially contingent creatures, individuals only acquire meaning within a system of sociosyntactic relations; it is through participation in a particular social community of speech that the individual becomes a person—that individuality becomes personality. In other words, the public sphere, with its discursive terms of incorporation, is a social world of convention in which individual "contemplation" and "action" are given generic forms of expression and thereby made generally intelligible and meaningful[53]—a world where an individual's natural capacity for speech is translated into communicative speech acts, where raw human sociability is converted into sociality and narratability is activated as narrativity. Under the prevailing nation-statist model of citizenship, statelessness amounts to a state of human rightlessness, in which the human rights personality is reduced to bare individuality, as Hannah Arendt knew from her study of the fate of ethnonational minorities in Europe between the two World Wars: "A person becomes a human being in general—without a profession, without a citizenship, without an opinion, without a deed by which to identify and specify himself—*and* different in general, representing nothing but his own absolutely unique individuality which, deprived of expression within and action upon a common world, loses all significance."[54] For Arendt, who esteemed classical publicness as the highest form of human sociality and personality, statelessness–rightlessness precipitates a "civil death" that is also a "social death," a form of public nonexistence in which the individual is disbarred from "the entire social texture" of the nation-state and confined to its own socially and civically insignificant individuality.[55] According to the liberal model of human sociality and citizenship, expulsion from the community of speech represents the fiercest assault on the human personality because it excludes the individual from "a place in the world which makes opinions significant and actions effective."[56] Exclusion or eviction from the common world of convention forecloses, then, access to the very institutional machinery that designs to convert personal will into collective will—to transform the pre-social, human personality into the human rights personality and to give individual opinion and freedom official, historical, and public significance. Disenfranchisement, with its attendant loss of legal rights, also has direct literary consequences: it expels the individual from the social texture upon which the *Bildungsroman* historically depends and "in which alone," as the UDHR declares, "the free and full development of the human personality is possible."

If the freely and fully developed human personality depends upon participation in a democratic social world, then individual persons are vulnerable to human rights abuses that target the public sphere and the social texture. When, as Adeno Addis has argued in his narratological defense of the communal rights of ethnic minorities, "the individual is seen to be at least partially constituted by the tradition to which she belongs, [then] those narratives the group tells about *itself* . . . are ones that enable her to continue to tell stories about *herself*" (emphasis added).[57] Thus, disruption of the discursive mechanics of the public sphere rends the social story texture that makes meaningful personal narratives possible. Indeed, restrictions on freedoms of assembly, thought, speech, the press, and education, as well as on the rights to public hearings and to participate in public elections (among others), amount to wholesale assaults on the public sphere that degrade the social texture, limit the possibility of its reproduction, disable the conventional forms that give social significance to opinion and action, and disincorporate (or depersonify) the person. Addis' linkage of group and individual narratives vis-à-vis ethnic minorities finds a legal basis in human rights law's recognition of not only the national public sphere as a space and engine of collective identity, but also of other sub- and supra-state public spheres in which communal identities are produced and reproduced. In all cases, a public sphere is the primary space where the individual is incorporated as a particular instance of a group's personality, whether the group be as large as humanity in general (thus the human personality) or as narrow as one of the "legitimate" variations of humanity (what we might call sanctioned human diversity: "national, ethnical, racial or religious" and, more recently, gender differences) that are recognized in treaties like the Convention on the Prevention and Punishment of the Crime of Genocide (1948). An example of human rights law's provisions for public spheres in addition to the conventional Habermasian adjunct to the nation-state appears in the Declaration on the Rights of Persons Belonging to National or Ethnic, Religious and Linguistic Minorities (1992), adopted on the quincentennial of Europe's encounter with the New World. The nonbinding declaration directs states to ensure that "persons belonging to minorities" have access not only to the dominant state public sphere but also to "national" (in the ethnological sense) sub-state publics that provide the "conditions for the *promotion* of [their] identity" by enabling them "to express their characteristics and to develop their culture, language, religion, traditions and customs" (Articles 1.1, 4.2). The Minority Declaration recognizes the importance of such sub-national publics and the dangers of even subtle economic and cultural assaults upon them; it provides for a cultural security to protect against cultural death (ethnocide) by safeguarding for minority national publics what the UDHR calls "the right freely to participate in the cultural life of the community" (Article 27).

Assaults on the public sphere have consequences for the individual and the possibility of constructing narratives of identification; reciprocally, assaults on the individual have consequences for the public sphere and its social texture. If the public sphere is a medium through which the rights of the individual may be violated, the individual is also a medium for social repression, through which the rights of the public may be violated. Human rights law treats the individual person as a figural embodiment of (a synecdoche for) a group of which it is a part and an effect. The individual person is an instance of group personality and the smallest unit of human sociality (which, as we shall see, is related to the logic of novelistic exemplarity); as such, the individual person also represents the most immediate and discrete point of a group's vulnerability to human rights violations. Indeed, many of the crimes committed against the ostensibly atomic individual are violations of the integrity of the group because they have profound implications for the vitality of the social texture and constitution of, and the possibility for participation in, the public sphere. For instance, both the Convention

Against Torture and Other Cruel, Inhuman or Degrading Treatment or Punishment (1984) and the Declaration on the Prevention of All Persons from Enforced Disappearance (1992) recognize that the individual person is embedded within, and enabled by, a complex network of social relations; thus, torture is "inflicted on a person for such purposes as obtaining from him or a third person information or a confession, . . . or intimidating or coercing him or a third person" (Article 1) and disappearance constitutes "an offence to human dignity" and a violation of a "right to recognition as a person before the law" that "inflicts severe suffering on them [the disappeared] and their families" (Article 1). The individual becomes both an object and instrument of human rights violation. The synecdochal, identitarian logic that configures the individual person as an embodiment of group personality and of the vulnerability of a social texture is the very basis of the Genocide Convention, which aspires to punish and prevent not only the killing of individuals as representatives of ethnic, racial, religious, and national groups but also acts of violence that target the modes and mechanics of group identity reproduction.[58] By the logic and letter of the law, to die as a victim of genocide is, precisely, not to die as an individual but as an instance of a racialized, ethnicized, nationalized, or sect-tionalized group.[59] The human rights person may be an atom, but it is not the atomized individual of libertarian Enlightenment philosophy; rather, the individual person is an atomic unit of social relations—the embodiment of group personality and vulnerability.

As Arendt's analysis of statelessness suggests, absolute and irreducible individuality is a consequence of expulsion from (rather than a precondition for participation in) the social texture. Like genocide, disappearance, and torture, many human rights violations, especially those most insistently focused on the individual, exploit the physical singularity of the individual to disarray the social texture and disarticulate the network of relations of which the person is a part and an effect. In other words, they instrumentalize and intensify the particularity of the individual as a means of dissociating The People. If human rights law promotes an image of socialized individualism that seeks to prevent certain collective actions and violence (as I described in the previous chapter), it also articulates an image of the socially contingent human personality that seeks to protect the individual from the predations of a radicalized (or hyper-) individualism. I am not claiming that the individual is *not* the object of human rights violation, nor that the individual is somehow merely accidental or ulterior to the motives of violation; rather, my insistence on the ways in which the individual is cynically manipulated as the discrete point of social vulnerability aims to make clear that the denial of individual rights—for example, asylum or the right of return (UDHR Articles 13, 14)—is as much about policing the texture of social relations and the scope of the public sphere as it is about stripping one particular person or group of their rights.

In international law, public spheres are transfigurative spaces of social reproduction inclined to perpetuate their own collective norms, personalities, and identitarian particularities. According to these legal assumptions, what publics ideally produce and repro- duce (along with public opinion) are themselves through the pro- motion of their conventionalized forms of public expression—the cultural, linguistic, religious, and customary characteristics that constitute group identity and personality. If the democratic state's primary interest (and constitutional obligation) is its self-perpetua- tion, each of the political, cultural, and social structures implied with the human rights package helps to perpetuate the values, as- sumptions, habits, dispositions, cultural narratives, ideologies, etc., that constitute the state's historical identity—the identity of The People. In the modern rights-based nation-state, the *Bildungsroman* plot tends to pattern not only the stories of the subjectivation of citizens but also those of the incorporation of the public and of the constitution of the nation itself. In theory, the national public sphere imbricates "narratives of person and nation" so that a per- son's life narrative is brought into approximate alignment with The People's narrative; the biography of an individual is harmonized (both thematically and formally) with "a nation's biography." "As with modern persons, so it is with nations," writes Benedict Ander- son of the "need" to compose "narrative[s] of 'identity'" after the eruption of modern secular, historical time precipitated by the eighteenth-century European human rights revolutions.[60] As we shall see in the following sections, Tununa Mercado's *In a State of Memory* and Michael Ondaatje's *Anil's Ghost* narrate a reciprocal thesis, so that the disintegration of the nation-state entails a correla- tive disarticulation of the life story of the person. Without a nomi- nally democratic nation-state and public sphere, there can be no

Bildungsroman, at least as late-eighteenth- and early-nineteenth-century Europe knew the form. The exclusion of part of the population from one of these democratic institutions usually entails that sector's exclusion from the entire cultural package of human rights; similarly, the foreclosure, deformation, or absence of any of these institutions generally coincides with the foreclosure, deformation, or loss of the others.

Circling the Square: Exile, Agoraphobia, and the Public Sphere in *Tununa Mercado's In a State of Memory*

> The post-war epoch has brought into wide currency the psychological biography, the masters of which art often pull their subject up out of society by the roots. The fundamental driving force of history is presented as the abstraction, personality. . . . If you remove from a personality . . . the content which is introduced into it by the milieu, the nation, the epoch, the class, the group, the family, there remains an empty automaton. . . . Unable to explain itself by means of historic processes, [the sovereign, human personality] tries to explain history from within itself.
>
> —LEON TROTSKY, "On Lenin's Testament"

In the Mexico City suburb of Coyoacán, the unnamed narrator of Tununa Mercado's novel of statelessness, *In a State of Memory*, inscribes her name in the museum guest book of what had been, forty years earlier, Leon Trotsky's home in exile. Her signature joins "dozens of inscriptions and slogans left by other [expatriated] Argentines . . . who unknowingly signed a pact, as we had, with the greatest of all exiles and with his vulnerability."[61] Trotsky's "house-museum," which the narrator imagines having "transmigrated [the decades] to offer me shelter" in her own exilic time of need, seems to promise her the possibility of reconstituting a textual, if not a fully sociological, imaginary community of Argentines forced to flee the military dictatorships of the 1970s and 80s.[62] Visiting the house every few months for five years with her family, the narrator reifies it as a unique and powerful public site where "personal experience [might] reach historic and collective dimensions," but like

her other many efforts to knit a meaningful texture of social relations outside of Argentina, her visits ultimately devolve into ritualistic rehearsals of the first visit, during which she "read and reread"
the newspaper announcements of Trotsky's assassination wherein
"the tragedy was repeated."[63] The disappointment of both the
promise of transcending the isolation of exile and also the unsatis-
fying compensation of "diasporic public spheres" is itself repeated
as tragedy throughout the series of *tableaux* that constitute Mercado's novel-memoir.[64] *In a State of Memory* presents a lyrical study
of the experience of exclusion from the Argentine state and a democratic public sphere—losses whose gravity, in the narrator's view, is
doubled by exile: she is once removed from a familiar social texture
that might give historical and collective significance to personal experience, and she is twice removed from the immediate scene of its
unraveling "happening in Argentina, . . . [where] it was others who
buried the dead, . . . others who continued belonging to that place
and to that present."[65] Her feeling of displacement and alienation
is intensified by her anguished sense that, with her two periods of
exile in Mexico and France, she is not present at the tragic site of
loss—that not even the loss properly belongs to her.

A ghostwriter, occasional adjunct professor of literature, and
sometime journalist, Mercado's narrator experiences the "destructuralization [*desestructuración*] of exile" as a distortion of both time
and space that forces her to live in the "suspended state" of a "long
parenthesis," in which "*el presente parecía detenido* [the present appeared to be detained]."[66] The parenthetic suspension of exile inter-
rupts biographical time just as it separates her from the physical
space of the Argentine state and the discursive space of its public
sphere. Thus, exile has consequences not only for her sociopolitical
sense of belonging to an Argentine community but also for the construction of her autobiography, which "became disjointed, and
pieces of myself somehow found their way into the writings of others, gestating and giving birth to unrecognizable monsters";[67] in
both the public sphere and her own biography, the narrator imagines herself participating *in absentia*. "We lived by proxy," she observes of the exilic condition, "through third parties, struggling
with the memory of a country that was thousands of kilometers
away."[68] This refracted image of the lost country and the vicarious,
commemorative modes by which the exiles attempt to reconstruct

"a country out of that Argentine limbo" as a basis for sociality, identity, and collective political activity abroad exacerbate the narrator's long-held sense that she is "not inscribed in the social text."[69]

As a "female ghostwriter," the narrator has learned, even before the perversion of Argentina's democratic institutions by two decades of military dictatorship, to be wary of the "empty framework" of public reception and reputation, where impostors "have forged a personality by pitilessly taking transfusions of the competence of others" and so "depersonified me [*me . . . ninguneaban*]."[70] Although she recognizes the public sphere under the dictatorship as a place where impersonators thrive by "nobodying" others, the narrator nonetheless remains—with the novel's other exiles—fixated on that sphere as the "object of our desires."[71] Unpersoned by profession and exile, Mercado's narrator offers an extended lament for a devastated national public sphere, which she fetishizes as a place of personal completion—the organizing center for history, identity, rights, and narrative; however, her incapacity to compose a coherent, linear biographical narrative is compounded by the fact that both the public and private spheres have become sources of mutually complicating phobias—an agoraphobia that is aggravated by the military's dictatorial assault on the public and a claustrophobia that manifests itself with the foreclosure of participation in the *polis* and the imposition of compulsory individuality. The narrator's simultaneous obsession with and fear of publicness is a symptom not of repressed personal trauma but of "psychosocial trauma" suffered in the public sphere itself—a trauma, as the liberation psychologist Ignacio Martín-Baró described it, that "resides in the particular social relations of which the individual is only a part."[72] That the narrator's profound sense of dispossession and depersonalization has a sociopolitical (rather than merely a psychological) etiology seems implicitly to drive her search for transcendence of exilic isolation and her various attempts to reweave a personifying social texture at the borders of a frayed public sphere and state.

In a State of Memory is a lyrical novel that wants to be a *Bildungsroman*, with a private lyricism that wants to be public narrativity. The disparity between the narrator's experience of exile and return and of her ideal of social incorporation manifests itself in a generic conflict (or discomfiture) between the progressive, teleological plot logic of cause and effect and an associative, lyrical "texture of imagery" that proceeds by analogy and homology.[73] The thickness of novelistic meaning accrues from the sedimentation of discrete episodes (which are not events in the narratological sense) that exposit various states of being and unbelonging as well as the failure to find social surrogates for the lost Argentine state that might act as alternative organizing centers for history, identity, rights, and narrative. For the narrator, to be expelled from the national public sphere is to be exiled from biographical and historical time, consigned to the detained present of "lyrical immediacy," which she suffers as a kind of suffocating, socially insignificant Arendtian individuality.[74] Left alone with a lyrical self that cannot, as the ideal of *Bildung* would have it, transform "the individual moment into the universal absolute," Mercado's narrator composes a collage of narrative fragments that cannot transcend the crushing isolation and imposed privacy of lyrical individuality to become the *Bildungsroman* for which she longs.[75] Locked in what she calls the "cellular chambers" of subjectivity—"the vague space of the so-called mind"—she produces texts in which "it was very difficult to breathe": "I was closing myself into spaces from which I had difficulty escaping."[76] Thus, rather than by the humanist narrative grammar of personality development, the novel acquires its texture according to the "precarious and provisory" psychoanalytic logic of "free" association[77]—each of the chapters explores the personal, social, and narrative costs of exilic dispossession and destructuralization, repeating scenes of the narrator's impossible, frustrated longing for incorporation. Only her steadfast desire for the vitality of democratic social relations and participation in meaningful collective activity interlace the otherwise fractured narrative, which ritualistically commemorates the lack of legitimate public modes of self-expression as if such obsessive circumnarration might somehow circumstantiate the lost public sphere, might bring the missing center of the narrative circle into focus.

The narrator's stubborn intellectual attachment to the public sphere—which is complicated by a well-earned distrust of "fallacious unity" and a deeply ambivalent psychical or "passionate attachment" to publicness—is perhaps the peculiar sensibility of the dislocated and disbarred journalist, who may be presumed to suffer the privations of involuntary privacy more urgently and acutely than others.[78] The events of Mercado's novel parallel much of her own biography: between the two periods of exile recounted in the novel, Mercado wrote for the progressive Buenos Aires newspaper *La Opinión*, whose editor, Jacobo Timerman, was himself arrested, detained, and tortured for his journalistic activities as part of the military junta's systematic measures to "prevent all public debate."[79] In an effort to disarticulate the public sphere, the regime privatized the *res publica* by criminalizing public discussion of its policies and activities in a series of directives; Communiqué No. 19, which gutted article 19 of the UDHR, made the publication of reports on governmental repression punishable by incarceration for "anyone who by any means emits, spreads or propagates news, communiqués or images with a view to upsetting, prejudicing or demeaning the activity of the Armed, Security, or Police Forces."[80] Among the activities proscribed from public discussion were the torture and disappearance of nearly 30,000 people during Argentina's Dirty War (1976–83)—the name initially given by the military junta to the activities of a small armed opposition that eventually attached instead to its own violent program for "National Reorganization," *el proceso*. Under the pretext of fighting a war against subversives and terrorists, which General Jorge Videla famously defined as "not just someone with a gun or bomb, but also someone who spreads ideas that are contrary to Western and Christian civilization," the junta's efforts to quash public dissent took two related forms:[81] direct assaults on the public sphere by curtailing freedoms of speech, assembly, and expression—which isolated individuals from each other—and focused, exemplary attacks on individuals designed to terrorize the public generally.

As privileged participants in public discourse, journalists, artists, authors, and professors were special targets of intimidation, forced exile, imprisonment, disappearance, torture, and murder. With the restoration of democracy in 1983, newly elected civilian president Raúl Alfonsín established CONADEP, the National Commission on Disappeared People (*Comisión Nacional sobre la Desaparición de Personas*) to document the fate of the *desaparecidos*, the generic term for those citizens abducted by the government, detained without trial or official acknowledgment, tortured, and often summarily executed. The truth commission's published report, *Nunca Más*

(*Never Again*), documents almost 9,000 testimonial cases of disappearance and other repressive methods of "paralysing public protest . . . by every possible means."[82] The quintessential crime of the Dirty War—and the "sad privilege for Argentina," as the novelist and CONADEP president Ernesto Sábato lamented, that the word *desaparecidos* is "frequently left in Spanish by the world's press"—disappearance is a liminal state of nonexistence;[83] in this zone of instability, the disappeared are neither functionally alive nor officially dead. This ambiguous state of present absence is key to the crime's disruptive effects; individuality (or, more precisely, the empirical singularity of the individual) became an instrument of repression. The *desaparecidos* were not merely individual victims but the most vulnerable point of the social texture; they were a means to terrorize the community, their uncertain status calculated to create a paralyzing combination of fear and hope that would "ensur[e] the silence of the relatives" and prevent "solidarity being shown by the population in general."[84] To heighten the effect of the terror, anonymized "nameless bodies" often reappeared in public, defaced and depersonified, "without identity, driving people distraught at the impossibility of knowing the specific fate of their loved ones."[85] By destroying both the body and personality of the individual (as well as official documentation of their existence and incarceration) disappearance assaults more than a discrete individual; its effects are both more concentrated and broader because it hyperindividualizes the victim to target the intersubjective relations of the community that give meaning to individual opinions, actions, and identity. That is, disappearance instrumentalizes individuality to disfigure the person as a civil and social subject by leveraging the individual against the relational texture of social signification of which it is a part.

During the Dirty War, the military regime promoted an organic vision of the nation-state, constructing the general populace as complicit with its vision of social reorganization while simultaneously and cynically assigning responsibility for state violence to its individual victims. Similarly, at their trials after the return to democracy, the generals resorted to the exculpatory logic of individual responsibility to blame the crimes of the regime on a few sadistic individuals rather than on the coordinated ideology and practice of a pogrom. Just as *Nunca Más* refuses to speak of the victims of disappearance and torture as simply individual victims, it also rejects the individualist excuses for the systemic "normal abnormality" of the violence, insisting that under the dictatorships "no such thing [as 'excesses'] existed" because "transgression was common and widespread . . . [and] dreadful 'excesses' were themselves the norm."[86] But if the military made participation in the public sphere a risky affair (whether one appeared *in propria persona* or *de persona ausente*), the normal methods of repression (whose extreme versions are torture, disappearance, and forced exile) made privacy itself a "terror"—a realm in which the individual is "'disappeared' from the fields of cultural and state discourse" and human rights.[87] Mercado's narrator suffers exile as depersonalization and dissociation, a disappearance that traps her between the social world of public personality and the self-absorption of lyrical subjectivity. The authoritarian state's perversion of both individuality and collectivity morbidizes in the narrator's claustrophobia and agoraphobia—a precarious complex of social and civil fears that sustains her conflicted "perpetual mania for enclosure and aperture."[88] The narrator can neither be with other people (although that is her deepest desire) nor comfortably alone in the "compartment of my persona," which is "overcrowd[ed]" with "morbid projections . . . of bodies lying neatly aligned in open graves."[89] The narrator is left with what she feels are the counterfeit social spaces of temporary and vicarious publics that rehearse "the exercise of lack" and the "re-creation of the void [that] was the characteristic condition [*el estado propio*] of living in exile."[90]

The parodic character of her efforts to fabricate meaningful social textures outside of Argentina consistently reveals itself in their failure to serve as satisfactory substitutes for that other, lost national public sphere to which their vicariousness seems insistently to refer. The narrator, for instance, depreciates the significance of her participation in occasional small demonstrations outside a closed Argentine Embassy in Mexico: "The rallies . . . were obviously cathartic, but, in the long run, they proved to be pathetic recourses; . . . this discharge and the illusion that we were fighting the dictatorship were a political ritual that compensated for the lack, through sheer dearth, of an effective political practice."[91] In contrast to the mechanical roles of the unnamed narrator and her anonymous compatriots, two protestors carrying photo placards of their disappeared family members receive proper names: Clara Gertel and Laura Bonaparte.[92] Recognizing the immediacy and scale of these women's loss, the narrator regards their protest as authentic—not merely a ritualistic copy of the form of political defiance inaugurated by that politically effective counterpublic, the Mothers of the Plaza de Mayo, who have marched at the symbolic center of Argentina's public sphere every Thursday since 30 April 1977.

For the narrator, her own participation in the Mexican demonstrations is a dislocated imitation of *Las Madres'* circling the public square and their successful occupation of "the quintessential site of the polis, as well as the tragedy of the polis."[93] Demanding both the reappearance of the disappeared and official accountability for their disappearance, *Las Madres* responded to the individual depersonification of their children by publicly identifying the disappeared and reincorporating them into public discourse; their practice insists on the importance of both individual identity and collective action. Refusing to accept "their own private losses and personal griefs as 'individual human rights abuses,'" the Mothers made public "both their children's disappearance and the disappearance of the public sphere itself" by asserting themselves as a "new kind of citizen," reclaiming the public sphere and repopulating it with the disappeared, dispossessed, and the historically disenfranchised.[94] The Mothers' protests began the revival of both the symbolic and functional legitimacy of a popular public sphere, and in Mercado's novel their "circles of madness"[95] become the gravitational center of exilic desires for personal reintegration and the mending of the social texture, "with all its cottony imperfections."[96] In the Mothers' circle, returning exiles "converged" and were "reunited" after the end of the dictatorships.[97] Although the urgency of claiming "the site of the polis" begins to wane for many returnees, the narrator herself retains "no other intention than that of occupying the reconquered space."[98] But even the promise of incorporation into the circle proves elusive for the narrator, who finds that there is no place in the public discourse for the story of exile, for the ones who were absent during the terror and time of loss.

The narrator's final return to Argentina in 1986, after the country's own return to democracy, confirms her constant feeling of disenfranchisement when she discovers that even her literary proxy in the national imaginary, a figure standing on a balcony with her husband and son in a scene from Tomás Eloy Martínez's *La novela de Perón*, has been abbreviated out of the new edition.[99] The narrator experiences exile in literary terms, as abridgment both *from* the social text and *of* her proper life story, which she imagines would proceed at the usual biographical pace if she still belonged "to that place and to that present"—to Argentine national space and time. A component of her libidinal fixation on the public sphere is her obsession with the German-idealist language of *Bildung* and its promise of harmonious concordance between personal desire and socio-institutional constraint. Indeed, the narrator consistently registers the disappointment of her desire for sociopolitical incorporation in ironic language that underscores the thematic and formal discrepancy between her disjointed life story and the idealist *Bildungsroman*. Thus, for instance, she holds out hope for the possibility of folding the individual experience of exile into the collective story of Argentina's emergent democracy even as she recognizes that "for those who return, the country is not an open container, and it is futile for them to try to lose themselves within the existing structures [*confundirse en las estructuras permanentes*]."[100] If the narrator cannot simply disappear into the post-dictatorial social formation, she also refuses to accept a psychiatrist's palliative diagnosis that exile (rather than reintegration) is the objective expression of her personal will—the form of life that "*corresponded to the form of my desire*."[101]

Mercado's narrator maintains a faith (of which she also remains characteristically circumspect) in the capacity of literature to transcend individuality—to mediate between her subjective desires and the objective world of social forms; she routinely turns to literature—to reading and writing—as surrogate forms of sociality. Books tantalize her with *Bildung*-like promises of "spiritual richness" and self-discovery, "invad[ing] my entire self as if, through unknown arts, [they] conformed perfectly to my being."[102] But the literary satisfaction of finding oneself in the structure of a book in such perfect conformity is fugitive, escaping "from [her] awareness from one day to the next"; what the narrator ultimately discovers in "the textual" is her "fundamental nudity," "vulnerability," and an awareness of "not knowing, the inability to fill the void or approach the universal."[103] Recreating a bourgeois reading society with "surreptitious friends" in Mexico, the narrator undertakes a projected thirty-year reading of Hegel's *Phenomenology of Spirit*, but even the activity of collective reading only reconfirms her sense of isolation and disconnection. While the *Phenomenology*'s account of the coming of universal self-consciousness through the arc of alienation and return resonates with the exiles, Hegel's philosophical *Bildungsroman* yields its "revelation of the Spirit" only sparingly and "unrepeatabl[y]" in the form of symmetrical but individuating epiphanies that occur to *"cada uno por su lado* [each in their own part]."[104] Like the narrator's other efforts at socialcraft, the epiphanic reading experience becomes ceremonial, producing both a "profound sorrow" and an unfulfillable "hope some day to return [to] that place [of the Spirit] that became a reality, instantaneously"—the collective philosophical search for the Spirit is called off after only fifty pages.[105]

The experience of return from exile is similarly disillusioning. The narrator not only discovers that "no person, organism, or institution has ever taken into account people who have been absent, estranged, or fugitive from reality";[106] she also finds that she cannot complete the image of completion that she projected for herself. Instead, returnees are received by the "motherland" with "nothing more than a formality" and an expectation that they "adapt" to the "new situation."[107] The narrator rejects the deformed version of the *Bildungsroman* that the years of repression have degraded into an obligatory story of sociocultural adaptation, as if "a person is like malleable putty that yields to circumstances merely by softening up."[108] In particular, she resents the social imperative to narrate her return as a series of "temporal segments"—of "periods and intensities"—that construe the experience as progressive personal "improvement," refusing to credit the palliative anticipatory logic of novelistic plot: that "there will be a future time of adaptation in which everything will be ordered in a satisfactory way." The novel's fragmented structure resists that compulsion, calling into question the very possibility of formulating a traditional *Bildungsroman* story of personal incorporation when the state is disrupted and there is no room in the national imaginary for the "prisoners, the ill, or the alienated."[109] Mercado's narrator resents the dominant cultural narrative of adaptation not simply because it arrives preformed but because, in repeating the expected story, its narrator performatively consents to accept singular responsibility for both her present marginalization and her future assimilation.

The novel refuses to endorse the dominant narrative's individualistic, teleological ideology that, as far as the narrator is concerned, obfuscates the disappearance of legitimate state and civil institutions and perpetuates the same sociopolitical arrangements that necessitated her exile and make it possible for Argentine society to ignore its continued collective complicity in the crimes of the dictatorship. Given the narrator's simultaneous fears of exclusion and inclusion, it is, however, difficult to imagine withholding such consent in the social world. When returning exiles are asked "if they have adapted," as much as they might like "to meet [the question] with a sharp remark or a refusal to answer, . . . one rarely has the urge."[110] The codes of social formality compel the narrator to parrot the required response, even though she recognizes that the question is "anodyne"—"a cliché used by an entire social class seeking to ease its conscience." For Mercado's narrator, adaptation is performed in the very act of narrating the socially acceptable story of adaptation, which publicly certifies that she has indeed "adapted to a requirement" and "an environment." The inevitability of narrating the pre-scripted story is all the more distasteful because the exiles recognize that with their command performance they have again "let themselves be trapped into insignificance"—they have acquiesced to the conventions of "the existing social structures" and consented to play the role of the narrator in *their* hegemonic narrative of adaptation.[111]

The narrator's profound ambivalence toward the social world of convention is repeated in her distrust of literary forms and symbolic acts of representation. Much of that suspicion is a residual effect of the dictatorship's distortion of the tropes of republican political representation—its abuse of the ways in which the figures of metaphor and metonymy enable one to speak, act, and write in the name of others. Some of that skepticism can also be traced to the normalization of the post-dictatorial public sphere that is partly conditioned on "the erasure and forgetting of the experience of the victims."[112] That is, if the *desaparecidos* underwrote the authority of the authoritarian state, their continued palpable absence haunts the new order—their still-unsettled state threatens the restoration of the democratic state. In an effort to avoid representation's tendency for misrepresentation, the narrator refuses to accept any symbolic compensation for such losses, which amounts to a wholesale rejection of "any metaphorical transaction." Struggling with the imperative to write "after the catastrophe," she anguishes over the question of how to write without either relapsing into the suffocating privatism of her exilic texts or replicating the dictatorship's figural usurpations of collectivity.[113] As much as she resists tropological acts of substitution, Mercado's narrator also eschews saturated literary conventions, "overpopulated," as Bakhtin writes of the social condition of language generally, "with the intentions of others."[114] She finds, for instance, "the inevitable trappings" of conventional novelistic scenes of women suddenly recognizing their mortality in a mirror to be contrived, and yet she recounts this epiphany about literature at the moment she discovers the sudden descent of the time spent in exile in her own mirrored image.[115] Searching for an effective political and aesthetic practice for the occupation of public space, the narrator struggles with a resentment of rhetorical and literary conventions, not merely because they are conventional and therefore in some way trite or inauthentic, but also because they reflect, and even anticipate, her own experience.

The narrator's anxious resistance to literature becomes critical after her return to Buenos Aires, when she is enthralled by the "situation of exposure" of a man who lives in a public plaza and with speculation about "what kind of message the man . . . and his circumstances [of vulnerability] were sending."[116] The man, who spends his days diligently writing in a notebook, seems to symbolize a willful state of marginality encrypted in the heart of public space—a deliberate mode of occupying the public sphere without dominating it or being swallowed by it. The man's public exposure puts the narrator in "*un estado de excepción o, por lo menos, de emergencia* [a state of exception or, at least, of emergency]" and inspires in her a "literary emotion" and a compulsion to put the image of the homeless man writing into her own writing.[117] "The scene demanded to be written," writes the narrator, adding that "the pitiless clarity of that image arrived prewritten, yet I refused to translate it." Torn between the imperative to transcribe the scene and her suspicion that it is too apt "for transference onto paper," the narrator articulates her fear of simply "convert[ing] the exposure of the man into a literary theme, . . . a topic, or, much worse, an object."[118]

From the narrator's perspective, the man's circumstances make him vulnerable not just to the elements and the government but to her "literary and unwholesome curiosity"—to the cupidity of literature and the conventional devices of literary signification.[119] Her anxiety stems not from a sense that literature can never adequately translate or represent the image of the man, but from a sense that, like the institutions of the state, it is only too eager to do so, and in fact already does so. The ready-made image of the homeless man writing in the park already appears to signify according to the codes and conventions of literature, and any derivative rendering would likely reduce that significance to a vicarious, redundant reproduction. As with the account of her self-fascination in the mirror, the narrator smuggles the prewritten image of the writing man into her story surreptitiously—its literary vulnerability re-presented in the narrative of its own conventionality. The narrator never fully reconciles herself to the world of convention, although she does come to recognize that to write is necessarily to enter a saturated social world of objective forms—a practice whose stakes are public exposure and personal vulnerability.

The narrator finally manages to write in earnest after exile, on a wall outside the window of her Buenos Aires apartment. Her public graffiti, as Jean Franco suggests, does not represent "the kind of self-discovery that we often encounter in women's writing in which, after the trials of growing up, the girl finally puts pen to paper and thus arrives at a consciousness of her own personhood";[120] nor is it the kind of transcendent writing that has pretensions to approaching the universal. Instead, she writes on the wall in "small awkward letters" and "clusters of text," in "spewing slashes" and "overlapping texts, on lines and between lines, with blank areas and areas configuring representations beyond their own relevance."[121] The wall is transformed as these texts accumulate, until, in the novel's final sentence, it slips "down into the line at its very foundation, like a sheet of paper sliding vertically into a slot." The narrator's ultimate act of writing assumes the symbolic significance of an act of balloting—that quintessential democratic activity that links the individual to the community, not in the ethereal realm of the Spirit but in the mundane, sociohistorical world of the practical, plebiscitary "universal." She writes in the smallest unit of popular sovereignty and democratic publication—the grapheme of citizen-subjectivity—through which private opinion ideally emerges as popular will and the singular becomes collective. The only nonvicarious activity of the novel, the narrator's final writing is both an act of resistance to authoritarianism (and presumptive democracy) and a responsible performance of civic duty that contributes to the restoration and maintenance of a legitimate democratic social order. The act is relatively modest and its effect ambiguous, but in Mercado's text it is politically, personally, and literarily profound in its insistence upon the institutions of deliberative democracy and the reincorporation into the state and the public sphere of their historical victims. It reclaims the political and literary tropes of representation as it also aspires to recuperate the discursive machinery of the public sphere that might make the idealist promise of the *Bildungsroman* once again sensible. If we recognize the novel as an absentee ballot finally delivered in person, the intensely private writing becomes public, the lyrical collective, and in the act the narrator emerges from her state *of* memory to cast her literary vote for a state *with* memory.

Form, Conformity, and Deformation: Public Conventions and the Dissensual Bildungsroman

> Now, every relation of representation is founded on a fiction: that of the presence at a certain level of something which, strictly speaking, is absent from it. But because it is *at the same time* a fiction and a principle organizing actual social relations, representation is the terrain of a game whose result is not predetermined from the beginning.
>
> —ERNESTO LACLAU and CHANTAL MOUFFE,
> *Hegemony and Socialist Strategy*

The narrator's final act of writing in Mercado's novel gestures modestly toward a renewal of the state/citizen bind that sustains, and is sustained by, the Habermasian public sphere and the idealist *Bildungsroman*. Throughout the novel, the narrator can neither imagine for herself a linear autobiography outside of the state/citizen bind nor plot for herself a realist *Bildungsroman* with its progressive movement from the private to the public sphere. Yet she stubbornly refuses to abandon that ideal and to accept the compensation of alternative public spheres, whose sociality and opportunities for personal expression are, in her assessment, vicarious—hollow echoes of that other public sphere that persists only in her romantic imagination. Her inauthentic, ritualistic publics are provisional, never offering the narrator more than fleeting impressions of belonging, of transcendence of Arendtian individuality, or of a form of life that conforms "perfectly to my being."[122] If, through the modern institution of the public sphere, The People usurped the place of Nature and Nature's God as the guarantor of social order and meaning, the loss of that democratic institution—like the earlier death of God—induces an existential vertigo that, in Mercado's novel, manifests itself in the deformation of the story form of human personality development. The lyrical texture of Mercado's novel constitutes a kind of pre-*Bildungsroman*—a preamble that anticipates the restoration of the sociocivil conditions that might make a narrative of socialization and personalization something more than a story of compulsory adaptation and might make it once again possible to imagine a narrative of constructive (and legitimate) reconciliation between the proclivities of the individual and the democratic demands of society.

The idealist *Bildungsroman* gave narrative structure and voice to certain assumptions about the emergence of a social order constituted on a particular vision of rights; if its realist representation seemed to correspond to the ideal, this was because the novel had abstracted a narrow slice of the "real" and called it ideal—it had "romanticise[d] certain parts of reality and abandon[ed] others to prose, as devoid of meaning."[123] Indeed, Goethe's narrative realism corresponds to his theoretical humanist idealism (and thereby satisfies the strictest criteria of the generic type that his novel is said to have inaugurated) because he took the incorporated, bourgeois male and the public "virtues of the citizen" for the ideal—the concrete embodiment of the universal. The traditional genre aimed to reconcile the discrepancy between idealism and realism; in contrast, the sociological vitality and thematic substance of contemporary *Bildungsromane* derive from precisely this discrepancy, which sustains the literary form. As I have been arguing, the *Bildungsroman* is best understood not as a form but as a function—as the name of a form of literary social work; it is as much the name of a reading as of a writing practice that situates the realist story of human personality development in relation to an ideal of that development. Like the reading of Hegel's *Phenomenology*, which reveals for Mercado's narrator a short-circuiting of the Spirit, the continued salience of the *Bildungsroman* is nourished by the variance between a poetic promise of incorporation and the prosaic experience of exclusion. International human rights derive their energy from a similar discrepancy that emerges when the proposition that such universal things exist is confronted with the historical evidence and experience that they do not; that is, the struggle for human rights occurs in the space between the world that the law and discourse (including the idealist *Bildungsroman*) imagine and the one that they address in fact. In the alliance between literary form and legal norms, the *Bildungsroman* negotiates between an ideal of human rights (not always, or necessarily, coextensive with that articulated in international law, although that is my narrow focus) and the sociohistorical condition of rights on the ground—the improbability of realizing the ideal in any real public sphere.

Like *Bildung* and human rights discourse, the liberal public sphere celebrates itself in universalist rhetoric that envisions an egalitarian imaginary—"a space in which [private] differences [are] erased through the universal equivalence of citizens."[124] As Ernesto Laclau and Chantal Mouffe have argued, for liberal philosophy (and the democratic ideal that Mercado's narrator maintains) the public sphere constitutes a conventional social world in which "a *positive* and *unified* conception of human nature . . . would have to manifest the effects of its radical liberty and equality." This reification of "a public space linked to the idea of citizenship,"[125] institutionalized with the eighteenth-century bourgeois revolutions, made it possible, even necessary, to imagine publicness in emancipatory terms. Thus, publicness and public expression become the hallmarks of human equality and freedom. Ideally, the democratic public sphere is a transformative space of social reproduction—the site where The People produce and reproduce the norms and forms of themselves as citizen-subjects—that is inclined to normalize and perpetuate its own deliberative practices and discursive forms. As we saw in the previous chapter, the affirmative, idealist *Bildungsroman* conventionalizes this liberating conception of publicness and intensifies the egalitarian fiction of the public sphere's democratic inclusiveness and responsiveness to the individual, in part by naturalizing its *Bildung* hermeneutic and dialogical ethic as the proper mode for reconciling the potentially conflicted desires and designs of the individual and society. That is, the affirmative *Bildungsroman* plots the story of an individual's training in the dominant modes of public debate and discursive sociality; it seeks to convince both the *Bildungsheld* and the reader that its particular narrative of personality development, modernization, and socialization is the natural form for encoding the story of the individual's emergence in the public world of convention.

The public sphere is so crucial to the thematic and formal consistency of the *Bildungsroman* and the rest of the human rights cultural package that one way to describe and delimit the genre as a subfield, or constellation, of the modern novel is to classify novels according to their treatment of the egalitarian imaginary that underpins the public sphere. Rather than focus primarily on "how the image of the main hero is constructed," as Bakhtin did in his dissection of the genre, we can consider the image of the other half of the dyad: the social world of convention.[126] The ideological pressures and problematics of the *Bildungsroman* (its generic "frameworks of expectation"[127]) are socialization, normalization, and incorporation; the genre assumes that either the individual or the social world is malleable, or both. (If neither is, we have a version of the *picaresque*.) The attitude or position that a particular novel takes toward the public sphere's shape, scope, flexibility, rigidity, etc., establishes the text's "identity relationally, against other important resolutions of the problematic."[128] "*Bildungsroman*" is a rather capacious generic label, as Franco Moretti has recognized: "Even those novels that clearly are *not Bildungsroman* or novels of formation are perceived by us against this conceptual horizon; so we speak of a 'failed initiation' or of a 'problematic formation.'"[129] If, however, we stress the social end of the process of formation rather than its outcome, novels of both successful and failed initiation will be seen to be concerned with similar questions of the legitimacy of social formations and relations—and, thus, of human rights. Indeed, stories of frustrated incorporation are possibly more important for the social work of the genre than are *exempla* of normative assimilation. Recognizing this continuity of the generic social function, and its relation to human rights, allows us to situate novels from various sociocultural and historical circumstances within a field of *Bildungsroman* possibilities while respecting the heterogeneity (or thematic and formal diversity) of individual examples.

The idealist *Bildungsroman* envisions a dialectical relation between the individual and society in which the two achieve a mutual
accord in the consensual, conventional forms of the social texture
and the public sphere (which respond to, reflect, and refine the
inclinations of the human personality). By contrast, realist variants
of the genre tend to depict the social order as intractable, and in
such cases the plot of personality development appears as a process
of assimilation, or "accommodation *to the existing society*";[130] these
versions of the genre (which still may be called affirmative, since
they represent processual incorporation) image the social texture
as aprioristic—as the "immobile background of the [ready-made]
world" against which the protagonist becomes heroic by adapting
(to a greater or lesser extent) to its exigencies.[131] This is the degraded form of the narrative of incorporation that Mercado's narrator rebels against because she recognizes that the story of
adaptation, promulgated by an entire social class seeking to assuage
its conscience, "functions as a form of symbolic legitimation, valorizing existing power relations by narrativizing the process of socialization . . . in such a way that young men and women *fit into
society*."[132] The affirmative *Bildungsroman* is, as I suggested in the
previous chapter, a fundamentally "conservative genre, confident in
the validity of the society it depicts, and anxious to lead both the
hero and reader toward a productive place within that world."[133]

The idealist and the realist variations of the *Bildungsroman* represent two poles on a continuum of possible solutions to the problematic of modern socialization that ranges from consensuality on the
one hand to conformity on the other—from maximum malleability
on the part of society to maximum malleability on the part of the
individual. An additional axis of plot possibilities bisects the first
and can help us graph the field of the *Bildungsroman* genre with
greater complexity. This second dimension ranges from full incorporation (acceptance) to complete disenfranchisement (rejection)—
from citizenship to individuality (the condition of being "nothing
but a man," in Arendt's words[134]). In any *Bildungsroman*'s representation of the process and possibility of socialization, the *Bildungsheld*'s integration or exclusion is not merely a matter of having "the
choice of accepting or rejecting th[e] projected resolution" of some
form of accommodation with society;[135] instead, the social order
may be so deformed and insular that no admission for the postulant

is possible, no matter how much they are willing to compromise. Indeed, in novels of disillusionment—anti-*Bildungsromane* that narrate the failure of incorporation—it is often difficult, if not "impossible," as Lukács claimed, "to tell whether the inadequacy of the structure of the individual is due to the individual's success or failure or whether it is a comment on the structure itself."[136]

I posit that among contemporary examples of *Bildungsromane* (especially from the Global South) the most common variation of the genre lies at the crux of these two axes, which, appropriately for a genre whose primary work is demarginalization, places an ambivalent, double-edged marginality (like that of Mercado's man-in-the-park) at the center of the field of *Bildungsroman* possibilities. This dissident subgenre depicts the imperatives of modernization, socialization, and human personality development not as an idealist process of consensual harmonization, but neither does it discount such concordance as an absolute, abstract impossibility. Like Mercado's narrator, it neither accepts the grossly compromised terms of enfranchisement (the story of adaptation, for example) nor rejects them outright; instead, it holds onto the ideal of harmonious integration even as it narrates the unfulfillment of the promises of human rights and idealist *Bildung*. In contrast to the consensual ideal of the affirmative genre, we could call this variant a "dissensual *Bildungsroman*," after the form of political dissensus that Jacques Rancière describes as taking place after the French Revolution. French women, he writes, made a "twofold demonstration" against the discriminations of the Declaration of the Rights of Man and of the Citizen: "They could demonstrate that they were deprived of the rights they had, thanks to the Declaration of Rights. And they could demonstrate, through their public action, that they had the rights that the constitution denied to them, that they could enact those rights."[137] Like the Mothers of the Plaza de Mayo after them, these French women exploited a logical and legal inconsistency in the formulation and application of the "universal"—"*tous les membres du corps social*" (DRMC)—to stage their dissensus in a public performance of the paradox: "They acted as subjects that did not have the rights that they had and had the rights that they had not." The dissensual *Bildungsroman* performs a similar double-demonstration by making a twofold rights claim that protests the protagonist's exclusion from the public realm of rights, yet articulates this

protest within the normative genre of the rights claim, thereby asserting a right to make such a public narrative demonstration and
to do so in the dominant novelistic technology of incorporation.
Like Mercado's narrator, the genre affirms the ideal of the egalitarian imaginary as the basis of its narrative demonstration (both an
exposition and a protest) of the *Bildungsheld*'s actual exclusion from
a social texture in which she is theoretically, and rightfully, included. The dissensual *Bildungsroman* insists upon the abstract legitimacy of human rights principles and expands the effective
compass of their universality through a generic "act of translation"
in which, as Judith Butler has written, "one with no authorization
to speak within and as the universal nonetheless lays claims to the
terms" in order to "demand that the universal as such ought to
be inclusive of them."[138] The dissensual *Bildungsroman* inverts the
affirmative rights claim of the idealist genre by publicizing the discrepancy between the rhetoric of liberty, equality, and fraternity
and the inegalitarian social formations and relations in which that
rhetoric is put into historical practice.

A transformation in either the ideal of the public sphere or in
the sociohistorical condition of human rights in a particular circumstance registers in a correlative transformation of the *Bildungsroman*'s generic conventions. Likewise, in the dissensual *Bildungsroman*'s negotiation of the ideal and the real, it is not only the
sociohistorical condition of human rights that is criticized; the egalitarian ideal itself is called into question by a rights claim for inclusion that effectively reveals the ideal to be a Gramscian "concrete
universal." The very articulation of this rights claim as a narrative
assertion of a right to have rights rearticulates the sociohistorical
category of the "universal" in human rights. Typically, the dissensual *Bildungsroman* narrates the frustration of incorporation to publicize the social, political, cultural, and economic assumptions about
normativity that determine the constituency of the historical public
sphere and that underpin, and are perpetuated by, the traditional
conventions of the affirmative *Bildungsroman*. In other words, the
dissensual *Bildungsroman* demonstrates the gender, racial, ethnic,
religious, class, and other "minority" biases and exclusions that are
institutionalized in the historical world of convention and that are,
as Nancy Fraser and others have argued, constitutive of, rather than
incidental to, the liberal public sphere's hegemonic functioning.

For Mercado's narrator, the idealist *Bildungsroman* is both an enabling and disabling fiction: it fortifies her refusal to accept anything less than full enfranchisement, even as its inconsummable promise of incorporation deepens her sense of disenfranchisement from an Argentine social world of convention that presents itself in the duplicitous egalitarian image of an "open container."[139] Similarly, the Habermasian ideal of a public sphere that is open to all comers not only animates the narrator's obsession with an Argentine national public sphere but also makes it impossible for her to find fulfillment in alternative publics. The narrator's disappointing search for alternative forms of collectivity, public life, and political expression in Mexico leads her to the conclusion that the common condition of exile—based upon symmetrical vulnerability to the predations of a repressive state rather than upon mutual recognition and positive equality—is a feeble foundation for the formation of a viable counterpublic. Her subgroup fails "to reach agreement" primarily because the forms of "verbal constructions" among the participants prove too "numerous and varied" to achieve and sustain consensus.[140] Indeed, as Mercado's narrator recognizes, a public sphere is a verbal construction (a discursive formation) that is constituted of shared verbal constructions.

A public—in its function as a deliberative community (a debating and reading society) that is, ideally, consensual in character—enables, conventionalizes, and canonizes some verbal and conceptual forms for the expression of public opinion over others, and these forms tend to abstract and reproduce the contingent assumptions, norms, and social relations generally shared by its members. A public frames its collective opinion in public narratives (or, more accurately, *cultural* narratives, since they represent a particular public culture's particular common sense that passes itself off as transcendent, universal truth). Whether a public sphere is inflected as bourgeois, literary, partial, alternative, feminist, subaltern, or counter, it maintains a "publicist" orientation (quoting Fraser), a deliberative ethic, and a discursive threshold of membership that institutionalizes the terms of group incorporation and exclusion in its favored speech genres. In other words, the conventionalized hermeneutic codes and modes of a public's cultural narratives tend to reenact at the level of rhetorical form and generic structure the

often-undeclared rights and responsibilities assumed with public affiliation; they also tend to discriminate (as the story of adaptation
does for returning exiles in Mercado's novel) between "natives" and
"aliens," between those who can be naturalized and those who will
remain disenfranchised—the demarginalizable and the perpetually
marginal. In this sense, the socially acceptable discursive forms pattern the canonical modes for the expression of public opinion and,
perhaps more importantly, set the effective shape and scope of the
public itself—the parameters of belonging to its ostensibly voluntary association.

Nancy Fraser has persuasively argued that Habermas's valorization of a singular national public—which shadows the state and
takes the citizen as its categorical subject—monologizes the actual
multiformity of public discourse by disregarding the important
presence of competing publics within the domain of the nation-
state. In her analysis, these alternative publics challenge the dominant cultural narratives of the state and its hegemonic public
sphere, constituting—as Fraser says of her "subaltern counterpublics"—"discursive arenas where members of subordinated social
groups invent and circulate counterdiscourses, so as to formulate
oppositional interpretations of their identities, interests, and
needs."[141] In this regard, the dissensual *Bildungsroman* is a particularly effective political demonstration because it puts "two worlds
in one and the same world," straddling the divide between the dominant class and a subordinated group;[142] it appropriates the incorporative form and egalitarian promise of the hegemonic group to
rewrite it in the interests of the subordinated. The dissensual *Bildungsroman* puts in circulation a countercultural narrative that seeks
to rearticulate the sociohistorical universal and the political terms
of antagonism between a marginal group and the dominant group.

Although the *Bildungsroman* (and the realist novel more generally) tends to be the bourgeois public sphere's hegemonic form, I
am not arguing that it is the only narrative basis upon which the
Habermasian public sphere (projected in human rights law) constitutes itself as a public; nor am I suggesting that the dominant discursive form within any given public is exclusive to that public or
that it provides its singular discursive pattern and deliberative
focus.[143] I am, however, arguing that the specific rights and duties
constitutive of both a particular public sphere and its patterns of

social relations manifest themselves in the discursive forms that predominate within it, and that these forms in part determine the public's particularity and constituency. Although counterpublics tend to incorporate themselves around counterforms, such countercultural narratives and literary countergenres similarly abstract and reinforce the specific rights, duties, and social relations of their respective publics, even if at a broader level they represent alternatives to the dominant society's deliberative and narrative ethics, and therefore make it possible to imagine alternative constructions of human rights.[144] As we shall see in *Anil's Ghost*, the predominance of a particular formalization of common sense within a given public can be appreciated by the regularity with which it submits various phenomena, events, and objects to its normalizing and narrativizing conventions.

Marginal(ia) Publics: Narrative Remains and the Disarticulation of Human Personality in Michael Ondaatje's Anil's Ghost

> *Dans un sens le Bildungsroman n'est donc qu'une sorte de préroman, de préambule. En fait, à la fin de l'oeuvre le héros nous apparaît armé pour l'existence, prêt à vivre son roman.*
>
> [In a sense, the *Bildungsroman* is nothing more than a sort of prenovel, a preamble. Finally, at the end of the work, the hero appears to us armed for existence, ready to live his novel.]
>
> —FRANÇOIS JOST, "La Tradition du 'Bildungsroman'"

Michael Ondaatje's novel *Anil's Ghost* (2000)—about a forensic anthropologist on contract with a Geneva-based nongovernmental human rights organization sent to Sri Lanka to uncover evidence of government-sponsored murder, torture, and disappearance of civilians during an ongoing civil war—is an unfulfilled, or post-, *Bildungsroman*. Anil Tissera, the novel's thirty-three-year-old heroine, returns to Colombo for the first time since she left Sri Lanka fifteen years earlier to pursue her medical studies overseas in the former colonial capital. Anil has passed most of those years—the height of the violence in Sri Lanka—in England and the United States, where "she felt completed."[145] These *Bildungsroman*esque plot details that are scattered piecemeal throughout Ondaatje's disjointed narrative constitute a "preamble" to *Anil's Ghost*, a "prenovel" from which the protagonist would appear to emerge "armed for existence, ready to live [her] novel."[146] Yet Ondaatje's novel "violat[es] the codes that are its [apparent] point of departure," and in doing so it takes a position in relation to the "generic horizon" of conventional *Bildungsroman* expectations evoked by the promise of a postcolonial homecoming.[147]

These disarticulated pre-novelistic, biographical events allude to a conventional story of Anil's personal and social "completion" that, when reconstructed, narrates the "typical *Bildungsroman* plot" of human personality development.[148] In fact, if we allow for a shift in the genre's traditional gender and geographical orientation from the nation to a postcolonial international order, these biographical details fit neatly into Jerome Buckley's normative description of the "typical" patterns and "principal characteristics" of the *Bildungsroman*, with little alteration or elision to either his schema or her story:

> [Anil,] a child of some sensibility[,] grows up in the country or in a provincial town, where [s]he finds constraints, social and intellectual, placed upon the free imagination. . . . [S]he therefore . . . leaves the repressive atmosphere of home . . . to make [her] way independently in the city (in the English [and postcolonial anglophone] novels, usually London). There [her] real "education" begins, not only [her] preparation for a career but also—and often more importantly—[her] direct experience of urban life. The latter involves at least two love affairs or sexual encounters, one debasing, one exalting, and demands that in this respect and others the hero[ine] reappraise [her] values. By the time [s]he has decided, after painful soul-searching, the sort of accommodation to the modern world [s]he can honestly make, [s]he has left [her] adolescence behind and entered upon [her] maturity. [Her] initiation complete, [s]he may then visit [her] old home, to demonstrate by [her] presence the degree of [her] success or the wisdom of [her] choice.[149]

Anil's Ghost will not, in the end, honor this generic contract with the reader: neither Anil's wisdom nor her professional success (which would also represent a symbolic victory for international human rights) will be demonstrated in the novel; her return is not triumphal, and the political and personal frustrations of her human rights efforts call into question the hermetic novelistic individualism that Buckley describes, the universality of human rights norms, and the propriety of the *Bildungsroman* plot in the context of Sri Lanka's war.

Despite the appearance of her name in the title, it is debatable whether Anil is an eponymous protagonist or the novel has a single (or living) protagonist at all. And although the book's dust jacket promises a story of a search for "identity" and a "quest to unlock the hidden past," precisely whose identity and past, and what manner of search, remain ambiguous throughout Ondaatje's narrative. The novel ultimately troubles the categories of fictional protagonist and juridical person as well as the metonymic literary convention of eponymity. The possessive form of Anil's proper name in the novel's title actually unnames any potential individual protagonist, foregrounding instead the novel's concern with social relations and relationships—the modes of group affiliation and the terms by which people mutually consent to be "bound together . . . by language, law, and literature" in a common community and story.[150] The novel's title therefore emphasizes its interest in sociality (rather than individuality) and in the terms of consociation that sustain its ambivalent genitive of possession and incorporation. In many ways, the novel uses Anil as a narrative device to study the mechanics of sphere-making and the discursive conditions of possibility for forming democratic, paranational collectives in the absence of both a legitimate democratic-state formation and an operative egalitarian national public sphere.

Superficially, however, two conventional novelistic questions drawn from two different generic forms of a search for identity propel the narrative: the first, taken from the repertoire of the *Bildungsroman*, poses the problem of Anil's identity in terms of a conflict between her Sri Lankan past and her contemporary cosmopolitan habits and assumptions as a "citizen of the world" who represents a court of world opinion; the second, borrowed from the genre of detective fiction, seeks to discover the identity of a disinterred skeleton provisionally called "Sailor," to determine his cause of death, to give a name to this individual "representative of all those lost voices"—"the unhistorical dead"—and thereby, as Anil hopes, to "name the rest" of the victims of human rights abuse.[151] The novel is deeply interested in questions of history, truth, and

identity, as well as in the narrative modes of their production, veri-
fication, and legitimation, but Sailor's story never reaches a national
public sphere where it might become justiciable history (or social
truth) and might indict the government in human rights abuses.
Likewise, the projected harmonization of Anil's cosmopolitan desires and Sri Lanka's national needs never materializes. Those generic horizons remain narrative tantalizations, and the two plot-
driving questions eventually give way to variations on the theme of
reading—vignettes that explore various modes (forensic anthropology, medical diagnostics, archaeology, paleontology, reconstructive
history, imaginative sculpture, and psychobiography) by which such
questions might be answered. All of these finally prove insufficient
for fulfilling the forensic anthropologist's clinical desire for (and
the *Bildungsroman*'s generic promise of) truth in identity. The process of excavating this pre-novelistic *Bildungsroman* plot from its
fragmentary, narrative remains in Ondaatje's text parallels Anil's
own forensic interpretive attempts to reconstruct the elements of
Sailor's narrative. Confronted with the setting for a political murder and a skeleton that she presumes is the victim in a crime story,
Anil is herself a character in search of a plot—the presumed governmental plot to kill Sailor and the plot of her own cosmopolitan
Bildung. The novel aligns its reader with Anil, a professional reader
not just of bones but of human rights reports from the Third World
that are "copied and sent abroad to strangers" in a way that, as I
will argue, has disturbing implications for an imagined international
community founded on the language, law, and literature of human
rights.[152]

Set against the backdrop of violence in late-1980s Sri Lanka, the
plot of the novel unfolds under a declared permanent state of emergency that suspended the 1978 constitutional protections of human
rights. The obliteration of any functional, open, democratic, national public sphere is partly the effect of the "continual emergency" and partly the result of insurrectionary terrorism. The
modes of reading that Anil takes for granted, as well as the generic
expectations of the *Bildungsroman*, become problems under such a
state of emergency and in the absence of any semblance of a democratic state or public sphere. Sarath, the government archaeologist
assigned to work with Anil's investigation, frames the emergency as

a necessary deformation of political forms: "Whatever the government is possibly doing now, it was worse when there was real chaos. . . . The law abandoned by everyone. . . . Terror everywhere, from all sides. We wouldn't have survived with your rules of Westminster then. So illegal government forces rose up in retaliation. And we were caught in the middle."[153] The Indemnity Act, No. 20 of 1982, which presaged the 1983 state-of-emergency regulations, cleared the legal way for the government's "illegal" and violent anti-insurgency response to this "chaos":

> No action or other legal proceeding whatsoever, whether civil or criminal, shall be instituted in any court of law for or on account of or in respect of any act, matter or thing, whether legal or otherwise, done or purported to be done with a view to restoring law and order . . . , if done in good faith, by a . . . person holding office under or employed in the service of the Government of Sri Lanka in any capacity. . . ."

The indemnity effectively legalized government-sponsored "good faith" execution, torture, and disappearance.[154] Moreover, the Emergency Regulations permitted public officials to dispose of dead bodies without requiring the usual "inquest of death" (ER 55FF 1989). Where the regulations dispensed with *official* inquest, the severe limitations placed on freedoms of speech and the press proscribed *public* inquest. By foreclosing the ordinary democratic modes of history and identity production, the emergency regulations, rather than some poststructuralist axiom or postmodern stylistic narrative effect, transformed bodies like Sailor's into dehistoricized masses, sociopolitical enigmas—potentially interpretable, but still officially unread, narrative remains.

For Anil, unearthing Sailor's body is discovering an untold story of torture and extrajudicial killing—a story that wants to be told. The reading of Sailor's bones becomes a contest between (and within) Anil's team and the Sri Lankan government over the modes of reconstructing the narrative of his life and death and of interpreting its meaning; that is, Sailor's appearance creates a series of conflicts over how to read the "truth" of the exhumed body—over the hermeneutical "means by which the facts are [to be] settled."[155] Sarath, who "can read a bucket of soil as if it were a complex historical novel," applies an archaeological model of interpretation to Sailor's anonymized and dehistoricized skeleton.[156] Ananda, the artificer and the novel's silent subaltern, brings an artistic approach to give Sailor "a distinct personality" by sculpting an imaginative reconstruction of his head.[157] Anil undertakes "her reading of the bones" with expectations about what she will find based on reading human rights reports and with a predetermined forensic methodology for interpreting and narrativizing those findings.[158] Anil's project of identification is to "give the skeleton a name" by reading his "markers of occupation" and turning him into a "representative . . . of race and age and place" and to plot those into a historical biography.[159] Anil hopes to reinscribe Sailor into the social text—to reincorporate him as an instance of a particular group's vulnerability and personality; thus, she seeks to repersonify, rehistoricize, and reanimate the dead by giving Sailor back a name, a face, and a voice—in short, a juridical personality—that can speak for itself, testify to the crimes against it, and implicate the government in his torture and execution.

The more Herculean task, of which Anil remains largely unaware despite Sarath's repeated cautions, is to rectify a democratic public sphere that could invest Sailor's body with national and historical meaning. A public sphere is not only a community of speech whose social norms are abstracted in the communicative practices and conventionalized story forms that it favors; it is also an "interpretive community"[160] with its own hermeneutic norms that define the methods and manners by which those forms are made meaningful. Thus, membership in a public depends upon at least a tacit agreement to treat particular texts, topics, problematics, and phenomena as what Miguel Tamen calls "interpretable objects" and to deliberate on those objects according to shared interpretive codes.[161] Although Anil succeeds in reconstructing a convincing plot of Sailor's death and giving it a conventional story form, there is no such shared, official story space for that narrative and her interpretation—a fact vivified in the novel, which also makes little space for Ruwan Kumara's (Sailor's real name) story in a concise, but belated and practically incidental, paragraph.[162] Fully convinced of the objective, scientific truth of Sailor's narrative that she has reconstructed, Anil insists that his body be recognized as a historically interpretable object, but she misjudges the institutional resistance to her personifying efforts. During a presentation to an audience of government bureaucrats and state scientists, Anil discovers the enormity of official refractoriness when her counternarrative of Sailor's death is met with coordinated insistence that his fate be properly read not by the codes of forensic pathology, which intends to make the past justiciably relevant to the historical present, but by the codes of conventional archaeology, which would rebury his story in the sediment of natural—and finished—history. At this hermeneutical impasse between the international human rights community and a state that asserts its sovereignty, Anil is forced from the country, Sarath is killed for having reentered "the intricacies of the public world" by assisting Anil, the Sri Lankan president is killed by a suicide bomber, and Ananda returns to the pastoral, consecrative work of opening the eyes on statues of the Buddha.[163]

Despite Anil's suspicion that her interpretive tools may not be adequate to "give meaning" to Sailor's narrative remains or "logic to the human violence," with its "surreal turns of cause and effect," she stubbornly holds to her forensic methodology and her necessary, but anodyne, faith that *"One victim can speak for many victims"*[164]—which is also the republican, metonymic ideology of the realist *Bildungsroman*'s exemplarity: "the law that it should take as its object the representative individual."[165] Like the projected consummation of her *Bildungsroman*, Anil's personification of Sailor is doomed to fail because his rehistoricization is predicated upon a democratic, nation-statist framework; that is, the orientation of Anil's recuperative project remains fundamentally nationalist. Her failure to make Sailor speak highlights the degree to which the project of human rights incorporation—and the human personality that it aspires to realize—presupposes an egalitarian national public sphere, a functional democratic nation-state, and a common national narrative, whose formations are the primary objects of contest in the Sri Lankan conflict. *Anil's Ghost* dramatizes the tenuity of these grand narratives of identification and the historical dependence of the traditional plot of human personality development on the public social institutions of the nation-state. In the absence of those structures, the conventional novelistic plots—that patterned Anil's pre-novel—are lost, so that neither the *Bildungsroman*'s quest narrative of a search for social identity nor its perversion into the detective novel's inquest narrative of the re-search for social identity appears viable without the sanctioning body, deliberative mechanics, and social horizon of a legitimate, democratic, national public sphere.

Ironically, perhaps, Ondaatje's novel is not particularly interested in characters as individuals; as Anil's long-distance friend, Leaf, asks rhetorically, "I'm just a detail from the subplot, right?"[166] Instead, individuals provide a point of entry for the novelistic representation of social relations, the dynamics of social binding, and the contingent conditions that make certain kinds of biographical stories about individuals and groups possible and meaningful. Although Anil's forensic team never manages to turn Sailor over to History, its investigative activity of reading a common "text" has the unintended incorporative effect of producing an alternative public in which, through a comity of readers, Anil is "citizened by friendship."[167] The novel explores the possibilities of cultivating this fellow-feeling of citizenship dynamically, through shared reading and shared interpretive practices; it depicts a panorama of spontaneous Sri Lankan reading societies, alternatives to the deformed national public sphere that has been degraded in the contest over the state. Such paranational publics proliferate in the novel, emerging with their own implicit and consensual codes of sociality and undeclared rights and duties of citizenship. The novel's characters combine and recombine in impromptu associations centered around some form of text or some principle of textuality that adjudicates their local truths and the narratives that bind them together as groups.[168] These hermeneutic circles incorporate their participants as coactors in a common story through the collective act of reading common texts and through the shared interpretive modes that emerge from that reading, settling not only the means by which meaning is to be given to the text but, more importantly, establishing the tacit terms of enfranchisement and the discursive lines of the group's binding force. Ondaatje's novel proposes a dialectical view of the relation between a text and a public sphere in which the two are interconstitutive: the group determines what counts as an interpretable object that in turn describes, through the collaborative activity of interpretation, the shape and scope of the collective. If terrorism, insurrection, and counterterrorism have rendered the national public sphere anamorphic, these surrogate micropublics not only substitute for it in complex ways that cross national, political, linguistic, ethnic, class, and gender boundaries; they also offer a counterperspective on the nation-state that brings to light the deformation of the national public sphere and the destruction of both a common, national public text and a coherent social texture. The disarticulation of grand historical narratives is reflected in the temporal and spatial disjunctions and unconventional conjunctions that plot Ondaatje's novel and that replay, at the level of literary form, the recombinant associations that spawn counterpublics.

An idealized version of these parastatal public spheres enters the novel surreptitiously. In temporary field hospitals that sprouted up in remote areas of Sri Lanka during the civil war, there developed among the doctors and nurses what Ondaatje's narrator parenthetically calls a "habit" of "critical marginalia"—a social-reading practice conducted in the margins of the books in the hospital's ad hoc library.[169] This practice of "critical marginalia" develops its own complex of semantic and syntactic rules that regulate the terms of an individual's engagement with the texts and with the other anonymous scribblers' contributions. The spontaneous conventions of commentary, dialogue, emendation, and annotation to some degree establish the conditions for membership in the group, the generic forms of participation, and the norms of its sociotextual decorum. At the simplest level, a critical marginalist might, for ironic emphasis, inscribe in "medical texts as well as novels" an "exclamation point beside something not psychologically or clinically valid." A novel with a scene "of outrageous or unlikely physical prowess or sexual achievement" receives an equally hyperbolic and sarcastic affirmation: "*This happened to me once.*" In a book "somebody once brought" on Carl Jung, "someone had underlined *Jung was absolutely right about one thing. We are occupied by gods. The mistake is to identify with the god occupying you.*" The narrator reports that the meaning of the aphorism never becomes clear to its readers, but the emphatic underlining makes the commentary on Jung collectively, if unconsciously, memorable—"a thoughtful warning, and they let the remark seep into them." The participants are mutually personified through their social reading and writing, and although some marginalia habits seem to evince individualized idiolects and personalities that the narrator attempts to attribute to particular persons, the practitioners remain largely anonymous: "somebody" brought a book; "someone" underlined. From the practice of critical marginalia emerges an interpretive community with a shared set of literary references and marginal social relations. In the process, the participants are incorporated into a unified (albeit anonymous and marginal) social body, grouped together under the generic, third-person plural pronoun "they" in the narrator's single account of their plural biographies: "*They* all knew it was about the sense of self-worth that . . . had overcome them. *They* were not working for any cause or political agenda. *They* had found a place a long way from governments and media and financial ambition. *They* had originally come to the northeast for a three-month shift. . . . *They* had stayed for two years or three, in some cases longer" (emphasis added).[170]

The anonymous marginalists' practice constructs an imaginary community that is regulated by its own dynamic codes of interpretive literary manners and social civility. The form of their communicative activity literally makes their marginality legible. Explicitly located outside the realm of the national public sphere, away from ordinary "governments and media," these "marginalia criminals" (as the narrator quips) constitute a counterpublic that, in refusing to abide the authoritarian imperatives of the state, the insurgents, or the separatists, deliberately rejects their legitimacy. Their interpretive practices repeat their disenfranchisement from the national social text with their scribblings in the margins of books, to which, however, they adopt a relation similar to that which the Habermasian public sphere takes to the institutions of state authority; collectively, in the graphical production of their public opinion, they doctor, nurse, debate, revise, regulate, and ultimately cosign the "dominant legalities" of the texts.[171] Their collective rejection of the dominant, nationalist norms and forms of civil and political activity available during the Sri Lankan conflict is reflected in their "criminal" irreverence for the bourgeois prohibition against writing in library books. Nonetheless, reading matter matters, and the critical marginalists' literary rejections say as much about their collective constitution as do their selections. For example, despite its outwardly appropriate title, Goethe's *Elective Affinities* sits unread "throughout the war," resting among better-thumbed novels on a table, its potential readers never getting past the "back-cover description."[172] Perhaps it is the blurb describing Goethe as Germany's foremost *national* author, rather than the lurid plot synopsis, that recommends to these politically and civically marginalized readers "the other, more porous paperbacks." The gang of marginalia criminals, whose story is itself set in an extended parenthesis to Ondaatje's text, are communalized neither by a transcendental, or archetypal, human personality associated with Jung nor by the nationalist appeal of Goethe but by their common practical choices to read the one and not the other.

Ondaatje's novel is profoundly antinationalist (though not necessarily antistatist) in its rejection of ethnonationalist claims of predetermined group filiation based on a mythicized primordial cultural coherence and distinction. For example, the novel all but refuses to name either Sinhala or Tamil as anything other than languages, dismissing the essentialist terms typically evoked by both domestic and international media to simplify the brutal civil struggle over the shape and machinery of the Sri Lankan state as merely an ethnic conflict. Instead, the novel offers somewhat idyllic visions of alternative, ghostly publics that haunt the destabilized nation-state and that serve their associates as temporary discursive safe-havens. The spontaneous generation of these ephemeral, paranational publics represents a withdrawal from the conventional terrain of politics, although Western reviewers of the novel have tended to insist upon its nationalist engagements, ironically by invoking an ultimately ethnocentric image of a supranational court of world opinion in which *Anil's Ghost* speaks to an imaginary community of cosmopolitan readers without borders: "More effective than a documentary," *Anil's Ghost* puts the Sri Lankan "tragedy on the map of Western consciousness," and the "outrage[s of] the civil war . . . will touch even those of us to whom its capital, Colombo, signifies a brand of yogurt."[173] Ondaatje's "Author's Note," which sets the terms of novelistic correspondence between its fiction and the abstract historical outline of the Sri Lankan conflict, also tacitly situates the novel in relation to the "international authority" and "independent organization" of an international public that Anil professionally represents.[174]

The novel, however, ironizes this gesture at its conclusion when Anil hurriedly boards a plane to Europe with her British passport and little to show for her efforts—a departure foretold by Sarath's brother Gamini, who anticipates it as the inevitable fulfillment of a conventional Hollywood-film plot: "The American or the Englishmen gets on a plane and leaves. That's it. The camera leaves with him. . . . So the war, to all purposes, is over. That's enough reality for the West. . . . Go home. Write a book. Hit the circuit."[175] In contrast to the novel's numerous mutually constituted interpretive communities in which individuals bind themselves together over shared texts and dynamically negotiated reading methods, the international human rights community, bound together in imaginary relations by the shared texts of international law and a jurisprudential tradition for their interpretation, reads Sri Lanka generally and Sailor's body specifically according to predetermined conventions agreed upon in the supranational court of world opinion. As earnest as Anil may be, she embodies the common sense and hermeneutic assumptions of an international community constituted elsewhere that attempts to impose its international will from on high, without regard for or dialogue with the people it seeks to assist. Indeed, the novel demonstrates the practical irrelevance of presumptuous international public opinion to the attitudes and activities of the Sri Lankan government, the insurgents, and the daily lives of the people. Despite her cosmopolitan pretensions, Anil's human rights and humanitarian assumptions are cultivated in an international order that is based on the Westphalian culture of national sovereignty and the "good of the nation," and her interpretive efforts to inscribe Sailor in a still-contested national social text ultimately reinforce the logic of the nation-statism that fuels the war.[176] Anil becomes a symbolic extension of an internationalism (or cosmopolitanism) that has forgotten its own enabling condition, which it reencounters in the recalcitrant sovereignty of the state. In many ways, the novel exposes the indifference and quixotism of an imaginary international community of human rights sentiment that can neither effectively insinuate itself between the people and the state nor act as a viable surrogate for a devastated, national public sphere to activate its universal human rights norms and forms and to translate its common knowledge into official, local acknowledgment.[177] In *Anil's Ghost*, the international community, with which the novel aligns its reader through the synecdoche of Anil, is not the democratic public sphere projected in its enabling fiction.

The aspiration of contemporary human rights law, and one shared by Anil, is to incorporate the individual within a national (and ultimately an international) system of human sociality and its complex of constitutional rights and duties, in which the human personality will assume its fullest potential form in the public subjectivity of the citizen. In its exploration of alternatives to the traditional human rights model of human sociality and personality that exist below and beyond the nation-state, Ondaatje's novel reminds us that the dominant paradigm is historically contingent upon the fortunes of the nation-state (both in its particular and abstract forms) and the democratic operations of its public sphere. The novel's alternative micropublics are ultimately too idealized, too utopic, and too intimate to be sustained, except when completely removed from the infringements of the nation—far away from "where the main purpose of war had become war."[178] Nonetheless, in its study of substitutes for the state/citizen bind, the novel highlights the fact that personality, subjectivity, and citizenship are sphere-bound. If Anil can be "citizened" among Sarath, Ananda, and Sailor through discursive friendship, then personality development becomes a process of socialization that takes place within a particular sphere and relative to its specific social relations and its attendant rights and duties of citizenship. *Bildung* remains relevant here, but rather than think the free and full development of human personality in the universalist, monolithic, German-idealist terms as the unique event and effect of a citizen-subjectivation anchored by the nation-state, the proliferation of more modest publics in Ondaatje's novel recognizes a multiplicity of individual subjectivities and human personalities: forensic personality, national personality, international NGO personality, literary personality, marginal personality, etc. From this perspective, Anil's post-*Bildungsroman* turns out not to be a failed *Bildungsroman* but a collection of more modest, paranational *Bildungsromane* that narrate the various processes by which the individual is incorporated (or citizened) as a person within diverse paranational publics. Indeed, the biographies of the novel's characters are largely narrated according to the hermeneutic principles that dominate in the publics in which they participate: the anonymous marginalists are given a collective, anonymous biography; Anil, Sarath, and Ananda (like Sailor) are first identified by their most prominent "markers of occupation" (the swimmer-pathologist, the archaeologist, the miner-artificer) that are only fleshed out with a complex biography and personality in retrospect—after their departure or death.[179] Personality is a social condition, a capacity to act within a particular social formation as a subject who bears the specific sphere-bound rights and duties of its citizens. Personality thus belongs neither to society nor to the individual as such, but to the social texture of which the person is a part and an effect—not to

Anil or her ghost, but to the genitive relation of incorporation between the two.

Joint-Stock Companies: Cultural Narratives and the Discursive Constitution of Publics

Both thematically and formally, Mercado's and Ondaatje's novels
are interested in the generic deformation of the idealist *Bildungsroman* in the context of political repression—when the state is a destabilized, contested site of competing corporate interests and the
public sphere is under siege. In these novels, governmental assaults
on the public sphere and the perversion of its role in manufacturing
national common sense register in a generic struggle with the normative form of the *Bildungsroman*. As part of their thematic fascination with the discursive dynamics and constitution of public
spheres, both novels explore the historical sociocultural conditions
and metaphysical assumptions that enable and sustain—or corrupt
and foreclose—the idealist, generic story form of personality development. In *Anil's Ghost*, the early invocations of the *Bildungsroman*
establish a tension between the novel and the general expectations
of the generic form. As I suggested in my reading, *Anil's Ghost* is a
kind of post-*Bildungsroman*, in which the productive place in the
social world toward which her biography has so far led her as a
representative of "the international authority of Geneva" turns out
to be a place in another world that "mean[s] nothing" amid the
"crisis" of the Sri Lankan civil war.[180] More particularly, the humanitarian and professional principles that Anil has learned from
formal education and personal experience to take for granted prove
unworkable in the confrontation with the "chaos" of her homeland.
This undoing is perhaps best exemplified by the novel's invalidation
of the axioms that "one victim can speak for many" and "the truth
shall set you free," which represent more than disciplinary tenets of
forensics;[181] they have become Anil's personal doctrine—articles of
scientific faith that, despite all contradictory evidence, she stands
stubbornly by until the fateful end. In a moment of frustration with
her inability to convert her knowledge of Sailor's murder into official acknowledgment, Anil expresses her disappointment with Sarath in an accusation that could just as well apply to her: "I thought

you represented more than you do."[182] The novel thereby underscores the social and structural contingency of the synecdochal logic that underpins international human rights law and the republican ideology of representation that sustains the traditional *Bildungsroman*'s logic of novelistic exemplarity.

Mercado's novel is perhaps more explicit in its engagement with the *Bildungsroman* form, given the narrator's obsession with publicness and the German-idealist language of *Bildung*. If Ondaatje's novel presents a relatively optimistic vision of the sublimation of an assaulted Habermasian public sphere into post- or paranational possibilities for the collective production of social and political meaning and personality development, Mercado's narrator's fixation with the state and a national public sphere exacerbates her sense of chronic dispossession and depersonalization, and it prevents her from accepting the compensation of alternative publics or resigning herself to post-dictatorial Argentina's hegemonic narrative of adaptation that is required of returning exiles. Rejecting the "anodyne" cliché that "the exiles had it good"[183] and the dominant narrative terms of reintegration, the narrator insists that the experience of exile properly belongs to the Argentine national story. In its fascination with the relations between personal (or narrative) truth and social truth, Mercado's novel challenges what she regards as the premature stabilization of the post-dictatorial narrative of the Dirty War and exposes the discursive mechanics of hegemony—the means by which a particular group's formulation of common sense comes generally "to be taken-for-granted as the natural and received shape of the world."[184] In her novelistic rebuttal to the narrative of adaptation, the narrator foregrounds the sociopolitical contingency of dominant public opinions, whose commonsensical appearance is the result of a "cultural battle" in which, as Gramsci explained, particular conceptions of "the world and man" manage to "demonstrate themselves to be 'historically true' to the extent that they become concretely—i.e., historically and socially—universal."[185] Mercado's narrator consistently seeks to explain the sociopolitical motivations and class interests that sponsor the dominant cultural narratives against which she struggles.

In both of these novels, the social struggle over the hegemonic narratives that articulate the terms of inclusion in and exclusion from a public sphere are replayed at the level of form. If the narrator of the classical *Bildungsroman* represents a structural surrogate for society—the voice of public opinion that establishes the dominant legalities of the text with "a discourse that feigns to make the world speak itself and speak itself as story"[186]—that explains why Mercado's self-deprecatory narrator is perpetually anxious about her own role in naturalizing the narrative norms and forms of common sense. She stages a dissensus not only against the dominant narrative legalities of the Argentine social text but against those within her own narrative. Ondaatje's narrator, on the other hand, is relatively at ease with his role in reinforcing the banal common sense of the novel's tautological refrain: "*The reason for war was war*" (43). Ondaatje's narrator assumes personal responsibility for naturalizing this common international diagnosis about the Sri Lankan conflict, which implies that it is senseless, incomprehensible, and, in some fundamental way, insoluble. Indeed, the narrator's tautological articulation of the novel's common sense is made redundant by the thematic and formal properties of the text; Anil's failure to make public sense of Sailor's murder, and the narrator's fragmentary plotting of the story, habituate the reader to ratify the axiomatic senselessness of war.

Ondaatje's narrator openly declares the tautological common sense that underpins the narrative, but, as I discussed in the previous chapter, tautologies represent the most compact, irreducible, and logically irrefutable forms of "things that [mostly] go without saying because, being axiomatic, they come without saying";[187] they are, in part, made redundant by the cooperation of cultural narratives that tend to normalize a society's unstated common sense. We might even say that the proverbial tautologies tend to spawn and structure socially acceptable narratives. That is, while the axioms of common sense generally remain undeclared, they generate a virtual public library of cultural narratives whose social work (from a systemic perspective) is to test, revise, sustain, substantiate, and naturalize the tautological things that generally go without saying. These hegemonic cultural narratives tend to validate and reproduce public opinion by conventionalizing the normative forms in which events, agents, and figures are emplotted and made meaningful for the group. They thereby serve a regulatory function, modeling and normalizing the literary themes, devices, plot structures, imagery, tropology, symbology, diction, grammar, etc., for the articulation of socially acceptable narratives. But, as I have been stressing throughout this chapter, they also perform a constitutive function, establishing the discursive terms for incorporation into the community of speech—the public norms and forms of common sense that incorporated citizens treat as if they were their own, like Anil's mantric recitation of the gnome: "'The truth shall set you free.'" This is the consolidating social work of "bourgeois myth" in the modern rights-based nation-state, whose institutional "transform[ation of] history into nature" incorporates, in Roland Barthes' felicitous phrase, the "bourgeoisie as a joint-stock company."[188] With incorporation, the individual presumably acquires a vested interest in maintaining the group's "tenuous sense of common sense."[189] If human rights law positivizes nature, the public work of cultural narratives is a renaturalization of the contingent positive assertions about "the world and man" that circulate without any transcendental or executive guarantee of their legitimacy.

As Mercado's narrator recognizes with the story of adaptation, these narratives are saturated with the intentions of others—with the particular interests and motivations of a particular corporate group that has achieved hegemony by successfully "present[ing] its own aims as those realizing the *universal* aims of the community."[190] Such narratives are cultural because they re-present the common sense of a particular group and are activated within "structural formation[s] larger than the single individual, [within] intersubjective networks and institutions, however local or grand."[191] Thus, cultural narratives are saturated with the ostensibly shared intentions of the group's incorporated citizens, which is to say that, from within a particular corporate formation, they also appear to be empty, neutral, and natural. They present themselves as "innocent speech," unmotivated by ideology, and freely available for appropriation by the individual;[192] they appear to be statements of "simple fact": that "man" is "man," in the fundamental human rights tautology.[193] That is, a cultural narrative is simultaneously saturated and empty: saturated because, as a narrativization of common sense, everybody already knows what it has to say, and therefore the guarantee of its "truth" is simply its saturation; empty because, appearing as merely an accurate (tautological) reflection of the accepted state of things, it has no need of a sanctioning authority to guarantee its sense. This is the formal gamble that the drafters of the UDHR took when they transformed human rights law into a set of tautological principles aspiring to become universal cultural narratives.

Cultural narratives appear to be unmediated by a narrator who would produce and constrain their meaning and to whom the selection and arrangement of the story elements might be attributed. Thus, paradoxically, cultural narratives are narratorless. A narratorless narrative operates without the ordinary personal guarantee for the "facts" of the story—without a narrator who can be held responsible for "the language that constitutes the text."[194] In narrative theory, the narrator may be made redundant when there appears to be a complete congruity between the *fabula* and the *sjuzet*—between the way things are and the way things are said to be.[195] From this narratological perspective, we could describe hegemony as the naturalizing process by which the *sjuzet* (the positively plotted story) comes to be perceived as the *fabula* (the natural order of things), which, in the process of producing a cultural narrative that endorses public opinion, obviates the function of the narrator. As Mercado's narrator recognizes, the evacuation of the office of the narrator in a cultural narrative leaves a vacuum: an injunctive force that summons the individual to narrate the story for herself—to assume the function of the narrator and thereby to assume some personal responsibility for the validity of the hegemonic narrative's common sense.[196] In this transference, socially accepted "historical truth" becomes "personal truth," averred by the individual's performance in the role of the cultural narrative's narrator. The authority of cultural narratives borrows its legitimacy from the precarious sovereignty of the human personality, and individuals become fully incorporated citizen-subjects of a particular social formation when they narrate for themselves its cultural narratives—when they "consent" to occupy the office of the narrator in a social formation's cultural narratives. This is the hegemonizing process that the idealist *Bildungsroman* repeats as both fable and form, narrating the story of how the protagonist comes to share the text's socially dominant understanding of the novel's events—an understanding typically held and voiced by the already-incorporated narrator. That is, within the world of the novel, the traditional *Bildungsheld* arrives at a retrospective comprehension of its story that the narrator already has and actively naturalizes. The affirmative *Bildungsroman* stages a consensus—an alignment of the protagonist's perspective with that of the narrator. In the dissensual *Bildungsroman*, the two perspectives never achieve complete concordance or congruity. As we shall see in the following chapter, the structure of narrative self-sponsorship in the first-person *Bildungsroman* gives form to the story of how the protagonist comes to occupy the office of the narrator in the text's dominant narrative of human personality development and so comes to take responsibility for the narrative process of incorporation.

The human rights plot of inherency-in-becoming is another name for the hegemonizing process by which individuals are expected to partake of the sociohistorical universal and become the instances of universal humanity that they are (pre)supposed to be by right. Contemporary human rights and the classical theories of *Bildung* both subpoena the individual to occupy the role of the narrator in their cultural narratives of human personality development, but they imagine this process of occupation as a consensual, dialectical harmonization of the individual and the sociopolitical world of convention. Thus, in their idealist formulations, the individual is supposed to come to perceive social institutions as manifestations of the self—as the forms that the individual would have freely chosen for itself. In Ondaatje's and Mercado's novels, these structures have failed or have been violently co-opted at the state level, and the novels' anxious negotiations with the conventions of the *Bildungsroman* ironically illustrate the dependence of the story form upon the democratic social relations and institutions promised by the bourgeois rights-based state. In its ideal role as the engine of consensus in the democratic nation-state, the public sphere is the social and civic organ tasked with emptying the office of the narrator, thereby naturalizing the cultural narratives of the story of human emergence in which the saturated institutional forms are to be recognized, experienced, and incorporated as expressions of personal volition—as that which the person would have instituted and demanded for itself if it were in a position to do so. However, in Ondaatje's and Mercado's narratives, consent and compulsion have obverted to coercion—hegemony has obverted to repression. Within a modern rights-based state, the *Bildungsroman* story of human personality development is the hegemonic narrative for the affirmative human rights claim, the story form of hegemony itself, of how the particular and the contingent strive for the status of the universal and the natural, of how the individual is to become the international human rights person. It is in the bourgeois public sphere that the hero of the *Bildungsroman* and the human person of human rights are expected to emerge in their freest and most fully developed form as a voluntary narrator of the hegemonic story of citizen-subjectivation.

CHAPTER 4

Compulsory Development:
Narrative Self-Sponsorship and the
Right to Self-Determination

The human person is the central subject of development and should
be the active participant and beneficiary of the right to development.

—UN Declaration on the Right to
Development (1986), Article 2

Development means the development of *people*. . . . A new road extends a man's freedom only if he travels upon it.

—JULIUS NYERERE, *Freedom and Development*

When Actors Become Narrators: The Central Subjects of Development and Human Rights

"DEVELOPMENT IS A LIE" protests a placard carried by Manu,
a recurring character in Epeli Hau'ofa's satirical short stories, *Tales
of the Tikongs* (1983), about the euphoria of developmentalism that
washed over Tonga and other Pacific-island nations in the 1970s,
during the heyday of internationally sponsored development projects.[1] As "the only teller of big truths in the realm," Manu peddles
his "lonely message against Development" throughout the island
of Tiko, a fictionalized version of Tonga.[2] Recounting parables of
the pitfalls and failures of progress, Manu broadcasts his warning
that "Tiko can't be developed . . . unless the ancient gods are killed"

to anyone who will listen, and he shouts his message that "TIKO
HATES YOU" to the "new gods" who will not: the Bank of Tiko,
the Doctor of Philosophy who "works on Research for Development," the Great Secretary of the Great Development Project, and
all other "Appropriate Authorities."[3] Manu manages to resist the
seductions of developmentalism brought with the waves of "alien
experts" and "technical advisers" from the Great International Organization—"established to provide first-class employment for the
excess, over-educated elites of destitute lands"—and the "Greatest
Nation on Earth," which "occasionally takes a giant step or two for
mankind even though mankind may not have asked."[4] Preaching
the gospel of economic and social modernization and "policing
human rights," the international organizations encounter meek cultural resistance to such "foreign things" as development and human
rights from a few island elders who, like Manu, maintain that "Democracy and Tiko don't dance"; to the patronizing insinuation that
he is "underdeveloped," the motto on Manu's T-shirt retorts
crisply: "Over Influenced."[5]

Hau'ofa, a professor of social anthropology and first director of
the Rural Development Centre in Tonga, sets his stories in the
postcolonial aftermath of the island kingdom's 1970 return to full
political sovereignty, which it conceded to the British in a 1900
treaty designed to preempt German imperial advances. Hau'ofa's
stories explore the absurd contradictions within and inconsistencies
between the discourses and practices of development and self-determination in an uneven international order systematically divided
between developed and underdeveloped peoples—between those
"carrying . . . heavy global responsibilities" for human rights and
those who have "never heard of such things."[6] Hau'ofa burlesques
the inflated rhetorics of humanitarianism, developmentalism, post-
colonialism, and internationalism, as well as the various Tikong responses to these imports. Thus, the narrator's account of Tiko's day
of "independence from the shackles of colonialism" mocks not only
the ex-colonial power and its "running dogs of Imperialism and
Capitalism" but also the hyperbolic, anti-imperialist, and nationalist rhetoric of His Excellency the Paramount Chief's self-important
"Historical Proclamation," which rails against the perditions of soft
British colonialism and disingenuously promises to restore "the direction of National Development" to "indigenous hands."[7] The

neocolonial character of Tiko's nominal sovereignty and self-determination becomes evident when national development reveals itself to be a program of international dependency. If sovereignty and self-determination mean the right of peoples to "freely dispose of their natural wealth and resources" and to "freely determine their political status and freely pursue their economic, social and cultural development" (as the identical first articles of the International Covenant on Civil and Political Rights and the International Covenant on Economic, Social, and Cultural Rights affirm), then Tiko is technically self-determining: The local comprador Tikongs put the island's natural wealth and resources at the disposal of international development predators with proud nicknames like "Sharky," who are responsible for "Bottom Development."[8]

On the island of Tiko, the pursuit of economic, social, and cultural development becomes a short story—a very short story—in which the developmental promise of self-determination is betrayed almost before it is extended. Indeed, at the end of the international plot, the people "to be developed" find themselves as destitute as they started and burdened by a mounting debt that they have no hope even of servicing. For the majority of "Bottom" Tikongs, the more things change, the more they stay the same: development loans are granted to purchase goods from firms that the loan officers also represent; fishermen who cannot afford the maintenance on boats bought with such loans end up sinking them and returning to the days of endlessly repairing worn out dinghies; the vacuum created by the brain drain of "over-skilled Tikongs" is filled by "Third World elite employees of the Great International Organization"; old British colonial officers, who "for more than a century" worked to "modernize" the "indigenous personality," are recycled as career administrators in a retooled "Bureau for the Preservation of Traditional Culture and Essential Indigenous Personality."[9] In *Tales of the Tikongs*, the benefits of modernity and the beneficiaries of progress are shuttled from one "underdeveloped" location to the next, creating a global circulatory system of development assistance that promises to "improve" the lives of the natives but ultimately "reproduces endlessly the separation between the reformers and those to be reformed by keeping alive the premise of the Third World as different and inferior."[10] In the context of these international development schemes, the fragile tautological–teleological complex that characterizes the human rights narrative of personality development unravels into two separate plot strands of advancement and redoubled impoverishment. The international machinery of development offers the Tikongs only the circular stasis of tautology without the progress promised by teleology.

If development is not exactly a lie in *Tales of the Tikongs*, it is an exaggeration (whose promises are not to be taken seriously) that is incapable of sustaining a full novelistic plot of steady, prosaic evolution and accumulation. The foretold deaths of the ancient gods do not lead to the "loss of providential plots" or to the emergence of modern, secular "narrative plot" that "organizes and explains the world" as a historical, progressive process of unfolding consequence and causality.[11] Instead, in Tiko, development is subsumed within the mythological story forms of "revealed plots," operating according to the figurative logic of other tropes: hyperbole, metalepsis, catachresis. In principle, this cargo-cult tropology is incompatible with the "rationalized" discourse of developmentalism that the Great International Organization promotes, but not with its practice, which Manu fiercely (but futilely) contests.

The idea of rational modernization—which views development as a "technical problem" to be managed by social scientists and technicians as much as a natural tendency of the human personality or of peoples (as nineteenth-century sociology had it)—emerged as a dominant principle of international affairs with the decolonization boom of the 1960s and in the context of the Cold War rivalry between the First and Second World industrialized nations that staged their ideological, political, social, cultural, and economic battles in the "underdeveloped" countries of the Third World.[12] With the admission of dozens of newly independent states into the UN, the General Assembly embraced "economic and social development" as a practical panacea to the perpetual global disparities between rich and poor nations that the UN identified (hyperbolically perhaps) as one of the gravest threats "to the attainment of international peace and security" (GA Res 1710 [XVI]). Thus, recalling its Charter obligations "to promote social progress and better standards of life in larger freedom," on 19 December 1961 the UN greased its "international machinery" and inaugurated the current era of developmentalism by declaring the 1960s to be the "United Nations Development Decade in which Member States and their peoples will intensify their efforts to mobilize and to sustain support for the measures required on the part of both developed and developing countries to accelerate progress towards self-sustaining growth of the economy of the individual nations and their social advancement" (GA Res 1710 [XVI]). In an effort to hasten what many perceived to be the inevitability of global modernization and the emergence of what Lucian Pye foresaw as "a *world culture* based upon modern standards and technology, modern practices of organization, and modern standards of governmental performance," the UN fostered development strategies that, "although couched in terms of humanitarian goals and the preservation of freedom," became "powerful instrument[s] for normalizing the world" (emphasis added).[13] The affluent ex-colonial nations and international NGOs styled themselves as so many Societies of the Tower, claiming the authority and moral responsibility to manage the inevitable process of development in the Third World and the disposal of its natural and human resources.

During the UN's Decade of Development and the era of decolonization, political scientists and sociologists began to speak in earnest, if exaggeratedly, of world cultures—e.g., of modernization, human rights, and a mediated global village. But Pye's overly eager assessment of the emergence of a world culture of development in his study *Politics, Personality, and Nation Building* (1962) links socioeconomic modernization with human personality development, *Bildung*, and human rights in a way that would not be formally articulated in international law until the Declaration on the Right to Development (1986), adopted against the lone objection of the United States.[14] In language echoing the UDHR's right to participate in the cultural life of the community ("in which alone the free and full development of the human personality is possible"), the declaration proclaimed development to be "an inalienable human right by virtue of which every human person and all peoples are entitled to participate in, contribute to, and enjoy economic, social, cultural and political development, in which all human rights and fundamental freedoms can be fully realized" (Article 1). Pye recognized that modernization entails more than socioeconomic national development, and his use of the word "culture" was intended to describe not merely the globalization of developmentalism but its internal logic: "For from the point of view of the society as a whole or of the individual personality [the elements of modernization] are related to each other in much the same coherent fashion as the elements of a culture are felt to be. . . . [T]he process of change and . . . the act of becoming a part of the modern world [are] in essence a process of acculturation."[15] Pye recasts the technical structural and infrastructural adjustments of modernization as a late industrial *Bildung*—as a process of acculturation through which the "becoming . . . modern world" and the becoming-modern human personality adequate themselves to the expansive internationalist "culture" of developmentalism, to its hegemonic vision of modernity, and to its transition narrative of modernization. *Bildung*, human rights, and human personality development become species in the genus of modernization; or, to use Manu's conceptual language, development and self-determination (as we shall see in this chapter) join the human rights package as "new gods" in the international pantheon of modernity.

The narrow socioeconomic notion of modernization sanctioned in the 1961 UN resolution has evolved over the past half century. Indeed, the UN Decade of Development was such a success—or such a failure—that, in an absurd illustration of the affinity between teleology and tautology that Manu would appreciate, the General Assembly renewed its dedication in 1970 with the declaration of a "Second Decade of Development" and re-upped in 1980 for a third. The 1970 resolution greatly expanded upon its predecessor, adding pages of detailed policy measures and goals that take into account the role of culture in development and recognize the process of modernization as itself cultural (GA Res. 2626 [XXV]). The resolution speaks of "human development," rather than merely social and economic advancement, as a primary objective of modernization and human rights, and it includes provisions for transfers of technology that are aimed at effecting epistemic, not just industrial, revolutions in the "underdeveloped" world. In this more holistic human- and culture-sensitive version of development, the "mobilization of public opinion" becomes a key force in disseminating and naturalizing the logic, promise, and process of modernization. Thus, public spheres, both national and international, in both developing and developed countries, are impressed upon "to deepen public understanding of the interdependent nature of the development efforts . . . , of the benefits accruing to them . . . and of the need to assist the developing countries." The 1970 resolution imbricates individual and national development, and it devolves upon states a duty to develop both "human and natural resources." The resolution obliges the international community to assist the underdeveloped, although it also insists that "[t]he primary responsibility for the development of developing countries rests upon themselves."

Since the 1960s, when the United Nations Development Programme (UNDP) was instituted, the international discourses of human rights and development have steadily converged under the rubric of "human development," which, in the words of the UNDP's first Human Development Report (1990), "is a process of enlarging people's choices . . . to develop their potential" that "brings together the production and distribution of commodities and the expansion and use of human capabilities."[16] As the discourse of development has claimed a greater stake in the discourse of human rights, their lexicons have become practically synonymous and functionally interchangeable in the legal formulae of international human rights. Thus, the Declaration on the Right to Development asserts that "[t]he human person is the central subject of development and should be the active participant and beneficiary of the right to development"; the Vienna Declaration and Programme of Action (1993) makes the same assertion about human rights more generally and about the centrality of the human person to its project by "[r]ecognizing and affirming that all human rights derive from the dignity and worth inherent in the human person, and that the human person is the central subject of human rights and fundamental freedoms, and consequently should be the principal beneficiary and should participate actively in the realization of these rights and freedoms." More recently, human rights and development (in its many forms) are twin projects and entwined themes in the United Nations Millennium Declaration, which set the institution's aspirational agenda for the twenty-first century according to what it calls the "proved timeless and universal. . . . purposes and principles" of human rights and development put forward in the UN Charter.

Fifty years after the adoption of the UDHR, human rights have been rearticulated explicitly as a program for development; nonetheless, the human person(ality) remains both the fundamental principle behind the law and its ultimate referent—the projected vanishing point of the convergence of human rights and development discourses. According to international law, the rights to development and self-determination (like all human rights) derive from and realize the dignity and worth of the human person and the sovereignty of the human personality. The econometricized discourse of development therefore represents not so much a displacement of the humanist project and plot of personality development as a translation of its terms into the instrumentalist language of technical management. In the "global information age," human personality development (*Bildung*) becomes quantitative as well as qualitative.[17] The relatively recent appointment of a right to development (along with a right to self-determination, with which it is historically aligned and upon which it depends) among the list of fundamental human rights makes explicit some of the unstated assumptions about the human personality and its free and full development that underpinned the UDHR. In other words, the image of the freely and fully developed human personality projected in the UDHR presupposes the capacities for development and self-determination that the law now retrofits to the human person as endowments of nature; through their articulation in positive human rights law, development and self-determination become, retroactively, fundamental and natural aspects of the human person.

As the technical discourse of development has expanded to encompass cultural and personal advancement, the language of socioeconomic development has become fully entangled with the liberal humanist vocabulary of personality development. As we shall see, contemporary international law retains its basic commitment to the plot of human personality development—the story of the individual's becoming, and learning to recognize itself in, the international human rights person; however, that project is now subsumed in the more general human right of development that consists, as the Development Declaration has it, in "a comprehensive economic, social, cultural and political process, which aims at the constant improvement of the well-being of the entire population and of all individuals on the basis of their active, free and meaningful participation in development." This absorption of *Bildung* by comprehensive development has important qualitative consequences for the concept and narrative grammar of human personality development that I have been tracking in these chapters. For one thing, the right to development imposes upon the individual a correlative responsibility for development that makes development itself an obligation of (and to) the individual, the nation, and the international community. Thus, development is configured as a social compulsion. Additionally, the human right to development complicates the traditional logic of *Bildung*—which implies an end to the developmental process with the individual's social integration—by imagining the "improvement" process, for the individual and the nation, to be "sustained" and "self-sustaining" (GA Res. 2626 [XXV]). Both of these modifications to the idiom and emphasis of international law have thematic and formal implications for the human rights plot of incorporation that are legible in contemporary postcolonial *Bildungsromane*, many of which situate the narrative of personality development at the discursive intersection of the older, humanist logic of *Bildung* and the emergent technical process of comprehensive development (*Entwicklung*).[18] In these novels, the tensions and complicities—the continuities and discontinuities—between a project of personality development that is (self-)cultivated and one that is managed play out in the narrative form.

Although late-twentieth-century human rights law posits a relatively unproblematic symbiosis between development and self-determination (as we shall see in the next section of this chapter), Epeli Hau'ofa's Manu signals some of the ways in which they collide in practice and on the ground. The often-conflicting imperatives of development and self-determination put pressure on the impossible—but conceptually indispensable—tautological-teleological temporal complex of human rights personality development, which is prone to disarticulation in the context of unequal power relations between managers and beneficiaries of development that distribute the responsibilities and benefits of development differentially and that reinforce a hierarchical disparity between "developed" and "underdeveloped." To transcend this patronizing division, the idealist *Bildungsroman*, which is conventionally narrated in the third person, contrived the narrative device of a wholly benevolent overseer who manages the protagonist's development behind the scenes. In *Bildungsromane* like *Wilhelm Meister's Apprenticeship* and *Coming to Birth*, the narrator (along with other philanthropic social institutions) sponsors the developmental process, withholding the secret of that sponsorship until the *Bildungsheld* is judged to have completed its social apprenticeship and to have thereby become capable of self-narration and self-determination, at which point the story and the narrator's work end. This humanitarian plot is, as we have seen, both tautological and teleological because it posits a process of inherency-in-becoming by which individuals are to become the human rights persons that they ostensibly already were by nature—by which the human personality is to recuperate its fabled, originary, natural sovereignty.

In first-person retrospective *Bildungsromane*, this structure becomes reflexive and retroactive through the conventional figure of the seemingly self-identical manager-beneficiary of personality development, who assumes distinct, though related, narratological functions as both the story's protagonist and narrator. These novels plot the acquisition of self-narrative agency in stories that circle back to where they began after bringing the past into conjunction with the present and an earlier protagonist self into correspondence with the later narrator self, producing the ostensibly self-substantiating figure of the narrator-protagonist, a self-determinative literary agent. The elder narrator thus acts as a Society-of-the-Tower-like guarantor of the younger protagonist's incorporation, and this narratorial agency bends teleological linear development into a reflexive structure of narrative self-sponsorship that formally repairs the diegetic split between narrator and protagonist that is the founding subjective condition of autobiographical novelistic plot (just as the citizen–subject divide is the founding condition of a rights-based democratic social formation).

The narrative grammar of the first-person *Bildungsroman* appears to drive toward sustained and self-sustaining personality development. In the abstract, this structure of *Great Expectations*—in which, in the end, the *Bildungsheld* (like Pip) assumes "undivided responsibility" for its development and story[19]—might seem to consummate formally the sovereignty of the human personality promised and projected in the UDHR (and finessed in the idealist *Bildungsroman*). But in practice the structure of narrative self-sponsorship (particularly in postcolonial *Bildungsromane*, which are suspicious of the genre's traditional missionary plot logic) tends not to affirm the modern emancipatory lesson that the "*Bildungsheld* . . . is free to sponsor himself";[20] rather, the diegetic split that inaugurates the retrospective, autobiographical form of narrative and the tautological–teleological (temporal) plot complex that attempts to bridge the diegetic divide are both novelistic symptoms of a lingering anxiety about the still-uncertain sovereignty of the human personality. The split narrative personalities can only be tenuously reincorporated within the limits of the first-person *Bildungsroman* in the frail, artificial figure of the self-sponsoring narrator-protagonist. The structure of narrative self-sponsorship more typically represents a reaction to the ideological fiction of personal sovereignty and self-sustaining *Bildung*. In many postcolonial *Bildungsromane*, for instance, the genre's traditional conclusive event of social, civil, and self-integration is perpetually postponed, so that the sovereign, undivided human personality remains a vanishing (plot) point beyond the frame of the text.

I am suggesting that, despite first appearances, this structure of narrative self-sponsorship does not produce the self-sufficient, sovereign subject of Enlightenment philosophy; rather, the conventional form of first-person, retrospective *Bildungsromane* closely approximates the tautological form and hypothetical (or aspirational) character of human rights law, which pretends to legislate for tautological (self-same and sovereign) subjects in the hope of realizing such human rights subjects. (The legal tautologies are seen, then, as simply a matter of matching form and content.) The narrator-protagonists of the two novels that I examine in this chapter, Zimbabwean Tsitsi Dangarembga's *Nervous Conditions* (1988) and South African Christopher Hope's *A Separate Development* (1980), both learn the hard lesson that the atomistic, self-sufficient individual is a hyperbole that is not to be taken literally—or, more precisely, that it is an effect of fiction and its figurative technologies. If sovereignty means the sustained and self-sustaining capacity to legislate and execute for oneself the disposal of one's human and natural resources, both novels suggest that the human person is not a self-determinative literary agent—is never free to sponsor itself. Instead, the narrator-protagonists discover what Manu knew: Development is always sponsored elsewhere, and the sovereign human personality is, at best, suzerain. Contemporary first-person postcolonial *Bildungsromane* tend to be novels of disillusionment, in which the promises of developmentalism and self-determination are revealed to be empty, or at least exaggerated; *Bildung* thus becomes the process of recognizing the limits of personal development and the sociohistorically contingent condition of the idea and project of *Bildung* itself.

This chapter traces the implications of the addition of development and self-determination to the package of fundamental human rights in relation to the transformations that the first-person, dissensual *Bildungsroman* makes to the traditional narrative grammar of human rights incorporation. The following section offers a historical overview and a formal analysis of these relatively young human rights and of the revisions they make to the legal configurations of the relations between individuals, the community, the state, and the international order. Both rights internationalize the individual human person as a synecdoche of a nation's developmental potential; thus, they intensify the state/citizen bind even as they reposition individuals in new relational networks of international rights and responsibilities. The tension between the nationalist, instrumentalist discourse of development and the idealist, transcendental vision of *Bildung* creates some of the conflict that sustains the plot of Dangarembga's *Nervous Conditions*. Set in the waning years of white-minority rule in Southern Rhodesia, the novel suggests that hyperbole is the basic trope of developmentalism, which, in the context of late colonialism, distorts and distends the tautological–teleological complex of human personality development. Dangarembga's characters are obsessed with the language, promises, and pitfalls of self-determination and development. Although the young, female protagonist is fixated on an image of self-fulfillment that she gleans from reading classic British *Bildungsromane*, the temporal structure of novelistic self-sponsorship opens the "narrative distance [that] creates irony"[21] and enables her older-narrator self to historicize her seduction by the exaggerated, fictive promises of development as part of the discursive systems that maintain colonial and patriarchal domination.

I am particularly interested in what happens to the *Bildung* plot of free and full human personality development when the discourse of development, with its obligation to develop, is overlaid onto human rights. These developmental responsibilities overlap with duties that are attached to the human right to education, which, taken together, reconfigure human personality development as an imperative to acquire what I call human rights literacy; that is, the social obligation to develop one's personality (to modernize) implies a correlative obligation to recognize oneself and others as (central) subjects of human rights with symmetrical potential for self-determination and development. Yet as we have already seen, historically these rights-cum-responsibilities are often experienced not as personal compulsion but systemic coercion. If human rights are rationalized on the teleology of human (personality) development, their violation is often rationalized through appeals to the good of the nation and the requirements of national development. This chapter concludes with an examination of Christopher Hope's *A Separate Development*, which demonstrates the fallout for the *Bildungsroman* form when the state abuses the humanist discourse of development for the systematic repression of human rights. Arrested and tortured for his ontological defiance of apartheid South Africa's racial classifications, Hope's protagonist becomes a reluctant, but cagey, narrator of a coerced (dissensual) *Bildungsroman*, responding to the demand for his confession with a metaleptic narrative that plots a series of unrelated accidents as a "career" of causal and consequential events leading to his personal apartheid. The circular narrative staves off his execution and superficially satisfies the state's insistence that he take personal responsibility for his social aberrancy—for his "separate development."

From Bildung *to* Bandung *(and Back): Development, Self-Determination, and the Narrative Return of Personal Responsibility*

> *Internally*, self-determination . . . [is] a vehicle for enfranchisement, for ever expanding circles of citizens against all manner of *ancien régimes*. . . . *Externally*, self-determination has been no less of a challenge to established authority—that of the small circle of 'civilized nations' which constituted the international legal order.
>
> —ANTONIO CASSESE, *Self-Determination of Peoples: A Legal Reappraisal*

During the 1960s, the rights to development and self-determination entered international law together as mutually enabling and reinforcing conditions for participation in the modern world and as preconditions for the free and full development of the human personality. Between 1948 (when the UDHR was adopted) and 1966 (when the two International Covenants featuring self-determination were completed), the UN more than doubled in size from the admission of sixty-four new self-determining states whose human rights priorities soon found their way into international law, reconfiguring the historical relationship between development and self-determination. In a series of influential speeches theorizing these new priorities, Julius Nyerere, president of the newly independent United Republic of Tanzania, cogently articulated the integral interdependence of development and self-determination, whose internal, nationalist aspects and external, internationalist dimensions he glossed with the single word "freedom"—"the ability of [a people] to determine their own future, and to govern themselves without interference": "Real freedom for the people requires development, so real development of the people requires freedom."[22]

As head of the Tanzanian state, Nyerere aligned with the Non-Aligned Movement, an international coalition of Third World (mostly young decolonized) states who rejected modes of development that undermined their political and economic autonomy, seeking to avoid the "neo-colonialist trap[s]" of dependence laid by the two Cold War empires.[23] Both the shape and scope of the international human right to self-determination owe much to the Movement's political skill in playing the geopolitical interests of the two superpowers against each other. Thus, the human right to self-determination combines both the principle of internal self-governance identified by Woodrow Wilson as "a standard [and regulatory criterion] of democracy" and also the Leninist (anti-imperial) principle of a people's right to rid themselves of external—or foreign—domination.[24] In 1960, with scant support from the Soviet Bloc and outright resistance from the ex-colonial Western democracies, the newest members of the General Assembly successfully pushed the adoption of the Declaration on the Granting of Independence to Colonial Countries and Peoples (DGICCP), which linked self-determination and development by articulating the rights of peoples to "freely determine their political status and freely pursue their economic, social and cultural development."

Much of the language and militancy of the DGICCP is drawn directly from the Final Communiqué of the Asian-African Conference that met in Bandung, Indonesia in 1955 to establish inter-South cooperation for the promotion of social, economic, and cultural development. The forerunner of the Non-Aligned Movement, the Bandung conference symbolized, in the judgment of the Philippine delegate Carlos Romulo, "the coming of age of Asia and Africa."[25] Its Communiqué pressed the international urgency of the "right of peoples and nations to self-determination," condemning colonialism, "in whatever form it may be," as a "denial of the fundamental rights of man" that "suppresses the national cultures of the peoples" and "hampers the development of their personality."[26] Although Bandung was perceived as a threat to Western interests and ideals, the final document actually echoes the UDHR when it characterizes "the fundamental principles of human rights as a common standard of achievement for all peoples and all nations";[27] indeed, since neither "self-determination" nor "development" (as such) appears in the Universal Declaration, to legitimate their commitments to those "human rights," the Bandung conferees found it necessary to appeal to the authority and language of the UN Charter—language that Romulo himself had been instrumental in formulating and that, ironically, provided the legal basis for the exclusion from the UN of some of the states represented at Bandung.[28]

According to the Wilsonian logic of the UN Charter, self-determination (self-governance and sovereignty) is not a right; rather, it is the primary criterion for state membership in the international body—for official recognition of a people's legal personality. Using sovereignty as a developmental metric, the Charter also renewed nineteenth-century civilizational-threshold arguments about what counts as a capacity for self-determination.[29] Thus, under the International Trusteeship System (which updated the League of Nations' Mandate system), some sovereign states were assigned responsibility "to develop self-government" for "non-self-governing" peoples (Article 73). Entrusted states assumed a legal obligation (not in relation to underdeveloped peoples but to the international community) "to promote the political, economic, social, and educational advancement of the inhabitants of the trust territories, and their

progressive development towards self-government or independence" (Article 76).[30] These "sacred trusts" formalized both new
and existing colonial arrangements and revitalized the tutelary logic
of the *mission civilisatrice*, which placed development before self-
determination in the teleology of modernization. In other words,
socioeconomic and cultural development were regarded as preconditions of civil and political self-determination, the capacities for
which were imagined to be the democratic fruit of modern
development.

Trusteeism's rhetoric of humanitarian responsibility evolved
from (rather than rejected) the language and spirit of the nineteenth-century international law of imperialism elaborated in treaties like the General Act of the Conference of Berlin (1885). It also
refurbished the contractual obligations that gave colonial Charter
Companies their social and civilizing missions to promote the welfare of colonized peoples. The charters of corporations such as
Cecil Rhodes' British South Africa Company (1889)—whose peculiar role in colonial education I examine in my reading of Dangarembga's *Nervous Conditions*—granted monopolistic trade rights in
return for the promise that "the conditions of the natives inhabiting
the said territories will be materially improved and their civilisation
advanced" by the company's activities. Under both the Trustee system and classic colonialism, "self-determination became connected
with the imperative to 'become civilized'";[31] ideally, development
would prepare dependent peoples for eventual self-governance and
the right to practice self-determination among the "civilized" peoples. But by making colonial relations a matter of official, international—rather than merely domestic—concern, the Trust system
implicitly recognized (if only proleptically) the international legal
personality of "non-self-governing" peoples by acknowledging
their potential for development and self-determination. In this
sense, contemporary human rights law articulates self-determination according to the paradoxical logic of enabling fictions that I
have been describing throughout this book: a people must be presupposed to be self-determinative for them to be legally recognized
as a people, but they acquire such legal capacity for self-determination only at the moment that they coalesce as a recognizable people.

The Bandung Communiqué reversed the colonial logic of the
UN Charter by declaring self-determination to be "a prerequisite

of the full enjoyment of all fundamental human rights,"[32] and the international law that followed from it is even more strident in its dismissal of colonialism's missionary logic: "Inadequacy of political, economic, social or educational preparedness should never serve as a pretext for delaying independence" (DGICCP, Article 3). The Declaration on the Granting of Independence to Colonial Countries and Peoples recodes the emancipatory teleology of modernization and liberation, which it characterizes as "irresistible" and "irreversible," as a warning to the international community of the "serious threat to world peace" posed by any continued "denial of or impediments in the way of the freedom of [colonial] peoples" (preamble). Presented as "an authoritative interpretation of the [UN] Charter"[33] rather than as a postscript to the UDHR, the declaration opened a new international legal front in the prosecution of anticolonial liberation struggles for self-determination. Indeed, coming at the height of the Algerian War of Independence (1954–62), it was regarded by many legal analysts as a victory for the Army of National Liberation (ALN), which "conduct[ed] an international war" while the French government was mired in the outmoded parochial warfare of counterinsurgency.[34] In principle, the right of self-determination makes it possible for peoples subjected to "alien domination" to broaden their liberation struggle and internationalize their human rights claims to recognition of their legal personality.

International jurist Antonio Cassese has described self-determination as "a vehicle of enfranchisement for ever expanding circles of citizens against all manner of *ancien régimes*."[35] Translated into literary terms, self-determination is a tropological vehicle of incorporation whose tenor is legal personality (both for persons within states and for peoples at the international level). In other words, enactment of the right to self-determination conveys international personality, and its figurative work traces the developmental trajectory of the human personality toward its expression in international citizen-subjectivity. Self-determination becomes a facet of and a factor in the human rights plot of human personality development as both a precondition and consummation of development. Indeed, the Declaration on the Right to Development (1986) expands on the relations among self-determination, development, and the fulfillment of the human personality. Like the human right of self-determination, the development declaration reverses the paternalist promise of colonialism and trusteeship—that a process of tightly supervised development could eventually qualify subjugated peoples for self-determination—with the assertion that the right to development "implies the full realization of the right of peoples to self-determination" (Article 1). Also like self-determination, development is a right "both of nations and of individuals who make up nations." Individual persons, like the nations they constitute, are presumed to have a natural inclination (both a desire and a design) for development, which the law normalizes as the *telos* of modernity and modernization. Thus, "obstacles to development"—including "the denial of civil, political, economic, social and cultural rights"— are construed as obstacles to "the complete fulfillment of human beings and of peoples." The development declaration posits a right to self-determination as prior to its "realization" in the freely and fully developed human personality.

The 1960 declaration represents the first formal and comprehensive recognition of a people's human right to self-determination, and although the principle had been in circulation at the UN since at least 1952—when the Commission on Human Rights published drafts of the two International Covenants—it would acquire real justiciability only with the entry into force of the ICCPR and the ICESCR in 1976.[36] The two binding Covenants conjoin the Wilsonian and Leninist principles of internal and external self-determination, and they maintain the anti-imperialist stance of the previous declaration by affirming self-determination as "a necessary precondition for the enjoyment of individual rights."[37] Indeed, the appearance of self-determination among what are generally regarded as the individual rights of the ICCPR and the ICESCR implicitly extends its application to both peoples and the individuals who constitute peoples. Historically, as I have previously argued, human rights are borne by individuals (persons) who acquire international personality as members of groups (peoples). Thus, by the same synecdochal logic that configures the individual as an instance of a people's vulnerability in, among others, the Convention on the Prevention and Punishment of the Crime of Genocide (1948), the two international Covenants construct the individual person as the smallest unit of a people's self-determinative capacity and potential for development.[38] In this sense, international law constructs the individual as a kind of teleoeme of human self-determination and development more generally. (This synecdochal configuration is the foundation of the allegorical structure of human rights claims to recognition, in which the individual represents both itself and a class of people, laying personal claim to rights belonging to a group.[39]) As with the Westphalian logic of the classical theories of *Bildung* that I examined in chapter 2, international law posits the state as the ideal medium for and highest form of (collectivized) expression of the human personality's self-determination;[40] as such, self-determination becomes one of the names for the incorporative process by which the person transcends its individuality and amplifies into the community and the state to emerge in the international sphere as a bearer of human rights and duties.

Paradoxically, perhaps, as contemporary human rights law has become increasingly (and thematically) a discourse of development over the past fifty years, it has also become more formally tautological. The 1986 Declaration articulates its developmental common sense in the traditional tautological form of self-evidence, but it surpasses all earlier human rights treaties in this regard. The chiastic balance of its preamble and its body of articles formulates a perfect tautology. Thus, the final preambular paragraph confirms, in a constative speech act, "that *the right to development is an inalienable human right* . . ." and anticipates Article 1.1 in which the same content is now proclaimed in the declarative: "*The right to development is an inalienable human right* by virtue of which every human person and all peoples are entitled to participate in, contribute to, and enjoy economic, social, cultural and political development, in which all human rights and fundamental freedoms can be fully realized" (emphasis added). Beyond their internal tautologies (a right is a right), each of the preambular statements of recognition and confirmation has a corresponding statement within the body of the text that proclaims the same idea, often verbatim.

As we saw with the legislation of dignity and personality in the UDHR, the legal documents inscribe their moment of enunciation in the transitive space between the preamble and the text—in a "therefore" that marks the rhetorical turn where natural law becomes positive and the constative becomes performative, so that what the preamble recognizes as historically or universally valid and desirable in the past is enacted in the present and issued into the future. Conventionally distributed between the preamble and the

text of the articles, these two speech acts—the constative that confirms and the declarative that enacts—interact to imbue the tautological construction with a kinetic potential and temporal
dimension that initiates a teleology-in-tautology. This tautological–teleological configuration is repeated for each of the Declaration on the Right to Development's preambular paragraphs; the
content of their statements remains the same, but their illocutio-
nary mode changes as they cross the transitive space into the body
of the text. Thus, the preamble first recognizes "that *the human
person is the central subject of the development process*" and then declares
in the body of the text that "*the human person is the central subject of
development* and should be the active participant and beneficiary of
the right to development" (Article 2.1, emphasis added). In effect,
the human person is declared to be the central subject of development that it was presupposed to be by both prior right and the
disposition of the human personality.

Despite dispensing with the tutelary logic of development for
self-determination in its characterization of the human person as
both "active participant" and "beneficiary" of development, the
declaration holds onto the roles of patron and client distributed
unequally in the colonial relation. But it seeks to transform that
relation into a structure of self-patronage by describing an ideal
developmental narrative in which the person represents both the
impulse of development and its plot product. The declaration presupposes a human person capable of developing (and being developed) by participating in the process of development, through
which the person accrues the benefits of development itself; thus,
the human person is both the engine of development and an effect
of that developmental agency—its agent and beneficiary. The suspension of the right to development across the anticipatory preamble and the retrospective text plots a project by which the human
person is to realize itself as a subject with a right to development—as the central subject of development (the agent-beneficiary)
that it already was in the preamble and always already was by nature
and right. Thus, the tautological structure of the intentional teleology of human rights developmentalism animates inherency and inalienability as developmental plots by which the human person
comes to be the same as itself (or to persist as itself) by which the
human person is to become, and to be recognized as, *the* subject of

development: the international human rights person. The infusion of temporality into the human rights tautologies changes their aspect from natural to positive—from expositive to narrative—describing the structure of self-sponsorship that makes the individual at least partially responsible for its own development. In fact, the tautological–teleological structure of development reproduces and reinforces the paradigmatic narrative form of the first-person *Bildungsroman*; both the law and literature balance anticipation with retrospection and thereby transform the subject of development and self-determination into a narrative projection (a project, a projected image, and a vehicle) of the fully developed human personality.

Alexander Nékám anticipated this structure in a rather brilliant, though largely forgotten, 1938 thesis on the figurative character of legal personality and what he regarded as a historical confusion of the "legal image" of the person for the "so-called 'natural' person."[41] As a legal category, personality is an abstraction that, he argues, "cannot be the source . . . out of which every right evolves."[42] Indeed, "person" is an elastic, aspirational figure, and in recent international law it becomes the legal name for creatures endowed not only with dignity but with the capacity for development and self-determination. To account for the discrepancy between legal poetics and common sense, Nékám explains that, by describing the "human personality as somehow the natural subject of rights," the law initiates a split between the "administrator of rights" (the already-capacitated person) and the "beneficiary of rights" (the yet-to-be-incorporated individual).[43] Thus, he concludes that it is "only a coincidence that these two conceptions seem to overlap in our system of today in the case of the rights belonging to the normal adult person."[44] But, in the case of international human rights law, the visionary overlap is no coincidence; the breach between the beneficiary and the administrator—a late-capitalist "business model" of the subject–citizen divide enacted in the French Declaration of the Rights of Man and of the Citizen—is precisely the fracture that contemporary human rights law seeks to repair in the figure of the international citizen-subject by making them coincident manifestations of the same person. In the late twentieth century, international human rights law translates this sociopolitical, tropological problematic and structure into the dominant language of economics as a technical problem of management.

Contemporary human rights plots a narrative of *Bildung* in which the administrator and the beneficiary ideally conjoin in the proleptic figure of the human rights person. This transition narrative of modernization is an idealized developmental story of narrative self-sponsorship in which the human person becomes a self-administering beneficiary of development and rights—a self-sustaining and self-determinative creature of both social life and law, where "self" is understood as a social category and condition. The social nature of this "self" is further evident in the crucial revision that the Declaration on the Right to Development makes to our formula of free and full human personality development: "All human beings have a responsibility for development, individually and collectively, taking into account the need for full respect for their human rights and fundamental freedoms as well as their duties to the community, which alone can ensure the free and complete fulfillment of the human being" (Article 2.2). The individual's right to development entails a reciprocal obligation on and to the community, the nation, and the international order. The rights of self-determination and development not only reverse the missionary logic of colonialism, they also invert—or redistribute—the terms of responsibility. Thus, the beneficiaries of development become responsible for its administration; individuals share with communities and states the obligation and responsibility for their (and others') social, political, economic, and cultural advancement. The individual is obliged to the community (local, national, and international) and to itself not only to participate in collective socioeconomic development but to develop the human personality. In other words, the individual is *compelled* to become the international human rights person that it already was by right.

In terms of the plot of incorporation, this reconfiguration of responsibility is ultimately the most dramatic revision that the addition of human rights to self-determination and development makes to the story form of free and full human personality development; the individual human person is expected to assume narrative, social, economic, and political responsibility for an emancipatory process of incorporation that the law already describes as irresistible, irreversible, imprescriptible, and natural. We have seen in previous chapters how the idealist, third-person *Bildungsroman* responds to the modern imperative to "become civilized"—to become what

Foucault described as self-regulating subjects; it refashions the civilizing mission as a model of benevolent social assistance to construct a personal story of the individual's acquisition of narrative self-determination and citizen-subjectivity. The shift in human rights law toward a discourse of sustained and self-sustaining development appropriates the social and political structure of popular sovereignty as a model for the realization and management of the sovereignty of the human personality; it posits a citizen-subject who is already a narrator-protagonist and who assumes responsibility for its own incorporation into the rights and duties of international human personhood—that is, who assumes responsibility for the figurative work of the law itself. In other words, as plots of autoincorporation, the human rights of self-determination and development charter narratives of responsibilization by which individuals are to become personally responsible for the tropological force of the law—for guaranteeing the common sense and "rightness" of the human rights tautologies. This shift has a formal correlative in the first-person *Bildungsroman*, where the narrative structure of self-sponsorship literally takes the rhetorical and logical form of tautology—what George Puttenham glossed in 1589 as "selfe saying."[45] The affirmative, third-person *Bildungsroman* offers an idealistic image of the social and narrative responsibilization of the subject—of how the protagonist comes to occupy the seemingly empty place of the narrator in the cultural narrative of human personality development, assuming retroactive personal responsibility for the invisible hand of fate in natural law and the institutional demands of the state in positive law that compel the individual's development. The first-person *Bildungsroman* takes the form of international law itself; the technology of narrative self-sponsorship becomes a literary device that labors to realize, at least formally, the promised reconciliation of the citizen and subject in the singular figure of the narrator-protagonist—to make the uncertain sovereignty of the human personality appear certain. But, although this fabled reunification constitutes the genre's central problematic and formal accomplishment, the emancipatory promise tends to remain a thematic mystification (a hyperbole) under a contemporary regime of rights and responsibilities in which the theoretical inevitability of development and self-determination has the character of an imperative to become freely and fully developed.

"Loose Connections": Colonial Bildung *and Hyperboles of Development and Self-Determination in Tsitsi Dangarembga's* Nervous Conditions

> Now *therefore*, we, the Government of Rhodesia, do hereby declare:
> That it is an indisputable and accepted historic fact that since 1923
> the Government of Rhodesia have exercised the powers of self-gov-
> ernment and have been responsible for the progress, development and
> welfare of their people. . . .
>
> —*Unilateral Declaration of Independence*,
> 11 November 1965

Recalling her excitement at finally being permitted to pursue her schooling after her older brother's sudden death, Tambudzai Si-gauke, the narrator-protagonist of Tsitsi Dangarembga's *Nervous Conditions* (1988), remembers the image of the "clean, well-groomed, genteel self" that she "expected to find" at the American mission school headmastered by her uncle, Babamukuru.[46] Given to "excesses and flights of fancy," Tambu describes her arrival, in the exuberant poetry of her fourteen-year-old imagination, as a "rein-carnation" expected to add "wisdom to my nature, clarity to my vision, glamour to my person": "I was going to be developed in the way that Babamukuru saw fit, which in the language I understood at the time meant well."[47] For Tambu and her extended family, that language of development and self-determination is practically an obsession, and the novel traces the effects of the inflated rhetoric of modernization on a Shona girl coming of age in Southern Rhodesia during the 1960s and 70s, the last years of white minority rule. Dangarembga's partially autobiographical *Bildungsroman* explores the inconsistencies and contradictions between colonial education's exaggerated promises of "mental and eventually, through it, mate-rial emancipation" and their systemic frustration by the colonial formation itself.[48] The novel narrates an ironic version of how the liberation struggle (*Chimurenga*) that precipitated Zimbabwean in-dependence in 1980 was, from the perspective of the colonial sys-tem, supposed to have been avoided through the strategic "peaceful promise" of native development—the "step by step" assimilation of problematic black Africans, "on an honorary basis," into the domi-nant, white Rhodesian society and culture.[49]

Narrated in a retrospective first-person voice, the novel focuses on Tambu's "escape" from, and her cousin Nyasha's unsuccessful "rebellion" against, the conflicting and confounding imperatives of development for young women caught between the racist regime of colonial Rhodesia and the traditions of Shona patriarchy.[50] Tambu's story of escape is counterpointed by those of her mother's and aunt's entrapment. On its surface, then, the novel appears to tell a conventional story of "self-discovery and [the] consolidation of a subjectivity," with Tambu being merely a black, African female variant of the affirmative European *Bildungsroman*'s "traditional protagonist."[51] The novelistic form seems to be performing its traditional social work of demarginalizing the marginal subject—of enfranchising the individual as the normative, national citizen-subject that Tambu espies "as a sunrise on [her] horizon" and that is intimated at the story's close with her securement of a full scholarship to the Young Ladies College of the Sacred Heart, a prestigious, multi-racial convent school that offers "the privilege of associating with the elite of that time."[52] Indeed, Tambu is in the "fast lanes" of qualification for one of "the strategically small number of . . . places the Government gave us," not only for educational opportunities but for black citizenship.[53]

But the apparent generic conventionality of the novel is misleading because the narrative traces the protagonist's "anticipation" not to the projected threshold of sociocivil integration (or the reunification of the narrator and protagonist) but to the verge of "disappointment."[54] Its opening lines articulate the implicit narrative contract of the first-person *Bildungsroman*, which promises its reader a story of how the narrator became a narrator: "I shall . . . begin by recalling the facts as I remember them . . . , the events that put me in a position to write this account."[55] But the novel deliberately reneges on its generic contractual obligation, as the narrator announces abruptly in the text's closing lines: "Something in my mind began to assert itself, to question things and refuse to be brainwashed, bringing me to this time when I can set down this story. It was a long and painful process for me, that process of expansion. It was a process whose events stretched over many years and would fill another volume."[56] Thus, the narrative dissolves into a significant ellipsis that leaves unnarrated the process of critical expansion that might account for the narrator's sardonic disposition and her recognition of the fact that, although as a young girl she had managed to escape some of the restrictions of Shona patriarchy, the plot of incorporation she had so eagerly anticipated is strategically foreclosed to a black African woman in colonial Rhodesia. This ellipsis becomes a meaningful part of the narrative itself, and it undoes the seamlessness and formal certainty expected with the plot structure of self-sponsorship, "suspend[ing] the adoption of a final stance."[57]

Dangarembga disrupts the *Bildungsroman*'s smooth linear circularity of narrative development, placing the emergence of the historical and narrative consciousness that hallmarks the genre outside the scope of the story in a period after the narrative and before the narration. In other words, the narrator gives an account of herself, but only up to a point that does not fully reconnect either the closing lines of the novel with its opening lines or the time and events of the narrative with the time and tone of their narration. Unlike in the classic *Bildungsroman*, there is no narrated handover of narratorial agency, and this elision opens the space not only of irony but, as I will argue, of history. Indeed, the diegetic gap turns the form of narrative self-sponsorship into a device for resocializing Tambu and rehistoricizing her personal story of development as the story of an illusion. The conventionality of Tambu's story of apprenticeship for self-narrating citizen-subjectivity is, then, a literary feint, a preamble to a story of *Bildung* that remains unwritten—a process that is, the novel seems to suggest, systemically unwritable for a Shona girl in colonial Rhodesia and unassimilable to the conventions of the idealist *Bildungsroman*, whose democratic norms of citizenship do not match the forms of social and civil participation available either to the marginalized black majority generally or to native women specifically. The diegetic gap is indicative of the improbability of free and full human personality development under a colonial regime that is unable (and unwilling) to foster either real development or real self-determination.

The novel's generic conformity (like the colonial promise of development itself) becomes a sort of technical school exercise that satisfies certain readerly expectations. In fact, the novel attributes those expectations to an explicit narratee—the figure of an "implicated reader"[58]—who comes to the story with particular presumptions, presentiments, and prejudices about development, colonialism, and African social, racial, and gender relations, as well as a general bourgeois humanitarian and *Bildungsroman* literary sensibility. Tambu-the-narrator addresses this reader from the first lines of her story: "I was not sorry when my brother died. Nor am I apologising for my callousness, as *you* may define it, my lack of feeling."[59] The novel's main plot—the story of Tambu's schooling and her citizen-subjectivation (so far as it goes)—seems to endorse the egalitarianism of the *Bildungsroman* form and to legitimate, at least formally, the affirmative educational action of the Rhodesian state in its narration of her exceptional assimilation and her progressive exemption from the colonial "rule" of native backwardness. But this façade of generic conventionality fronts for the displaced, or deferred, plot of Tambu's unschooling—the not-yet-narrated "process of expansion" that "would fill another volume"—by which she comes to recognize that the socioeconomic discourse of development and the form and ideology of the traditional *Bildungsroman* are themselves implicated in the patriarchal and racist structures of colonial domination. This historicizing, "submerged plot," which "encodes rebellion" against the imperatives of colonial development and the constraints of the *Bildungsroman* genre, contravenes the "surface plot" that "affirms [such] social conventions."[60] The submerged plot, which perhaps legitimates her "callousness" as a product of the same structures of domination that constructed her brother as an obstacle to her education, is detectable both in the narrator's ironic interventions into young Tambu's story of normative development and in her running invocation of the implicated reader's literary, social, and cultural expectations for that story.

Rhodesian history consists of a series of contested claims to self-determination. Founded by Cecil Rhodes and his British South Africa Company (BSAC), Rhodesia was originally governed according to the narrow democratic principles of Rhodes's famous dictum: "Equal rights for all civilized men south of the Zambezi [River]." Vested by Royal Charter (1889) with monopolistic trade rights and command over the country's natural resources, the BSAC also enjoyed the extraordinary powers to "make ordinances" and to "maintain a police force" so long as it supervised, "in the interests of humanity," the civilization and development of the natives. The BSAC lost its Charter in 1923, when the settlers, whose immigration it had encouraged, voted for self-rule as a British colony. In the

1950s and 60s, feeling the pressure of black nationalism in all of its African colonies, Britain began to entertain the possibility of Rhodesian independence, but it insisted, against the will of the white minority, on fulfilling its civilizing mission with the extension of universal suffrage to the black population. On 11 November 1965, in an attempt to preempt black majority rule, the white supremacist regime of Ian Smith announced its own self-determination in the Unilateral Declaration of Independence (UDI). The UDI co-opted the language of human rights (mimicking the rhetoric of the American Declaration of Independence) to justify its claim to self-determination, and it drew the first-ever sanctions from the UN Security Council, who cited the right of "all peoples" to self-determination from the Declaration on the Granting of Independence to Colonial Countries and Peoples to substantiate its refusal to recognize the independence of the "illegal racist régime" of Southern Rhodesia (S/RES/232). Despite increasing international diplomatic pressure and the widening armed liberation struggle of the Second *Chimurenga* (1966–79), the Rhodesian Front managed to retain power until 1980, when the country's first democratic election made African resistance leader Robert Mugabe the president of independent Zimbabwe.[61]

Dangarembga's novel is set in the tempestuous period between the UDI (1965) and the establishment of Zimbabwe (1980), at the height of the *Chimurenga* and the government's counterinsurgency campaign; however, like the process of expansion that occurs in the narrative gap, that historical violence remains mostly outside the novel and the characters' lives. Many readers have noted the novel's elision of this history, and the young Tambu herself seems rather oblivious to these historical events, preferring, as her cousin Nyasha charges, the "fairy-tales" of British *Bildungsromane*—Louisa May Alcott's *Little Women* and the novels of Enid Blyton and the Brontë sisters—to the "reality" that absorbs Nyasha, who reads books about "the condition of South Africa . . . compare[d] with our own situation . . . ; about Nazis and Japanese and Hiroshima and Nagasaki . . . whether the Jews' claims to Palestine were valid . . . [and] exactly why the UDI was declared and what it meant."[62] But beyond those oblique references to (inter)national history, the important biographical dates identified in the novel are themselves historically overdetermined—1965: Babamukuru returns to Rhodesia, and the UDI is enacted; 1968: Tambu begins school after her brother's death, and UN sanctions are made permanent; 1971: Tambu enters Sacred Heart, and British-Rhodesian negotiations for a formal independence collapse once and for all.

The history that most captivates Tambu is encrypted in the form of an episodic "fairy-tale of reward and punishment, cause and effect" about her family's experience of colonialism that Tambu's grandmother narrates as they tend the fields of the homestead.[63] This "romantic" allegory of invading "white wizards . . . versed in treachery and black magic," "glittering gold mines," "holy [missionary] wizards" and native "princes" and "princesses" on a desperate quest to recuperate their land, has a pair of heroes and a "tantalising moral that increased your aspirations, but not beyond a *manageable* level" (emphasis added). Tambu's heroic grandmother, "being sagacious," had the "foresight" to have Babamukuru "educated in [holy] wizardry"; while, for his part, her uncle proved to be "cultivatable, in the way that land is, to yield harvests that sustain the cultivator," winning a scholarship to South Africa and England to pursue a master's degree and returning "well enough salaried to reduce a little the meagreness of his family's existence." Tambu recalls this recurrent scene of storytelling at the moment in her own narrative when she begins to cultivate the plot of land that her grandmother farmed as her "own plot" to earn money for her school fees. The material connection between the cultivation of land and the cultivation of personality (configured implicitly in the freedom to dispose of one's "natural and human resources" that partially constitutes the human right to self-determination) serves as a *leitmotif* that links plots of land to plots of development and to the narrative act of plotting. The novel is especially attentive to the social, material, and cultural conditions that enable, or disable, a people and an individual "to organise his immediate world and its contents as he wished," as the young Tambu romanticizes Babamukuru's self-determinative narratorial agency.[64] As a student, Tambu misreads those conditions, imagining development as a process that culminates in total narratorial self-control, but the older narrator seeks to recuperate the historicity of the cultural narratives of development and self-determination that beguile Tambu beyond a manageable level.

These various narratives of development, which prescribe the dominant norms and forms of female socialization, are each sustained by their own legislative regimes and regulatory institutions. Shona traditional patriarchy, whose unreformed mouthpiece is Tambu's father, insists that general education is not for girls, who are to "learn to cook and clean [and] grow vegetables," and to "efface" themselves in marriage;[65] this domestic-marriage plot is enforced through the patriarchal family council (*dare*) that promotes images of women that are "no more than reflections" and teaches them "to recognise these reflections as self."[66] The patriarchal pressure of Shona culture is largely reinforced by the educational expectations of dominant Southern Rhodesian society, which inherited the BSAC's two-tiered pedagogical policy of providing a British-styled "literary education" for all whites (and a few blacks) while offering "industrial training" for "natives" that would "improve" their condition and civilization by teaching them "habits of order, discipline and obedience . . . [and] to look upon work *as the natural means* of earning a livelihood."[67] Thus, except for what Nyasha calls the "precocious few who might prove a nuisance if left to themselves . . . . [and are] made a little [honorary] space into which [they] were assimilated,"[68] Africans "should NOT be thrown into the turmoil of academic western [literary] education" but should, according to the Commission on Native Education (1951), be given "elementary education" in "manual labor" and domestic "servant work for girls," "where their natural abilities can be assisted" and they can "thereby find a place for themselves within a democratic social structure."[69] The demands of colonial education are generally said to contradict those of "traditional" native culture, but from the perspective of the developmental imperatives for girls, the two are variations on a "universal" theme of "inferior" "femaleness."[70]

Tambu places herself in the category of the "precocious" exception to each of these deterministic plots, and her romantic, Goethean vision of "emancipation"—the "extension and improvement of what I really was"—holds that the "evil wizards' spell" that keeps the African in servitude can be broken by "hard work and determination";[71] this didactic "heady transition" narrative of "sublimation" is "represented," "laid out," and "taken care of" by Babamukuru, but it is intensified by Nyasha's "extensive library" of

British *Bildungsromane* that introduces Tambu to "places where reason and inclination were not at odds."[72] Reading these emancipatory fictions enables her to recognize the arbitrariness of the gender and race plots of "underdevelopment," leading to both her admission into Sacred Heart (based partly on her mastery of *Little Women*) and her hasty dismissal of her mother's insight that the female Shona condition entails a double burden of poverty and subservience.[73] Nonetheless, she draws suspect lessons from her enabling misreadings of both her grandmother's fairytale (which teaches that individual education should serve group development) and the *Bildungsromane* (which she reads as stories of personal fulfillment rather than of social responsibilization). Tambu-the-narrator subtly underscores the slippage between the "fairy-tales" and social "reality," between the romantic rhetoric of the *Bildungsroman* and the strategically limited plot of colonial assimilation that it conceals, between the idealistic vision of personal self-determination that a young Tambu gleans from those tales and the need for collective emancipation.

On the plane of the surface plot, the novel enacts this rupture between "rhetoric" and "reality" by splitting the figure of the traditional *Bildungsheld* into two protagonists: Tambu, believer in "fairy-tales"; and Nyasha, student of "reality." Beyond the marked divergence in their reading tastes, this formal and generic partition represents the most immediate symptom of the novel's "nervous conditions," literalizing the "bewitching" of the colonized that Sartre described in his preface to Frantz Fanon's *Wretched of the Earth*: "The status of the 'native' is a nervous condition introduced and maintained by the settler among colonized people *with their consent*."[74] The *Bildungsroman* plot and the hyperbolic promises of native development are part of the discursive technologies that manufacture that consent. Colonialism, Sartre and Fanon suggest, pretends to offer the colonized a choice between Western and native cultures that cannot, in practice, be made. Nyasha and Tambu each respond differently to this false dilemma, with consequences that manifest themselves in a second set of nervous conditions. Nyasha, who recognizes that she is in no historical position to choose, suffers from *anorexia nervosa*; Tambu, who believes she has already freely chosen British culture, shows signs of aphasia. Nyasha's mother attributes her eating disorder to "her head [being] full of loose connections that are always sparking"; the narrator, however, intimates that it is Nyasha's "multi-directional mind" and her ability to "glue . . . together facts for herself" about "real peoples and their sufferings" that give her too much to stomach.[75] In other words, her anorexia is a somatization of her historical consciousness—of the implications she draws from her reading of history; in the climactic scene of her nervous breakdown, Nyasha "rampages," "shredding her history book between her teeth ('Their history. Fucking liars. Their bloody lies.'). . . . 'They've trapped us. . . . But I won't be trapped . . . I've tried to keep it in but it's powerful. It ought to be. There's nearly a century of it.' "[76]

Where Nyasha's recognition of her conflicted historical position and her struggle against the compulsions of both assimilation and nativism manifest themselves in anorexia, Tambu's eager and uncritical acceptance of "their" plot of development leads progressively to aphasia. The older, articulate narrator comes to recognize that her younger self had followed the same path of incapacitation that she despised in her late obsequious brother, who became "more aphasic . . . . the more time [he] spent at Babamukuru's," ostensibly losing his fluency in Shona.[77] In the young Tambu's case, the narrator reports that the loss of language—of a sociocultural voice and a historical sensibility—"happened insidiously" and "stunted the growth of my faculty of criticism":[78]

> I had grown much quieter and more self-effacing than usual. . . . I hardly ever talked unless spoken to, and then only to answer with the utmost respect. . . . I did not question things. It did not matter to me why things should be done this way rather than that way. I simply accepted that this was so. . . . I was not concerned that freedom fighters were referred to as terrorists, did not demand proof of God's existence nor did I think that the missionaries, along with all the other Whites in Rhodesia, ought to have stayed at home. As a result of all these things that I did not think or do, Babamukuru thought I was the sort of young woman a daughter ought to be.[79]

In *Nervous Conditions*, colonial education prepares black individuals to be subjects but not citizens—actors but not narrators; the promise of incorporation obscures a plot of incapacitation. The process of native development (of African "assimilation") is a project of "forgetting" and unsaying—a disarticulation of the social and cultural relations of the Shona traditional world for which the "exceptional" individual is to be compensated with a contingent enfranchisement into the elite world of dominant Rhodesian society, so long as she consents not to articulate the "loose connections" between racism, sexism, colonialism, and the historical condition of the natives.[80]

Tambu-the-narrator recalls the seduction of her father by Babamukuru's argument that her brother's education "would lift our branch of the family out of [our] squalor": "My uncle's gesture was oceanic, and my father, who liked hyperbole, did not need much persuading to see the sense of the plan."[81] The characters in the novel have various grandiloquent names for this oceanic notion of development: improvement, uplift, expansion, extension, emancipation, reincarnation, progress, sublimation, centripetence. But, as the narrator ultimately recognizes, these figures are all hyperbolic; indeed, she suggests that, in Southern Rhodesia, hyperbole is the central trope of a development discourse that not only overstates the possibilities for black African incorporation but also construes development as a project of amplification—a hyperbolization of its subject. The rhetoric and process of exaggeration perverts the tautological–teleological complex of development by configuring the plot without a recursion, distending the teleological component of self-realization into a plot of alienation and isolation, directed toward an unattainable, fabled honorary whiteness. Young Tambu takes these hyperbolic and hyperbolizing narratives literally, envisioning herself on their "path of progress," which she objectifies in the gates of Sacred Heart college, "those gates that would *declare* me a young lady" (emphasis added).[82] Thus, she confuses her "escape" from traditional patriarchy and her avoidance of being "screened out of school" as confirmation of the "emancipating lesson" of her individual and exceptional achievement.[83] Considering herself "living proof of the moral," young Tambu conflates the strategically restricted plot of assimilation and the romanticized fiction of personal fulfillment with the idealized plot of emancipation that she takes away from Babamukuru's story and the library of English *Bildungsromane*.

Tambu's misapprehension is understandable in light of the state's equivocatory official discourse on native education. In the wake of the UN's adoption of the UDHR, the Rhodesian Department of Native Development and African Education articulated its educational policy in the humanist rhetoric of *Bildung* and legislated in

the spirit of apartheid. In 1951, the Rhodesian government conscripted a version of the human rights formula of personality development from the liberal pedagogical principles of the country's
more progressive missionary schools: "Native education means the
development of the human personality in the native child . . . for
the ultimate purpose of human life, and for life in society."[84] This
Bildung formulation is belied by the historical practice of native education for social, political, and economic control: here "native development" intends to undercut, rather than enable or realize,
African self-determination.[85] The idealistic plot elaborated in the
classical *Bildungsroman* and appropriated from the rhetoric of British liberal education is a "misplaced idea" in Southern Rhodesia, an
"ideolog[y] of the second degree" that, as Roberto Schwarz suggested about the nineteenth-century Brazilian novel's adoption of
the codes of European realism, does "not describe [local] reality,
not even falsely."[86]

Forgetting that her educational opportunity is sponsored by Babamukuru (whose own development has an entire colonial apparatus behind it), young Tambu is so smitten with her vision of *Bildung*
that she gets ahead of its usual plot, prematurely concluding that
her "present propitious circumstances were entirely of my own
making."[87] As with the plots available to her, Tambu's sense of narrative self-control is inflated. In her anxiousness to realize the
promise of self-determination, Tambu presumptuously imagines
herself the coordinator of the plot—the occupant of the narratorial
office in the cultural narrative of emancipation. Her mother has
other names for this process of development—"fattening . . . for
slaughter," "Englishness" that kills—and Nyasha insists that the
assimilative story is a captivity narrative that traps one in a space
that, as she warns Tambu, "one ought not to occupy."[88] Thus, the
colonial promise of development (for the chosen few) proves hyperbolic in another way that the novel underscores to ironize the Rhodesian discourse of development, the situational ideology of the
affirmative *Bildungsroman*, and the racist and sexist stereotypes that
portray the educated African woman as an anomaly. The discourse
of development is formulated in universalist, egalitarian rhetoric,
but its tropological work figures the "improved" native woman as a
singular entity that somehow exceeds its class: she is catachrestic,

both culturally and socially improper and exceptional. Her irregularity results in a double disenfranchisement—from "tradition" and from colonial society. The "fairy-tale" morals that Tambu digests from her Dilthean misreading of British *Bildungsromane* offer symbolic legitimation of this narrative of (de)marginalization as exemption and of her own burgeoning individualistic sense of exceptionality.[89]

Tambu-the-narrator recognizes that her earlier egotistical sense of personal achievement is an effect of the same hyperbolic, individualist discourse of development and self-determination that holds her father personally responsible for his "underdevelopment." She also recognizes that her view of the Rhodesian social formation—which regards the traditions of Shona patriarchy (rather than the entire colonial complex) as the lone obstacle to her emancipation—is distorted by an inflated humanist rhetoric of universalism that conceals narrow political motives. However, Tambu-the-student only begins to have such "suspicion, no more than the seed of a suspicion" at the end of the novel.[90] If Tambu escapes capture in the egotistical trap of the évolué, she does so outside the purview of the novel, in that other, unwritten volume where the seeds of suspicion, sown in her grandmother's plot and cultivated by Nyasha and her mother, eventually fructify. Within the surface plot, the planting of those seeds begins to intimate for the young Tambu that "I was not the person I was expected to be" and ends up "splitting" her mind "into two disconnected entities that had long, frightening arguments with each other."[91] This bisection of Tambu into "a paragon of female decorum" and a critically conscious woman who is "able to perceive implications" manifests itself in another of the titular "nervous conditions," and replicates another separation of "romance" from "reality" through the temporal disjuncture and diegetic split between Tambu-the-protagonist and Tambu-the-narrator.[92]

The novel appears to perform the traditional social work of the *Bildungsroman*, in which a narrator oversees the development of narrative self-sufficiency by bringing the beneficiary-protagonist and the administrator-narrator (in the novel's language, the "cultivatable" and the "cultivator") into conjunction in the singular figure of the freely and fully developed citizen-subject: the narrator-protagonist. However, what is narrated in the guise of the *Bildungsroman* is not the fusion but the fission of the narrator-protagonist.

Yet the diegetically split personality opens the space between the time of the narrative and the time of narration from which emerges Tambu's historical consciousness, which finally enables her to make the "long leaps that Nyasha's mind made between . . . events past, present and future," to recognize patterns of "cause and effect."[93] It is therefore also the space of narration—the place of expansion in which Tambu overcomes her colonial aphasia and assumes the post of the narrator in her story of development that makes it possible for her to plot a retrospective narrative that historicizes her naive anticipation of self-emancipation as a "historical artefact" of the colonial condition.[94] Ironically, the extratextual process of expansion (*Bildung*), which enables the narrator to recognize the ideological distortions of the *Bildungsroman* in the Rhodesian context, is unassimilable to the generic conventions of the *Bildungsroman*; instead, it cultivates the capacity to historicize *Bildung* and the *Bildungsroman* as a generic glass ceiling—a hyperbolic fairy tale that helps to sustain colonial domination.

This revisionist process is exemplified in the narrator's recollection of her first impressions of Babamukuru's mission house: "Had I been writing these things at the time that they happened, there would have been many references to 'palace' and 'mansion' and 'castle'. . . . but I have learnt, in the years that have passed since then, to curb excesses and flights of fancy."[95] The self-reflexive and recursive structure of the novel attempts to curb hyperbole by taking a second pass at the story of development and self-determination to escape the trap of egocentrism. In the process, the tautological–teleological temporal complex of retrospection and anticipation that sustains narrative self-sponsorship is converted into a technical literary device for defending against the hyperbolic discourse of development and the distended, exceptional individualism that tantalized the young Tambu with romantic promises of emancipation. The curve of self-sponsorship seeks to rectify her improper and personal unilateral declaration of independence by reattaching tautology to the teleology of development, thereby also resocializing her within "the community of women in whose company she comes of age" and who facilitated the actual development of her historical consciousness, which could not emerge within the official Rhodesian plot of self-determination.[96] Thus, as with contemporary human rights law, this narrative act of reclamation recognizes (confirms and enacts) the mutual responsibility that Tambu and the community share in her personal and social development. The recursiveness of the narrative ultimately insists that independence and self-determination are not unilateral projects (this was the rhetorical and tropological problem with the UDI that met with international sanctions) and that the individual is not an atomically self-substantiating subject (a free-standing tautology)—that the human personality is not itself sovereign.[97]

In its refusal to narrate the emergence of Tambu's critical, historical consciousness, Dangarembga's novel undoes the certainty and self-assurance usually associated with narrative self-sponsorship, foregrounding instead the indeterminacy of self-determination. It resists closing the circle of the story of citizen-subjectivation, not drawing a straight line of cause and effect between the events of the narrative and the critical voice and perspective of the narrator. The narrative gap that elides the emergence of Tambu's historical consciousness figures the process of expansion as deferred and discontinuous, refusing to accredit the paternalistic colonial plot of development and ensuring that the narrator and protagonist are not merely extensions (or dimensions) of a predetermined self-same subject. The historicizing and socializing (re)cyclical structure of Tambu's narrative undercuts the "definitive stabilization of the individual" narrated by the traditional *Bildungsroman*, "where the meaning of events lies in their *finality*."[98] Instead, the recursive narrative structure rejects the unilateralism of a self-declared independence, and it subverts the individualizing and exceptionalizing hyperbolic plot of colonial development by insisting that self-determination is a social practice: not a final state or a pre-given capacity, but a reflexive and collective process of self-revision. The narrator acts as a surrogate for an absent democratic social order, and the novel models self-determination as a perpetually incomplete project of self-saming and self-saying that depends upon a sustained and self-sustaining act of narration to articulate the social and historical relations of which the individual is a part and an effect. In *Nervous Conditions*, the fragile figure of the self-sponsoring narrator-protagonist represents not the consummation of the plot of incorporation but an attempt to rectify a corrupted process of human personality development and self-determination.

The narrator rejects the stunting half-education (what Adorno called *Halbbildung*) that Rhodesian society offers the black African woman, but the novel ultimately affirms the humanist principles that ground the form and ideology of human rights personality development and the idealist *Bildungsroman*.[99] If, as Wendy Brown has perceptively noted, "rights secure our standing as individuals even as they obscure the treacherous ways that standing is achieved and regulated," Dangarembga's narrator seeks to uncover the hidden costs of Tambu's seduction by the language of personal rights and the romance of the *Bildungsroman*, which, like human rights themselves, "promise increased individual sovereignty" at the risk of "intensifying the fiction of sovereign subjects."[100] Dangarembga's novel is a critique of the *Bildungsroman* in the form of a *Bildungsroman*; her dissensual *Bildungsroman* challenges the exclusionary and narrow universalism of the classical form (particularly as it is deployed in Rhodesian missionary education) by reactivating its historical social work as the novel of human rights incorporation. The novel also affirms, albeit ambivalently, the social utility of the genre in its pursuit of narrative self-determination over violent revolution. Indeed, the *Bildungsroman* story form—those Tambu reads and Dangarembga's novel itself—appears to make the *Chimurenga* literally avoidable. In narrating Tambu's story within the *Bildungsroman*'s general conventions, the novel makes a double human rights claim in its attempt to reconstruct and resocialize Tambu—to regroup her as a synecdochal instance of Shona self-determination and developmental capacity. The split narrative personality vivifies the historical discrepancy between the rhetoric and practice of self-determination and human rights in Southern Rhodesia, and it articulates a demand for the right to collective and individual self-determination with development, where the "cultivatable" might become "cultivators" of plots that "yield harvests to sustain" themselves.[101]

Written and published after Zimbabwe's independence, the novel has been enjoined to perform the *Bildungsroman*'s traditional civilizing mission to catalyze development and self-determination through its promotion by the ex-colonial Literature Bureau, whose postcolonial mandate includes disseminating "[m]aterial for new literates . . . [that] reflects Zimbabwe's national goals and priorities . . . [and] act[s] as a vehicle for the social, economic, cultural and political transformation of the nation."[102] Thus, as Heather Zwicker observes, the novel becomes an instrument of "national literacy," whose social tutorial effect is intended "to school citizens in the language of nationalism" and to "cultivat[e] particular kinds of national subjects."[103] We might therefore read the novel's self-sustaining architecture of narrative self-sponsorship in terms of a traditional topos of the genre: a recursive scene of reading (in which a *Bildungsheld* reads others' *Bildungsromane*) that Benedict Anderson regarded as the literary symbolic confirmation of the imagined national community.[104] The novel literalizes this structure, with the diegetic split, as a scene of self-reading in which the narrator reads, revises, and historicizes her own *Bildungsroman*. To some degree, this self-contained structure of autoliteracy that produces both a *Bildungsroman* and its own reader is necessitated by the historical lack of Zimbabwean *Bildungsromane* and the imposition of "misplaced" British *Bildungsromane* in the curriculum of Southern Rhodesia. This reflexive structure of narrative self-sponsorship abstracts the self-reflexive democratic dynamics of a projective Zimbabwean popular sovereignty, and the novel retrospectively prefigures in some way the "institutions that stood in for the political institutions yet to be, . . . forming citizens in anticipation of the founding of the state of which they were to be citizens," as David Lloyd has described the historical role of literature in the colonial Irish context.[105]

Although the ascension to self-determination potentially opens plots of development for young Zimbabweans that were unavailable to Tambu in Southern Rhodesia, the novel's treatment of Zimbabwean national history and the *Chimurenga* does not readily foster a sense of national historical consciousness. Susan Andrade has suggested that the novel's historical allusions may be recognizable only by "a reader already familiar with Zimbabwean history [who] might be aware that a historical narrative undergirds the more literary tale."[106] Indeed, this history enters the novel as obliquely as it might have entered a colonial Rhodesian classroom in the 1960s and 70s. That is, for readers (like Tambu and Nyasha themselves) tutored in *Oliver Twist*, *Jane Eyre*, *Middlemarch*, and perhaps some "historical" African texts written by missionaries and European travelers,[107] the fleeting intimations of historical context represent and reperform some of the very pitfalls in the way of acquiring a Zimbabwean national consciousness that the protagonists themselves struggle with as students of the same dislocated anglocentric curriculum. When, in the 1960s, the Cambridge Syndicate proposed an alternative syllabus that included "the Rise of Modern African Political

Consciousness," the Rhodesian Ministry of Education rebuffed them, arguing in the idealist language of *Bildung* that such "local" topics tended "to militate against" the cultivation of "children's own consciousness, . . . their inward development, the awakening of their creative faculties as subjects and not just objects of the universe, capable of making and re-making the world."[108] If colonial education seeks to produce a subject outside of itself—outside of (its) history—then the historico-narrative gap in the novel replicates the difficulty of historical emergence in a place where history has not yet become one's own.

As Zwicker notes, *Nervous Conditions* circulates not only in a literary economy "regulated by . . . the Literature Bureau within Zimbabwe," but also in a broader economy regulated largely by "the international women's press and its attendant feminist vision."[109] But, for both national and international readers, the novel's complex narrative structure should trouble its easy consumption as an emancipatory tale of self-sponsored development and self-determination. The novel is, at least partly, a dissensual *Bildungsroman* about the allure of the consensual *Bildungsroman*, and this self-reflexive pattern (like that of narrative self-sponsorship) is taken to extraordinary formal heights in the text's vertiginous, *mise en abyme* layering of readers reading *Bildungsromane*. On top of the scene of Tambu-the-narrator reading Tambu-the-protagonist reading British *Bildungsromane*, the novel constructs another storey with its invocation of an implicated reader who shares the young Tambu's assumptions about development, modernization, and her taste for the *Bildungsroman*. Thus, the novel implicates that reader in the discursive structures of colonial domination and in the propagation of the romantic cultural narratives of self-determination that fascinated the young Tambu. If the *Bildungsroman* is an interactive social technology that performs for its reader the civicizing process that it narrates for its protagonist, the didacticism of Dangarembga's novel is as elliptical as its historical allusions. The novel does not tell of the "long and painful process" by which Tambu finally disabuses herself of the fairy tales of colonial development to become capable of seeing the story we are reading within a larger national and international system of sociopolitical relations of domination; rather, it reperforms for the implicated reader the difficulties obstructing that process of disabusement. Indeed, given the narrative gap, it might be said that the novel does not explain anything at all, at least not in terms of the ordinary conventions of the *Bildungsroman*. The surface plot reproduces the seductions of the idealist *Bildungsroman*, conforming Tambu's story to the generic expectations and sociocultural prejudices of its implicated reader, until it abruptly refuses to deliver the cultural and civil incorporation that the narrative form and Tambu anticipate. If, as Susan Fraiman has hypothesized of female *Bildungsromane* generally, "[t]he improbability of the *Bildung* plot . . . heighten[s] its appeal for the heroine and for female writers and readers," part of what Tambu has to unlearn in order to become her own narrator in the patriarchic colonial context is the appeal of the genre and its distortions of social reality.[110] The novel therefore leaves its implicated reader where it leaves Tambu-the-student: with no more than a seed of suspicion about the relationship between the cultural narratives of self-determination and the historical "nervous conditions" of the natives. It makes readers responsible for plotting the "loose connections" between the conventional, postcolonial, female *Bildungsroman* of the surface plot and the sardonic voice of the narrator in the submerged plot—for articulating the relations that an aphasic Tambu could not and for disabusing themselves of hyperbolic, ahistorical fantasies of unilateral self-determination.

Human Rights Literacy: Scenes of Narrative Recognition and Self-Determination

> Education (*Erziehung*) is to educate oneself; cultivation, or formation, (*Bildung*) is self-cultivation. . . . Cultivation (*Bildung*) cultivates itself. . . . All that is involved here is what has already formed itself in a hidden way.
>
> —HANS-GEORG GADAMER, "Education is Self-education"

> To recognize the individual as a person is to respect her power for self-determination.
>
> —DRUCILLA CORNELL, *Just Cause*

Both thematically and formally, Dangarembga's *Nervous Conditions* underscores the conspicuous role that reading plays in the formation of human personality in the *Bildungsroman*, whose traditional protagonists are, like Tambu, not only "avid readers" of literary texts but "intensive readers of their own lives."[111] It may be the case generally that "in post-colonial novels of development reading almost prevents development";[112] however, in Dangarembga's novel, the narrator's act of rereading the events of Tambu's life becomes a strategy for undoing the effects of Tambu's reading of *Bildungsromane*. Like Tambu, the implicated reader is urged to learn, from the submerged plot, to unlearn the generic expectations that predetermine our reading of the surface plot as an affirmative *Bildungsroman*. In presenting the reader with some of the same interpretive challenges that face the young protagonist, the novel rearticulates the didactic effect of the classical *Bildungsroman*, "which aims to convince the reader of the legitimacy of a particular interpretative framework, bringing her or him to a cumulative and retrospective understanding of the events narrated in the text."[113] Such a process of convincement amounts to a training in literacy, "a training as a reader of narrative" that involves tutoring in the operations and meaningfulness of a particular syntax of emplotment.[114] Contemporary human rights law envisions an analogous pedagogy that educes a human rights literacy by which the individual learns, also retrospectively, to recognize itself and others as human rights persons—a literacy whose acquisition the law posits as the culmination of free and full human personality development. This reading project is perhaps most clearly legible in the notion and act of recognition in the human rights documents.

Replicating the dialectical temporality of tautology and teleology that I have traced throughout this book, human rights law recognizes that the human personality and dignity have substantial existence prior to the law that are also enabled through the law. "Recognition" becomes a consummative speech act, modeled concisely in the "therefore" that transitions between a document's preamble and the text of its articles; it thus combines the two primary speech acts of human rights law: preambular constatation and articular declaration. Like the diplomatic recognition of a state or an emissary, human rights' recognitive speech act simultaneously confirms the existence of a prenominated entity and confers upon it a certain positive, official legitimacy that invests it with a corresponding set of rights and duties. In other words, it both acknowledges and activates an existential condition, endorsing and bringing into effect a status and set of capacities that the recognized object presumably already has, even if it does not yet enjoy them. The speech act of recognition makes historical what the law posits as natural or transcendental.

Across the body of international human rights law, this structure forms the basis of its self-referentiality; over the sixty years of human rights legislation, these speech acts of recognition function cumulatively as self-consummating acts of legal reading. In the two 1966 covenants, for example, the objects of reading are not only the dignity and human personality projected in the UDHR (1948), but also the text of the UDHR itself. Thus, the UDHR characterizes "recognition of the inherent dignity and of the equal and inalienable rights of all members of the human family" as the essential precondition for the realization of human rights and the "foundation of freedom, justice and peace in the world." In contrast, the two 1966 covenants convert this legal pretext into a temporally (and grammatically) progressive activity by "*Recognizing* that these rights derive from the inherent dignity of the human person. . . ." The legally binding covenants actively recognize (both confirm and redeclare) the human personality's dignity as both the fundamental condition and consummation of human rights that the nonbinding UDHR aspired to make recognizable. Perhaps more neatly than the elaborate relay of readings of *Bildungsromane* presented in *Nervous Conditions*, this recursive act of self-reading and self-citation completes a rhetorical event of self-recognition, closing the hermeneutic circle of the law and formally reproducing the plot of inherency-in-becoming that the law projects for the human personality. The human rights documents routinely repeat this act of self-recognition in an effort to make the law self-substantiating by making it formally self-referential—that is, tautological and sovereign, not dependent upon the traditional extratextual guarantors of natural and positive law. In the human rights treaties, the double recognitive speech act of confirmation and declaration labors to realize the legal self-sufficiency and rhetorical independence of "the rule of law" that is supposed to protect human rights (UDHR).

As important as the "juridical revolution"[115] that international human rights law represents is the epistemic (or sentimental) revolution that it undertakes in transforming the terms through which the individual frames its relation not only to national and international society, but also to itself. In its didactic capacity, human rights law thematizes the recursive process of reading that it models. The rhetorical structure of self-reading, which advances the formal sovereignty of human rights law, articulates the process of human rights literacy that the law prescribes for the human person, to whom it assigns responsibility for the act of self-recognition. Self-reading becomes a crucial part of the plot of human personality development in the ICESCR (1966), which makes primary education free and compulsory; more poignantly, the ICESCR charges states to ensure that "education shall be directed to the full development of the human personality *and* [of] *the sense of its dignity*, and shall strengthen the respect for human rights and fundamental freedoms . . . [and] that education shall enable all persons to participate effectively in a free society, promote understanding, tolerance and friendship among all nations and all racial, ethnic or religious groups, and further the activities of the United Nations for the maintenance of peace" (Article 13.1, emphasis added). The state's obligation to provide an education for national and international citizenship is paired with a reciprocal obligation on the part of individuals to fully develop their human personality; the right to mandatory education further modifies the plot of human rights incorporation with the direction that such development entails also the full development of *a sense of* the human personality's dignity. In other words, the ideal of human personality development involves a training in human rights literacy that cultivates a sensitivity to the dignity of one's own (and others') human personality as well as a profound feeling for human rights—their project and fundamentality—more generally. Thus, the sentimental education of human rights *Bildung* becomes compulsory—an obligation of the individual (to the community and to itself) to learn to read, recognize, and respect the signs of (among others) the inherency of human dignity, the fundamental worth of the human personality, its capacity for self-determination, and its developmental potential.

If the two 1966 international covenants style themselves as payments on the promissory note of human rights that was taken out with the UDHR, the scenario of self-recognition takes the form of a promise made and kept. The tautological–teleological complex that underpins the structure of self-recognition, and its novelistic corollary, narrative self-sponsorship, also supplies the logic of the human rights pedagogy for inherency-in-becoming, which prepares the "natural" human person to recognize itself in the "artificial" person of human rights law. In other words, the goal of human rights literacy is to teach the human being to recognize the human person as its legal representative: the rightful and real bearer of international human rights and duties. Thus, the plot of free and full human personality development, for which the acquisition of human rights literacy represents the fulfillment of its promise, anticipates a time when the human rights person will have renaturalized for itself (as second nature) the natural-law categories of inherency and inalienability that the UDHR positivized when it dispensed with the traditional, transcendental guarantors of modern human rights law. In making the human personality and recognition of its dignity matters of cultivation, these promising forms of human rights situate the human person capable of bearing rights and duties as their product in the mode of a subject-yet-to-come—a subject not-yet-fully capable of recognizing the inherent dignity of the human personality nor itself as a person before human rights law. In this sense, the human personality that the law posits as sovereign in its enabling fiction is not precisely a tautology because it is not *yet* a tautology—because the human person is not yet the human person of human rights.

The teleology of human rights personality development describes a progressive project of learning to recognize what one already is by right, but this process of recognition is figured in the later human rights documents specifically in terms of a responsibility that links reading to writing, recognition to narrative. The self-saying, self-incorporating citizen-subject that the law anticipates is itself predicated upon a reading proficiency in the semiotics of human dignity and the human personality, but this human rights literacy is only acquired through the social apprenticeship of human personality development figured according to the trope of incorporation. We can understand this plot of incorporation as a narrative responsibilization of the human person: human rights intends to educe in its incorporated citizen-subjects—as part of the process of becoming those citizen-subjects—a personal sense of responsibility for the figurative act of incorporation itself. Thus, human rights law makes individuals not only responsible for the plot of development (mediated through the nation and the community to which they have duties); it also obliges them to do so in narrative rather than in violent modes of self-determination. This, then, is the primary duty that the human rights person owes to the community and its law for enabling free and full human personality development; it is the fundamental sociocivil imperative from which the others derive: to recognize itself (and others) in the figurative work of the law, in its plot of human personality development, and to accept personal responsibility for that plot by occupying the role of the narrator in the human rights story of personality development. This recursive narrative structure makes the individual retroactively responsible for having become the bearer of international human rights and responsibilities that, in principle, it always already was.

The paradoxical temporality of this narrative of responsibilization and self-recognition obeys the generic Hegelian laws of all enabling fictions and narratives of subjectivation, which represent a circular "process that attains its true beginning only in its completion."[116] This is the impossible narrative grammar of the free and full development of the human personality that the conventions of the first-person *Bildungsroman* render and aspire to make sensible. This is also the vision that seduced the young Tambu and whose constructedness the older Tambu historicizes by recognizing its situational dependence on a particular set of social formations and relations—specifically, that its narrativity consists of "representational practices by which society produce[s] a human subject peculiarly adapted to the conditions of life in the modern *Rechsstaat*."[117] I will return at the end of this section to the first-person *Bildungsroman*'s elaboration of narrative self-sponsorship and its relationship to the imperatives in international law of human rights literacy and narrative responsibilization. But it is important to note that human rights law treats the grammar of inherency-in-becoming not merely as the fictional form of a story told in retrospect about citizen-subjectivation but as the form of the process itself—a process reenacted in each tautological–teleological speech act of self-recognition that simultaneously asserts a narrative claim to human rights and assumes responsibility for them.

In strict narratological terms, the teleological line of development is proper to the *fabula* (the series of transformational story events as they "really happened") and is emplotted tautologically in the *sjuzet* (the version of those events as they are organized in the narrative for meaning or effect).[118] However, in its idealized version of the human-personality-development narrative, human rights law makes no distinction between the *fabula* and the *sjuzet*; that is, the historical process of incorporation and its narrative representation are complementary and coextensive facets of a single grammatical pattern, imagined to unfold in perfect parallel, repeating the same biographical events in the same order. These two diegetic levels of the idealist narrative are distinguished not by their content or organization but by the responsibility that the law distributes differently for each. Thus, the *fabula* is construed as the product of nature, the irresistible progression of the human personality to its freest and fullest expression in the figure of the self-narrating citizen-subject, whose development is motivated by an inherent force of the human personality. Whereas the citizen-subject is ostensibly produced as an effect of the *fabula*, the plotting of this story in the *sjuzet* assigns responsibility for that process to the citizen-subject itself, who confirms its incorporation with an obliging narration of the story of citizen-subjectivation. The law treats both the process that configures the citizen-subject of human rights and its narrativization that formally recognizes (confirms and produces) the human rights person as if they were the products of positive personal effort. Thus, human rights project a complete correspondence between the *fabula* and the *sjuzet*, the responsibility for which they attribute, after the event, to the personal will and agency of the citizen-subject. The social contract imagined in human rights law may be universal and entered (in the classical mode) before will, but the corollary narrative contract that follows from it requires a self-recognitive story about the process in which the individual assumes retroactive responsibility for having entered into the rights and duties of personhood by describing its enfranchisement as the consummation of its own personal anticipation. In other words, the individual joins the speech community of human rights readers (for whom the dignity of the human personality is presumably already legible) by narrating the mandatory story of incorporation as if it were the result of personally orchestrated desire and design. This is the compulsion of human rights literacy: the already-incorporated human rights person must articulate a narrative speech act of self-recognition by which the citizen-subject consents to be civically—

and thereby to take personal responsibility for—what it was otherwise (inevitably and imprescriptibly) by natural right.

The human rights legal process of narrative responsibilization has its formal correlative in the first-person *Bildungsroman*'s conventional structures of narrative self-sponsorship and self-determination, in which the narrator emplots the story of how she or he "consented" (in the Gramscian sense) to assume narratorial responsibility for that story. "The paradox of emplotment," writes Paul Ricoeur, "is that it inverts the effect of contingency . . . by incorporating it in some way into the effect of necessity or probability exerted by the configuring act."[119] In this sense, the narrator is a plotting device that converts the contingency of personality development into fatality, standing surety for the protagonist against the risks that she may not survive the figurative process of incorporation or, if she does, that she may not "recognize [her]self after having taken so many confusing [turns]" (as Tambu writes).[120] The structure of narrative self-sponsorship that responsibilizes the subject puts the narrator in a position homologous to that which Nature and the Sovereign occupied in natural and positive law. The narrator functions as a discursive surrogate for fate and the state, underwriting the human rights tautologies by ensuring that the protagonist becomes (and recognizes herself as) the narrator-protagonist–citizen-subject that she already was from the first words of the novel. In this sense, the narrative speech act of self-recognition in both the literature and law positions the narrator-protagonist as a citizen-subject *derrière la lettre*—that is, behind the plot, both coming after (or emerging from) it and organizing it, in a Society-of-the-Tower-like conspiratorial sense. Indeed, the retrospective narration formally substantiates the protagonist's proleptic claim (or promise) to have personally willed and ordered its plot of citizen-subjectivation. This was the presumptive leap of narrative faith that the young Tambu made in prematurely imagining herself as the singular agent (central subject)—both participant and beneficiary—of her own development.

One of the virtues of the *Bildungsroman*—and the reason why I suggest that this generic "carrier . . . of humanist ideology" has been doing some of the cultural work that the law cannot do for itself to make human rights tautologies compelling[121]—is its technical capacity to make the convoluted, esoteric, and improbable narrative grammar of citizen-subjectivation not only legible but ordinary, so ordinary that it often goes unremarked, seeming merely to conform to common sense. In fact, part of the historical literary social work of the *Bildungsroman* is to naturalize and universalize the impossible temporality and contorted conceptual grammar of human rights personality development, so that the rules of its composition appear commonsensical—becoming, as it were, second nature. This is the emancipatory process of citizen-subjectivation that human rights law tacitly constructs as narrative self-determination—the "freedom to pursue a story line, a life plot."[122] The first-person *Bildungsroman* represents the acquisition and exercise of this freedom as a transfer of "the operation of emplotment" from the narrator to the protagonist that makes the "identity of the character" of the narrator-protagonist "comprehensible"—that is, that accounts for its self-personifying capacity to act as its own narrator.[123] The conventional structure of this novelistic dénouement, which is telegraphed by the presence of the fully capacitated narrator-protagonist at the opening of the novel (and thereby undercuts the Aristotelian element of surprise in the recognition scene that constitutes the climactic moment of the third-person idealist *Bildungsroman*), rejoins the developmental circle of citizen-subjectivation by transforming the right to plot into a responsibility to narrate the already-completed story of human personality development as if it were a voluntary expression of the individual's newly acquired freedom to plot.

Traditionally, the *Bildungsroman* posits as the culmination of modern subjectivation the cultivation of a democratic, humanitarian sensibility—a profound fellow-feeling that enables the *Bildungsheld* to recognize the equal humanity and fundamental dignity of the human personality in both the self and others. It is through this social training in human rights literacy, narrated in the idealist *Bildungsroman* as the proper career of the modern subject, that "the abstraction of personality in a formal legal sense is achieved."[124] The acquisition of human rights fluency climaxes in a recognition scene in which the individual formally recognizes itself as a subject of human rights—as one subject among others—and this discovery (or *anagnorisis*) typically corresponds to the moment when the protagonist assumes responsibility for its narrative. In Goethe's novel, for example, Wilhelm receives the consecration of his citizenly virtues and his articles of apprenticeship at the same time that he becomes aware of the existence of the Society of the Tower and its massive collection of similar indentures, of which his is only a small part. Thus, the (self-)recognition scene—the moment of personification (or incorporation) when the individual becomes conscious of being a subject to and for the rules of law and narrative—is also a moment when the abstract symmetricalness of the law reveals itself; that is, ideally, the newly incorporated citizen-subject becomes aware of "the right [of everyone] to recognition everywhere as a person before the law" (UDHR). The *Bildungsroman* seeks to disarm the surprise and forestall the tragic reversals (*peripeteia*) that attend the scene of recognition in classical drama by plotting a smooth evolutionary process of self-recognition, over the course of which the individual progressively encounters its own inner nature in the objective, conventional world of law and society.[125] But in *Nervous Conditions*, the anticipated *anagnorisis* remains unnarrated, perhaps because Tambu's recognition of what she has become is "painful," maybe even tragic.[126] This peripety precipitates Tambu's refusal to accept full narrative responsibility for the conventional plot of the *Bildungsroman*, effectively rejecting the limited terms of incorporation prescribed by the sociopolitical discourse and practice of native development in Southern Rhodesia. Nonetheless, the novel's story grammar of narrative self-sponsorship ultimately demonstrates Tambu-the-narrator's fluency in human rights (gained outside the text) with her insights about the various systemic forms of violation of the dignity, self-determination, and developmental potential of the human personality in the patristic colonial context.

The pedagogical logic of human rights literacy can help us better grasp the implication of the reader within the *Bildungsroman* structure of narrative self-sponsorship and self-determination. Unlike third-person *Bildungsromane*, in which linear plot appears to round out the complexity of the protagonist's personality that was only implicit at the beginning of the novel, in first-person *Bildungsromane* the full complexity of personality is conventionally present in the *Bildungsheld* before the story of its rounding even begins. The plot of personality development is elaborated for the benefit of the reader and the narrator, who is also a reader and is making sense of the narrated events. With its re-presentation of the process by which the protagonist becomes the narrator-protagonist introduced at the beginning of the *Bildungsroman*, the form accustoms the reader to the subjective plot dynamics of modernization—to the reflexive grammar of anticipation and retrospection that character-izes the emergence and narrative performance of citizen-subjectiv-ity. For the tutelary effect to work, fate must appear as chance—the foregone conclusion must be treated as if it were still in doubt—so that the reader (like the protagonist) moves through the plot with what Peter Brooks calls an "anticipation of retrospection," awaiting a time when the events of the narrative will have assumed meaning, but (also like the protagonist) already accepting proleptic responsi-bility for the necessarily retrospective construction of that mean-ing.[127] The narrator, of course, already possesses the experience and literacy that the reader and protagonist require to make sense of the narrative, and the usually inevitable consummation of the antici-pated moment of meaningfulness where the *fabula* and *sjuzet* inter-sect (foretold from the very beginning) is enacted in the handover of plot responsibility from the narrator to the now-capacitated nar-rator-protagonist. This handover also entrusts the reader with re-sponsibility for the plot—with the interpretive capacity "to go about the construction of the text's specific meanings . . . [and] to grasp past, present, and future in a significant shape."[128] Tutelage in the narrative grammar of inherency-in-becoming is also tutelage (of the reader and the protagonist) in human rights literacy that develops and exercises the proleptic and analeptic imagination nec-essary for projectively recognizing the dignity of the human person-ality in both the self and the other—that is, for recognizing individuals as the human rights persons they always were. The re-flexive, socializing structure of this form and temporality images an improbable human rights legal creature that the first-person *Bildun-gsroman* accustoms us to regard as ordinary: an already-incorpo-rated citizen-subject perpetually awaiting citizen-subjectivation but already accepting responsibility for that process in advance of its own figuration.

Contemporary human rights law, like the classical *Bildungs-roman*, idealizes a process of narrative self-(re)formation as the so-cially acceptable mode of citizen-subjectivation. This process is imagined to obviate the need for violence in the assertion and ex-pression of an individual's and a people's self-determination. But when the irresistibility of human development and narrative self-determination become obligations, the human rights imperative has the potential to turn violent. In the final section of this chapter, we see the predicament of the *Bildungsroman* and human rights in the context of apartheid South Africa, where the compulsion of self-determination reverts to coercion, the responsibility for narrative subjectivation becomes a liability, and the obligation to recognize oneself as a person before the law produces a scene of forced recognition. With the perversion of a democratic order and the humanist language of *Bildung*, the *Bildungsroman* becomes dissensual—both a form imposed by force and a potential space of refuge from and redress of state violence against the noncompliant individual.

The Sense of No Ending: Torture and the Forced Narrative Links of Bildung in Christopher Hope's A Separate Development

> **"coloured person"** means any person other than a white person;
> **"white person"** means any person who in appearance obviously is or who by general acceptance and repute is a white person.
>
> —South African "Immorality Act"
> (1957, amended 1969)

The novelistic logic of plot is sustained, wrote Frank Kermode, only by a sense that the "end will bestow upon the whole duration and meaning."[129] If definitive meaning only emerges with the completion of a plot, "clos[ing] the sentence as a signifying totality,"[130] then the South African system of apartheid, as it operates in Christopher Hope's novel *A Separate Development* (1980), is a narrative regime obsessed with enforcing "endings," with hastening the end of meaning. "This is a statement of endings," writes Hope's protagonist, Harry Moto, in the opening pages of his *Bildungsroman*, a "statement of *fact*" produced under duress of torture in response to *the* question posed by apartheid: "Who are you the same as?"[131] Arrested on the pretext of having violated the Immorality Act, which regulated sex between the races, Harry finds that his real crime is the existential one of not conforming to "the great colour chart in the sky"—of not "belong[ing] to anything."[132] For a legal system that bristles at ambiguity, Harry is "a danger to the order of things" and a living oxymoron: a kinky-haired Catholic boy with an uncertain skin tone, breast buds, and a vaguely East Asian name. The apartheid authorities demand from Harry an account of the "odd case that I am" and "just what it is that I have done," which the chief of police, Dekker, describes as a reverse-progress narrative (a kind of regress narrative): the story of a boy who "started off life as white as wedding lace and ended up as some kind of kaffir."[133] As Harry sees it, the law's real regulative force is its "great powers of definition," by which apartheid's "enemies" are "classified, registered and consigned to one of the official, separate racial groups which give this country its uniquely rich texture."[134] Under a legal regime obsessed with racial purity, such power is exercised as much on the basis of "appearance" or "general acceptance" as on genealogy (as my epigraphic citation of the tautological "definitions" of race from the Immorality Act dramatically illustrates). Without an official "identity card," Harry's social and legal status is more-than-usually subject to the capriciousness of common opinion, which is delivered most succinctly by a bus driver who defines Harry's "identity" as a "white kaffir."[135] Apartheid perverts the developmentalist logic of inherency-in-becoming, policing the synecdochal relation between individuals and the groups into which they "fall naturally"; under its existential racial imperative to become what one already is by *sight*, Harry is consigned to "an identity in search of a group."[136]

"Nobody will deny that for the Native as well as for the European complete separation would have been the ideal if it had developed that way historically," opined future South African prime minister Hendrik Frensch Verwoerd to parliament just after his National Party assumed power in 1948, the same year that the UN adopted the UDHR, from which South Africa abstained on the grounds that many of the declared freedoms (of movement and assembly, for example) were not fundamental human rights.[137] At its inception, apartheid was rationalized as a humanitarian amelioration of the effects on the natives of cultural alienation and detribalization that the white man's mere presence in South Africa was supposed to have catalyzed. After its electoral victory, the National Party began legislating its "practical" solutions for a partial restoration of the "ideal" and "natural" segregation of the races, framing its policies of "apartness" (*apartheid*) in the humanist language of *Bildung*: "The party . . . desires to afford the non-European races the opportunity of developing themselves in their own fields, according to their . . . national character, [natural] abilities and destiny."[138] In practice, apartheid was a system of taxonomic laws designed to "purify" and stabilize the particular "personality" of each of South Africa's "racial groups" while insuring an ample supply of cheap black labor for white South Africa by regulating the public and private interactions between the "races." In its obsession with racial classification, apartheid codified an increasingly rigid system of legal personality that constructed the individual with differential and variable sets of rights and duties based on its assignment of racial identity (White, Bantu, Coloured, Indian) and on a correlative racialization of space: "The Native in our urban areas must be regarded as a 'visitor', who will never have the right to claim any political rights or equal social rights with the Europeans in the European areas."[139]

In the mid-1950s, the National Party formulated its racial and spatial regulations as a policy of "separate development" that provided the theoretical basis for the establishment of semiautonomous "homelands" in which black Africans would supposedly have, as the Tomlinson Commission celebrated, "the fullest opportunity for self-expression and development."[140] According to the organic logic of apartheid, groups (and their particular "natural" and "national characteristics") preexist and predetermine the individuals who compose them, and so the purity of apartness demanded not only a policing of group identity (both psychoaffective and geographical) but systems of socialization intended to produce group identification. Thus, in the name of modernization, apartheid was an antimodern legal practice of forced filiation, in which individuals were configured as sociocultural embodiments and carriers of racialized group characteristics.

Set during the years of Verwoerd's prime ministership (1958–66), when the National Party had consolidated both its hold on power and the legislative and judicial instruments of "separate development," Hope's novel exposes the absurdities of what Rey Chow calls "coercive mimeticism," of compulsory personification and racialized incorporation.[141] The coercive effects of separate development register in the generic perversions of the plot in Harry's forced *Bildungsroman* that is *A Separate Development*. Published and banned in South Africa (for its depiction of the police), Harry's *Bildungsroman* is in many ways a novelistic elaboration of Althusser's thesis that the Repressive State Apparatus intervenes to discipline "bad subjects" when the Ideological Apparatus (schools, churches, and literature) fails to "recruit" properly interpellated subjects who work "all by themselves."[142] In Harry's case, the *Bildungsroman* joins the Repressive State Apparatus to give organizational form and predetermined meaning to his confessional statement, which tenuously strings together aleatory "things . . . not connected except in time" into a narrative series of "accident[s] that turned out to be a career."[143] Harry formally embarks on his "career" as an apartheid pariah at his high school matric celebration, when the discrepancy between his racially ambiguous body and his white upbringing becomes critical; his disastrous attempt to straighten his hair brings "into the open a dreadful secret that my parents must have known about and tried to hide."[144] Although the "question of skin colour" had been a source of some mild anxiety throughout his childhood, it is his failed attempts to conform to the phenotypic expectations of whiteness that publicly "broadcast" his social aberrancy.[145] Harry's skin condition receives its definitive diagnosis when, during an intimate moment with his girlfriend (whose father is "convinced that it's only a matter of time before [she's] raped" by an "African"), the schoolmaster startles the young couple, and she confirms both her father's "mad prophecy" and Harry's father's worst fear by yelling "rape";[146] the outcry fixes Harry's social identity as a black man and publicly indicts him for his ontological crime.

An apartheid outlaw, Harry goes on the run, with dreams of "achieving that invisibility I so admired in the [black] cleaners at [school]," which he imagines to be "nature's gift to your common or garden kaffirs."[147] In pursuit of a social and vocational invisibility to match his lack of legal personality, Harry stumbles into a series of jobs in which he becomes increasingly invisible, not just to the official overseers of apartheid but to the ubiquitous "watching world" of properly interpellated, racialized citizen-subjects: his father, school friends, and teachers.[148] In Koelietown, he "passes" as a coloured errand boy for the Indian shopkeepers until he is hired as a shill for a Jewish skin-lightener salesman, for whom "the trouble with Harry" proves a virtue since he is "light enough to pass for white in the country hotels and yet dark enough to impress my customers" as a "successful kaffir" on whom "the bleach really worked."[149] Just before his arrest, Harry seems to have finally achieved his own menial ubiquity, staying out of sight in plain sight by blending into the social texture of the "invisible" black majority in his job as a roadhouse "tray collector"—"kaffir work" that requires an ability "to come and go like a shadow."[150] The trajectory of Harry's "separate development" is plotted as the cultivation of invisibility—a staging of his own social and civil death with his successful apprenticeship in racial mimicry. Harry's "career . . . of being different," as the police chief describes it, is actually a career of impersonation, of fitting in—forever passing but never proper.[151] His existential crime against apartheid is his extraordinary racial and spatial mobility—his capacity to pass without an official pass.

For some time, Harry manages to evade detection by the "dark forces" of apartheid, and his arrest results only from a series of fateful "accidents," in which, under torture, each of his ex-employers and racial mentors falsely implicate him as the "missing link" in their criminal activities; but the dark forces are obsessed with Harry as a "living link between separate but equal races," as "[l]iving proof that oil and water don't mix."[152] What the police chief, Dekker, requires of Harry is not "a 'statement' in the usual sense" but a "biography" that "documents in the fullest possible way everything that I have been, everything I am."[153] The account of himself that the law demands, and that it elicits through torture, is a statement of personal responsibility for being an apartheid "mutant." A "student, hygienist, and philosopher" of apartheid, Dekker is an avid reader of antiapartheid literature by authors like Trevor Huddleston and Alan Paton, and he expects Harry's *Bildungsroman* of social invisibilization to reveal the cracks in the ideological and repressive systems through which he slipped so that the regulatory and reproductive taxonomical instruments of apartheid might be refined.[154] The police anticipate from Harry's forced narration "a pattern [to] emerge which will enable others to work out just what it is that I have done."[155] This "poisonous, romantic notion," says Harry, is the "ultimate sentimentalism of a people increasingly desperate for a link, a connection with something—correction, with *anything*, that makes some sense." In fact, as the traditional *Bildungsroman*'s compulsion becomes coercion, Harry is forced to read and write his life by the codes of apartheid—to make his own "connections"; his coerced "confession" becomes an exercise in plotting—in canalizing the social critique and episodic, incidental plot structure of his *picaresque* experiences into the socially affirmative and intentional trajectory of the *Bildungsroman*. This forced "transformation of the 'picaro' into the 'confessor'" (or *Bildungsheld*) converts Harry's experience of apartheid's systemic social and racial exclusions into a story of his voluntary self-marginalization by tracing a direct line from his childhood to prison.[156] Harry's metaleptic narrative, which configures his detention and torture as the preposterously inevitable consequences of having accidentally "exposed" himself at a swimming pool as a child, is made plottable (and sensible) as a series of causes and effects only by the racial and social hermeneutics of apartheid.[157] That is, apartheid makes definitive narrative sense of the otherwise senseless, disconnected events that Harry is forced to plot as "a life."[158]

"Some things you get only from books," insists Dekker, as he gears up the literary ideological apparatus and repeats the injunction to have Harry's "story from his own lips," adding emphatically: "Knowledge is power."[159] The apartheid philosopher-policeman holds to the anodyne classical Greek notion (of which we too have failed to disabuse ourselves adequately) that torture produces "truth," maintaining an equation between confession and facticity.[160] This enabling fiction of torture underpins the UN's 1975 Declaration on the Protection of All Persons from Being Subjected to Torture and Other Cruel, Inhuman or Degrading Treatment or Punishment, which defines the practice as "any act by which severe pain or suffering, whether physical or mental, is intentionally inflicted by or at the instigation of a public official on a person for such purposes as obtaining from him or a third person information or confession, punishing him for an act he has committed or is suspected of having committed, or intimidating him or other persons" (Article 1.1). By positing violence to the body as a means to speech, torture obliterates the violence–speech dichotomy that human rights law tries to enforce and that the *Bildungsroman* tries to naturalize. But if the coerced "confession" is regarded as an act of "coming clean," as Dekker explains to Harry, its utility to the torturer rests less in its content than in the dissociative, disarticulative, and disincorporating "cleansing" effects of the confessional speech act: "It is not that the torturers get no information from their interrogation. . . . It is rather that the useless information they generate is rendered useful tautologically by being used *as though* it were valuable."[161] "The nonsense of torture," writes Ñacuñán Sáez, abides "a certain logic": "It is repeated, consistent, almost predictable, never exactly 'absurd.'"[162] Torture is predictable because the torture victim has been prejudged to be guilty, and torture seeks to confirm, through a coerced confession, that prejudgment—what the torturers think they already know. By this logic, what matters at the scene of torture is the speech act of confession—its form, or performance, rather than its content—which, by a sleight of voice, the torturer translates into an "insignia of [state] power."[163] The UN recognized this performative quality of the confession and sought, in the Convention Against Torture (1984), to weaken the information-retrieval logic that rationalizes torture. The convention limits the legal use of a confession in Article 15: "Any statement which is established to have been made as a result of torture shall not be invoked as evidence in any proceedings, except against a person accused of torture as evidence that the statement was made." The convention empties the confession of any informational content; confession under torture becomes a pure speech act, a performative tautology that, at least legally, attests only to the fact that the confessor has been tortured—that is, coerced speech becomes evidence only of coerced speech.

In forcing an individual to bear witness against itself, torture is self-destroying, dis-integrating the "physical and mental [systems] that people ordinarily maintain, mostly without thinking about it, to keep themselves together as independent beings" and dissociating the networks of social relations that make such individual "independence" meaningful.[164] Torture tends to effect an abnegating split between body and mind, making the one, as Elaine Scarry vividly explains, "emphatically and crushingly *present* by destroying it, and . . . the other . . . *absent* by destroying it."[165] Torture forces the victim to speak in a falsetto, adopted voice (often supplied by the torturers themselves) that says whatever it can to end the pain. Torture is therefore also subject-making, generating particular kinds of abnormal and abject subjects required to justify the work of the torturers, for whom the "confession" serves as a speech act of self-recognition that claims personal responsibility for the tortured individual's social abjection and thus for the torture (and its "legitimacy") itself.[166]

In Harry's case, the torture precipitates a forced recognition scene, in which Harry is to become in narrative what he already is by sight—an abject apartheid subject who is outside the sphere of civil rights; "I'd never be heard of again," he writes, and then remembers that, with his vocational invisibility, "I'd never been heard of again once *already*. . . . They'd just be making it official."[167] Harry is pressured to name names, but mostly he is compelled to name himself as a subject of apartheid law and thereby to take personal responsibility for his exclusion from the regime of white rights and for the law's powers of definition. The form imposed upon this self-incriminating narrative of (mis)identification is the *Bildungsroman*, which gives the shape of a fated career to the accidents of Harry's misfortune, individualizing the burden of apartheid's racial configurations and sociopolitical segregation. In other words, the *Bildungsroman*-as-confession superimposes the form and plot logic of narrative self-determination on the disparate effects that follow, as Harry says, from apartheid's systemic and "sacred belief in sundered, severed, truncated, fractured, split, divided, separate selves."[168] Ironically, here the force of torture is not directed to splitting the subject in the usual sense; rather, the coerced *Bildungsroman* confession seeks to reintegrate the Arendtian individual—to bring Harry back under the spell of apartheid law, if only as a disenfranchised criminal. Nothing is to be left outside the scope of apartheid's comprehensive racial and spatial legislation, and the police seek to make Harry's narrative identity match his body, so that apartheid's "insanity will be miraculously proved to be wise policy."

"Meaning," insists Harry's torturer and primary reader, "is what other people make of things."[169] The conflict between the demands of the state and the freedom of the individual that Hope stages in an apartheid torture chamber is a contest over the right to make meaning of the events of Harry's life and ultimately a struggle over the norms and form of the *Bildungsroman* itself. The perverse irony of Hope's novel is that the apartheid police are asking little more of the *Bildungsroman* form than that it perform its traditional social work to legitimate the state's legal norms. Like its abuse of the humanist rhetoric of *Bildung*, human rights, and self-determination to rationalize the segregationist policies of "separate development, or parallel freedoms, or equal opportunities,"[170] the apartheid regime conscripts the historically democratic form of the *Bildungsroman* to substantiate its antidemocratic norms, to validate the legal tautologies that incorporate the individual with racialized rights and responsibilities, and to make this racialized apartheid nonsense compelling. The traditional didactic role of the *Bildungsroman* is perverted into a form of reeducation imposed to forcibly tutor Harry in an apartheid, rather than a human rights, literacy.

When Dekker dismisses Harry's "serious charge" that his statement has been produced under torture with the claim that it was "done . . . of your own free will, . . . [w]ithout pressure from us," Harry vows to "put it into writing."[171] Harry is well aware that the story he narrates is artificial, whose value, for both him and his torturers, lies not in its content but in the act and fact of its telling. A master of forms, Harry cannily mimics the literary conventions that the police expect, capitalizing on the torturers' conflation of confession and truth and on the *Bildungsroman*'s historical complicity with state power to articulate his human rights claim. But, because he realizes that "as long as I have a story to tell, life goes on," he tries to separate the conventional form, or performance, of the *Bildungsroman* from its content.[172] If Harry's narrative voice assumes the confessional falsetto of the torture victim in the surface plot of his *Bildungsroman*, the submerged plot indicts the apartheid regime in *sotto voce*—under his narrative breath, as it were. While the surface plot superficially satisfies the demands of his torturers with a metaleptic narrative of self-determination that appears to take personal responsibility for the figurative work of apartheid law with a forced recognition of the "odd case that I am," the submerged plot undermines the conventional *Bildungsroman* narrative by stressing the absurdity and compulsory character of its plot connections, thereby reversing the ordinary logic of plotting itself. The submerged indictment undoes the certainty and inevitability of novelistic plot, literally decomposing the form's anticipated fatality into contingency in an attempt to forestall the sense of its ending. Thus, Harry underscores the hypothetical, metaleptic, performative aspects of his self-saying, self-naming, self-responsibilizing narrative; "Let's say it began . . . ," begins his dissensual *Bildungsroman* confession, but this is his consummate act of passing—a strategically contrived novelistic opening that alerts the reader to its artificiality.[173] Harry converts confession into testimony, reversing the polarity of the *Bildungsroman*'s assignation of responsibility. Harry thereby recodes his confessional speech act as the "statement of fact" that he ambiguously declared it to be at the beginning of his narrative, an affidavit that attests not to the "facts" of "everything that I have been" but to the fact that he has been tortured—to the fact that he has been forced to narrate his experience of disenfranchisement as a "life."[174] The surface fiction of the *Bildungsroman* smuggles into the record the submerged fact of his torture; in the end, Harry takes advantage of the imposed novelistic form to obvert its traditional work of social legitimation and file a charge of human rights abuse. Harry empties the genre of its ordinary symbolic content; his forced speech becomes a tortured performance of confession—his coerced *Bildungsroman* becomes evidence only of a coerced *Bildungsroman*.

"I am the beginning and the ending," writes Harry at the end of his narrative, simultaneously imaging himself as apartheid's sacrificial lamb and asserting his continued defiance of the state by rejecting the isolating, segregationist plot of separate development and reconnecting the developmental circle of narrative self-sponsorship. However, Harry narrates his *Bildungsroman* as a story of depersonalization and disincorporation, in which he appears to "consent" to play the role of the narrator in the cultural narrative of separate development, as if it were the expression of his "own free will," but he undercuts the naturalness (and naturalizing) of the form and resists its stabilizing, finalizing injunctions. Harry composes his statement by the dictates of the conventional, first-person *Bildungsroman*'s narrative grammar to avoid his physical decomposition under torture: "I shall write until I drop. . . . While I write I'm safe. . . . While it goes on I will *never* stop."[175] As Sherezade manipulated the story cycle and Penelope exploited the material quality of weaving to forestall a definitive end, Harry turns to his advantage the narrative technology of the *Bildungsroman*'s circular linearity to keep the dark forces absorbed with "Harry on the paper" so that they might ignore "Harry in the flesh, . . . the form to which I'm especially attached."[176] Harry exploits the reality effect of fiction to invisibilize himself within the story space and paper time of the first-person *Bildungsroman*; in other words, he disappears behind the mask of the artificial literary and legal person that his narrative confession constructs, counterfeiting a story of self-recognition to survive in the device of its diegetically split personality. The narrative structure of self-sponsorship becomes not a sign of the individual's self-sufficiency or self-determination, but a symptom of its vulnerability—a desperate act of narrative self-preservation. Ironically, this protective, self-sustaining narrative is necessitated by a predatory legal regime that both refuses to recognize any real right of black African self-determination and is all-too-eager to sponsor the end of Harry's imposed separate development.

The addition of self-determination and development to the collection of internationally recognized human rights transformed the archetypal thematic conflict between man and society into a contest of competing human rights claims by assigning those rights to both nations and individuals who make up nations. In theory, international law made the state and the individual human person coequal partners in the struggle for self-determination and the pursuit of development; in practice, it reinforced the primacy of the state as "the privileged apex of a form of collective identity" and the only legitimate "structural expression of democratic self-determination."[177] During the Cold War, the legal and moral obligation to develop one's "human and natural resources" (repeated in the socioeconomic structural adjustment demands of institutions like the World Bank and the International Monetary Fund) often became an excuse for the state's curtailment of individual human rights. As Arturo Escobar writes, "development grew to be so important for Third World countries that it became acceptable [to the West] for their rulers to subject their populations to an infinite variety of interventions, to more encompassing forms of power and systems of control."[178] National development was reprioritized in the teleology of modernization; the individual's struggle for self-determination and personal development was again subordinated to the will of the state, and the realization of other human rights was deferred into a future when the socioeconomic conditions might be imagined capable of sustaining their norms. In this context, the imperative of modernization enjoins the individual to claim its rights to self-determination and development along the figurative lines of the Jamesonian "national allegory" as a micro-unit (or synecdoche) of the state's self-determination and developmental potential.

The conversion of a right to "free and full development of the human personality" into a state-mediated individual responsibility and obligation also reconfigures both the character of the historical alliance between human rights and the *Bildungsroman* and the novel's role in legitimating the structures and institutions of the nation-state. As we saw in Dangarembga's and Hope's dissensual *Bildungsromane*, the novel of incorporation becomes available as a technology not merely of ordinary democratic compulsion—a literary "vehicle for acquiring and exercising power"—but of extraordinary repressive coercion, one of many measures imposed in the name of human rights and development as part of the repressive forms of state power and systems of social control.[179] This corruption of the historical social work of the *Bildungsroman* takes advantage of the association between the literary form and human rights norms that I have been charting throughout this book to proffer an image of an egalitarian imaginary that is entirely fictional; the antidemocratic state abuses this complicity to give its sociopolitical deformations the stamp of democratic legitimacy. In other words, the form becomes purely formalistic—an ideology of the second degree that refers to and substantiates wholly nonexistent democratic norms. Yet, through a perverse bait and switch, the state attempts to claim this improper image of institutional legitimacy that the *Bildungsroman* fosters as its own.

If the *Bildungsroman* has the historical capacity to render legible a human rights vision of the world, it also has the capacity to falsify that vision and to obscure actually existing uneven social relations. The *Bildungsroman* is a situationally ambivalent novelistic technology that, as I have suggested, simultaneously naturalizes the terms of exclusion from the human rights franchise while normalizing the conditions of incorporation. In Dangarembga's and Hope's novels, for example, the literary genre naturalizes the nonsense of social, political, cultural, economic, and civil inequities by making the individual both the lone agent and sole beneficiary of its own development and self-determination—by making the individual singularly responsible for its own incorporation and disenfranchisement. In both cases, the literary form is enlisted to legitimate the dominant inegalitarian social relations and antidemocratic formations of the state by presenting an appearance of formal equanimity, of equal access to the socially acceptable narrative of human personality development, and of equal opportunity to become socially acceptable narrators.

Both human rights and the idealist *Bildungsroman* articulate visions of human personality development that valorize a process of narrative self-(re)formation as the proper mode of citizen-subjectivation and social self-expression, through which the individual is incorporated as a person into the nation-state and thereby recognized (confirmed and activated) as a subject of international rights and responsibilities. Thus, human rights law seeks to displace the act of collective violence that historically founds the rights-based nation-state with communicative speech acts, declarations of independence, and narrative self-determination. We can describe this configuration of the state/citizen bind in generic narrative terms as an effort to inaugurate an international order in which the epic no longer has any viable social work to perform. That is, if the epic is a story of collective self-determination, in which a body politic is founded on extreme acts of violence and a singular sense of national duty (emblematized by an extraordinary hero who excels at both) the *Bildungsroman* offers a prosaic vision of an ordinary individual who, through dialogue and social interaction, realizes its half-formed personal desire for incorporation by submitting to the discursive mechanics of self-determinative popular sovereignty to become one citizen-subject among others.[180] In this regard, both of the novels that I have examined in this chapter formulate narrative petitions for a national and international order in which the historically disenfranchised individual might plausibly stand as a legitimate representative of The People (and their collective potential for development and self-determination), in which the national allegory might be more than a stock, predetermined, Western reading practice for Third World *Bildungsromane* and become, rather, a legitimate novelistic institution of republican representation.

The cooperation of human rights and the *Bildungsroman* means that the novel form is an arena of political, social, cultural, and economic struggle, as Harry's confrontation with his torturers over the generic form of his confession and Tambu's hard-won demystification of its discriminatory ideology should remind us. Both novels have conflicted relationships with the *Bildungsroman*; the narrator-protagonists reject the genre's legitimating obfuscations and its ahistorical, universalist pretensions even as they affirm and lay claim to the humanist presuppositions of the form and the fundamental norms of human rights. Their appropriations of the form are cultural extensions of the *Chimurenga* and antiapartheid struggles for human rights and self-determination. As part of that emancipatory effort, both novels attempt to unsettle (or denaturalize) the ordinariness of the genre from within the genre itself by consistently disrupting the alliance of the *Bildungsroman* with cynical systems of power and social control and by stressing the historical contingency of its idealistic vision of social reconciliation. In doing so, these novels also attempt to resuscitate the literary form, to reclaim its legitimate social function, and thereby to demand the reformation of the state and the institution of human rights. This double-voicing, which is characteristic of the dissensual *Bildungsroman*, exploits the ironies and paradoxes that are reconciled in the consensual genre to expose the inequities institutionalized in discriminatory systems of social exclusion while making a claim for incorporation.[181] Narrative self-sponsorship here becomes a historicizing and socializing activity that defends against the isolating individualist assignation of personal responsibility that the Rhodesian and South African authorities sought to inculcate through the injunction to narrate a story of self-determination. The narrative of the acquisition of historical consciousness becomes (self-)reflexive, so that the development of historical consciousness entails a consciousness of the historicity of the forms of historical consciousness. In other words, the emergence of historical consciousness, which in both novels occurs outside the text's boundaries, becomes a consciousness of the sociopolitical complicity of the *Bildungsroman* with particular dispensations of power, which amounts to a consciousness of the contingency of the universal, hegemonic narrative of self-determination and human personality development promoted by human rights law. *Bildung* becomes *Bildung* of the second degree, in which the *Bildungshelden* affirm the right to free and full human personality development even as they recognize the historical uses and abuses of *Bildung*, the *Bildungsroman*, and the human rights discourse of self-determination and (personality) development. Both novels attempt to postpone the definitive ending that typifies the classical *Bildungsroman* by insisting upon the circularity of human personality development and reforming the tautological–teleological plot complex of human rights incorporation. Thus, these novels also insist upon "the sense of [no] ending," on the sense that avoiding preemptive, narrative closure makes in the struggle for human rights, self-determination, and development.

CHAPTER 5

Clefs à Roman: Reading, Writing, and International Humanitarianism

1. Everyone has the right to read.
2. Books are essential to education.
3. Society has a special obligation to establish the conditions in which authors can exercise their creative role.
4. A sound publishing industry is essential to national development.
5. Book manufacturing facilities are necessary to the development of publishing.
6. Booksellers provide a fundamental service as a link between publishers and the reading public.
7. Libraries are national resources for the transfer of information and knowledge, for the enjoyment of wisdom and beauty.
8. Documentation serves books by preserving and making available essential background material.
9. The free flow of books between countries is an essential supplement to national supplies and promotes international understanding.
10. Books serve international understanding and peaceful cooperation.

—Charter of the Book, UNESCO 1972

Humanitarianism: The Highest Stage of Human Personality Development

In a racially mixed school in a predominantly African-immigrant neighborhood of Paris, Mamadou Traoré, the young protagonist of

Calixthe Beyala's novel *Loukoum: The 'Little Prince' of Belleville* (1995), gets his first official lesson in international relations and French humanitarianism. "The world," instructs his teacher with the kind of Caesarean confidence and precision that once trifurcated Gaul, "is divided into developed countries and developing countries. The industrialised nations must help the poorest ones."[1] Appealing to the children's "generosity," "courage [gallantry]," and "sense of solidarity," Mamadou's teacher proceeds to recreate that world in microcosm within the classroom and to reenact the moment in 1948 when the International Bank for Reconstruction and Development (the World Bank) formulated an official definition of poverty, with which, "almost by fiat, two-thirds of the world's peoples were transformed into poor subjects."[2] Applying to the classroom the geopolitical logic of economic relations between states, Mademoiselle Garnier separates the children into groups of "developed" and "developing" nation-students with the intention of instituting a mentoring program to redress the educational disadvantages that, she says, arise from "culture, religion, and social differences."[3] A little white girl, suggestively named Lolita, disrupts the partitioning when she begins to disrobe, carefully placing her sweater, shoes and socks on the teacher's desk, to the approval of Mamadou who "hop[es] she'll also take off her dress."[4] When Mlle. Garnier intercedes, Lolita explains the international humanitarian logic of her divestment: "All I'm doing is handing you my contribution to help the underdeveloped countries, Mademoiselle. That's what my mum does with her organisations that send aid to poor countries." Mademoiselle clarifies the character of the donation she envisions: "The help we're asking for here is of the intellectual, not the material kind. Get dressed and sit down." The aid that Mademoiselle has in mind is literacy. Thus, she assigns to the "developing" Mamadou—who, "contrary to the French lifestyle," knows only how to read and write the Arabic of Koranic verses—a "developed" intellectual benefactor with the "face . . . of a little French boy in the time of kings and princes" to train him in the proper French of Antoine de Saint-Exupéry.[5]

In contrast to the English translation that I cite above, the French original of Beyala's novel, *Le petit prince de Belleville* (1992), parses differently the distinction between the assistance that Lolita's mother, as one of the world's "*plus favorisés*," renders to "poor countries" and the educational project that Mamadou's teacher proposes.[6] Instead of contrasting material aid (that ministers to the body) with intellectual relief (that ministers to the mind), Beyala's French text characterizes the distinction in temporal terms as the difference between a timely, pointed, but transient humanitarian assistance (*"aide ponctuelle"*) and the durable good of literacy.[7] That is, in contrast to the acuity and comestibility of material aid, literacy is configured as a gift that keeps giving. It is a technology, rather than a product, of development—an aspect and means, not merely an index, of modernization. Thus, intellectual intervention is imagined to initiate a sustained and sustainable development—a causal and consequential *plot* of personal and socioeconomic progress, rather than a single life-story *event*. Beyala's novel (despite the discrepant English translation) configures literacy as a technological bridge between material and immaterial development. Reading and writing are valorized both as tools for acquiring the knowledge necessary for socioeconomic advancement and as the primary media of modern transcendental personal fulfillment through the imaginative extension of the individual into the world.

Beyala's novel ultimately endorses, although it also problematizes and ironizes, a common assumption about the role of literacy as a link between the material (socioeconomic) and spiritual (cognitive–epistemic) aspects of modernization that reflects a modern democratic orthodoxy about the benefits and effects of reading and writing that coalesced over the course of the nineteenth and twentieth centuries, conjoining two post-Enlightenment conceptions of the organization, operation, and expectations of modern society itself. On the one hand, literacy is viewed as the communicative precondition of "modernity and rationality"—the necessary equipment not only for socioeconomic development but for the "establishment and maintenance of democratic institutions," as the literacy scholar Harvey Graff has written.[8] In this Weberian "functional conception of modernity" as organizational efficiency, literacy is valued as an instrumental modern(izing) technology—both the primary mode of communication that organizes social relations and the fundamental medium of civil and political participation in modern society.[9] On the other hand, literacy is also configured as a crucial component in an Enlightenment-liberative view of modernity that concerns "not the functionality of structures but the emancipation of individuals." This emancipatory view of modernity envisions literacy as a project of release from Kant's self-incurred tutelage—a primary means to enlightenment itself. These dual conceptions of the benefits and effects of literacy combine in the educational ideal articulated in the International Covenant on Economic Social and Cultural Rights (ICESCR: 1966), where a model of functional literacy that intends to "enable all persons to participate in a free society" coordinates with an emancipatory model of what I called in the previous chapter a human rights literacy that is directed to "the full development of the human personality and the sense of its dignity." This relation is reinforced in the Vienna Declaration and Programme of Action (1993), which encourages states "to eradicate illiteracy" and to "direct education towards the full development of the human personality and to the strengthening of respect for human rights and fundamental freedoms" (Article 79). The association of literacy with modernity, democracy, and liberty not only reifies reading and writing as keys to socioeconomic modernization—to a "fuller life . . . and to higher income"; literacy also comes to be regarded as a primary means to "greater independence and protection of the individual" and to "the full attainment of human rights"—the necessary equipment both for the enjoyment of human rights and for the articulation of a right to have rights.[10]

Literacy is bound with the other responsibilities delivered through the international legal formulation of a right to development that, as I discussed in the previous chapter, entails on the individual a double obligation: to develop one's human personality and to assist others with their own development. Thus, literacy is a part of the educational technology that is to be directed not only toward the free and full development of the human personality but also to the development of a sentimental sensitivity to the signs of the universal dignity of the human personality, in both the self and others. Indeed, the human rights legal formula of personality development from Article 29 of the UDHR that I examined in chapter 1 was rearticulated explicitly as a responsibility by the UN General Assembly on the occasion of the fiftieth anniversary of the UDHR in Article 18 of its weak Declaration on the Right and Responsibility of Individuals, Groups and Organs of Society to Promote and Protect Universally Recognized Human Rights and Fundamental Freedoms (1998): "Everyone has duties towards and within the community, in which alone the free and full development of his or her personality is possible," including a duty to develop that human personality.[11] In each of these formulations, the acme of human personality development is the voluntary assumption of responsibility to the other—the refinement of a humanitarian sensibility, a refinement most fully manifest in the idealized figure of the citizen-reader. Historically, the *Bildungsroman* similarly posits the cultivation of a democratic, humanitarian sensibility as the culmination of *Bildung*—the acquisition of a profound fellow-feeling necessary to appreciate human rights and to recognize the equal humanity and fundamental dignity of the human personality in the self and others. I have attempted to capture, and to telegraph, some of the problems with these valorizations of humanitarian sensibility in the subtitle to this section—"Humanitarianism: The Highest Stage of Human Personality Development"—which tropes on Lenin's *Imperialism: The Highest Stage of Capitalism* (1917). Humanitarianism is not, of course, the precise contemporary equivalent of classical imperialism, but, as I will argue throughout this chapter, they share enough structural features that they are, though imperfectly, homologous.[12] Similarly, although human personality development is obviously not the same as capitalism, it is inflected by and expressed within a heavily marketized international economy of both human rights and "world" literature. The rights to education and development entail humanitarian obligations both to become literate and to assist others with their own acquisition of literacy. Helping someone learn to read and write may be a humanitarian act, but, as I will argue, international human rights law and discourse, like Mamadou's teacher, construct a humanitarian model of reading that complements the scientific, functional model promoted in the international mass literacy campaigns of the mid-twentieth century. The humanitarian model, what Lynn Festa has called in another context a "sentimental model of reading," configures reading generally as the practice of a human rights literacy—an act of imaginative, affective "extension of humanity to hitherto disenfranchised subjects" including, as I have suggested, a self-reflexive extension of humanity to readers themselves.[13]

Within the programs of the international agencies of the UN (and for many NGOs), literacy also becomes one of the primary technologies for the production of what French critic and symbolist poet Paul Valéry, troping on the League of Nations, characterized as an international "League of Minds," an international community of mutual understanding.[14] The scene of Lolita's public undressing offers a comic allegory for the politics and dynamics of the redistribution of social, cultural, and economic goods and technologies entailed in "the full realization" of the international legal ideal of a world founded on "universal respect for and observance of human rights and fundamental freedoms" (UDHR). Literacy is thus valorized in international human rights discourse both as an essential technology for balancing the asymmetrical geopolitical conditions of an emergent international world system and as an engine of the internationalist teleologies of human personality and socioeconomic development imbricated in the articles of UNESCO's Charter of the Book that I have reproduced as an epigraph to this chapter. In the charter, "national development" and "international understanding and peaceful cooperation" seem to flow directly from the guarantee of an individual's "right to read," which comprehends both a libertarian right to be free from governmental interference in the practice of literacy and a social right to the resources necessary for the acquisition and enjoyment of literacy. Although literacy occupies a fundamental place within the rights to education and freedom of expression articulated in international law, UNESCO is characteristically more exuberant than the General Assembly in its promotion of literacy (and the book more specifically) as a "link between peoples and cultures," "a passport to the world," and the primary means of "initiation into today's society."[15] The Charter of the Book condenses these functions into an implicit plot of personality development; through the transformative powers of literacy, the individual journeys from singularity into a national community and from the nation into a cooperative international order of fellow readers.

This imagined international community of human rights holders is projected in the image, and by means of the literary and legal technologies, of the nation-state, based on an idealized model, and the enabling fiction, of a liberal public sphere as an egalitarian space of democratic intercourse. Indeed, the Enlightenment "master narrative" of emancipation presupposes, as Arjun Appadurai suggests, an integral "relationship between reading, representation and the public sphere."[16] This chapter considers the role of literacy (and literature more generally) in the projection and constitution of an international order based on the recognition and observance of human rights. More specifically, it examines the geopolitical and socioeconomic conditions, dynamics, relations, and formations out of which international literacy (as a sociocultural technology) and literature (as its artifactual product and object) are expected to coalesce. Universal literacy, it is imagined, would mitigate the asymmetry of global sociopolitical relations, yet an analogous asymmetry manifests itself in the unevenness of the international economies of literary and "human rights goods and services [as they are] produced, circulated, and 'consumed'" in our contemporary era of globalization.[17] The *Bildungsroman* is an international commodity shaped by the uneven forces of supply and demand and the market fortunes of human rights. I have described the production of the *Bildungsroman* as the culmination of a process of development in which a subject writes a novel, claims human rights, and thereby joins an imagined humanitarian community of readers. Such a process responds (perhaps only implicitly) to a developmental imperative that, under the current marketized configuration of the "global" literary industry, is often issued through the "soft" imperialist force of consumer demand by humanitarian readers based largely in the northern hemisphere. As I will argue, the Western "market reader" of *Bildungsromane* that are written in the global spaces of historical marginality literally buys in to the business of human rights through a practice of literary consumption that in turn intensifies an editorial demand for *Bildungsromane*.[18] As I demonstrate in my reading of Beyala's *Loukoum: The 'Little Prince' of Belleville*, these disproportionate international market relations are thematized and abstracted as novelistic form in many contemporary postcolonial *Bildungsromane* that offer a metacritique of the literary and human rights economies in which the books themselves are subsumed. That is, the contemporary global market dynamics that have commodified both human rights and the *Bildungsroman* constitute part of the uneven international conditions of (im)possibility for human personality development and its novelistic form of expression, conditions that these novels make legible in their narratives of an individual's (willing and unwilling) incorporation into an international society of readers—a "World Corporation of Letters, Ltd." that advertises itself in the egalitarian image of a "World

Republic of Letters" as the instantiation of "peaceful [intellectual] internationalism, a world of free and equal access in which literary recognition is available to all writers."[19]

Literacy in Development: Transfers of Technology, Technologies of Transfer

> TECHNOLOGY TRANSFER: Has been defined as 'the transfer of knowledge generated and developed in one place to another, where it is used to achieve some practical end.' Technology may be transferred in many ways: by giving it away (technical journals, conferences, emigration of technical experts, technical assistance programs); by stealing it (industrial espionage); or by selling it (patents, blueprints, industrial processes, and the activities of multinational corporations).
>
> *—International Relations Dictionary*,
> U.S. Department of State (1980)

Mlle. Garnier's physical and intellectual partition of the students is merely giving pedagogical expression to the lore of literacy scientized in the "modernization theory" of the mid-twentieth century: "that social and economic progress follow [or, are *almost sure* to follow, in Kant's phrase] from a change in persons from illiterate to literate."[20] In her implementation of this thesis, Mlle. Garnier duplicates in the classroom a paradigm of international relations that was, in part, derived from this "exaggerated estimation of the power of literacy" and normalized through the agencies of the UN. If the World Bank's 1948 definition of poverty redrew (or at least reshaded) the demarcations of the globe into masses of rich and poor peoples (nations), UNESCO's 1946 program for "Fundamental Education" institutionalized an equally dramatic bisection that mapped international geopolitical and socioeconomic disparity in terms of literacy. In the emergent globalist discourse of the UN, illiteracy assumes the character of an international problem; that is, illiteracy represents not merely a domestic impediment to modernization and the industrialization of individual nation-states but also a global obstacle to the smooth operations and socioeconomic dynamics of a projected world system based on human rights.

Describing the intellectual condition of the planet in Abraham Lincoln's menacing U.S. Civil War imagery as "a house divided against itself" that "[can]not stand," UNESCO Director-General Julian Huxley introduced the program for "Fundamental Education" in 1946 with a dire warning that "the existence of immense numbers of people who lack the most elementary means of participating in the life of the modern world" represents "not only a threat to peace and security, none the less real because indirect, but also a barrier and a challenge to science and culture."[21] UNESCO's principles of "Fundamental Education" provided the pedagogical grounding for the UDHR's articulation of the goals of compulsory education: "Education shall be directed to the full development of the human personality and to the strengthening of respect for human rights and fundamental freedoms" (Article 26). As part of its efforts to create the conditions of "mutual understanding" deemed necessary to avoid a third World War in the twentieth century, UNESCO proposed a "radical revolution" in the name of "human betterment" and the "spirit of brotherhood," entreating the literate world to "launch" a global humanitarian "war on ignorance," with an especial "attack on illiteracy."[22]

The international problematization of illiteracy, as Arturo Escobar writes of the contemporaneous problematization of poverty with which it is typically partnered, "brought into existence new discourses and practices that shaped the reality to which they referred";[23] the specific links that UNESCO forged between literacy, "human betterment," and international "brotherhood" drew upon a more general algebraic relation among knowledge, development, and peace that the UN had already enshrined in its charter. This conceptual configuration isolates ignorance as something more than the antithesis (or lack) of knowledge; ignorance becomes knowledge's antagonist and, by association, an enemy of humankind's emancipation, development, fraternity, and peace. Thus, in international affairs, one nation's underdevelopment is imagined to pose a threat to other nations' development; poverty poses a threat to wealth; illiteracy to literacy; nonscientific culture to the progress of science and culture. The systemic remedy identified to solve these potentially explosive Manichean conflicts was the transfer of technology—including the transfer of what Walter Ong called the "technologized word"—from the industrialized West to the underdeveloped "rest." Thus, literacy joins the cultural package of mutually reinforcing and revered modern goods, goals, and means identified in the UN Charter as the purposes for which the international body was incorporated: "economic and social advancement of all peoples," "better standards of life in larger freedom," "international peace and security," and "fundamental human rights."

Like Mlle. Garnier's humanitarian literacy project in Beyala's novel, UNESCO's intellectual bipolarization of the globe divided the world into readers and nonreaders; or, in geopolitical terms—based on a sort of Gross National Literacy Product—into modern reading nation-states (with citizens in a "highly interiorized stage . . . of consciousness") and premodern, illiterate huddled masses "immersed unconsciously in communal structures."[24] At the level of postwar international relations, illiteracy becomes the hallmark of *national* deficiency, not merely (as early-nineteenth-century colonial rationales had it) of a people's supposed cultural and civilizational inferiority—described in the classical anthropological literature as the prelogical, prescientific, and prehistorical mentality of primitives—but also (as late-colonial discourse had it) of its social and political immaturity; thus, the illiterate peoples are doubly relegated to what Walter Ong called "an earlier state of affairs" in humanity's progress narrative.[25] With its discursive, idealized alignment with modernity, democracy, and liberty, literacy becomes the primary qualification and capacity for participation in what the ICESCR calls "a free society"—a society that writes about itself as a "lettered city." Such a configuration of the contrast between illiteracy and literacy, and a functionalization of the relation between literacy and modernity, defines orality against literacy as the negative condition of and a menace (or affront) to literacy, which is itself naturalized as the normal state of modern social affairs both intra- and internationally. Literacy, historically utilized in modern democracies as a discriminatory qualification for the franchise, is reified as the functional boundary—globally as much as locally—between the disenfranchised and the incorporated, the de facto city limit of a lettered society. If reading and writing are among the Goethean virtues of the modern bourgeois citizen (as *Wilhelm Meister's Apprenticeship* implies), illiteracy is construed as a vice of the disenfranchised—invoked variously as the cause of, the cause for, and the effect of exclusion from modern society in an age "that imprisons and impoverishes illiteracy and ignorance," as Paul

Tiyambe Zeleza writes of the economic and literary marginalization of Africa in our contemporary era of globalization.[26]

However, UNESCO's program for "Fundamental Education"
transformed the "Grand Dichotomy" of classical anthropology—
that distinguished between "traditional," "undeveloped" oral
cultures and "modern," "developed" literate ones[27]—from a taxonomic schema into a sociological metric that enabled international
agencies to chart the relative location of people(s) on the path to
literacy and modernization, "*en voie de développement*," in Beyala's
text.[28] Thus, the mid-twentieth-century international and sociological pejoration of orality animated the classical dichotomy by imagining it along an emancipatory vector of modernization that
inclines from the constraint of illiteracy to the liberty of literacy—
from "the prison of the mythopoetic imagination" to the rationalized freedom of "scientific and technological civilization"[29]—a
process that Jack Goody famously dubbed "the domestication of
the savage mind." I suggest, however, that we should read the international institutional transformation of anthropological orality into
sociological illiteracy not as a sign of the actual hegemony of literacy in so-called modern society (which has never been as wholly or
fully literate as it claims) but as a discursive effect of the hegemony
of *the idea of the hegemony* of literacy. That is, the institutional arrangements created to manage illiteracy on an international level
were founded upon, and in turn intensified, what Harvey Graff has
called "the literacy myth"—the orthodoxy that reading and writing
have a necessary interrelation to urbanization, industrialization, and
modernization, and that participation in the modern social texture
is primarily, and properly, conducted in and through writing and
reading, as Weber's analysis of modernity and Habermas' account
of the liberal public sphere that took the historical form of a bourgeois reading society suggest.[30] Nonetheless, the institutional
internationalization of this conceptual association of literacy with
modernity—already at work within the domestic discourses of
Western welfare states—rewrites the nineteenth-century colonial
missionary disposition of "civilized" European nation-states toward
"savage" peoples in terms of intellectual, technical assistance, as a
humanitarian interventionist posture of the literate, industrialized
world toward the illiterate peoples of the Third World. Thus, as I
have already suggested, at the international level, national illiteracy

becomes a scourge—a mental and social condition to be remedied; to paraphrase the humanitarian injunction (the writing man's burden) of Mamadou's teacher: reading nations must help the nonreading ones (to read).

In the decades following the wave of decolonization, developmentalism coalesced as the predominant discursive paradigm in the industrialized West not only for "making statements about" and "dealing with" a nascent Third World but also for "dominating, restructuring, and having authority over" the socioeconomic and geopolitical asymmetry of an emergent postcolonial international order (to borrow from Edward Said's characterization of the work of Orientalist discourse).[31] In some ways, like Mlle. Garnier, developmentalism naturalized the disproportionalities of the world system as the effects of cultural difference that translated into a geopolitical asynchronism—the social organizational difference between "primitives" and "peoples of the book." As humanities and social-science professionals began to participate with their economist colleagues in theorizing development, the instrumental (functional) and the spiritual (emancipatory) conceptions of modernity and the vectors of modernization were increasingly routed together through the technology of literacy, and more specifically through the artifactual form of the book, which became something of a fetish within certain humanitarian strands of development discourse and human rights.

Thus, for example, in 1964, Dan Lacy, the managing director of the American Book Publisher's Council, opened a USAID-sponsored international conference on the role of "Books in Human Development" by rehearsing the individual benefits of literacy and by proposing that "a nation's production and consumption of books is likely to be a very good index of its general stage of social and economic development."[32] UNESCO sought to fortify the conceptual connection between literacy and development—and illiteracy and underdevelopment—with its declarations of the Charter of the Book and of 1972 as International Book Year. Literacy (and literature more generally) appears as the missing link between intellectual and material welfare in the pithy phrases the organization coined to publicize what it regarded as an almost invisible "poverty" in which "half the world's population" languished—a poverty

"so acute in some countries as to be characterized as a 'book famine.'"[33] The numerous conferences, pamphlets, and events associated with International Book Year attempted to inscribe the global
"crisis" of illiteracy within the same moral, humanitarian economy
that motivates people to give their old clothes and unused canned
goods to the poor, by encouraging the creation of "irrigation
schemes to end the book drought" in the Third World.[34] "Book
philanthropy" was officially introduced to the international development agenda as part of the programs for technology-transfer to
the developing "book hung[ry]" countries from the industrialized,
book-sated nations.[35] These technology-transfers included not only
literacy—in the form of mass literacy projects—but literature, in
the form both of books and of the machinery to start a book industry. These linkages between development, literacy, and humanitarianism make it possible for Alan Hill, long-time director of
Heinemann Educational Books, to characterize in his autobiography the company's lucrative business in the ex-British colonies as
"a form of aid to developing countries" while also triumphally pro-
claiming that the Empire "which British soldiers and administrators
had lost was being regained by British educators and publishers."[36]
    Within the discourse of development, the book is a singular tech-
nology in which, as the Charter of the Book asserts, "information
and knowledge" *and* "wisdom and beauty" reside, awaiting their
activation and transference through reading. Reified as a delivery
device of scientific and spiritual enlightenment (as well as of the
technology of literacy itself) the book becomes both the quintessential technology and symbol of modernity; "To live in a library,"
writes Gianni Vattimo, exploiting a "double meaning of the Latin
homonym *liber*," "is perhaps . . . the image itself of perfection, of
humanism, of the experience of the truth which renders us, according to the word of The Book, The Gospel, free."[37] Before we conclude that this literary vision of liberty as confinement in a library
is just the peculiar eccentricity of utopic humanities professors and
idealistic organizations like UNESCO, we should note that, with
the functionalization of literacy in the international arena, institutions like the World Bank—which established a donation program
called the World Bank Book Project—took at least a nominal interest in world literacy. We should also recall that the drafters of the

UDHR believed that the free trade of information was such a potent antidote to fascism that they established a subcommittee to articulate a human right "to seek, receive and impart information and ideas through any media and *regardless of frontiers*" as a civil and political—rather than a cultural or social—right (Article 19, emphasis added).[38]

According to these developmental, liberative visions of literacy, the immaterial takes material form and becomes portable in the artifact of the book, a vehicle not just for the "domesticat[ion of] science and technology" but for the conveyance of "the scientific spirit itself."[39] As the Charter of the Book suggests, the book is regarded as a vehicle of intellectual and socioeconomic advancement, human betterment and national development, and international understanding and peace. Indeed, it is the physical mobility of the book, UNESCO notes, that has "enabled [it] to fulfill more completely its function as a means of reflection . . . relaxation . . . . [and] action," as Lukács would have appreciated;[40] in other words, it is the reified medium and agent of modern international *Bildung*. Capable of circulating beyond the sociocultural and physical location of its imprint, the book is seen as a supplement (in the Derridean sense) not only for democratic social relations, but for both the relative immobility of people (especially of impoverished peoples) and the locational nature and evanescence of oral events. A technology capable of being transferred, the book is itself regarded as a technology of transfer; "[t]he act of reading is at once an initiation into today's society"—an imaginative "passport to the world" and a practical "means of participating in the life of the modern world."[41] This conception of the book as a technology of transfer underpinned the logic by which the drafters of the UDHR cited *Robinson Crusoe* to underwrite their articulation of the ideal relation between the individual and society, as I discussed in chapter 1. Not only do they affirm this view of the book in their own use of Defoe's novel as a library of (European) civilization's knowledge and wisdom about modern socialization; they also affirm it in their reading of Crusoe's social interpellation through the books he salvaged from his ship, the "products of human industry and culture" that made it possible for him "to live and [fully] develop his personality."[42] The idealization of personal transformation and socioeconomic development through the practice of literacy is predicated upon, and sustained by, the anthropological distinction between orality and literacy and the sociological dispensation of the world into readers and nonreaders.

Historically, the plot dynamics of the *Bildungsroman* depend upon a similar, if not always explicit, stratification (or classification) of the world into nonreaders and readers for its teleology of human personality development. The genre typically depicts "the passage from orality to writing"[43]—from the communal catechistical spaces of oral social training to a writing and reading room of one's own—as part of the modernizing transformations undergone by the *Bildungsheld*. With the acquisition of literacy, the protagonist obtains a social promotion from the familiar, and dependent, realm of illiteracy (whether imaged as a function of age, class, gender, race, or religion) into a presumably independent world of letters—a world of literature and literary convention, already reading and already saturated with literary signs and significance. The classical *Bildungsroman* generally replays the grand civilizational transition to modernity as the personalizing process of literary socialization that must be repeated in the life narrative of every modern individual. Topically, the idealist *Bildungsroman* was much more concerned with social and cultural literacy—which, as I have suggested, usually means national literacy—than with the acquisition of the rudimentary skills of reading and writing (functional literacy); but, even in those early novels, learning to read (or to read well) both emblematizes and catalyzes the vagarious processes of modernization and personality development. An apprenticeship in reading is a constitutive feature of the *Bildungsroman*'s plot; however, "we have grown [so] used to identifying literacy with development"[44] that the process rarely receives notice in the critical and theoretical literature on the novelistic form, appearing almost incidental to the genre's more holistic interest in human personality development and its imbrication with what Bakhtin described as the "historical emergence of the world itself"—that is, of the bourgeois world.[45]

The social act of writing a novel presupposes the existence of a critical mass of readers, and literary historians have long connected the form's rise with the social expansion of literacy among the emergent bourgeoisie. If we can describe the emergence of the novel form as a sociocultural effect of the transfer of literary technology (like the dissemination and popularization of human dignity in the French revolution) from the aristocracy to the bourgeois citizenry, the *Bildungsroman* is the novelistic genre that takes that transference as a central problematic—as both its theme and extra-textual pedagogical objective. "[O]ne of the cardinal documents of bourgeois literacy," the *Bildungsroman* narrates the story of an individual's mastery of literacy in the very medium through which such proficiency is acquired and practiced.[46] As a social text, the novel is addressed to a group of readers (that surely is a truism); like the novelistic artifact itself, the *Bildungsroman*'s protagonist is similarly destined for a society of readers, a society of which the novel's reader is already (or is fast becoming) a library-card-carrying member.

The *Bildungsheld* and its story(book) follow parallel paths; both are to be published (in the broadest sense of that term) among a society of readers. Within the *Bildungsroman*, the portability of books resembles, but also complements and facilitates, the social mobility of the protagonist, who through literal and literary wandering learns "to recognize himself as an inhabitant of the 'cosmopolis.'"[47] The novel narrates the story of an individual's initiation into a modern society of readers and his or her incorporation as a reader—very often as a reader of other *Bildungsromane*. But, like their critics, the earliest *Bildungsromane* took literacy mostly for granted. The prototypical Wilhelm Meister, for instance, begins his apprenticeship already functionally literate, but his socialization is overseen by a masonic society of avid readers who pronounce his freedom in the Tower's chapel-cum-library—a vivid image for the secularization of both novelistic plot and *Bildung*. At the symbolic moment in which his mastery of sociocultural literacy is certified, Wilhelm is granted borrowing rights to all of the scrolls containing the documentation of members' apprenticeships (including his own) that have been deposited in the archives of the Society of the Tower; he becomes the custodian of his own narrative of socialization only when the society deems him capable of appreciating (that is, reading well) his articles of apprenticeship. Goethe's novel, like most canonical European *Bildungsromane*, tells a "literacy narrative of progress" that forges and reinforces the linkages among literacy, liberty, and modernity with "a story about being empowered by books"—a story that promises "self-improvement and cultural uplift" through reading, as R. Mark Hall has recently written of the ethos of Oprah Winfrey's popular televised book club.[48] If training in the technology of literacy (both basic literacy and literary reading) constitutes part of the ordinary process of transformation undergone by the traditional *Bildungsheld*, the relative critical silence about its role within the story form is a telling silence that speaks not only to the depth of the assumption about the place of reading in modern development but also to the almost invisible literacy privilege (ordinarily conceived of as a class privilege) that the reader of the *Bildungsroman* shares with the representative protagonist as fellow citizens of a lettered city.[49]

However, contemporary postcolonial (and metropolitan minority) *Bildungsromane* rarely take literacy for granted; instead, they tend to foreground the process of learning to read and write as a significant part of the *curriculum vitae* of modern personality development and to make it a primary topos of the novelistic genre. The prominence of the literacy topos is partly a reflection of the sociohistorical condition of education in the global (and national) "provinces" under which these novels are composed, where the relative scarcity of the technological resource of literacy—and what the Charter of the Book calls "national supplies" of literature—makes reading an act of conspicuous consumption. That is, the process of learning to read and write tends to become visible as part of the *Bildungsroman*'s study of modernization in social formations where there is a substantial disproportion in the number of nonreaders to readers; namely, where nonliterate forms of media predominate, where a colonial language is imposed on a populace, where universal primary education is lacking, where the economic resources and material conditions necessary to enjoy a "right to read" are absent—in short, where contemporary human rights have not been widely realized. In such contexts, the contrast between the world of readers and nonreaders is especially stark, and the lettered society into which the literacy myth seems to promise the protagonist incorporation (and among whom the book is most likely to circulate) is very often the exclusive ranks of the social and political elite or of the foreign power that "brings" literacy (or both), whose dominance subsists and is perpetuated, at least partly, by such educational disparities.

Many *Bildungsromane* from what Pascale Casanova calls "the literarily deprived territories" (or, alternatively, "the literarily dominated spaces") of her "world republic of letters" are reactions to, rather than merely effects of, the spread of mass literacy.[50] They tend to recognize the instrumental and historical use of literacy as an "enormous sorting device" that "grinds out a humanity sorted into categories consistent with the way the world economic system divides the same humanity" according to the requirements of the capitalist division of labor.[51] Literacy becomes a site (a topos) of conflict—a personal, social, political, economic, and cultural battleground. Thus, the struggle *for* literacy is also a struggle *with* literacy, with the modern institutional developmental imperative to read and write, and with the literary forms through which the technology is acquired. Developmentalism and the idealist *Bildungsroman* typically mythologize literacy as a neutral technology—an almost magical transformational practice that makes beguiling promises of "human betterment" and socioeconomic advancement. But these promises will not, or cannot, be kept (at least on a mass scale) in colonial, neocolonial, authoritarian, or predatory capitalist social orders that are sustained by and profit from the dispensation of the world into readers and nonreaders—that is, in a world system that is predicated upon and perpetuates such socioeconomic and educational disparities.

In contrast to the emancipatory vision of reading and writing underwritten by the idealist *Bildungsroman*, many of these novels depict the acquisition of literacy as an ambivalent achievement—a sign as much of alienation as of incorporation and as much of disenfranchisement from a traditional social texture and the displacement of nonliterary modes of socialization as of enfranchisement into a republic of letters. Indeed, as we saw in the previous chapter, in Tsitsi Dangarembga's *Nervous Conditions*, literacy is associated with aphasia as much as with fluency, and the *Bildungsroman* form itself operates as a literary genre of ideological domination and social control in its promotion of an ideal of development that is largely foreclosed to the black African woman by the civil, political, and economic structures of Rhodesian colonialism and by the social dynamics of traditional Shona patriarchy. Given the sociohistorical context of literacy, and the colonial content of the literature on and in which it is practiced, the act of reading becomes both an agent of and an obstacle to the fulfillment of free and full human personality development and to the realization of the "literacy myth," whose palliative moral seems to promise that "better literacy necessarily leads to economic development, cultural progress, and individual improvement," as a young Tambu herself might have written.[52] The conflicted literacy narratives of dissensual *Bildungsromane* innovate formal literary devices to express ambivalence toward literacy. In Dangarembga's novel, for instance, the ironic distance—established through the diegetically split narrative personalities of the protagonist and the narrator—offers a formal solution that enables her to depict a naive protagonist who follows the conventional, progressive trajectory of the literacy narrative while demystifying the literacy myth by emphasizing the historicity of reading and writing as social practices that are "implicated in power relations and embedded in specific cultural meanings."[53] In other words, the novel underscores the personal and social costs entailed in Tambu's learning to read and write; it denaturalizes the accepted linkages between liberty and literacy by situating its acquisition and practice within larger systems of domination. Reading perhaps "*almost* prevents development," but full human personality development (*Bildung*) is recoded as the achievement of a postliteracy (or postcolonial literacy)—an ability not only to recognize and recombine letters but also to recognize the sociocultural inflections of literacy and the historical conditions in which it is prescribed, practiced, and prized as the primary means of initiation into (and exclusion from) modern society.[54]

"Words like hammers": Literary Human(itarian)ism and Implicated Readers in Calixthe Beyala's Loukoum: The 'Little Prince' of Belleville

> What will happen will happen beyond my power, without me. . . .
> French legislation anticipated it all.
>
> —Mamadou's father Abdou in a letter from
> a Belleville jail (Beyala, *Loukoum*)

To read and write, "you've got to struggle [*il faut te battre*]," goads Mamadou's young French literacy tutor "endlessly"; "he makes me read [*il me fait lire*]," writes our narrator: "It's cool but it's hard."[55] In the French edition of Beyala's novel, Mamadou's teacher draws a connection between intellectual and material aid—between the struggles for literacy and socioeconomic development—and she attempts to instill in him a faith in the "fantasy of [personal and social] transformation" through reading and writing.[56] Based on his experience with the lives of the residents of Belleville, Mamadou is justifiably suspicious of the claims of the literacy myth, and he initially accepts his tutor's humanitarian assistance more out of boredom than commitment, unconvinced that "forcing" himself to stop speaking "*petit nègre*" and to start writing proper French will enable him either to "become something other than a street sweeper" like his father or to feel "a lot more comfortable with [him]self."[57] Despite Mamadou's doubts about the promise of becoming "a gentleman," literacy seems to offer him the only possible mode of reconciling the contradictions between the illegal, abject underworld of his childhood and the world of legality and French social legitimacy; writing eventually becomes the "work" that he "live[s] for," a means "to fill the gaps" in his life while he "just wait[s] for my fate, seeing that it's none of my business."[58]

Mamadou's literacy narrative is set in the late 1980s and early 1990s, at the height of what his elders call the "fascist crisis" of backlash against African immigrants. This backlash was fomented by the xenophobic slogans of ethnonationalism popularized by the National Front, Jean-Marie Le Pen's right-wing political party: "France for the French"; "One million immigrants equals one million jobless." Mamadou's novel is about the experience of the gap between the civil-political constitution of France and the sociocultural, mediated construction of the French, to whom France apparently belongs; it is about the difference between the liberal, official state ideology of liberty, equality, and fraternity and the social formations and practices that preclude their enjoyment by an African immigrant; and about the social relations inflected by an asymmetrical distribution of human rights and humanitarian rights, "the rights of those who cannot actualize them," as Jacques Rancière has written.[59] Although Mamadou has internalized much of the racism and sexism of both mainstream French society and what he affectionately calls "the tribe"—the cohort of hustlers, prostitutes, pushers, and working-class Muslim African immigrants with whom his Malian father associates in Belleville—he nonetheless imagines himself to be a part of both the French nation and state, included within, rather than debarred by, the seemingly redundant, tautological formulation of a France for the French. But the one thing that both the National Front and Mamadou's father, Abdou, agree upon is that the tribe is not French, and the first hard lesson of Mamadou's social apprenticeship is learning the difference between France (to which he "belongs," if only as a welfare charge) and the French (from which he is excluded). This racialized difference between France and the French is policed at the local level—for instance, in the segregation of Mamadou from his "girlfriend," Lolita, in which their parents join with school officials to enforce. It is the effective and affective difference between the state and the racialized nation that he ultimately seeks not only to unlearn but to undo through his reading and writing. In other words, Mamadou seeks to perform with his story a novelistic intervention in the dynamics and content of the French national imaginary.

Mamadou's "revered father" is more or less habituated to the daily discrimination he experiences in France. But when his father rails against French governmental hypocrisy and Le Pen's "Nazism," threatening to bring on a "general strike" with his fellow sanitation workers, Mamadou imagines the full text of a letter that he would like to compose to President François Mitterand, the gist of which would read: *"It's not Monsieur Le Pen's fault if he suffers from misinformation, for social separation makes all people stay in their own district without intending any harm."*[60] Not yet capable of writing in French, Mamadou is nonetheless already familiar with epistolary formalities, and his imaginary letter humbly petitions the president to *"organise a committee . . . to do a census of Negroes in distress . . .* [that] *would nail the mouth of the President of the National Front shut."* Mamadou's frustration at his inability to transcribe his imagined letter simultaneously intensifies his sense of disenfranchisement and impels his begrudging acceptance of the democratic functional necessity of literacy as well as a budding faith in its transformative social power. This emergent faith is expressed in both his act of epistolary imagination and his naive, UN-esque belief that a census revealing the actually existing conditions of Blacks in France might foster mutual racial understanding and social peace.[61] Mamadou's book compiles an imaginative and imaginary census in which "Negroes in distress"—African immigrants and unemployed "illegal residents"—count, rebutting the popular perception that "things

are a mess in France . . . because of us."⁶² Such an accounting aspires
to rectify some of the unintentional "harm" and "misinformation"
that result from habitual, systemic segregation by drawing readers
out of their "own district" to cross the racial, spatial, and social
divide in an attempt to reimagine and re-mediate a French sentimental community—"a community of individuals to whom human
rights are to be extended."⁶³

Born to his father's prostitute-mistress in Mali, Mamadou immi-
grated with her to France, where she "entrusted" him to Abdou
until she could "g[e]t the hang of it" in Paris.⁶⁴ Abdou apparently
accepted this arrangement to claim the child-welfare benefit. But
Abdou is falsely accused of having murdered his second wife by a
White feminist social worker (who regularly comes out of her own
district to enlighten his two wives on the inherent misogyny of po-
lygamy and "what rights they have" in France) and is jailed after
state investigators discover that Mamadou is the son neither of Abdou's legally recognized first wife nor his customary second.⁶⁵
Charged with welfare fraud, Abdou is imprisoned because of a conflict between civil and customary law—between state-recognized
paternity and maternity and Malian tribal traditions of parenthood.
Attuned to stories about the parasitism of immigrants, inquiring
newspapers swarm Mamadou and his siblings, publishing their pic-
tures under headlines that bombast: "A FAMILY OF IMMI-
GRANTS REGISTERS FALSE BIRTHS AND DIVERTS
SEVERAL MILLION CENTIMES TO FAMILY BENEFITS."⁶⁶
Humiliated by this scandalous introduction to a French society of
readers and his public infamy, Mamadou turns off the television
and turns to "writing a real book. About my life," consoling himself
with the thought that "one day . . . they'll make a film out of it."
His *Bildungsroman* is precipitated by his social embarrassment, and
it constitutes his narrative response to public demand that he give
an account of himself—that, literally, he account for his cost to
French society.

Mamadou's narrative and letter—which imagines asserting a yet-
impracticable petitionary right to write to the president and establishes the literacy-narrative trajectory of his desire for an ordinary
French adolescence and for his pursuit, as he tells Santa Claus, of
"a little happiness"—are counterpointed with letters written by his
father from prison.⁶⁷ This dialogic novelistic structure incorporates

two common plots of the story of postcolonial migration to the metropole in its tenuous oscillation between the poles of assimilation and alienation. The generational divide is enacted as a narratorial split decision that responds to the stereotypical dilemma of the postcolonial immigrant caught *"entre la nécessité de s'intégrer et celle de préserver ses racines* [between the necessity of integration and that of preserving one's heritage],"* as the back cover of the French edition advertises it; these dual narratives act as counterweights that keep the novel's plot from finalizing in either full enfranchisement or complete disenfranchisement. Heading each chapter, Abdou's letters express his increasing sense of dispossession, emasculation, and despair over what he regards as the "loss" of his son to France's "perfected machinery"—formal, mandatory liberal education, "the vocabulary of Paris," and the culture of "the stars on television."[68] These are media whose modes of transmission show little regard for the spatial, racial, and social frontiers within Paris—media that are "in the air." Registering his complaints against "so much outside interference" in his letters from a Belleville jail, Abdou imagines himself engaged with French society in a full-blown culture war, of which his son is a casualty and he a prisoner.[69]

Where Mamadou's imagined letter to President Mitterand invokes a real reader through direct address, the imagined reader for his "real" *Bildungsroman* is interpellated through a series of apostrophes in which he "wonder[s] what you're going to think of all this."[70] These rhetorical appeals configure what I called in the previous chapter an implicated reader who personifies the public demand that Mamadou account for himself and who serves as a synecdoche for (the shared assumptions of) a more general French society of readers. Mamadou's appeals to this implicated reader repeatedly—and strategically, as I will argue—seek assistance in the reader's area of presumed social expertise: reading. His solicitations range from a request for factual information about how Saint-Exupéry's *The Little Prince* ends—"If you know anything about it, write to me at the above address"—to an exasperated confession of confusion at his discovery that "my mothers aren't my mums [*mes mères sont pas mes mamans*]."[71] Indeed, both Mamadou's novel and Abdou's letters configure such an implicated reader, but each addresses this figure differently. Abdou politely salutes his reader as "friend," but he holds his addressee in contempt, as a party to the

French legal and social conviction—that Mamadou's familiar "mums" are not his official "mothers"—that put him behind bars. In contrast, Mamadou seeks aid in untangling this civil–customary technicality, and he entreats the reader to help him solve the juridical and cultural puzzle: "So if you can explain this to me, I'm at your disposal."[72] The implicated reader summoned by Abdou and Mamadou stands in for an ethnonationalist society that declaims its commitments to universal liberty, equality, and fraternity even as it erects discriminatory social, economic, cultural, racial, legal, and literary-generic barriers to their incorporation. In both cases, the literary device gives textual form to an implicit social injunction that they account for their "scandalous" sociocultural aberrancy— that they narrate their own stories and thereby take personal responsibility for their "choice" to live "contrary to the French lifestyle."[73]

If social pressure dictates a story in which Mamadou is to become the image of ignominy that has precirculated in the newspapers, official French-rights rhetoric seems to embrace his inclusion, prescribing a developmental narrative of voluntary cultural assimilation for the incorporation of the immigrant. *"Culture is for everyone,"* writes Abdou with irony, impersonating the voice of liberal French ideology in the opening line of both the novel and his first letter.[74] But beneath the rights rhetoric of this declaration of the impartiality and universality of culture, Abdou detects a French imperialist commandment: *"La culture c'est pour tous. De gré ou de force* [By choice or by force]."[75] In other words, Abdou senses an imperative mood in this assertion of French cultural egalitarianism. Thus, he interprets the rights dictum not as a banal anthropological axiom about the universal phenomenon of culture—that, like ethnicity, everyone has one—but as a sociological directive that has implications for a whole sociocultural industry of "perfected machinery," institutional arrangements, social formations, and relations. From this cultural imperative, Abdou derives the human rights developmental injunction: *"Education is OBLIGATORY."* Abdou identifies a tension (even a hypocrisy) in the official state ideology between the rhetorics of freedom and compulsion—rights and requirements—that emerges from the simultaneous articulation of these two facets of the fundamental social-contract principle for the maintenance and reproduction of modern democracy. "The magic of this contradictory reasoning escapes me," claims Abdou, suggesting that the apparent paradox is intrinsic to the French cultural logic of a culture that is for everyone but not for him.

In Abdou's Althusserian vision of the perfected machinery of social domination, overt physical coercion enters to discipline bad subjects when covert systems of culture have failed to interpellate good citizens. For Abdou, his confinement is a demonstration of the violent imposition of French culture through the repressive force of law; he is being penalized for a cultural crime—for the fact, as he writes in one of his letters, that "*your legislation . . . has not integrated my customs.*"[76] Law and culture are not here two entirely different discursive orders; they are at once complements and expressions of one another. Indeed, the magic of this "contradictory reasoning" is the alchemy of consent, the process of convincement by which social force is transmuted into personal choice—the work assigned specifically to culture in the idealist theories of *Bildung* by which "I [come to] *desire* to do what I in any case *should* have done."[77] Mamadou's apparent choice to adopt French culture is a cultivated disposition produced by his media consumption and literacy training. This compulsory education in French cultural literacy enacts, in the words of Pierre Bourdieu and Jean-Claude Passeron, a "symbolic violence" through its "imposition of a cultural arbitrary"—a contingent norm that expresses, "though always indirectly, . . . the objective interests (material and symbolic) of the dominant groups or classes."[78] In Bourdieu and Passeron's sociology of the "reproduction of the structure of power relations within a social formation," the system of education is an engine of hegemony that gives culture a law-like force through the sustained training in a *habitus*—the "internalization of the principles of a cultural arbitrary" that "legitimate [the] exclusions and inclusions which form the basis of the social order."[79] The magic of this habituating process—ordinarily euphemized as socialization, acculturation, or free and full human personality development—converts compulsion to volunteerism and, as we saw with Goethe, makes a bourgeois, citizenly virtue of social necessity.

In Beyala's novel, the primary "cultural arbitrary" that both school and society seek to install is the notion that French culture is not arbitrary; that *culture is for everyone*; that culture is impartial, universal, and equally accessible to all; and that one's relationship to culture is voluntary, a matter of choice—or that one has rights in the matter of culture. This kind of rights talk pervades the novel, mouthed in one form or another by most of the novel's White French citizens who, like ideology itself, prate the equanimity of the French culture of individual rights—"He's free to talk," an old woman on the Metro reprimands Mamadou's teacher: "In this country, there's no way those rights can be denied."[80] "Women have the same rights as men. They are free. They work. They realise their dreams," insists the feminist social worker to Mamadou's mums.[81] Between the lessons of compulsory education and the popular recitations of its cultural arbitraries, the right to culture and the right to have rights become personal responsibilities— obligations of the individual to assert his right to liberty, equality, and fraternity by articulating a claim of inclusion. The language of individual rights ultimately disavows society's responsibility for the African immigrant's disenfranchisement by insisting that the French tradition of human rights has manifested itself in a social environment of equal opportunity that invites Mamadou to assert his right to become what he was not by the birth-accident of nature—to claim his right to culture and to be French. Mamadou never loses sight of the historical discrepancy between the official rhetoric of cultural inclusiveness—that culture is for everyone—and its popular implementation in social and political practices of exclusion; nonetheless, as we shall see, he tactically appropriates the rhetoric to articulate his own dissensual novelistic claim for inclusion in a France for the French on the implicit grounds that he, like everyone else, consumes its culture.

The mixed messages sent by official French ideology and social practice constitute a dual narrative mandate that sets the parameters for the socially acceptable story of a young African immigrant in Paris. Mamadou summarizes this double bind in the account of his first encounter with Lolita's mother:

> White people listen to [B]lack people when you tell them your woes [*misères*]. But when you tell them that all is well, that you don't need them, then they don't listen any more.
>
> Well, I wasn't going to do [Lolita's mother] that favour and tell her that my dad has two wives and a lot of mistresses, that my mother is a whore. No, I told her a story [W]hite people don't like to hear. That we were well off. [*Que nous*

sommes des gens bien.] That my dad works in the mayor's office. That my mum is a cashier at Ed's.[82]

Thus, on the one hand, the French human-rights rhetoric prescribes a *Bildungsroman* narrative of the individual's escape from the *demi-monde* to join the ranks of the *"gens bien"*—the respectable classes; however, in practice this story may be articulable but it is generally inadmissible in the liberal public sphere. On the other hand, the story of "miserable wretches" satisfies the expectations of public demand because it "replicate[s] the very banal preconceptions that have been appended" to Blacks.[83]

Whereas French liberalism urges a narrative of voluntary assimilation, popular demand expects from Mamadou a story of deliberate abjection in the literary form that Rey Chow has called an act of "confession" that legitimates his social exclusion, a "captivity narrative" whose "socially endorsed, coercive mimeticism . . . stipulates that the thing to imitate, resemble, and become is none other than the ethnic or sexual minority herself."[84] Reciting the expected social imagery of Black dependency and abjection also reconfirms the banal (self-)preconception of humanitarian White bourgeois French citizens who listen "reverently" to stories about the wretched of the earth that they presume already to know.[85] This "contradictory reasoning" of the dual-narrative mandate presents Mamadou not with an existential dilemma—to be *or* not to be French—but with an impossible ontocultural imperative: to be *and* not to be French. In his novel, Mamadou indulges the tacit demand of the implicated reader by deploying, within the officially sanctioned form of the *Bildungsroman*, the stereotypical images about the wretchedness of the Blacks and the altruism of the Whites that everyone already knows from the repository of cultural narratives in the national, humanitarian imaginary. In other words, his dissensual *Bildungsroman* complies with, at least superficially, both the social and the state narrative imperatives, doing them the "favour" of telling a miserable story of abjection that they will listen to in the respectable form that they claim to prefer.

The novel's implicated reader gets to have it both ways; Mamadou articulates a claim for inclusion in French society (thus demonstrating his protoassimilation) that will not be recognized as a claim but as a common complaint about eternal Black miserableness (thus confirming the "legitimacy" of his social exclusion). The novel's conclusion encapsulates this discord between normative form and abnormal content. At the end of his story, Mamadou is euphoric; his literacy narrative seems to have been consummated when the most intimate of implicated readers, Lolita, writes back to him. He reads her billet-doux with the same enthusiasm with which Wilhelm Meister received his articles of apprenticeship, taking the letter as a sign that he has breached the racial barrier and been confirmed in his French address—that he is a person with a French address who can be addressed in French. Moreover, the story closes with his family on the verge of civil legitimacy and French social normalcy. His birth mother announces that she has quit prostitution and is engaged to be married, and his father has become monogamous. Indeed, the novel closes not with the social conflagration of the threatened general strike for immigrant rights, but with a peaceful Bastille Day celebration of that earlier rights revolution against the *petits princes* of the *ancien régime* on 14 July 1789. The final scenes resemble a collection of pastoral snapshots of French propriety. But if Mamadou feels that he has found his sought-for happiness in these idyllic images, this is because for a few hours one afternoon he has lost sight of their social framing while he was transported "towards the gap in the heavens" by reading Lolita's letter.[86] Lolita, however, writes from a "mental" institution where she has been committed by her mother, ostensibly because of the racial transgression of her inappropriate affection for Mamadou;[87] Abdou's conversion to monogamy was effected not by the force of French law or culture but by the force of nature—the ultimately fortuitous death of Mamadou's second mum; and the celebration of the day that "[t]he French had their Revolution" takes the form of a separate, although perhaps oddly equal, tribal picnic in the Bois de Boulogne.[88] These qualifications to his picture-perfect afternoon in the park suggest that the trajectory of Mamadou's "path . . . of happiness" is at best asymptotic to the idealist *Bildungsroman*'s normal and normalizing plot curve, approaching but never quite intersecting with its generic promise of incorporation.[89]

Mamadou's narrative claim for inclusion in the French franchise is not immediately rights-based—the traditional logic borne out as plot in the affirmative *Bildungsroman*, in which one becomes positively what one already is by natural right; rather, Mamadou's asymptotic narrative makes an implicit claim of a right to enjoy the rights that correspond to what he has already become by his habits and practices of cultural consumption. In other words, Mamadou's novel asserts a civil, social, and political right to be recognized as (and with the rights that seem to belong to) a co-consumer of French culture—of a mediated national imaginary (e.g., literature, school culture, the vocabulary of Paris, radio, television, film, etc.). Like Benedict Anderson, Mamadou imagines "the French" as a society of readers—a society into which the (cultural) literacy myth and liberal rights rhetoric seem to promise incorporation. In some ways, his narrative carries out the logic of the ideological insistence that culture is for everyone to its absurd consumerist (and racist) conclusion. If the nation as imagined community is a sentimental republic that hypostatizes in the nation-state the affective, imaginary relations between individuals produced through the "figures of speech and thought found in [common] cultural artifacts,"[90] then Mamadou's fluent deployment of the racist and sexist images of Blacks—parasitic, criminal immigrants, prostitutes, welfare babies, and cheats—drawn from the repository of the postcolonial national imaginary suggests that he is as sentimentally French as his stereotyped, implicated, humanitarian reader who will only hear stories of Black wretchedness. Ironically, then, Beyala's novel enjoins the implicated reader to recognize what Mamadou himself already "knows" implicitly: that, on the basis of contemporary practices and dynamics of common cultural consumption (rather than on an essentialist myth of common cultural descent), he and the reader already constitute a sentimental community, even if the particular sentiments of their shared cultural citizenship reinforce and reproduce the legitimacy of Mamadou's historical exclusion from the social order and the national imaginary.

As problematic as this consumerist model of cultural citizenship and its reimagination of the French nation surely is, it nonetheless disrupts the revanchist, ethnonationalist tautology that delivers France to a mythical French bloodline by disrupting the traditional national borders—and official international order—of rights and culture. In Beyala's novel, the African immigrant child who imagines himself as an incorporable citizen of postcolonial France has already oriented himself with a transnational cognitive and affective compass and located himself within an international cultural system of rights.[91] This reimagination of community simultaneously extends and takes advantage of a long liberal French tradition that celebrates France as the birthplace of human rights and French society as the concrete embodiment of the abstract universality of the rights of man. Through the rights of man and the sociocultural impact of colonialism, the national and the international are imbricated under the sign of postcolonial "France." Thus, Mamadou's novelistic claim for inclusion in the French society of readers is premised on an impeccably logical (if not reasonable) conclusion to be drawn from a historical, colonial equation that the French civilizing mission drew between France and the "universal" culture of the rights of man. If to be French is to be universal, and to be Parisian is to be cosmopolitan, then being literate in a culture that is "for everyone" must make one French, and being fluent in the vocabulary of the cosmopolis must make one Parisian. Mamadou rearticulates the modern citizen-subject as a postmodern citizen-consumer who exercises the rights and responsibilities of citizenship, at least partly, through practices of consumption.[92] In the cultural terrain of the egalitarian imaginary, Mamadou asserts his right to be recognized as part of a French France, expanding the scope of its universality by speaking "from a split situation of being at once authorized and deauthorized" as "one who is excluded from the universal, and yet belongs to it nevertheless."[93] Although his dissensual appeal disturbingly deploys racial stereotypes for its effect, Mamadou's rights claim entreats its implicated readers to "think [themselves] beyond the nation" (in Arjun Appadurai's words)—to recognize the particular historical internationality of France and to reject the counterhistorical, ethnonationalist political forces that refuse to acknowledge the linkages between French colonialism and postcolonial immigration.[94] Mamadou's imaginative, transnational projection does not black out the hyphen in the nation-state (as Appadurai's does); rather, it imagines a reformation and remediation of the notion of "the French" to incorporate a transnational immigrant community as part of what might be imaged as a Sixth French Republic of France.[95]

Addressing his literary rights claim to a particular, already-incorporated, implicated reader, Mamadou constructs that reader as a humanitarian literary agent vested with the capacity to authorize or deauthorize his claim, to sponsor his membership in a sentimental community, and to broker his admission into the French society of letters—a society to whom he concedes its presumptuous self-image as the "capital" of the "World Republic of Letters." Rather than narrating the story of successful incorporation, Mamadou takes advantage of the implicated reader's banal preconceptions about "miserable" Black African immigrant "wretches" in France as well as of the reader's self-image as a humanitarian to get a hearing for his story and to put some flesh on the image of misery.[96] Mamadou converts the social imperative to give an account of himself into a dissensual *Bildungsroman* that deploys both the affirmative genre's conventions and the racial stereotypes of abjection and humanitarianism already at work in the national public sphere to activate in the implicated reader what Kay Schaffer and Sidonie Smith call "the ethics of recognition": "to recognize the disjunction between the values espoused by the community and the actual practices that occur . . . [and] to recognize the humanity of the teller and the justice of the claim; . . . to take responsibility for the recognition of others and their claims."[97] With this summons, Mamadou invites the reader to notarize his novelistic "class-action" suit in the hope that his *Bildungsroman* (and, for nonreaders, perhaps a future film) might influence the construction of and the terms by which "the French" claim the rights to and of France for themselves. The narrator rearticulates the literary and social "relations of subordination" between himself and the implicated reader (who personifies a bourgeois French society of readers) as "relations of oppression" in an effort to denaturalize the image of Black abjection as a sign of cultural difference and to politicize it as "the site of an antagonism."[98] Thus, Mamadou's novel does not contest the portrait of himself that circulates in the media; rather, he reframes it against the background of social formations and conditions that make the image to some degree both mimetic and predeterminative—something that, as Abdou suggests, French law and culture prefigured.

If the novel's recitation of stereotypes seems to confirm the prejudices of its implicated reader, it does so to undercut what Stanley Cohen and Bruna Seu call "implicatory denial"—a form of denial that "makes no attempt to deny either the facts or their conventional interpretation" but rather their "psychological, political, [social,] or moral implications."[99] In other words, "the facts"—or some condensed, oversimplified, stereotyped version of "the facts"—of Black wretchedness are already "known," but the implicated reader "bracket[s] off" the systematicity of those "facts" and the reader's own implication in the social structures (of which the reader is, in fact, a beneficiary) that reproduce as living human beings society's preconceptions about those human beings. Thus, the novel articulates an indictment not of some wholly abstract or bureaucratized social hypocrisy but of the particular hypocrisy of the White humanitarian reading classes that claim to care. In this sense, Mamadou's story is not (or not primarily) conceived of as consciousness-raising; rather, it is affect-raising—a literary effort "to move you beyond knowing by moving you to feel" a more complex sentimentality than the trite humanitarianism of implicated readers who congratulate themselves for listening to stories about Black abjection that are already foretold. But this sentimental education in human rights literacy is secondarily consciousness-raising, since such feelings are to be translated into a recognition on the part of the implicated readers of their own structural complicity in the systems that reproduce (ready-made images of) Black wretchedness and White humanitarianism.

In its attempt to use "words like hammers"—words like those that Mamadou says "would be needed to make me understand" the "moral depravity" of his and Lolita's love—Mamadou's novel patronizes its patron through its appeals to the humanitarian good will of the implicated reader.[100] In repeatedly seeking interpretive assistance to help him discover things like the "fault" in his having regarded his mums as his mothers—"I keep looking for my mistake but it's no use, I don't see it"[101]—Mamadou rejects the traditional individualistic thrust of the *Bildungsroman* genre, in which the freely and fully developed individual comes to take personal responsibility for his story of socialization and his place in the social order; instead, Mamadou charges the reader with the responsibility for making the events of his life coherent and his social abjection sensible: "If you can explain all this to me, you will have my eternal gratitude," he writes, somewhat sarcastically.[102] That is, the novel insists that the repeated frustration of Mamadou's attempts to inscribe himself within the French social text and texture cannot be explained by any personal choice or mistake on his part; rather, his continued disenfranchisement makes sense only in the context and as an effect of systemic discrimination in a French social order that has institutionalized the liberal ideology of the universal rights of man and citizen as the de facto privilege of the dominant classes.

Like the groups of women who publicly demonstrated against the sexist exclusions formalized with the Declaration of the Rights of Man and of the Citizen after the French Revolution, in the very act of formulating his literary petition, Mamadou writes as if he had the right. In so doing, he inscribes himself in the social imaginary with his insistence on his right to write in the genre of incorporation; he dramatizes the injustice of his historical and generic exclusion with this dissensual performative act of what Irène Assiba d'Almeida has called a *"prise d'écriture,* a 'taking of writing,' in the sense of a militant appropriation or seizing" of the tools of literacy and literature.[103] Thus, Mamadou formally projects himself into the company of the implicated reader, imaginatively insinuating himself, by a rhetorical forced entry, into the very society of readers from which he has been excluded. This imaginative, literary feat reconfigures the character of the fraternity of French readers and converts the figure of the implicated reader from a social antagonist who obstructs his incorporation into a potential sponsor—an accomplice and confederate reader of his *Bildungsroman.*

The texture of the egalitarian imaginary is both sociological and literary, and Beyala's novel represents the interdependency, interaction, and imbrication of those two realms in its deconstruction of the line between literary fiction and sociocivil petition. If the imagined community model of "the French" as a society of readers sustains, and is sustained by, the dictum that culture is for everyone—that everyone has the right to be a consumer of French culture—then Mamadou's attempt to inscribe himself within the textual order of the national imaginary also represents an attempt to reconfigure the social relations and formations between the African immigrant and normative French society in its assertion of a "right" not just to receive but to impart "information and ideas." This *prise d'écriture* may not accomplish the social "liberation" for Mamadou that d'Almeida suggests occurred when Francophone "women were at last, through fiction, able to represent themselves fully and earn recognition as full-fledged human beings."[104] But, in some sense, this "taking [up] of writing," which presumably obviates the need to take up arms, does represent an awareness (however tacit) of the ideological and social distortions promulgated by the egalitarian myth of cultural consumerist citizenship, in which, to modify Appadurai's insight, "the consumer [of the national imaginary] is consistently helped to believe that he or she is an actor, when in fact he or she is at best a chooser."[105] Within the literary economy of the national imaginary, Mamadou's seizure of writing enables him to convert his experience into a potential literary commodity: a novel to be circulated and consumed within the French national imaginary. The success of this literary intrusion (or extrusion) in remediating the national imaginary cannot be measured within the text of the novel itself; it could only be evaluated at the level of an actual French society of readers, in the extent to which *Le Petit Prince de Belleville* (as an artifactual form of Mamadou's eponymous story) takes hold of and in the national imaginary to become itself a figure of French thought and speech.[106]

The appeals to the implicated reader break the fourth wall of fiction to address directly a society of readers outside the world of the literary text—a society that is also represented within its discursive terms so that it is simultaneously both extra- and intradiegetic. Similarly, the compositional conceit of the first-person literacy narrative—which, like the first-person *Bildungsroman* more generally, can only be written after the acquisition of the reading and writing skills necessary to document the story of the protagonist's struggle with and for literacy—figures the fictional protagonist not merely as the narrator but also as the author of his *Bildungsroman*. The novel's compositional conceit assumes a special significance in its attempt to give sociological affect and effect to textual affects and effects, denying the implicated reader sanctuary in the convention of aesthetic distance by insisting that Mamadou himself writes the novel we read and that we are the implicated readers addressed in the text. In blurring the line between fiction and petition, the novel suggests that the possibilities and conditions for Mamadou's socio-civil incorporation are imbricated with those for the emergence of Beyala's novel into the postcolonial French *imaginaire*. In other words, the novel itself is implicated within similar (if not precisely the same) sociocultural dynamics, market relations, and power disparities that Mamadou experiences in his struggle for literacy and enfranchisement. Thus, the novel is not just about the social relations and formations that inflect an African immigrant's struggles for recognition and incorporation into a society of readers; it is also about the conditions of its own composition, publication, circulation, and consumption as a real cultural artifact—both a product of and a commodity within the social formations and cultural relations that define much of Mamadou's personal experiences. Mamadou's *Bildungsroman* thematizes the historical conditions of his and its own improbable emergence as a literary artifact in a French republic of letters, foregrounding both the remedial sociocultural work that the novel aspires to perform while dramatizing and "commenting ironically on the material conditions under which [it is] produced, distributed and consumed."[107]

Clefs à Roman: *Marketing Humanitarianism, Human Rights, and the Bildungsroman*

> For many years now, the majority culture has sought to image the fringe in dubious productions often termed 'autobiographies'. . . . [T]he subject matter tightly controlled and rendered down for public consumption, . . . [they] were written by altruistic people for reasons such as to show the white majority that Aborigines were human beings capable of achievement, or to serve as models for Aboriginal youngsters. . . . [Recent] life stories [written by Aborigines] . . . . might be a sign that Aboriginal literature is moving from the fringe towards the centre. Perhaps; but if it is, it is moving into a place already created.
>
> —MUDROOROO NAROGIN, *Writing From the Fringe*

Mamadou's figuration of the implicated reader as a potential literary humanitarian identifies an agency, or authority, that devolves upon the already-incorporated reader (and upon the act of reading more generally) in sociocivil political formations of an imagined democratic community of rights holders that are constituted as much on reading as on speech acts. This collective appears as the modern liberal public sphere that took the form of a bourgeois reading society in Habermas, the imagined community of the nation in Anderson, and transnational "diasporic public spheres" or a "postnational political world" in Appadurai.[108] In its idealized, communalizing form, a "sentimental model of reading" is supposed to "forg[e] collective identities among readers as consumers in a literary marketplace" through mutual "imagination as a social practice."[109] That is, according to the model of the imagined community, "an affectively charged association among distanced readers" is produced through individuals' experience of reading commonly shared texts by which they come to imagine themselves in mutual relation to other readers and thereby constitute a community of sentiment.[110] Such a model, of course, assumes a basic distribution of the technology of literacy and the material of literature (or access to other consumable media) for the cultivation of common sense, if we understand "sense" in its double sense; that is, the modern imagined community is constituted as much by common sentimentality as by popular rationality—as much by what everyone feels (or should feel) as by what everyone already knows (or should know), to paraphrase the opinion of John Humphrey with which this book began.

The sentimental model of reading, which historically facilitated the affective and effective formation of the modern democratic nation-state, was among the legal and literary technologies transferred by the UN for its projection (and realization) of an international order based on human rights. But, in an international sociopolitical formation that dispenses power differentially to the already and the not-yet incorporated (to citizen-readers and disenfranchised non-readers), these "cosmopolitan reading practices"—which K. Anthony Appiah suggests "are often undergirded by [an Enlightenment humanist] instinct . . . to learn 'mutual toleration,' even the sympathy and concern for others"[111]—tend to coalesce in a patronizing humanitarian model of reading that effectively reinforces the disparity between rights holders and those who cannot enact their rights. In a social order constituted even partially on reading acts, the incorporated readers' power to withhold or grant a "reading" (or hearing) may be tantamount to the power to retract or extend the community's franchise—to deauthorize or authorize claims for inclusion, to constrict or "expand the reference of the terms 'our kind of people' and 'people like us,'" as Richard Rorty writes in his advocacy for the "manipulation of sentiment" as an antifoundationalist program for the realization of an international human rights order.[112] These "generous imaginings" (as Elaine Scarry calls them), whose "unanchored good will" is fortified by the social and intellectual divide between the enfranchised benefactor-reader and the marginal subject in need of reading, are mediated in particular conceptual and cultural story forms;[113] indeed, in practice, they tend to both conform to and intensify normative generic conventions for the forms that "our kind of people" and their stories take.

In each of the novels that I have analyzed throughout this book, the protagonist responds to generic expectations about "people like us"—expectations expressed (however tacitly) as a social imperative to develop the human personality and to narrate an account of that development according to socially acceptable conventions. Rarely is the demand figured so overtly or heavy-handedly as it is when issued from the mouths and intensified by the thumbscrews of the torturers in Christopher Hope's *A Separate Development*. More typically, as we have seen, the *Bildungsheld* and its narrative respond to more subtle forces—to the interpellative demands of social formations, relations, and institutions. In the idealist version of the genre and in normative international human rights discourse, the social compulsion to develop (and to narrate the story of that process) is configured as fully corresponding to the predisposition of the human personality, making the modern social demand merely a correlative institutional expression of an innate human impulse to modernize; thus, in Goethe's novel, the Society of the Tower acts and speaks not in its own self-substantial name (in the name of society or the proto-nation) but on behalf of Wilhelm's desire to develop himself just as he is and in the assumed name of Nature. Indeed, the plot of the idealist *Bildungsroman* was supposed to effect this conversion, naturalizing both the process and story form of modern socialization by transmuting the social injunction into a personal compulsion—force into choice. Whether the developmental injunction is attributed to (human) nature (as it is in Goethe's novel) or to modernity—or, more precisely, to the institutions of nation-statist modernity (as it is in Marjorie Oludhe Macgoye's *Coming to Birth*)—it is generally given conventional literary form as the demand of a society of readers. It is, for example, emblematized in Macgoye's novel by both the voice of the altruistic, free indirect narrator and the Kenyan news media and, more insidiously, in Tununa Mercado's *In a State of Memory* by "an entire social class seeking to ease its conscience" by requiring from returning

Argentine exiles stories of "adaptation."[114] Similarly, Beyala, Dangarembga, and Hope insist upon keeping in view the historicity and particularity of the sociocultural motivations behind the imperative for (the story of) development, configuring its generic compulsion explicitly as a readerly demand personified by the implicated reader within the dissensual text. Thus, these novels ironize their own generic conformity even as they activate the historical function of the *Bildungsroman* as a rights claim.

Each of these novels figures the social relations and differentials between the already-incorporated and the not-yet-incorporated (the developed and the developing) as the relations between a society of readers and an apprentice of (social) literacy. In its idealized human rights form, as Abdou surmises from the official French cultural imperative, the demand is configured as humanitarian—a form of assistance that constitutes an insistence that the unincorporated, for his own good, become what he ostensibly already is by right. That is, in its ideal configuration, a society of readers assumes a benign humanitarian interventionist posture toward the unincorporated, pressing them to assert their right to claim a right to incorporation—a right to have rights. This disproportionality was imaged in the idealist *Bildungsroman* as a legitimate social difference that social literacy training and the cultivation of a literary sensibility were supposed to transcend. But, in our contemporary era of late capitalism and globalization, these social and power relations are also matters of market relations. The idealist developmental compulsion of human rights and *Bildung* in literature becomes a generic, narrative imperative that is formulated by popular demand and given institutional expression in the acquisition, editorial, publishing, marketing, and critical practices of the dominant literary industry. That is, in a heavily marketized and commoditized social economy, a society of readers' humanitarian pressure for social conformity (what it regards as liberation by enfranchisement) translates into a commercial pressure for generic conformity (liberation by literacy and publication).

Cultural critic and author Mudrooroo (Narogin) has described this process in relation to the treatment of Aboriginal writing and identity in Australia, where, over the course of the twentieth century, the ideal of incorporation was converted into a "humanitarian" social policy of assimilation and commercialized through the editorial, marketing, and critical machinery of an "altruistic" literary industry.[115] Mudrooroo argues that compulsory "conform[ity]" to "the fixed [European] categories of literature" becomes a literary weapon against Aboriginality when it constrains that part of "culture that lies outside European convention" in the novelistic "hallmark of character development."[116] The literary industry canalizes the Aboriginal life story, packaging it for popular consumption in predetermined categories like "the battler" genre, a variant of the *Bildungsroman* whose "plotline" Mudrooroo summarizes: "Poor underprivileged person through the force of his or her own character makes it to the top through own efforts."[117] Submitted to the "rationality" of a literary market, the ideological and social imperative for assimilation is converted into a generic imperative for a story of incorporation. Thus, "moving from the fringe towards the centre" typically means "moving into a place already created"—a place prefigured by both the law of human rights and the literary culture of the *Bildungsroman*. The commercialization of the traditional social work of the novel of incorporation converts the *Bildungsroman* into what I have called a *Clef à Roman*: an author's generic key to the lettered city that comes with a novel about a protagonist's attempts to gain admission into a society of readers.[118] In an era when both human rights and literature have been commoditized, the historically marginalized author's access to the dominant literary public sphere is very often conditioned on a novel about the tribulations of an individual's social apprenticeship in the culture of the dominant literary public sphere—that is, on a novel about the conditions of its own existential necessity and artifactual improbability.

Like the *Roman à Clef*, whose fictionalized depiction of actual people and events may be cracked with a key to its code, the *Clef à Roman* has an allegorical quality in its dramatization of the process by which both a book and its author find publication (in the double sense). This is not to say that these novels are simply coded authorial autobiographies (although many contain such elements[119]) nor that they are merely, or "necessarily," "national allegories" in the Jamesonian sense of a private individual's life narrative that stands in for the story of "*the public third-world culture and society*."[120] Both of those reading strategies have something to recommend them, since the *Bildungsroman* has always had an allegorical aspect as a novel about the sociohistorical conditions of its own possibility, thematizing the process by which the individual (both the reader and the protagonist) acquires the social literacy and literary sensibility required to become a part of the public social texture. But the *Clef à Roman* is a *Bildungsroman* that, at least implicitly, recognizes itself as a commodity in a socioliterary economy—as a vehicle for the commercial publication of the author that is about the social publication (the going public) of the protagonist. In the international context, these *Clefs à Roman* offer an international allegory because they allegorize the literary industrial generic constraints that prescriptive reading programs like the national allegory impose on historically marginalized authors as the condition of admission to the World Republic of Letters. Thus, the *Clef à Roman* is allegorical because it performs sociologically what it thematizes textually—it is simultaneously performative and figurative, repeatedly crossing the line between fiction and petition. These novels abstract as form and theme the conditions and dynamics under which they are produced, published, packaged, circulated, and consumed, which, given the alliance between the *Bildungsroman* and human rights that I have been describing throughout this book, also comments upon the current conditions and dynamics of human rights in "the global late-capitalist system of commodity exchange."[121]

Calixthe Beyala's novel is particularly rich in its representation of some of these ways in which social relations take the form of market relations in a postcolonial, capitalist (inter)national order that dispenses literary and human rights differentially. Beyala's novel foregrounds not only the sociocultural conventionality of the genre (her novel's own stereotypicality) but also its socioeconomic instrumentality (its commodification as a kind of generic shibboleth for the historically marginalized author who seeks access to the literary public sphere). Not only does the novel itself function as a *Clef à Roman*, it also thematizes the sociocultural and material conditions of that function through the compositional conceit by which Mamadou is figured as the aspiring author of his own *Clef à Roman*. Mamadou's use of the traditional genre of incorporation is both idealistic and tactical; he appropriates the *Bildungsroman* for its historical social work as the proper (both socially acceptable and obligatory) novelistic form for the articulation of a rights claim of inclusion in a bourgeois republic of letters, but he also exploits its commercial appeal to a society of already-incorporated readers—a society of book buyers—in the hope it might remediate the imagined community that sees him only as a drain on social resources. That is, although Mamadou responds to public demand for an account of himself, he trades on the commodity value of the genre as a vehicle of publicity to air his indictment of French social hypocrisy and his claim for enfranchisement in the public sphere. In appropriating both the commercial and the idealistic functions of the *Bildungsroman*, Beyala's novel thematizes the conditions and dynamics of its own production, but it does so with specific regard to the generic, social, and market fortunes of the novel and human rights in a late-capitalist commodity economy.

Fredric Jameson recognized something of both the incorporative social work of the *Bildungsroman* that I have described throughout this book and the genre's role as a *Clef à Roman* in the contemporary literary industry when he claimed in 1993 that the "archaeological canon of non-Western novels" assembled "in English translations some forty years ago, by patient librarians or adventuresome planners of humanities or great-books courses (generally junior faculty without tenure), consisted almost exclusively of bildungsromane from the immediate postwar period."[122] Jameson accounts for the prevalence of the *Bildungsroman* in the corpus of "Third World classics" in characteristic Marxian sociological terms by focusing on the production end of the supply line: "'That the novel of 'formation,' the educational novel, was somehow a formal solution of historical significance can be demonstrated by the frequency in which it appears in a range of different cultures, and at once becomes exportable to the West."[123] But rather than focus on the phenomenon of the form's instant exportability and its implication in a commodity economy, Jameson explains "that the emergence of a certain kind of storytelling documents the existence of a kind of social life in which these stories can be found—that, as a tautology, is surely an irrefutable position." I will not refute that position; however, the crucial part of Jameson's sociological-formal tautology is not, I believe, the eminently commonsensical notion that genres document "the existence of a kind of social life" but the begged second half of his formulation: "in which these stories can be found."

Jameson's Marxist account of the emergence of the *Bildungsroman* in the Third World largely ignores the role of the reader in a global commodity economy, who, as a consumer, makes generic demands that affect the modes of literary production and that are given effect through the editorial offices of the publishing industry. Although a society of readers is never fully homogeneous, neither is it as heterogeneous as its self-promotion might suggest; in our contemporary uneven, largely Western-capitalized global-literary-market economy, whose editorial authority and primary targeted readership remain rooted in the West, these novels still tend to be "found" precisely where Jameson seems to have encountered them: libraries, bookstores, catalogues, classrooms, and literary criticism of the Euro-American media empires.[124] Thus, I would suggest that the "kind of social life" that our contemporary, "at once . . . export-able" non-Western *Bildungsromane* are thought to "document" cannot be located simply by using the traditional comparative liter-ary and sociological coordinates and parametrics of the nation-state; nor should their abundance in the canon of Third World literature be taken as evidence either for the naturalness of the genre for rep-resenting the experience of the transition to adulthood or for the transcendental rightness and fundamental egalitarianism of human rights and the *Bildungsroman*. Rather, given the asymmetry of global literary production, distribution, and consumption, the pro-liferation of these novels in the lettered metropolis "owes as much to the relations of the marketplace as to the[ir authors'] conviction to 'testify' or 'bear witness'" to a "non-Western" social life, as Chandra Mohanty importantly warned eager Western consumers of "third world women's texts" against reading them as anthropo-logically or sociologically unmediated representations of women's lives in the Third World.[125] Indeed, aided by the mainstreaming of blunted, depoliticized versions of postcolonialism, multicultur-alism, and cosmopolitanism, the market value of and desire for these "marginal" literary commodities—for the latest Third World *Bildungsroman*—has only increased since Mohanty's admonition. Systemically, the proliferation in the so-called World Republic of Letters of *Bildungsromane* from the spaces of historical global mar-ginality says as much about readerly demands, critical desires, and "humanitarian" investments on this side of the "developmental di-vide" as it does about writerly predilections, human rights endeav-ors, and the enjoyment of free expression on the other side. Indeed, to be cynical, the *Bildungsroman* has come to serve a homologous gatekeeping function for the literary cosmopolitan postulant that proper responses to the asylum interview serve for the political refugee. Thus, given the differential power dynamics of the global literary industry that have more or less canonized the *Bildungsroman* as a compulsory novelistic genre for the historically marginal author, these novels may be understood to emerge from (and to be found in) a dislocated international marketplace of literature and human rights, where humanitarian imperatives and human rights claims are negotiated according to the logic of demand and supply. The contemporary globalization of international human rights principles and discourse is inseparable from the operations of market forces that have also facilitated the globalization of the *Bildungsroman*. As *Clefs à Roman*, these novels make legible the conditions of their own emergence—that is, the market relations of an asymmetrical global economy that has commodified not only the *Bildungsroman* and human rights but their historical alliance.

Jameson ignores the role of consumer demand (and the social politics of consumption) in the production of Third-World *Bildungsromane*, but his example of the prototypical "Third World Classic" is telling. "Camara Laye's *L'enfant noir* of 1953," he writes, "is both iterative and singular, characteristic of all that was to follow and itself something like the precursor text."[126] Laye's novel, which tells the story of a young African boy's coming of age in colonial French Guinea and emigrating to make his way in Paris, was not only modeled, as Laye himself claimed, on Flaubert's *Education Sentimentale*, but was supported, if not directly sponsored, by the office of the Ministry of France Overseas, "reworked by several people into a form that would appeal to the Western public," and first published and lauded in Paris.[127] According to Adele King, the Ministry "wanted to see this work published" because it showed "life in French West Africa in terms of the benefits of colonization" and therefore seemed to support "French policy on the overseas territories."[128] Thus, it seems Laye's *Bildungsroman* thematized the dynamics of colonial, "humanitarian" patronage and the imperatives of developmentalism that conditioned the publication of the novel itself.

In a contemporary international literary order still largely divided between book-producing and non-book-producing nations, too little has changed since the 1970s when UNESCO described this condition as a humanitarian crisis that required concerted international book-aid programs not just to transfer books to literature-poor countries but to transfer the publishing technologies to jump-start local literary industries. In fact, the increasingly concentrated and monopolistic media conglomerates of the West have tended to exacerbate the disparity, resulting in almost permanent book droughts—"catastrophically low levels of book production" in some parts of the world.[129] Given the metropolitan-dominated-market structure of the global literary industry, which in many ways replicates the classical colonial economy of resource extraction, it is not uncommon that many of the Third World novels and novelists that we read in the West were initially assisted by a development agency—either a governmental program or an international NGO. For example, Ngũgĩ wa Thiong'o's "first-ever attempt at a novel"[130] won a 1962 competition sponsored by the colonial East African Literature Bureau, whose official humanitarian mandate was to "facilitate the transfer of a viable literary system to the colony."[131] Similarly, Tsitsi Dangarembga's writing career was launched when she took third prize with a short story, "The Letter" (1985), in a competition for African women writers sponsored by the Swedish Office of Women in Development. The Swedish International Development Authority (SIDA) subsequently published "The Letter" in an anthology of new African women's writing that debuted at the third United Nations World Conference on Women held in Nairobi in 1985 to review the achievements of the United Nations' Decade for Women.[132]

In thinking about the role of consumer demand in the dissemination of the *Bildungsroman*, we should keep in mind the ambivalent historical alignment of the novelistic genre (like human rights themselves) with various predatory developmental projects and processes of globalization—e.g., colonialism, (neo)imperialisms, and consumer capitalism. Jacques Rancière offers a provocative description of the process by which human rights become humanitarian rights (rights that one claims in the place of an other who cannot realize them) that might illuminate the relations among cosmopolitan reading, generic compulsion, and the "new humanitarianism" that I am tracing.[133] Arguing that human rights "appear . . . empty" for incorporated members of the hegemonic class in the West, where the law has "become identical to the natural life of society,"

Rancière suggests that documents like the UDHR become purely tautological—declarations of rights for those who already enjoy such rights.[134] And when rights appear redundant, he writes, "You do the same as charitable persons do with their old clothes. You give them to the poor. Those rights that appear to be useless in their place are sent abroad, along with medicine and clothes, to people deprived of medicine, clothes, and rights. . . . They become humanitarian rights, the rights of . . . the victims of the absolute denial of right." If the *Bildungsroman* has, as many critics suggest, "played out its possibilities for males" and "outlived its usefulness and become virtually defunct in the European context," its marginalization—that is, its transportation to and use by globally disenfranchised subjects— represents both a translation (or transformation) and a renewal of the genre's historical social work in the overlapping global networks of literature and human rights.[135] Therefore what we might call the new literary humanitarianism—the Western desire for *Bildungsromane* of the non-Western other that is enacted through book markets—may be the latest in a series of globalizing forces that encourages the technology-transfers of human rights and the *Bildungsroman*.

I do not mean to suggest that the contemporary proliferation of non-Western examples is simply the product of a cultural imperialist imposition, nor do I mean to suggest that the "soft" imperialism of Western, or cosmopolitan, consumer demand for these novels is the single determinative factor in their production. The factors that contribute to the globalization of the *Bildungsroman* and the rest of the human rights package are more complex than such a unidirectional model of foreign intervention or (sentimental) investment would comprehend. Just as anti-imperialism and "resistance to power has a creationist role in the making of 'contemporary' human rights,"[136] the contemporary *Bildungsroman*, as a literary technology for making human rights claims, represents as much a contestation of as an acquiescence to the official terms of globalization, including the globalization of human rights discourse. Part of what has made the genre such a historically supple and vital novelistic form, from the eighteenth century to the twenty-first, is its technological capacity to negotiate contradiction. If the classical *Bildungsroman* mediated between the apparently conflicting demands of social conformity and individual inclination within the Westphalian para-metrics of the emergent nation-state, in a global context those com-pulsions might be understood in the terms of international humanitarianism and human rights. Indeed, I suggest that one way to describe the globalization of the contemporary *Bildungsroman* form is as a complex process of interaction between humanitarian-ism and human rights—that is, between an international sociocultu-ral intervention styled as humanitarian assistance and a rights claim often articulated to reject the patronizing terms and implications of that assistance. The *Bildungsroman* is the location and novelistic operation of international human rights globalization, the literary space in which the hegemonic norms of international human rights are being both naturalized and contested; this is also the space where candidates for the sociohistorical universal that have not yet been translated into international human rights norms are being negotiated and begin to become legible at the international level through the transformation of the conventions of the traditional *Bildungsroman*. (Indeed, the history of technology transfers suggests that while the tools may not be able to dismantle the master's house, they are useful for prying open its doors and windows.) Any *Bildungsroman* simultaneously asserts a rights claim and responds to the humanitarian imperative to assert such a claim. This is espe-cially evident when, as in many of the examples that I have exam-ined throughout this book, the dissensual *Bildungsroman* narrates the failure of social integration—when the generic and human rights promise of free and full human personality development re-mains unfulfilled.

In the abstract, an idealist human rights form of the contempo-rary *Bildungsroman* would novelize the aspirational narrative of in-corporation articulated in international law that takes citizenship as the ultimate expression of human sociality and personality. Rarely, if ever, does the story of human personality development narrated in any particular novel fulfill the plot ideal projected in the law. Such discrepancies between the ideal and novelistic realism have led many typologists of the novel to the skeptical conclusion that the literary form is an "unfulfilled" genre.[137] I suggest that such narrative unfulfillment—what Bakhtin called "unfinalizability," or that *"unfinalizable something in man"*[138]—has become a generic vir-tue and constitutive feature of the contemporary postcolonial *Bil-dungsroman*. A similar benchmark has long been employed by human rights critics who have argued that, since their ideal form is to be found nowhere in the historical (or natural) world, those rights must therefore not exist. Universal human rights themselves remain an unfulfilled genre of legal rights; however, we should think of this unfulfillment not as failure but as incompletion—the perpetual sociohistorical and narrative condition of a positive promise of a Blochian "not yet" that is "proper to an understanding of the universal itself: that which remains 'unrealized' by the universal constitutes it essentially."[139]

The United Nations conscripted (almost by default) the *Bildungsroman* both as the normative, ideal novelistic form of expression of the free and full development of the human personality and as the literary technology for the "realization . . . of a world in which human beings shall enjoy freedom of speech and belief and freedom from fear and want" (UDHR). Our contemporary postcolonial examples tend to register the discrepancy between an international human rights ideal and actual social practice. Therefore part of what these contemporary Third World *Bildungsromane* make legible are some of the exclusions, disparities, and inequities enacted when the *Bildungsroman* is canonized as the compulsory genre for incorporation into an international human rights society of readers and when its idealist image of human sociality is taken as the necessary paradigm for human personality development. Thus, we should recognize these novels not primarily as gauges of the triumph of human rights globally, or as intimations of the realization of an international order of human rights just over the horizon, or as evidence of global consensus on human rights principles; rather, what they make legible in their depiction of the ruptures between the ideal and the real and in their registration of human rights claims is the current state of the human rights promise—the location where (and the condition in which) the "not yet" of human rights universalism now stands.

CODICIL

Intimations of a Human Rights International: "The Rights of Man; or, What Are We [Reading] For?"

One of the messages I want to say to the people of Afghanistan is it's our country's pleasure and honor to be involved with the future of this country. We like stories of young girls going to school for the first time so they can realize their potential. . . . [T]he people of America have great . . . regard for human life and human dignity. . . . [W]e care about the plight of people. . . . I'm going to repeat what I said before: We *like stories*, and *expect stories*, of young girls going to school in Afghanistan.

—U.S. President George W. Bush,
Speech to the Afghan people, 1 March 2006

Eight days after the world's most notorious Baathist, ex-Iraqi President Saddam Hussein, was pulled from a spider hole by U.S. forces outside of Tikrit in December 2003, National Public Radio aired a review of a recently translated Saudi Arabian *Bildungsroman* entitled *Adama*. The short review by Alan Cheuse is worth reproducing, because it exemplifies a fairly typical metropolitan reception of non-Western literature as well as some of the discursive and historical linkages between the *Bildungsroman* and human rights that I have examined throughout this book.

Adama is the name of the neighborhood where the main character, a smart young Saudi fellow, named Hisham Ibrahim al-Abir, a rebellious late teenager, undergoes a formidable, and to Western readers by now rather familiar, transformation from homeboy to questioning intellectual. His mother and father of course want nothing but the best for him. And Hisham's got a good inquiring mind. He reads Western novels and a lot of philosophy; books are truly his life. But although he has a bunch of jovial male pals, and every opportunity to become an engineer or doctor, he eventually falls in with a crowd of clandestine

317

Marxists. With them he plots the overthrow of the Saudi government in the
service of the pan-Arab vision of the Baathists, but then he becomes disillu-
sioned with their radicalism. His story has its moments: a sexual initiation scene
both gross and pathetic; a spiritual night beneath the stars in the desert of Saudi
Arabia's aptly named "Empty Quarter." But for most of its length, the book
seems like a poor Middle Eastern relative of the traditional Western coming-
of-age novel. Scene by scene, *Adama* is talky, with never enough metaphors to
make it anything but a flat-footed account of one bright boy's education. Still,
I read it all the way through, and I think it was well worth it, to eavesdrop, as
it were, on an uncommonly free voice from a quarter of the world that usually
suppresses such pioneers: an empty quarter.[1]

The commentator introducing Cheuse's review notes that the novel
earned "a number of *fatwas*" for this Arab pioneer of second-rate,
derivative Western literature, the journalist and political science
professor Turki al-Hamad. There is nothing like a good *fatwa* to
boost sales, but compared to Rushdie's success, *Adama* remains a
relatively obscure novel in the United States and Europe, although
it is, as the book's dustjacket announces, a "bestseller in the Middle
East . . . despite being officially banned in several countries, including . . . Saudi Arabia." Cheuse himself dusts off Joseph Conrad's
Orientalist tropes not only to characterize the atmosphere of *Adama*
but to describe the encounter between a cosmopolitan Western
reader and an Eastern novel. He reduces the bustling city of Riyadh
(and by extension the whole of the Arabian Peninsula) to the
sparsely populated sands of the Rub' al Khali (Empty Quarter)—a
desert of nomads, silence, and secrets that reveal themselves to the
prurient, interloping gaze of the Western reader. Interestingly, the
urban characters in the novel use this same trope to mock one another's intellectual capacities as the sort underdeveloped by a premodern land where the "sense of place itself was banished, and time
seemed somehow to be suspended. . . ."[2] If the encounter with this
"uncommonly free voice from a[n empty] quarter of the world" no
longer induces the Western reader's Conradian fear of a "remote
kinship" with non-Western others—what Marlow described in
Heart of Darkness as the sneaking "suspicion of their not being inhuman"—part of the trouble with *Adama*, for Cheuse, is that it is all
too familiar.[3]

It is a curious phrase ("to Western reader's by now rather familiar") that Cheuse chooses to qualify our recognition of the story

form. What is familiar, it seems from these cultural, temporal, and geographic qualifications, is not so much the *Bildungsroman* form (which could hardly be described as only now becoming familiar) but the story of non-Westerners coming of age. So, on the one hand, the Third World *Bildungsroman* is a stepchild of a Western "original" (with, to complete the implication of Cheuse's metaphor, a rich uncle in the States) and, on the other, such novels of personalization have become characteristic of non-Western literature circulated in the West. Thus, *Adama* is simultaneously an uncommon, but pale, copy of an original and just one more of an innumerable canon of such knockoffs. This dialectic of familiar (form) and foreign (content)—of generic predictability and pioneering innovation—characterizes more generally the international literary relations between Western cosmopolitan readers and non-Western literature.[4] If, in the century since Conrad, the Global South is no longer the image of perpetual childhood (of "primitivism, abnormality, underdevelopment, non-creativity and traditionalism"[5]) it has been promoted, in the dominant transition narrative of modernization and development, to the land of problematic, antisocial adolescence; the *Bildungsroman* relocates to these demarginalizing territories of the world republic of letters and an international order of human rights to perform its historical social work of incorporation and emancipation. Freedom in the Middle East, as Cheuse's review esteems it, is the liberty to write (even flatfootedly) in the idiom of the Western novel, to submit oneself to the generic codes and conventions of the *Bildungsroman*.

    Adama is indeed a pedestrian male coming-of-age story, satisfying all of the plot elements that Jerome Buckley identified in the European *Bildungsroman*,[6] and Hisham's transformation from "homeboy to questioning intellectual" is even more prosaic than Cheuse suggests. Hisham is an avid reader not only of revolutionary theory by Lenin, Nasser, Fanon, Régis Debray, and Che Guevara but of canonical European *Bildungsromane* and novels by Dickens, Balzac, Flaubert, Dostoevsky, Gorky, and Hugo (among many others). The "crowd of clandestine Marxists" with whom he associates is little more than a semisecret bourgeois reading society with revolutionary pretensions that breaks up as much from a lack of common conviction and shared interpretations of the books they read as it does from the external pressure of a secret police seeking to keep the comrades from their "study of forbidden texts."[7] The conflict between Hisham's youthful ideals of social justice and the concrete form of revolution in which those are put into practice comes to a head when his reading group debates the blistering critique that "[t]hose in power in Iraq" have betrayed the pan-Arabic socialist cause and are nothing more than "a pack of opportunists and reactionary traitors with no relation whatsoever to [our] great revolutionary party."[8] If the evolutionary trope of *Bildung* (and its novelization) "implie[s] opposition to a barbaric political system and . . . offer[s] its proponents an alternative to revolution for realizing humanitarian goals," the revolution to be forestalled in *Adama* is a repeat in Saudi Arabia of that other July fourteenth revolution—the socialist Iraqi revolution of 1958 that eventually installed Saddam Hussein in power.[9] The plot accomplishes this displacement of social revolution by personal evolution with the disbandment of Hisham's Marxist reading group and his matriculation at the Faculty of Commerce in Riyadh, where he will "be able to read *Das Kapital* and understand it properly," not as the critical foundation for a proletarian revolution but as a theoretical analysis of capitalism indispensable to a future Saudi businessman. Hisham's youthful revolutionary fervor is ultimately redirected into his formal education in economics and politics, for which he hopes to "get a scholarship to study in America or Britain."[10] In the end, Hisham gives up the ideal of social revolution to become, as Hegel commented wryly on the dénouement of Goethe's *Wilhelm Meister*, "as good a Philistine as others."[11]

Eighteen months after the U.S.-Allied invasion of Afghanistan and the "fall" of the Taliban, another topical *Bildungsroman*, carefully packaged and produced by its editors and publisher, began its journey to the American bestseller lists in June 2003: Khaled Hosseini's *The Kite Runner*. This *Clef à Roman* tells the story of Amir, a refugee who flees Afghanistan during the Russian invasion of 1981 and who himself becomes a bestselling writer in the United States. Just months before 9/11, the narrator-protagonist sneaks into Kabul to rescue the orphaned son of his onetime best friend and houseboy, Hassan. His return is a quest for redemption—to repair a childhood lapse of judgment; Amir, an ethnic Pashtun, had abandoned his ethnic Hazara houseboy to be beaten by a gang of kids who years later become cruel leaders in the Taliban, killing

Hassan and taking his son for a sex slave. But Hassan turns out to be Amir's half brother, and, given their shared patrimony, Amir's redemption represents not so much an overcoming of ethnic prejudices—since Hassan is the mistaken object of those prejudices—as a reunification of the natural family. This plot logic (which updates the paternal recognition scene in Goethe's novel) does not suggest that Pashtuns should, in principle, treat Hazaras with dignity and equanimity despite ethnic or cultural difference; rather, it warns that some Hazaras may be Pashtuns, by nature (birth) if not by social convention. Thus, the suspect humanitarian moral is not that we should regard difference as irrelevant to our treatment of others, but that we should treat others as ourselves—that "[a]ll human beings . . . should act towards one another in a spirit of [half] brotherhood" (UDHR)—because they may not, in the end, be altogether (ethnically) other. The novel ultimately elevates the invasion of Afghanistan to an act of humanitarian intervention not only by representing the Taliban as a vicious sect of homosexual pedophiles intent on repressing the human personality; it also assures its American (and Allied) market readers that "we" are on the side of the people (and therefore that the aptly named "Operation Enduring Freedom" is a liberationist rather than imperialist venture) and, more pointedly, that these are people like us—people who "love . . . the *idea* of America" and freedom, enjoy Coca-Cola, appreciate John Wayne and Charles Bronson films, read *Les Miserables* and Ian Fleming novels, pursue happiness, and desire upward mobility.[12]

According to U.S. First Lady and literacy advocate Laura Bush, who recommends *The Kite Runner* as one of her and her husband's favorite books, the novel "tells a compelling story of how wounded people and wounded societies seek redemption and renewal" in a world of lost childhoods.[13] As the president's speech to the Afghan people during a surprise visit to Kabul in the spring of 2006 suggests, it is the possibility of childhood and normative *Bildung* that America supposedly seeks to restore with the forced installation of democracy and that it also *expects* to read about. In formulating a literary foreign policy from American reading tastes for Third World *Bildungsromane*, President Bush implies that at least part of what we are fighting for is reading—not only for a world in which young girls will have the opportunity to learn to read (and realize

their potential) but also for a world in which the philanthropic readers of the West will be well-supplied with stories about young girls
learning to read. Converting readers' taste into humanitarian expectation, Bush appeals to Americans to identify not with girls kept
from reading but with his own paternalistic desires and literary
magnanimity for those girls and their stories—with his own "cosmopolitan largesse."[14]

Bush presents himself as an empathetic figure of American humanitarian (literary) sensibility—a man who would rather be a
peacetime reader than a wartime president. In a sense, he merely
adopts as a policy of literary foreign relations what a survey of our
recent popular literature seems to suggest: that we do like and expect to read more of *Reading Lolita in Tehran*, more reading of Balzac by "little Chinese seamstress[es]," more *Bildungsromane* of
young girls (and boys) going to school in "the literarily deprived
territories" to realize their potential in the "world republic of letters."[15] These popular stories of literary incorporation package a
modicum of tolerable, even cherishable, cultural difference in a generic story form that insinuates a transnational affinity between the
novel's reader and its protagonist-reader. To put this in slightly
reductive, materialistic terms, the ethnic prints worn by the protagonists mark them as foreign, while the cloth binding of the novel
already outfits their stories in the generic trappings of the familiar.[16]

Most of the *Bildungsromane* that I have discussed in this book
were written by authors, and feature protagonists, "whose introduction to the very idea of the novel came from reading French and
English novels in the course of a colonial (and latterly a postcolonial) education."[17] These non-Western novels should not be read
as transparent representations of cultural, anthropological, or ethnographic difference, but this does not mean that they are simply
cultural derivatives of the Western novel. As Peter Hitchcock spec-
ulates about the apparent expansiveness of the novel form, "the
democratic instincts of the genre, nurtured by the democratic instincts of its genesis, are open to rearticulation and reformation
through content which is itself liberatory in its inclinations. . . .
[T]he postcolonial novel exists because it is in the nature of the
genre to provide form for content that challenges what constitutes
the genre."[18] Indeed, if we view the *Bildungsroman* as the generic
name of a social function, or incorporative technology, as I have

done throughout this book, then its vitality at the margins of what Pascale Casanova calls "world literary space" speaks to the character, operation, and relations of an international order in which both human rights and "world literature" emerge, are implicated, commodified, and determined.[19]

Thematically within *Adama* and *The Kite Runner*, and in their public reception (as with the other *Bildungsromane* that I have examined in this book), the worlds of geopolitics, consumer capitalism, literary subjectivity, and human rights law, discourse, and practice overlap in a single world. In *The World Republic of Letters*, Casanova attempts to compile a codex of the rules of emergence and operation of this world literary space; while its "literary geography," she says, "can never be completely superimposed upon the political geography of the world's nations," it nonetheless abides certain "international laws" of its own.[20] Like the "international treaty regimes" of human rights, the international law of world literary space is not yet "the expression of community but of power."[21] As I have argued throughout this book, international human rights law appropriated forms and institutions—e.g., the *Bildungsroman*, the public sphere, and human rights themselves—that historically served to legitimate the emergent European nation-state. In its conscription of the *Bildungsroman*, international law retasks the nationalist genre of human personality development to perform its work of incorporation at an international level, largely in advance of any administrative, institutional formation comparable to the nation-state. If contemporary human rights have failed to deliver fully on their transformative promises to internationalize the individual and to procure the effective "universal" recognition and observance of human rights themselves, this may be partly a consequence of having enlisted modern Westphalian institutions and cultural forms to imagine, and hypostatize, a projective Dumbarton Oaksian international order. Thus, the novels that I have examined must qualify as "world texts," since they refer to "a broader entity [than the nation-state]—a continent, or the world-system as a whole" (in Franco Moretti's terms); but, as Simon Gikandi notes, such novels "cannot [yet] do without the framework of the nation. What needs to be underscored . . . is the persistence of the nation-state in the very literary works that were supposed to gesture toward a transcendental global culture."[22] I would add that the nation-state persists as the organizing principle not only in the novels (and human rights law) but in the critical and reading practices that we perform on these novels. In other words, I am suggesting that the effective limitations of human rights are related not merely to the institutional frailty of the international legal regime but to the historically nationalist limitations of our literary imaginations—cognitive limitations that make it possible, in the era of a global "war on terror," to reduce *The Kite Runner* to "a story of two childhood friends in Afghanistan"[23] and to read *Adama* as the expression of a "free voice" from an "empty quarter" rather than to consider the places of the writers and their readers themselves within overlapping world systems.

The implicit cosmopolitan model of reading lurking within George Bush's statement of great novelistic expectations asks relatively little of our literary, humanitarian imaginations; it invites us to identify not with people unlike us but with our kind of people—people who "care about the plight of people." In a world where privileges and rights, as well as literary technologies and juridico-institutional resources, are unequally distributed, such cosmopolitan reading practices often serve to recenter the traditional subjects of history now as the subjects of benevolence, humanitarian interventionist sentimentality, and human rights—the literary agents of an international human rights imaginary.[24] "As more texts from elsewhere have entered the syllabus," observes Anthony Appiah, "we are naturally drawn to congratulating ourselves by describing our reading practices as more cosmopolitan."[25] If literacy and the consumption of the literary forms of print capitalism facilitated the individual reader's sentimental imagination of belonging to a national community of fellow reader-citizens, it remains to be seen whether the historically nationalist technologies conscripted by international human rights can crystallize an imagined international community of human rights holders.

In his Oxford-Amnesty lecture, philosopher Richard Rorty proposes that international human rights are not to be realized through more rationality, or "increased moral knowledge"; instead, he advocates a sentimental education in which "sympathy" is "manipulated" by reading or "hearing sad and sentimental stories."[26] In other words, the engagement with sad stories cultivates the humanitarian disposition that represents the apogee of *Bildung* in the human rights teleology of personality development. For Rorty, in the international context, "matters of justice become not legislation but literature," matters of mediation and the literary manipulation of readers' sympathetic imaginations that lead us to "see the similarities between ourselves and people very unlike us as outweighing the differences," or to sense that "anyone could assume the role of the subject endowed with rights," as Lynn Festa has described the affective work of the sentimental novel in the eighteenth century.[27] "By 'sympathy,'" explains Rorty, "I mean the sort of reaction that the Athenians had more of after seeing Aeschylus' *The Persians* than before, the sort that white Americans had more of after reading *Uncle Tom's Cabin* than before, the sort that we have more of after watching TV programmes about the genocide in Bosnia";[28] I note, rather crudely, that this is not the sort of reaction that we have had *more* of after watching similar programs about genocide in Rwanda or Darfur, or the daily sufferings of Palestinians in the Gaza strip.

The cosmopolitan solipsism of the Rortyan pragmatic model of sentimental (literary) education becomes evident when he explains that the stories of others suffering become texts for the training of "our" sympathetic moral imaginations; the edifying effects of "sad and sentimental stories," he says, "repeated and varied over the centuries, have induced us, the rich, safe, powerful, people, to tolerate, and even to cherish, powerless people—people whose appearance or habits or beliefs at first seemed an insult to our own moral identity, our sense of the limits of permissible human variation."[29] This sentimental model of reading has a tendency to become a patronizing humanitarianism that is enabled by and subsists on socioeconomic and political disparities. This model of humanitarian reading and sentimentality is essentially not very different from the one that Mamadou ascribes to Lolita's patronizing mother and the implicated reader in Beyala's *Loukoum*. In international human rights legal terms, this humanitarian reader is the freely and fully developed human person who has acquired the capacity to recognize perhaps not the "full weight and solidity" or "the reality of other persons"[30] but the abstract dignity of the human personality in both the self and others, whatever its concrete "human variation," and who is therefore positioned to assist others with the realization of their own human personality and dignity. The edification imagined here is the cultivation of an instrumental humanitarian disposition of the "powerful" (rights holders) toward the "powerless" (those who cannot enact their rights) that ultimately confirms the reader as a capacitated citizen-subject, a fully developed international human rights person.

If, as Casanova explains, a literary public sphere determines and trades in "literary value," then, given the alliance between literature and the law that I have elaborated, it implicitly determines and trades in what Upendra Baxi has called the "symbolic capital of human rights."[31] That is, in "set[ting] the limits and standards of what is and will be considered literary," an international literary public sphere has an implicit regulatory relationship to a projective international order, codifying the normative imagery in which it and the human rights person may be imagined.[32] In a global order that continues to equate literacy with modernity and liberty and that is effectively divided between full-rights holders and those who cannot enact the rights they have, we incorporated readers of contemporary postcolonial *Bildungsromane* must learn from these novels to recognize ourselves in the figure of the implicated reader, whose intentions may be humanitarian but whose reading practices make certain consumerist demands for generic conformity that influence the terms and conventions in which the world can be imagined and the observation and enjoyment of human rights realized. That is, we must learn to recognize not only our structural complicity in an international system that extends and denies human rights differentially, but also the triumphalist cosmopolitan pretensions and privileges of our humanitarian reading practices that can exacerbate the divisions between the incorporated and the disenfranchised that both we and these novels presumably aspire to remedy. Thus, a full sentimental education in human rights literacy would involve not only learning to sense the dignity of the human personality in "people very unlike us" but also unlearning the self-congratulatory sense of benevolence (or *noblesse oblige*) that seems naturally to attend such reading acts of recognition—"[s]till, I read it all the way through, and I think it was well worth it." If we take away from these novels only a heightened sensitivity to human misery and vulnerability and to the dignity and developmental potential of the human personality (whatever the concrete human variation) then we miss half the lesson that these *Bildungsromane* have to teach. These novels insist that, as beneficiaries of the social, economic, and political dispensation of the world and as image brokers of an international imaginary and world literary space, we are already implicated in the processes by which the imagined world is given conventional form in the regulatory regimes of law and literature—by our reading acts, we have already assumed, in Djelal Kadir's words, "the subject agency of the verb 'to world.' "[33]

If Rorty views the prospects of international justice and human rights as matters of literature rather than law, many other social historians, theorists, and literary critics have correlated the sentimental affect produced by particular texts at particular moments in the "last two hundred years of moral progress" precisely with humanitarian and human rights legislative projects.[34] For instance, David Rieff reminds us of "the astonishing and unexpected influence" of Jean-Henry Dunant's *Un souvenir de Solférino* (1862), which detailed the horrors of the Battle of Solférino (1859) during the Austro-Sardinian War and precipitated both the founding of the International Committee of the Red Cross and the adoption of the First Geneva Convention on "The Amelioration of the Condition of the Wounded and Sick in Armed Forces in the Field" (1864).[35] Legal historian Paul Lauren attributes at least part of the international humanitarian sensitization to conditions of "oppression and exploitation" in the nineteenth century to the translation and circulation of literature, including the work of Henrik Ibsen's *The Doll's House* in women's rights movements, *Uncle Tom's Cabin* in the international abolitionist movements, and Balzac's *Les Paysans* and Dickens' *Bleak House* and *Hard Times* in the "burgeoning public consciousness about the sufferings" of the working classes during the Industrial Revolution.[36] More cautiously, Elaine Scarry cites Stephen Spender's exceptional statement about the impact on the British imagination of E. M. Forster's *Passage to India* (1924)— that "overnight" the novel created popular support for the Independence of India Act (1947)—to suggest that very few novels have ever even had such claims made about their effect on legislation.[37] Notwithstanding Scarry's justifiable skepticism, as with the drafters of the UDHR's response to *Robinson Crusoe*, it seems that sometimes a literary feeling for others—or, rather, "the reaction to a book" that excites our sentimental imaginations—"translat[es] . . . into a body of law."[38]

Throughout this book, I have been concerned to elaborate a less spectacular and less immediately measurable set of interrelations and interdependencies between the *Bildungsroman* and international human rights law. I have attempted to show the mutuality, complementarity, and complicity of literature and the law as they cooperate in mundane, but important, ways to universalize and naturalize the normative image of the human in human rights—or, more precisely, the projected image of the international human rights person. Recognizing ourselves in the figure of the implicated reader and the implication of our reading practices in the imagination of an international order based on human rights means acknowledging the ways we collude to naturalize the generic forms in which "human variation" is felt to be socially acceptable. Recognizing the sociohistorical alliance between the *Bildungsroman* and human rights as mutually enabling fictions that institutionalize and naturalize the terms of incorporation in (and exclusion from) an imagined community of readers and rights holders means also recognizing that our reading acts have implications not only for the imagination but the legislation of an international human rights community; they partly determine the discursive parameters within which, and imaginative patterns with which, a human rights international might be realized. That is, the texts we read—and how we read, teach, speak, and write about them—have an effect (however unpredictable) on the possibility that the projection of a world based on human rights might become legible, articulable, and, perhaps, even commonsensical. To paraphrase H. G. Wells: if we are not reading for human rights, what are we reading for?

NOTES

PREAMBLE
The Legibility of Human Rights

1. John P. Humphrey, "The Magna Carta of Mankind," 31. The UDHR passed with no objections and eight abstentions. Of the eight nations that abstained—Byelorussia, Czechoslovakia, Poland, Saudi Arabia, South Africa, Ukraine, Yugoslavia, and the Soviet Union—six were communist Soviet Bloc countries who, despite their active participation in its drafting, felt that the document inappropriately recognized individual rights apart from the state. South Africa abstained because the document recognized rights, like freedom of assembly and movement, that were not, in its opinion, fundamental human rights. Saudi Arabia abstained primarily because some provisions on marriage and the right to religious conversion conflicted with Islamic law and seemed to permit proselytization (Johannes Morsink, *The Universal Declaration of Human Rights: Origins, Drafting, and Intent*, 21–28).

2. David Kennedy, *The Dark Sides of Virtue: Reassessing International Humanitarianism*, 111–48.

3. Jacques Maritain, *The Rights of Man and Natural Law*, 63.

4. For instance, Kenyan writer and critic Micere Mugo shows how traditional Gikuyu orature functioned similarly in precolonial society and in the struggle against British colonialism, facilitating the collective cultural imagination of "a more humane world in which they could reach a full realization of themselves as whole, dignified human beings" (*African Orature and Human Rights*, 22). But even Mugo's description of the social work of traditional Gikuyu orature resonates with the language of *Bildung*, and I contend that historically it would be difficult to imagine contemporary normative human rights law without some generic version of the *Bildungsroman*.

5. Lisa Lowe, *Immigrant Acts: On Asian American Cultural Politics*, 98.

6. Rita Felski, *Beyond Feminist Aesthetics: Feminist Literature and Social Change*, 168.

7. Ernesto Laclau and Chantal Mouffe, *Hegemony and Socialist Strategy: Towards a Radical Democratic Politics*, 159–60.

8. Martha Craven Nussbaum, *Cultivating Humanity: A Classical Defense of Reform in Liberal Education*, 88, 10, 67; Georg Lukács, *Goethe and His Age*, 62.

9. Questions of translation in human rights law are interesting and will recur throughout this book. In a paradoxical sense, human rights remains a kind of unwritten law precisely because it is so often written. Unlike most writing, there is no single authoritative text of international law; rather, the authority normally ascribed to written law is literally intertextual, distributed across and between the various translations of the legal conventions composed in the official languages of the United Nations.

10. Marc Redfield, *Phantom Formations: Aesthetic Ideology and the Bildungsroman*; Jeffrey L. Sammons, "The Mystery of the Missing *Bildungsroman*; or, What Happened to Wilhelm Meister's Legacy?"

11. Roberto Schwarz, *Misplaced Ideas: Essays on Brazilian Culture*, 53.

12. Fredric Jameson, "On Literary and Cultural Import-Substitution in the Third World: The Case of the Testimonio," 182.

13. Wendy Brown, "'The Most We Can Hope For . . .': Human Rights and the Politics of Fatalism," 459.

14. For a good overview of the disciplinary intersections between literary and legal study, see Julie Stone Peters, "Law, Literature, and the Vanishing Real: On the Future of an Interdisciplinary Illusion." For broader introductions to these movements, see the following anthologies of seminal essays. For Critical Race Theory, see Kimberlé Crenshaw, ed., *Critical Race Theory: The Key Writings That Formed the Movement*; Richard Delgado and Jean Stefancic, *Critical Race Theory: An Introduction*; and Mari J. Matsuda et al., eds., *Words That Wound: Critical Race Theory, Assaultive Speech, and the First Amendment*. For Critical Legal Studies, see Mark Kelman, *A Guide to Critical Legal Studies*; and Roberto Mangabeira Unger, *The Critical Legal Studies Movement*. On Feminist Jurisprudence, see Leslie Friedman Goldstein, ed., *Feminist Jurisprudence: The Difference Debate*; and Patricia Smith, ed., *Feminist Jurisprudence*. Finally, see the "Legal Storytelling" special issue of *Michigan Law Review*.

15. Austin Sarat and Thomas R. Kearns, "Editorial Introduction," 3. See also Duncan Kennedy, "The Critique of Rights in Critical Legal Studies."

16. Michel Foucault, "Two Lectures," 98.

17. Louis Althusser, "Ideology and Ideological State Apparatuses (Notes Towards an Investigation)," 182.

18. Immanuel Kant, "An Answer to the Question: What Is Enlightenment?" 58–59.

19. See "Guide to OED entries": http://dictionary.oed.com/about/guide/sense.html.

20. Saidiya V. Hartman, *Scenes of Subjection: Terror, Slavery, and Self-Making in Nineteenth-Century America*, 116–17.

21. Kenneth Burke, "Literature as Equipment for Living," 260, 259.

22. Raymond Williams, *The Sociology of Culture*, 142.

23. Margaret Cohen, *The Sentimental Education of the Novel*, 17.

24. Fredric Jameson, *The Political Unconscious: Narrative as a Socially Symbolic Act*, 20.

25. This phrase has become standard international legal fare since the Vienna Declaration and Programme of Action (1993) to describe the fundamentality of all human rights.

26. *Epigraph*. Douzinas borrows the phrase "only paradoxes to offer" from Joan Wallach Scott who, in turn, cites Olympe de Gouges' rebuttal to the

French Declaration of the Rights of Man and of the Citizen in her "Declaration of the Rights of Woman and of the Female Citizen" (1791) (*Only Paradoxes to Offer: French Feminists and the Rights of Man*).

27. Stanley Cohen and Bruna Seu, "Knowing Enough Not to Feel Too Much: Emotional Thinking About Human Rights Appeals," 188. See also Stanley Cohen, *Denial and Acknowledgement: The Impact of Information About Human Rights Violations*, and *States of Denial: Knowing About Atrocities and Suffering*.

28. Douzinas, *End of Human Rights*, 21.

29. Hannah Arendt, *The Origins of Totalitarianism*, 300.

30. Karl Marx, "On the Jewish Question," 167.

31. Wendy Brown, "Suffering the Paradoxes of Rights." On the politics of shame, see Robert F. Drinan, *The Mobilization of Shame: A World View of Human Rights*; and Thomas Keenan, "Mobilizing Shame."

32. Judith P. Butler, Ernesto Laclau, and Slavoj Žižek, *Contingency, Hegemony, Universality: Contemporary Dialogues on the Left*, 101.

33. Brown, "Suffering," 432.

34. Giorgio Agamben, *Homo Sacer: Sovereign Power and Bare Life*, 52.

35. Claude Lefort, *The Political Forms of Modern Society: Bureaucracy, Democracy, Totalitarianism*, 256–57.

36. Michael Ignatieff et al., *Human Rights as Politics and Idolatry*, 65.

37. Douzinas, *End of Human Rights*, 308.

38. Karel Vasak, "Pour une Troisième Génération des Droits de l'Homme"; Burns H. Weston, "Human Rights," 18.

39. Upendra Baxi, *The Future of Human Rights*, 24–41.

40. Ibid., 101.

41. Likewise, we should not conclude, because a particular cultural tradition of common sense may underpin their initial articulation, that the principles of the UDHR cannot be substantiated by cultural forms other than the *Bildungsroman* and other cultural constructions of common sense. For efforts in those directions, see Abdullahi Ahmed An-Na'im, ed., *Human Rights in Cross-Cultural Perspectives: A Quest for Consensus*. We also cannot presume that the geographical and ideological expansion of human rights common sense travels from the Western democracies, or that it is unidirectional at all.

42. Winfried Brugger has derived from the "image of the person" standard in German constitutional law a sort of "formula" to quantify the characteristics and capacities of the German human rights person, not as it necessarily ever took conceptual form in the intentions of legislators, but as it emerges from the legal codes (Winfried Brugger, "The Image of the Person in the Human Rights Concept"). My critical interest is in a more holistic image of the international human rights person and the narrative structures that sustain and follow from it.

43. For histories of these notions of "person," see Amélie Oksenberg Rorty, "Characters, Persons, Selves, Individuals"; Robert C. Elliott, *The Literary Persona*; and Gordon W. Allport, *Personality: A Psychological Interpretation*.

44. Immanuel Kant, *Groundwork on the Metaphysics of Morals*, 37 (4:428).

45. Human dignity is often cited by human rights commentators as the foundation of rights, the fundamental human quality from which liberty, equality, and fraternity are derived. However, dignity and personality are inextricably linked. "Person," by definition, is the proper name of creatures with dignity.

46. For detailed histories of legal personality throughout the Western tradition, see Raymond Saleilles, *De la Personnalité Juridique: Histoire et Théories: Vingt-Cinq Leçons d'Introduction á un Cours de Droit Civil Comparé sur les Personnes Juridiques*; James E. Hickey, "The Source of International Legal Personality in the 21st Century"; Sanford A. Schane, "The Corporation Is a Person: The Language of a Legal Fiction"; Peter Stein, "Nineteenth-Century English Company Law and Theories of Legal Personality"; and Joel Bakan, *The Corporation: The Pathological Pursuit of Profit and Power*.

47. Alexander Nékám, *The Personality Conception of the Legal Entity*, 40.

48. John Dewey, "The Historic Background of Corporate Legal Personality," 65.

49. Schane, "Corporation Is a Person," 565.

50. Excluding the title of the Declaration, the word "human" appears in the UDHR eleven times, and almost exclusively in the preamble—the rehearsal of what everyone supposedly already knows: twice it modifies "person"; once each "dignity" and "family"; five times it modifies "rights"; and only twice does it act like a noun to denote a "human being." "Person," on the other hand, appears eight times, always as a noun (person or personality) and almost exclusively in the articles, the part of the document that declares what everyone should know.

51. Adamantia Pollis and Peter Schwab, "Human Rights: A Western Construct with Limited Applicability," 8.

52. Charlotte Bunch, "Transforming Human Rights from a Feminist Perspective," 12. See also Charlotte Bunch, "Women's Rights as Human Rights: Toward a Re-Vision of Human Rights." In addition to Bunch's seminal critique of the gender bias of human rights law, see also Mutua on the Eurocentrism of its normative image of the individual.

53. Randolph P. Shaffner, *The Apprenticeship Novel: A Study of the "Bildungsroman" as a Regulative Type in Western Literature with a Focus on Three Classic Representatives by Goethe, Maugham, and Mann*, 8.

54. Ibid., 16.

55. Seyla Benhabib, *Transformations of Citizenship: Dilemmas of the Nation State in the Era of Globalization: Two Lectures*, 55.

56. For an excellent history of the emergence of contemporary human rights law from international colonial treaties and the nineteenth-century legislation that abolished the slave trade, see Paul Gordon Lauren, *The Evolution of International Human Rights: Visions Seen*, 37–71.

57. Schane, "Corporation Is a Person," 605.

58. Gregory A. Mark, "The Personification of the Business Corporation in American Law," 1470.

59. Barbara Johnson, "Anthropomorphism in Lyric and Law," 572.

60. Pheng Cheah, *Spectral Nationality: Passages of Freedom from Kant to Postcolonial Literatures of Liberation*, 235. See also David Lloyd and Paul Thomas, *Culture and the State*.

61. Paul de Man, *The Resistance to Theory*, 48; J. Hillis Miller, *Versions of Pygmalion*, 221.

62. Johnson, "Anthropomorphism," 551.

63. Miller, *Pygmalion*, 5.

64. Both Miller's trope of personification and the legal trope of incorporation tend to be teleological. These are not merely speculative theses but figurative patterns legible within the law itself. For instance, the UN's 1989 Convention on the Rights of the Child literalizes the figural work of human rights incorporation as coming-of-age story, following our accretive pattern by guaranteeing the child rights "to a name" (Article 7), then to an "identity" (Article 8), then "to freedom of expression" (Article 13), then "to freedom of association" (Article 15), and finally a responsibility to "respect . . . the human rights and fundamental freedoms of others" (Article 40).

65. Miller, *Pygmalion*, 5.

66. I provide here a short list of contemporary novels that offer formal refinements (and complications) to this generic structure: Kamala Markandaya, *Nectar in a Sieve*; Dany Laferrière, *Dining with the Dictator*; Turki al-Hamad, *Adama*; Zee Edgell, *Beka Lamb*; Arundhati Roy, *The God of Small Things*; Unity Dow, *Juggling Truths*; Mongo Beti, *Mission to Kala*; 'Biyi Bandele-Thomas, *The Sympathetic Undertaker and Other Dreams*; Romesh Gunesekera, *Reef*; Marcel Bénabou, *To Write on Tamara?*; Mario Vargas Llosa, *The Storyteller*; and Teresa de la de la Parra, *Mama Blanca's Memoirs*.

67. Richard A. Falk, "Reframing the Legal Agenda of World Order in the Course of a Turbulent Century," 47, 46.

68. Philip Gourevitch, *We Wish to Inform You that Tomorrow We Will Be Killed with Our Families: Stories from Rwanda*, 5–9.

69. Frank Kermode, *The Sense of an Ending*, 135.

70. Franco Moretti, *The Way of the World: The Bildungsroman in European Culture*, 16.

71. Ibid., 229–45.

72. Sammons, "Mystery of the Missing Bildungsroman," 237. Sammons concludes that the genre's existence is the matter of literary legend since, for

him, only Goethe's novel and "maybe two and a half other examples" qualify as *Bildungsromane* according to a strict idealist definition of the genre (237, 243).

73. Marc Redfield, "The Bildungsroman," 193.

74. Marianne Hirsch, "The Novel of Formation as Genre: Between Great Expectations and Lost Illusions," 300. See also Elizabeth Abel, Marianne Hirsch, and Elizabeth Langland, "Introduction," 13; Bonnie Hoover Braendlin, "*Bildung* in Ethnic Women Writers," 75; and Ellen Morgan, "Humanbecoming: Form and Focus in the Neo-Feminist Novel," 185.

75. Thomas Jeffers implicitly recognizes this social service of the genre when he situates his interest in "youthful white males" as endangered animals in the context of the contemporary "multicultural" American social scene, in which they comprise "the segment of our society that one needs to worry about" because, "guilt-heaped and feeling undervalued," they "test . . . lower, go . . . to college less often, and get . . . into legal trouble more than white females do" (*Apprenticeships: The Bildungsroman from Goethe to Santayana*, 7). Indeed, based on this apparent cultural disenfranchisement of the white male subject, Jeffers predicts the revitalization of an earnest (rather than ironic or vulgar) post-multicultural *Bildungsroman* that will dramatize "an acceptance of the liberal and (yes) free-market society in which everyman can become a *Bildungsheld*" (192).

76. Gauri Viswanathan, "An Introduction: Uncommon Genealogies," 16.

77. Thomas Keenan, *Fables of Responsibility: Aberrations and Predicaments in Ethics and Politics*, 38.

78. Barbara Harlow, *Barred: Women, Writing, and Political Detention*, 252–53.

79. Bruce Robbins, *Feeling Global: Internationalism in Distress*, 6.

80. Benedict Anderson, *Imagined Communities: Reflections on the Origin and Spread of Nationalism*, 36.

81. Jürgen Habermas, *The Structural Transformation of the Public Sphere: An Inquiry into a Category of Bourgeois Society*, 85.

82. K. Anthony Appiah, "Citizens of the World," 197.

83. Anderson, *Imagined Communities*, 32.

84. Adele King, *Rereading Camara Laye*, 52.

85. Joseph R. Slaughter, *Clef À Roman: Some Uses of Human Rights and the Bildungsroman*.

86. Pascale Casanova, *The World Republic of Letters*.

87. Emily Brontë, *Wuthering Heights: An Authoritative Text, with Essays in Criticism*, 15; Gourevitch, *We Wish to Inform You*, 6.

88. Jean-François Lyotard, *The Postmodern Condition: A Report on Knowledge*, xxiii–xxiv.

89. Ibid., 4.

90. Ibid., 20.
91. Baxi, *Future of Human Rights*, 121, 122.
92. Rey Chow, *The Protestant Ethnic and the Spirit of Capitalism*, 21.
93. Bakan, *The Corporation: The Pathological Pursuit of Profit and Power*, 153–56. In the reference to "Frankenstein monsters," Bakan cites Brandeis's opinion in Louis K. Liggett Co. et al. v. Lee, Comptroller et al. (19); Brandeis was himself alluding to a 1931 study of the corporation and the legal personality theory by I. Maurice Wormser, *Frankenstein, Incorporated*.
94. Sandra T. Barnes, "Global Flows: Terror, Oil, and Strategic Philanthropy."
95. Saro-Wiwa's inclusion is a fairly recent event, and the solipsistic irony that in Shell's eyes his fame has eclipsed those of the Nigerian Nobel laureate Wole Soyinka and internationally renowned novelist Chinua Achebe because of his hanging and his activism against Shell's inhumane practices in the Niger Delta goes uncommented. Royal Dutch Shell PLC also gets the literary facts wrong: Saro-Wiwa was known not for plays but for poetry, novels and, within Nigeria, a popular TV series. (http://www.shell.com/home/Framework?siteId = nigeria&FC2 = /nigeria/html/iwgen/nigeria_people/literature/zzz_lhn.html&FC3 = /nigeria/html/iwgen/nigeria _people/literature/dir_literat_0606_1050.html).
96. Abel, Hirsch, and Langland, "Introduction," 13.
97. Leigh Gilmore, *The Limits of Autobiography: Trauma and Testimony*, 2.
98. Kay Schaffer and Sidonie Smith, *Human Rights and Narrated Lives: The Ethics of Recognition*, 13.
99. Jameson, "On Literary and Cultural Import-Substitution," 173.
100. For Sabena airlines' own proud version of its colonial history, see http://www.sabena.com/EN/Historique_FR.htm. On the legacy of Belgian colonialism in the Rwandan genocide, see Mahmood Mamdani, *When Victims Become Killers: Colonialism, Nativism, and the Genocide in Rwanda*.
101. Irvin Muchnick, *Kite Bummer: Why Literary Fiction Needs Steroid Testing*; and Edward Wyatt, "Wrenching Tale by an Afghan Immigrant Strikes a Chord."
102. Soyinka, "Foreword," vi.
103. Douzinas, *End of Human Rights*, 2; Ernst Bloch, *Natural Law and Human Dignity*, 172.
104. Wayne Booth, "Individualism and the Mystery of the Social Self; or, Does Amnesty Have a Leg to Stand On?" 89.
105. Joseph R. Slaughter, "A Question of Narration: The Voice in International Human Rights Law."
106. Booth, "Individualism and the Mystery of the Social Self," 89.
107. Emmanuel Levinas, "The Rights of Man and the Rights of the Other"; Jean-François Lyotard, "The Other's Rights."

108. Slaughter, "A Question of Narration." In many ways, the so-called narrative turn in the social and human sciences in the 1980s replaced an ontological essentialism with a performative, discursive essentialism. Very often, analyses that invoke narratology tend to reify narrative as the founding articulation of *homo significans*, leaving the structures, capacities, and activities of narrative itself unproblematized. In other words, narrative becomes an Archimedean point by positing it as a universal, innate human capacity that is shared by all people, even when it is recognized as contingent upon particular socio-historico-cultural formations. Narrative, narrativity, and narratability then become the functional equivalents of universal dignity in a renaturalized law of the narrative human condition. As strategic as attentiveness to narrative construction has proved to be in exposing the discursive operations of disciplinary power–knowledge, we must also recognize that the idea that humans are narrative and narrating creatures (*homo narrativus* and *homo narrans*) is itself a notion that is implicated within the same structures that it is used to critique. Just as "narrative is not merely a neutral discursive form that may or may not be used to represent real events in their aspect as developmental processes" for historiography, human narrative capacity and activity are not simply traits of the human being; rather, they are constitutive of the category of human (or better, of person) as the subject of narrative and law (Hayden V. White, *The Content of the Form: Narrative Discourse and Historical Representation*, ix).

109. White, *Content of the Form*, 13. Barbara Johnson writes provocatively about the intersections of lyric and law, but hers is not a sustained study of the relations between poetry and human rights law ("Anthropomorphism," 556). Likewise, Teresa Godwin Phelps analyzes narrative and truth commissions, citing both modern and classical plays to unravel the dynamics of testimony, revenge, and forgiveness. But she makes nothing of the fact that her evidence is almost exclusively pulled from the drama genre (*Shattered Voices: Language, Violence, and the Work of Truth Commissions*).

110. Anne Cubilié, *Women Witnessing Terror: Testimony and the Cultural Politics of Human Rights*, 144. On the sociopolitical work of *testimonio*, see especially John Beverley, *Against Literature*; John Beverley, *Subalternity and Representation: Arguments in Cultural Theory*; John Beverley, *Testimonio: On the Politics of Truth*; and John Beverley and Marc Zimmerman, *Literature and Politics in the Central American Revolutions*. See also Schaffer and Smith, *Human Rights and Narrated Lives*.

111. On epistolary fiction, rights of petition, and women's rights more generally, see Joseph Slaughter and Jennifer Wenzel, "Letters of the Law: Women, Human Rights, and Epistolary Literature"; and Susan Staves, " 'The Liberty of a She-Subject of England': Rights Rhetoric and the Female Thucydides."

112. Upendra Baxi parallels "knight-errantry" with "adventures in human rights protection and promotion," arguing that the true vocation of human

rights is "to reenchant the world ... to address the human future" (*Mambrino's Helmet?: Human Rights for a Changing World*, xi–xii). I understand that a recent internal assessment by Human Rights Watch bears "La Mancha" in its title.

113. Peri Rossi's novel is set during the Dirty Wars of South America's Southern Cone in the 1970s and 80s. Arias' novel, set in the aftermath of the U.S.-orchestrated coup that ousted Guatemala's democratically elected socialist government in 1954, operates at the intersections of the *picaresque* and the *Bildungsroman*. It suggests what happens to the promise of *Bildung* in a sociopolitical formation where multinational corporations and a (foreign) military become the dominant legal persons. Just as the corporation is a parody of the human, the state becomes a farce of democracy, and writing one's life story as a *Bildungsroman* becomes a travesty of the classical humanist genre.

114. Lynn Festa, "Sentimental Bonds and Revolutionary Characters: Richardson's *Pamela* in England and France," 84, 91. See also Margaret Cohen, "Sentimental Communities."

115. Cohen, *Sentimental Education of the Novel*, 6–12.

116. Ibid., 99–110; David Miles, "The Picaro's Journey to the Confessional: The Changing Image of the Hero in the German *Bildungsroman*."

117. Hartman, *Scenes of Subjection*, 122. Cubilié, *Women Witnessing Terror*, 41.

CHAPTER I
Novel Subjects and Enabling Fictions: The Formal Articulation of International Human Rights Law

1. Ian P. Watt, *The Rise of the Novel: Studies in Defoe, Richardson, and Fielding*, 7, 92.

2. United Nations, "Third," 658.

3. At the urging of female delegates, most notably from Denmark, India, and Pakistan, "his personality" was to be replaced with the gender-neutral "human personality" (the form it takes elsewhere in the UDHR); through some bureaucratic oversight, the revision was never implemented (Morsink, *Universal Declaration of Human Rights*, 116–29; United Nations, "Third," 659). Early drafts of Article 29 used the term "state," but the drafters settled on the more benign and general "community," which, throughout the UDHR, signifies a range of "group units," from the family, society, and nation to the state (M. Glen Johnson, "A Magna Carta for Mankind: Writing the Universal Declaration of Human Rights," 57.) For a good summary of the debates around Article 29 in the Third Committee, see Morsink, *Universal Declaration of Human Rights*, 241–52.

4. United Nations, "Third," 656.

5. My translation; René Cassin, "Historique de la Declaration Universelle de 1948," 108.

6. United Nations, "Third," 659.

7. Ibid., 659–60.

8. Cassin, "Historique," 111.

9. Watt, *Rise of the Novel*, 74. Defoe's novel has a privileged place in the writings of both Rousseau and Marx. In his *Bildungsroman*–pedagogical treatise, *Emile*, Rousseau famously names *Robinson Crusoe* as the only novel he permits his eponymous charge to read until he comes of age. For his part, Marx takes Crusoe as a counterfigure to social man in his analyses of capital and labor.

10. In terms of property explicitly, Article 17 of the UDHR represents the banal compromise of the two positions: "Everyone has the right to own property alone as well as in association with others." On the relations between personality, property, and privacy, see Samuel D. Warren and Louis D. Brandeis, "The Right to Privacy." Reading British and American case law, they argue that the right to privacy, as a guarantee of immunity of the person and property from public intervention, is essentially "the right to one's personality" because the private belongs to the person as property.

11. Jacques Maritain, "Introduction," 14.

12. My translation; Cassin, "Historique," 109. This language becomes Article 26.2 in the French version of the UDHR: "*L'éducation doit viser au plein épanouissement de la personnalité humaine. . . .*"

13. Erich Auerbach, *Mimesis: The Representation of Reality in Western Literature*, 404; and Schwarz, *Misplaced Ideas*, 58–59. Schwarz presumably refers to the 1789 French Declaration of the Rights of Man and of the Citizen, since he writes about the development of the nineteenth- and early twentieth-century Brazilian novel. For Auerbach, in his magisterial *Mimesis* (published contemporaneously with the drafting of the UDHR), it is precisely a *Bildungsroman*—Stendhal's *The Red and the Black* (1830)—that epitomizes this formal development. Challenging Auerbach's "critical narrative that realism springs full-grown from the head of the Revolution," Margaret Cohen offers a provocative, gender-attentive account of the late eighteenth-century consolidation of, and contest between, novelistic codes of realism and sentimentality as a generic conflict over "one of the great impasses of [French] revolutionary ideology: how to accommodate both negative and positive notions of rights" (*Sentimental Education of the Novel*, 102, 10).

14. Watt, *Rise of the Novel*, 19.

15. Northrop Frye, *Anatomy of Criticism*, 308.

16. Ibid., 305.

17. Watt, *Rise of the Novel*, 60.

18. Lukács, *Goethe and His Age*, 55.

19. Watt, *Rise of the Novel*, 22; W. J. Harvey, *Character and the Novel*, 24.

20. Edward W. Said, *Culture and Imperialism*, 69, 71.

21. See Margaret Cohen and Carolyn Dever, "Introduction."

22. Daniel Defoe, *Robinson Crusoe*, 277. After his rescue, Crusoe reenters British civil society through a sworn statement attesting to his legal personality, by which he accepts, voluntarily, the English social compact and for which Defoe rewards him with an increase in wealth. The liminal period of his civil death makes possible Crusoe's incorporation as a person before English law by converting its demand of submission into an expression of his personal will. If Crusoe's story ended here, we might have a Rousseauvian social contract *Bildungsroman*, but the novel continues with a second visit to the island, and the sequels proliferate this pattern of remove and return. For this reason, Franco Moretti suggests that the *Bildungsroman* is an anti-Robinsonade because *Bildung* is only conceivable if it comes to mature conclusion (*Way of the World*, 26).

23. There is an inherent irony in the privilege the UN committee accorded to books in its vision of a new international human rights society, since, except for his Bibles, the books that Crusoe rescues are in Portuguese and therefore illegible to him. See Alberto Manguel, "The Library of Robinson Crusoe."

24. Ibid., 63.

25. Ibid., 13.

26. Ignatieff et al., *Human Rights as Politics and Idolatry*, 78, 66.

27. United Nations, "Plenary," 848.

28. Hersch Lauterpacht, *An International Bill of the Rights of Man*, 69.

29. H. G. Wells, *The Rights of Man; or, What Are We Fighting For?*, 14, 80–81.

30. Various brands of Personalism became popular across Europe and the U.S. by the mid-twentieth century—the Bostonian school followed the Protestant theology of Borden Parker Bowne; Max Scheler was the primary figure in Germany; Emmanuel Mounier and Jacques Maritain are generally cited as the major theorists of a French Catholic version. These social theologies intended to counteract the debasing and alienating forces of both a capitalist, bourgeois individualism and a communist collectivism. Personalist doctrine has remained influential. Martin Luther King, Jr. enlisted Bowne's teachings in the U.S. civil rights movement. The French strain persists in the Encyclicals of Pope John Paul II, particularly in *Veritatis Splendor* (1993), which argues that human personality is an essential substance that transcends culture and history. For some of this intellectual history, see Joseph Anthony Amato, *Mounier and Maritain: A French Catholic Understanding of the Modern World*; Borden Parker Bowne, *Personalism*; and Max Scheler, *Formalism in Ethics and Non-Formal Ethics of Values: A New Attempt toward the Foundation of an Ethical Personalism*.

31. See especially Charles Merriam, "The Assumptions of Democracy"; Charles Merriam, "The Ends of Government"; and Charles Merriam, "The Meaning of Democracy."

32. John Middleton Murry, "The Isolation of Russia: And the Way Out." Murry cites the phrase in a review of J. de V. Loder's *Bolshevism in Perspective* published in *The Adelphi*. Readers of the progressive British journal subsequently engaged in intricate theoretical polemics about whether Soviet communism or British parliamentary democracy had the more legitimate claim to being able to restore "the sovereignty of human personality."

33. UNESCO, ed., *Human Rights: Comments and Interpretations*, 107. The UDHR drafting committee viewed UNESCO's effort as a threat to its work precisely because it might open the Pandora's box of "metaphysical controversy." The study's publication was delayed until after the UDHR's adoption; see Johannes Morsink, "World War Two and the Universal Declaration."

34. Karl Marx, *Capital: A Critique of Political Economy*, 739.

35. Jean-Hervé Bradol, "Introduction: The Sacrificial International Order and Humanitarian Action," 6.

36. Rorty, "Characters, Persons, Selves, Individuals," 547.

37. Miguel Tamen, "Kinds of Persons, Kinds of Rights, Kinds of Bodies," 22.

38. Robert R. Williams, *Hegel's Ethics of Recognition*, 135.

39. Dewey, "Legal Personality," 656.

40. Fernando Volio, "Legal Personality, Privacy, and the Family," 188.

41. Nékám, *The Personality Conception of the Legal Entity*, 53.

42. Volio, "Legal Personality, Privacy, and the Family," 186.

43. Drucilla Cornell, *Just Cause: Freedom, Identity, and Rights*, 85; John Dewey, "Personality," 649.

44. Jean Piaget, "The Right to Education in the Modern World," 91.

45. Defoe, *Robinson Crusoe*, 147.

46. Bakan, *The Corporation: The Pathological Pursuit of Profit and Power*, 9.

47. Michael Seidel, *Robinson Crusoe: Island Myths and the Novel*, 43.

48. For a more detailed discussion of corporate personality, human rights, and *Robinson Crusoe*, see Joseph R. Slaughter, *The Textuality of Human Rights: Founding Narratives of Human Personality*. For histories of the South Sea Bubble and its impact on the law of corporations, see Malcolm Balen, *The Secret History of the South Sea Bubble: The World's First Great Financial Scandal*; Lewis Saul Benjamin, *The South Sea Bubble*; and Rudolph Robert, *Chartered Companies and Their Role in the Development of Overseas Trade*.

49. Mark, "The Personification of the Business Corporation in American Law," 1483.

50. See Schane, "Corporation Is a Person." That we naturalize corporations as persons who perform human-like actions suggests the degree to which the legal "person" has assumed a "real" (grammatical) life in both our speech and the social world.

51. Hickey, "Source of International Legal Personality," 10.

52. Baroody's observations were delivered as a partial explanation for Saudi Arabia's abstention on the UDHR vote in the General Assembly. United Nations, *Yearbook of the United Nations 1948*, 528.

53. M. Glen Johnson identifies these six positions that combined, overlapped, and diverged in not always predictable ways, as the major schools of thought represented in the UN committees in 1948 ("Magna Carta for Mankind," 42–48).

54. In the broad sense of the UDHR, social security protects against a living nonexistence not covered by "civil death," and a right to recognition as a person before the law. Thus, along with and through its more commonly recognized contents of welfare protections, social security responds to "social death"—what Orlando Patterson identified as the universal condition of slavery (*Slavery and Social Death: A Comparative Study*).

55. Maritain, "Introduction," 13.

56. Nékám, *The Personality Conception of the Legal Entity*, 36.

57. John Austin, *Lectures on Jurisprudence; or, the Philosophy of Positive Law*, 86.

58. Bloch, *Natural Law*, 182, 185.

59. Austin, *Lectures on Jurisprudence*, 89.

60. Bertrand de Jouvenel, *Sovereignty: An Inquiry into the Political Good*, 201.

61. Maritain, *Rights of Man*, 69.

62. Cited in Stephen P. Marks, "From the 'Single Confused Page' to the 'Decalogue for Six Billion Persons': The Roots of the Universal Declaration of Human Rights in the French Revolution," 463. Marks' nuanced study of the DRMC's "major impact on the form and content of the UDHR" reviews some of the foremost analytical sources of this narrative and its central role in the cultural relativist–universalist debates of the 1980s (460).

63. Ignatieff et al., *Human Rights as Politics and Idolatry*, 19. Ignatieff overstates his claim about the diversity of traditions behind the consensus that eventuated the UDHR when he taxonomizes the committee in identitarian terms: "Chinese, Middle Eastern Christian, but also Marxist, Hindu, Latin American, Islamic" (64). Beyond the fact that in 1946 the representatives of Marxism, Middle Eastern Christians, and Latin Americans were themselves representatives of forms of the Western tradition, the Hindu and Islamic traditions were represented during the review (not the drafting) process, where they made substantial contributions. The process was more multicultural than is ordinarily acknowledged, but of the UDHR's drafters, only P. C. Chang was "not representative of the Judeo-Christian tradition" (Marks, "From the 'Single Confused Page,'" 490). More pointedly, John Humphrey recalls that all but two of the national constitutions, legal documents, and proposals that he consulted for the first draft of the UDHR "came from English-speaking sources and all of them from the democratic West" (*Human Rights and the United Nations: A Great Adventure*, 31–32).

64. Pollis and Schwab, "Western." In many ways, Pollis and Schwab's essay launched the cultural relativist critique in 1979, but by 2000 they recognized that their charge depended upon an "overdrawn" essentialism of cultural difference that may be untenable and no longer strategic in the search for a "new universalism" ("Introduction," 2). Upendra Baxi usefully troubles the canonical narrative of contemporary human rights' Western provenance by recognizing the role of the local in "translating into global languages the reality of their [disenfranchised peoples'] aspiration for a just world" (*Future of Human Rights*, 101–2).

65. In Speech Act Theory, the "declarative" act presumably brings into effect the state, condition, or quality being declared and depends upon belief in the authority and capacity of the speaking subject to produce effects, while the "constative" is understood merely to confirm already-existing facts or conditions and is dependent upon a shared belief that such conditions actually obtain in the "real" world. See J. L. Austin, *How to Do Things with Words*; Mary Louise Pratt, *Toward a Speech Act Theory of Literary Discourse*; and John R. Searle, *Speech Acts: An Essay in the Philosophy of Language*, 66–67.

66. Benhabib, *Transformations of Citizenship*, 40.

67. These two functions of "therefore" (for the purposes of and in consequence of) are now marked by different spellings—therefore and therefor—although the *Oxford English Dictionary* notes that this orthographic separation of meanings occurred during the period in which the revolutionary declarations were made.

68. Costas Douzinas characterizes the long history from "classical natural law to contemporary human rights" that "transferred the standard of right from nature to history and eventually to humanity" as the "positivation of nature" (*End of Human Rights*, 20). This positivation is not merely the historical trajectory of human rights law—it occurs within the legal documents themselves, as an effect and trace of transcribing unwritten natural law.

69. Jacques Derrida, "Declarations of Independence," 49.

70. Ibid., 50.

71. Ibid., 49.

72. Agamben, *Homo Sacer*, 128.

73. Benhabib, *Transformations of Citizenship*, 23.

74. There are material examples of these speculative rhetorical structures. For example, the discursive moment of the UN's self-incorporation sits at the end of a chain of deferrals that antedate its founding by reference to earlier documents. Thus, the UDHR cites the UN Charter as part of its legitimation, but the charter itself refers back to the Atlantic Charter of mutual support concluded between Roosevelt and Churchill in 1941. This series of analeptic referrals traces the UN's origin to a point that is not itself a founding moment, that is, literally as well as figuratively, ungrounded, floating on a ship in the

North Atlantic. Fascinating to note in respect to this fabulous structure of retroactivity is the conclusion of the UN Charter, which establishes the terms of corporate membership, including provisions for states to become retroactively "original Members."

75. Douzinas, *End of Human Rights*, 202.

76. Ibid., 329.

77. The right to petition was another casualty of consensus in 1948. It went the way of rights to resist oppression, specific provisions on minorities and women, and an explicit statement about the UDHR's application to dependent territories. See Johnson, "Magna Carta for Mankind"; and Morsink, *Universal Declaration of Human Rights*.

78. For instance, the 1979 Convention on the Elimination of Discrimination Against Women was retrofitted in 1999 with an "Optional Protocol" that entered into force a year later. The ICCPR (1966) has two optional protocols; the second (1989), aimed at abolishing the death penalty, has not yet entered into force. The Convention Against Torture and Other Cruel, Inhuman or Degrading Treatment or Punishment (1984) has a justiciable option (2002) that also has not yet come into force. Two optional protocols, both from 2000, attend the Convention on the Rights of the Child (1989), covering separately the prohibitions against the involvement of children in armed conflict and the sale of children, child prostitution, and pornography.

79. Maritain, "Introduction," 17.

80. Georg Lukács, *The Theory of the Novel: A Historico-Philosophical Essay on the Forms of Great Epic Literature*, 56.

81. Schwarz, *Misplaced Ideas*, 53.

82. Fredric Jameson, "Third-World Literature in the Era of Multinational Capitalism," 78.

83. Eleanor Roosevelt, *Eleanor Roosevelt's My Day: The Post–War Years, 1945–1952*, 156–57. An astute rhetorician, Roosevelt framed her arguments defending human rights in terms calculated for the audiences of the various fora in which she participated, from *Liberty* magazine (in which she published a short story, "Christmas 1940," about the Nazi occupation of northern Europe and the triumph of the religious-human spirit) to *Foreign Affairs* (where she rebutted the legal arguments that the American Bar Association leveled against the UDHR). See Eleanor Roosevelt, *Christmas 1940*; and Eleanor Roosevelt, "The Promise of Human Rights."

84. The old guarantors of the law are sealed away and forgotten at the heart of the legal institution itself. Abraham and Torok call this process "incorporation," but Aeschylus' *Oresteia* already characterizes it as tragedy. If law in a democracy is untethered from its divine–natural moorings, the old transcendental sanction nonetheless remains part of the new civil law's formal structure, as in Aeschylus' Athens where the foundations of enforcement are

encrypted with the Furies just below—subtextually or subterraneously—the law's surface. In compensation for their entombment beneath the city and court of Athens, the Furies are forever re-membered within the formal architecture of the law, which becomes tautological and ambivalent when Orestes' trial results in a hung jury and must be decided by the goddess Athena (*The Wolf Man's Magic Word: A Cryptonymy*; and Aeschylus, *Oresteia: Agamemnon, the Libation Bearers, the Eumenides*).

85. United Nations, "Third," 114.

86. Gayatri Chakravorty Spivak, "Righting Wrongs," 174. Spivak argues that at the bottom of human rights there are, in fact, two seemingly contradictory begged questions. The first begs "the question of nature as the ground of rights"; the second begs the "assumption that it is natural to be angled toward the other, before will" (189). For Spivak, both assumptions are necessary, and their begging (and forgetting of that begging) characterizes the historical condition of contemporary human rights activity in a world that still does not share any stable, universal "proof that we are born free and proof that it is the other that calls us before will" (179). If the question of nature is somehow deleterious for the rights activist, this may be an effect not of forgetting per se, but of an equally less spectacular and unmarkable event: the passing of the UDHR from the aspirational realm into customary international law—when, in effect, it entered into effect by habit and citation.

87. Orlando Patterson, "Freedom, Slavery, and the Modern Construction of Rights," 175–76. Patterson dates this rhetorical deposition of Nature and God to the short period between Franklin Roosevelt's "Four Freedoms" speech (1941) and his "Economic Bill of Rights" (1944).

88. Talal Asad, *Formations of the Secular: Christianity, Islam, Modernity*, 148.

89. The rousing optimism of the quotation in the section header concludes Costas Douzinas' study of contemporary human rights: "The end of human rights, like that of natural law, is the promise of the 'not yet', of the indeterminacy of existential self-creation against the fear of uncertainty and the inauthentic certainties of the present." Douzinas, *End of Human Rights*, 308.

90. Jack Donnelly, *Universal Human Rights in Theory and Practice*, 9.

91. Humphrey, "Magna Carta of Mankind," 31.

92. Hans-Georg Gadamer, *Truth and Method*, 21.

93. Cited in Susan Maslan, "The Anti-Human: Man and Citizen before the Declaration of the Rights of Man and of the Citizen," 358. Maslan usefully demonstrates that the original duality of the DRMC lay not in a distinction between man and citizen but in the double sense of common sense—in the knowing/feeling dyad—with the "capacity to feel" being the "primary [French Enlightenment] qualification for inclusion within the category of the human." It is worth recalling also that in 1776 Thomas Paine defended his argument for the independence and constitution of the United States in the eponymous name of *Common Sense*.

94. United Nations, "Third," 225.

95. Roland Barthes, *Mythologies*, 152–53. Walter O. Wyrauch, "On Definitions, Tautologies, and Ethnocentrism in Regard to Universal Human Rights," 199.

96. Antony Flew, *A Dictionary of Philosophy*, 350.

97. On the empty content of the law, see *also* Jacques Derrida, "Force du Loi: Le 'Fondement Mystique de l'Autorité.'" My argument diverges from Derrida's because, at least historically, the emptiness of the legal signifier is not left empty; instead, it is precisely this empty place of warrant and sanction that begs to be occupied by the subject of law, the subject that positive law is itself charged with producing.

98. Barthes, *Mythologies*, 153.

99. I would venture that, at the bottom of all, cultural common sense (like law) is an often-unarticulated tautology, and we might understand the cultural relativist–universalist debates of the 1980s as a dispute about the culture-boundedness of such tautological common sense—of Maritain's proverbial "man is man." The cultural condition of tautology led to the gender critique of the UDHR that Eleanor Roosevelt recounted on its tenth anniversary: "A woman from—I've forgotten if it was a Near Eastern country or an Asiatic country . . . said, 'if you say "men", you tell us that "men" includes men and women, but our government will say it means just men.'" (*Human Rights: A Documentary on the United Nations Declaration of Human Rights*, record album). Although female delegates from many "Near Eastern" and "Asiatic" countries leveled this critique throughout the drafting process, Johannes Morsink credits the Danish chair of the Sub-Commission on the Status of Women, Bodil Begtrup, with being the driving force behind the declaration's gender neutrality (*Universal Declaration of Human Rights*, 116–29). See also Begtrup's speech to the General Assembly: United Nations, "Plenary," 892.

100. My reading of international law suggests that the difference between human rights' teleology and tautology is diaphanous. Its thinness is described in Aristotle's notion of entelechy: an entity is alike to itself only through the extensive process of its becoming what it is. See Hannah Arendt, *The Human Condition*, 206–7.

101. Although the "sense of [the human personality's] dignity" as a goal of sentimental education is ambiguous in the English text of the International Covenant on Economic, Social, and Cultural Rights, it is explicit in the other official language versions. For example, the French text reads: "*L'éducation doit viser au plein épanouissement de la personnalité humaine et du sens de sa dignité et renforcer le respect des droits de l'homme et des libertés fondamentales*" (Article 13).

102. Roosevelt, "Promise of Human Rights," 473.

103. Cornell, *Just Cause*, 18–19. See also Drucilla Cornell, "Bodily Integrity and the Right to Abortion."

104. Bloch, *Natural Law*, 174.

105. Falk, "Reframing the Legal Agenda," 46–47.

106. We could state this another way. If a lack of human rights violations can in any way be attributed to the effectiveness of the law, then the law may be said to receive its international force from local sociocultural habits and practices that do not violate its precepts; that is, it may be thought of as gaining legitimacy from the bottom up.

107. David Chandler, "The Limits of Human Rights and Cosmopolitan Citizenship," 127.

108. I have elsewhere argued that Joseph Conrad's *Heart of Darkness* is an invoicing narrative, which combines a general discursive principle of colonial writing with capitalist accounting methods ("'A Mouth with Which to Tell the Story': Silence, Violence, and Speech in the Narrative of *Things Fall Apart*"). *Robinson Crusoe* suggests that this narrative principle has as much to do with Protestant introspection as with imperialist economics. Michael Seidel makes a similar argument about *Crusoe*: "Everything is accounted for, recounted, counted up," and he argues that here at the beginnings of novelistic narration, "to tell . . . means to count as much as it means to narrate" (Seidel, *Robinson Crusoe*, 79, 77). The narrative accounting methods of Defoe's novel apply as much to the development of Crusoe's personality as to his excessive accumulation of material goods.

109. Richard A. Barney, *Plots of Enlightenment: Education and the Novel in Eighteenth-Century England*, 241.

110. The institutional vision and structure of the UN were sketched by the states that would become permanent members of the UN Security Council in meetings begun at Dumbarton Oaks, in Washington, D.C., in the summer of 1944.

111. It seems to me that most of the forms that have emerged to imagine an international order based on human rights are reactionary: urgent action bulletins, Amnesty International letters and petitions; concerts for famine and debt relief; documentary exposés about the failures of human rights internationalism and the predations of globalization. In some ways, popular internationalism is most fully expressed in the anti-globalization movements. However, Schaffer and Smith's *Human Rights and Narrated Lives* and Anne Cubilié suggest that perhaps the testimonial is explicitly an emergent internationalist genre written "from a post–Universal Declaration global positionality" (Cubilié, *Women Witnessing Terror*, 161). There is, of course, no lack of forms attending globalization, but those are mostly local (however broadly construed) forms that circulate and naturalize (Hollywood and Bollywood films, anime, CNN, jazz and many other musical forms, etc.). The dearth I am speaking of is one of forms that emerge from, and make legible and sensible, a domain called the international in its own right.

CHAPTER 2
Becoming Plots: Human Rights, the Bildungsroman, *and the Novelization of Citizenship*

1. Mary Robinson, "Realising Human Rights: 'Take Hold of It Boldly and Duly . . .'" (paper presented at the Romanes Lectures, Oxford University, 11 November 1997).

2. Ibid.

3. With the goal of humanizing economics, the analytical measures and methods—like the Human Development Index—created in the 1990s by Nobel-Prize-winning economist Amartya Sen and others for the United Nations Development Programme (UNDP) tend, instead, to econometricize the human personality. See United Nations Development Programme, *Human Development Report 1990*. Martha Nussbaum's "human capabilities" approach to development and human rights asks a more humanist, *Bildung*-resonant question—"What is A actively able to do and be?"—to measure the work of protecting and promoting "human agency" (Martha Craven Nussbaum, "Capabilities and Human Rights," 127). See also Martha Craven Nussbaum, *Women and Human Development: The Capabilities Approach*.

4. Robinson, "Realising Human Rights." There is a complex literary, in fact epic, subtext to Robinson's reproof. Her charge to "take hold" of the plot comes from an inscription in a copy of James George Frazier's *Golden Bough* that Irish poet Seamus Heaney presented to her on the occasion of her appointment to the UNHCHR. His inscription is itself a quotation of his recent translation of Virgil's *Aeneid*, from the instructions the Sybil offers the hero for safely entering and returning from the underworld.

5. Douzinas, *End of Human Rights*, 7.

6. Makau Mutua, *Human Rights: A Political and Cultural Critique*, 11.

7. Ibid., 22.

8. Cornell, *Just Cause*, 92.

9. Marx, "Jewish," 168. Marx argues that, because the French Declaration separated "man" from "citizen," true human emancipation can occur only with this reabsorption: "When man has recognized and organized his '*forces propres*' as social forces, and consequently no longer separates social power from himself in the shape of political power, only then will human emancipation have been accomplished."

10. Arjun Appadurai, *Modernity at Large: Cultural Dimensions of Globalization*, 1.

11. Peter Brooks, *Reading for the Plot: Design and Intention in Narrative*, 5–6.

12. Ibid., 12.

13. Lukács, *Theory of the Novel*, 77.

14. Ibid., 78.

15. M. M. Bakhtin, *The Dialogic Imagination: Four Essays*, 84–258.

16. Dorothea E. von Mücke, *Virtue and the Veil of Illusion: Generic Innovation and the Pedagogical Project in Eighteenth-Century Literature*, 162. For a fuller account of the notion of *Bildung*, see Gadamer, *Truth and Method*. Klaus Vondung, "Unity through *Bildung*: A German Dream of Perfection." Sven Erik Nordenbo, "*Bildung* and the Thinking of *Bildung*." Susan L. Cocalis, "The Transformation of Bildung from an Image to an Ideal." Walter Horace Bruford, *The German Tradition of Self-Cultivation: Bildung from Humboldt to Thomas Mann*.

17. Redfield, *Phantom Formations*, 38.

18. Wilhelm Dilthey, Rudolf A. Makkreel, and Frithjof Rodi, *Selected Works (V.5): Poetry and Experience*, 336.

19. P. Dahl, "The '*Bildungsroman*,'" 423.

20. Dipesh Chakrabarty, *Provincializing Europe: Postcolonial Thought and Historical Difference*, 34.

21. Ibid., 37. Chakrabarty suggests that the hegemony of this narrative pattern occludes alternative, subaltern "constructions of self and community [that], while documentable, will never enjoy the privilege of providing the meta-narratives or teleologies . . . of our histories." Subaltern or counter-configurations of the community/self complex conduce alternative visions of human rights and the human rights person; they also tend to reify other cultural and literary forms as abstractions of those social relations. My focus on the dominant, normative teleological version (allied historically to power) of the subject of history that conjoins human rights law and the *Bildungsroman* should not be mistaken as applying to those politically and institutionally subalternized forms.

22. Lukács, *Goethe and His Age*, 51. The 1947 chapter on *Wilhelm Meister's Apprenticeship* is part of a 1936 monograph on Goethe that, like Bakhtin's book on the author, did not survive World War II. Because Germany was excluded from UN membership after the war, German was not a drafting language for the UDHR. Nonetheless, Lukács' original phrasing corresponds almost verbatim to the declaration's later German translation (*Goethe und Seine Zeit*, 32).

23. Lukács, *Goethe and His Age*, 62.

24. Lukács, *Theory of the Novel*, 133.

25. Lukács, *Goethe and His Age*, 55. For discussion of the philosophical and political differences between Lukács' readings of Goethe in the 1910s and 30s, see Galin Tihanov, "The Ideology of *Bildung*: Lukács and Bakhtin as Readers of Goethe."

26. Lukács, *Goethe and His Age*, 60.

27. James N. Hardin, "Reflection and Action: Essays on the Bildungsroman: An Introduction," xxi.

28. M. M. Bakhtin, "The *Bildungsroman* and Its Significance in the History of Realism (toward a Historical Typology of the Novel)," 19.

29. Michael Minden, "The Place of Inheritance in the Bildungsroman: Agathon, Wilhelm Meister's Lehrjahre, and Der Nachsommer," 274.

30. Goethe, *Wilhelm Meister's Apprenticeship and Travels*, vol. 2, bk. 5, ch. 3, 8.

31. Robert Williams glosses this structure as the arc of "reciprocal recognition" from Hegel's *Encyclopedia of the Philosophical Sciences* in terms that resonate with my analysis: "The I is no longer simply self-identical, but is 'othered.' Prior to or apart from the other, self-identity remains abstract and immediate. The original I = I is a distinction without a difference, a merely empty and formal tautology. The self requires an other to objectify it to become conscious of its freedom" (*Hegel's Ethics of Recognition*, 69, 72).

32. Franco Moretti, "'A Useless Longing for Myself': The Crisis of the European *Bildungsroman*, 1898–1914," 45.

33. Goethe, *Wilhelm Meister's Apprenticeship and Travels*, vol. 2, bk. 7, ch. 9, 189.

34. Redfield, *Phantom Formations*, 71.

35. Goethe, *Wilhelm Meister's Apprenticeship and Travels*, vol. 2, bk. 8, ch. 1, 193.

36. Ferdinand Tönnies wrote the classic work on modernization as a shift from community to society. Edward Said recasts these terms as "filiation" and "affiliation," associative principles that he ascribes, respectively, to "the realms of nature and of 'life'" and "to culture and society" (*The World, the Text, and the Critic*, 20–21; Ferdinand Tönnies, *Community & Society [Gemeinschaft Und Gesellschaft]*).

37. Orphancy offers a particularly suggestive emblem of the modern condition, well-suited to the problematics of the *Bildungsroman*, so many of whose protagonists are literal orphans (Charles Dickens' Pip and Charlotte Brontë's Jane Eyre) or, like Wilhelm Meister and Robinson Crusoe before him, reject their biological family to choose their own—even if they ultimately choose their biological own.

38. Judith P. Butler, *The Psychic Life of Power: Theories in Subjection*, 112, 11.

39. Lukács, *Theory of the Novel*, 133–34.

40. Ibid., 137.

41. White, *Content of the Form*, 14.

42. The clunky device of the Tower is often regarded as symptomatic of the historical fact that, at the time of the novel, Germany was not yet a coherent nation-state. See Habermas, *Structural Transformation of the Public Sphere*, 12–13. See also John K. Noyes, "Goethe on Cosmopolitanism and Colonialism: *Bildung* and the Dialectic of Critical Mobility."

43. Michael Minden, *The German Bildungsroman: Incest and Inheritance*, 1. Minden offers an exceptional reading of the social and narratological role of inheritance and incest in twisting the teleology of development into a circle in

both Goethe's novel and in the classical *Bildungsroman* more generally. See also Minden, "Place of Inheritance in the Bildungsroman."

44. Brooks, *Reading for the Plot*, 6.

45. For Paul Ricoeur, the transmutation of "chance . . . into fate" is precisely the work of emplotment—the effect of a "narrative necessity" to synthesize the heterogeneous for the sake of meaning. Paul Ricoeur, *Oneself as Another*, 141–47.

46. Ibid., 124; Paul Ricoeur, "Self as *Ipse*," 106.

47. Lukács, *Theory of the Novel*, 88.

48. Ibid., 80.

49. Brooks, *Reading for the Plot*, 6.

50. Interestingly, this metaphysical movement from nature to personality is repeated in the history of the English translation of Goethe's novel. In 1824, Thomas Carlyle first translates Wilhelm's desire for *"harmonischen Ausbildung meiner Natur"* as "the harmonious cultivation of my nature." Goethe, *Wilhelm Meisters Lehrjahre*, bk. 5, ch. 3, 233–35. The translators for the 1989 edition of *Goethe's Collected Works* render this as Wilhelm's "irresistible desire to attain the harmonious development of my personality" (174–75).

51. Charles Taylor, *The Ethics of Authenticity*, 77.

52. My translation; François Jost, "La Tradition du 'Bildungsroman,'" 99.

53. Scholes and Kellogg, *The Nature of Narrative*, 256.

54. E. M. Forster, *Aspects of the Novel*, 69–78.

55. White, *Content of the Form*, 20.

56. The Tower not only serves a Foucaultian "author function," as Marc Redfield has suggested; it also serves a reader function, illustrating for readers who might not be fully literate in the workings of linear plot what Peter Brooks calls the "anticipation of retrospection" that drives the act of reading (Redfield, *Phantom Formations*, 94; Brooks, *Reading for the Plot*, 23).

57. Bakhtin, "Bildungsroman," 22.

58. Malik, *Man*, xxii–xxxvi. Malik, a professor of philosophy and student of Alfred North Whitehead and Martin Heidegger, saw little use for philosophy at the UN: "One wonders if the . . . 'the philosophers of history,' . . . Hegel, or Nietzsche, or Dilthey, for instance, [had] known personally and intensively what it meant to be responsible for actual historical-political decisions affecting the fate of a nation or a people or a culture, would they still have conceived history in the manner they did?" (xxii). Incidentally, this is the same Charles Malik whom Edward Said calls "Uncle" in his intellectual autobiography of homelessness, casting him, in good *Bildungsroman* fashion, as the mentor who must ultimately be superseded. (*Out of Place: A Memoir*).

59. David Lloyd, *Anomalous States: Irish Writing and the Post-Colonial Moment*, 134.

60. Michel Foucault, *The Archaeology of Knowledge and the Discourse on Language*, 21; White, *Content of the Form*, x.

61. White, *Content of the Form*, x, 1–25.

62. Bakhtin, "Bildungsroman," 25.

63. Ibid., 23.

64. Tamen, "Kinds," 6.

65. Williams, *Sociology of Culture*, 142.

66. Gadamer, *Truth and Method*, xxi–xxii.

67. Bakhtin, "Bildungsroman," 21.

68. White, *Content of the Form*, 13–14.

69. Bakhtin, "Bildungsroman," 25.

70. Margaret R. Somers, "Narrativity, Narrative Identity, and Social Action: Rethinking English Working-Class Formation," 596.

71. Bakhtin, "Bildungsroman," 23.

72. Foucault, *Archaeology of Knowledge*, 12.

73. Étienne Balibar, "Citizen Subject," 55.

74. Ibid., 46.

75. Habermas, *Structural Transformation of the Public Sphere*, 72.

76. Wulf Koepke advises against reading too strict a correlation between the *Bildungsroman* and eighteenth-century philosophical and pedagogical theories of *Bildung* ("Quest, Illusion, Creativity, Maturity, and Resignation: The Questionable Journey of the Protagonist of the *Bildungsroman*," 130). But as a matter of *realkritik*, the practice has been part of the analytical tradition since the genre's inception.

77. Gadamer, *Truth and Method*, 18.

78. Nordenbo, "*Bildung* and the Thinking of *Bildung*," 25.

79. Cocalis, "Transformation of Bildung," 400; and Nordenbo, "*Bildung* and the Thinking of *Bildung*," 25–26.

80. Cocalis, "Transformation of Bildung," 401. Although traditionally regarded as uniquely German, *Bildung*'s translational arc has an affinity with the *Bildungsroman* plot. *Bildung* reportedly entered England in Thomas Carlyle's 1824 translation of Goethe, but that channel crossing represents something of a reverse translation, a homecoming for Shaftesbury's idea, which, like the novels' protagonists, made the best of a prolonged stay among unexpected friends in Germany.

81. Todd Curtis Kontje, *The German Bildungsroman: History of a National Genre*, 2.

82. Friedrich Schiller, *On the Aesthetic Education of Man, in a Series of Letters*, 17–18.

83. For detailed discussions of the various inflections given to the German idealist theory of *Bildung* by eighteenth-century philosophers, see Kontje, *German Bildungsroman*; and Redfield, *Phantom Formations*. On Hegel, see John H. Smith, *The Spirit and Its Letter: Traces of Rhetoric in Hegel's Philosophy of*

Bildung. On Fichte and Hegel, see Cheah, *Spectral Nationality.* On the German-idealist heritage in English cultural thought, see David Lloyd, "Arnold, Ferguson, Schiller: Aesthetic Culture and the Politics of Aesthetics."

84. Wilhelm von Humboldt, *Linguistic Variability and Intellectual Development,* 131.

85. Ibid.

86. Wilhelm von Humboldt, *The Limits of State Action,* 64.

87. Ibid., 52.

88. Ibid., 51.

89. Cheah, *Spectral Nationality,* 235. See also Lloyd and Thomas, *Culture and the State,* 47.

90. Jameson, "Third-World Literature," 69.

91. Jameson, "On Literary and Cultural Import-Substitution," 172. In the question period of his keynote address to the American Comparative Literature Association (2004), Arjun Appadurai suggested that Jameson's national allegory was perhaps formulated too early ("Plenary Address"). We could, however, conclude from the classical theories of *Bildung* that his reading prescription was too late, or that it took too narrow a historical and geographical view of the "Third World" as its singular subject.

92. Agamben, *Homo Sacer,* 128.

93. Pierre Clastres, *Archeology of Violence,* 49.

94. Rita Maran, *Torture: The Role of Ideology in the French-Algerian War,* 142. The connections between the Rights of Man and French colonialism are well-documented. Perhaps more interesting is the palliative logic that surfaces among metropolitan sympathizers of anticolonial struggles who often credit both the rhetoric of the Rights of Man and the colonial power's refusal to apply them to the colonized with fomenting the independence movements. See, for instance, Pierre Cot, "Preface." For an excellent analysis of the paradoxical deployment of rights discourse in the context of colonialism, see John Comaroff, "The Discourse of Rights in Colonial South Africa: Subjectivity, Sovereignty, Modernity."

95. Kontje traces the proprietary nature of the genre and the universalist ideal from the eighteenth century to the cultural nationalism of Nazi organic ideology (*German Bildungsroman*). Witte takes the phrase "not for export" from a Swedish review of Thomas Mann's *Magic Mountain,* which was perceived to be too German to be comprehended outside of that nation ("Alien Corn—the 'Bildungsroman': Not for Export?"). See also Sammons, "Mystery of the Missing Bildungsroman"; and Vondung, "Unity through Bildung."

96. Moretti, *Way of the World,* 64. See "Evening Hours of a Hermit" in Johann Heinrich Pestalozzi, *How Gertrude Teaches Her Children: Pestalozzi's Educational Writings.* For similar arguments from commentators writing contemporaneously with the French Revolution, see Cocalis, "Transformation of Bildung."

97. Kontje, *German Bildungsroman*, 4.

98. The UDHR's drafters considered articulating a right to rebellion as a human right; instead they established an equation between respect for human rights and the prevention of revolution that serves as a preambular rationale for the declaration itself.

99. Appiah, "Citizens of the World," 229. On the history and effects of the sociopolitical and legal dissemination of "dignity" to the bourgeoisie and the lower classes "after the fall of the ancien regime," see Giorgio Agamben, *Remnants of Auschwitz: The Witness and the Archive*, 66–69.

100. Lukács, *Theory of the Novel*, 137.

101. Dilthey, Makkreel, and Rodi, *Selected Works*, 335. Dilthey apparently believed that he was inventing the term *"Bildungsroman,"* and he was generally credited with having done so until Fritz Martini excavated Karl Morgenstern's earlier definition ("Bildungsroman—Term and Theory").

102. Cheah, *Spectral Nationality*, 243.

103. Cited in Martini, "Bildungsroman," 18.

104. Eve Tavor Bannet, "Rewriting the Social Text: The Female Bildungsroman in Eighteenth-Century England"; Hirsch, "Novel of Formation as Genre," 298; and Dennis F. Mahoney, "The Apprenticeship of the Reader: The Bildungsroman of the 'Age of Goethe.'"

105. Jameson, "On Literary and Cultural Import-Substitution," 182.

106. Moretti, *Way of the World*, 15–16.

107. Gadamer, *Truth and Method*, 15.

108. Ibid., 13.

109. Democratic formalism is popularly regarded as a radical social constructivist position. Ironically, the same people who vilify it in the abstract tend to be those who most readily vocalize it to rationalize warfare in the name of democracy, human rights, and freedom. Suddenly, Foucault and Althusser return with a vengeance, and pundits opine endlessly about how "hard" (to quote George W. Bush) democracy is to establish, but that given the proper institutions, the people of "rogue" states will eventually be habituated to the practice of democracy and interpellated as good national and international citizens.

110. Lloyd, "Arnold, Ferguson, Schiller," 138.

111. Ngũgĩ wa Thiong'o, *Decolonizing the Mind: The Politics of Language in African Literature*, 9.

112. In the 91 countries in which the United Nations has assisted or sponsored elections, the trademark "purple finger"—the stamp of indelible ink that prevents electors from voting twice—inscribes the body of the voter as a subject of the institutions of statist democracy. With the 31 January 2005 elections in Iraq, the United States attempted to brand the purple finger as the watermark of its neoimperial legitimacy.

113. Humboldt, *Linguistic Variability*, 13. All recent English translations of this passage share the phrase "human rights," and although it is a retrojective translation of Humboldt's nineteenth-century German, it does capture his sentiment (Humboldt, *Humanist without Portfolio: An Anthology of the Writings of Wilhelm Von Humboldt*, 267; Humboldt, *Über Die Verschiedenheit Des Menschlichen Sprachbaues Und Ihren Einfluß Auf Die Geistige Entwicklung Des Menschengeschlechts*, 28).

114. Humboldt, *Linguistic Variability*, 14. John Noyes writes that "The philanthropic view of *Bildung* . . . was the motivating idea behind virtually all positive comments on colonialism in eighteenth-century Germany" ("Goethe on Cosmopolitanism and Colonialism: *Bildung* and the Dialectic of Critical Mobility," 453).

115. John Stuart Mill, *On Liberty*, 3.

116. Ibid., 11.

117. Gauri Viswanathan, *Masks of Conquest: Literary Study and British Rule in India*, 3.

118. Viswanathan's descriptions of the goals of nineteenth-century British colonial literary education in India resonate with the classical theories of *Bildung*: "to awaken the colonial subjects to a memory of their innate character, corrupted as it had become . . . through the feudalistic character of Oriental society. In this universalizing narrative, . . . the British government was refashioned as the ideal republic to which Indians must naturally aspire as a spontaneous expression of self" (132).

119. Leela Gandhi, "'Learning Me Your Language': England in the Postcolonial *Bildungsroman*," 59.

120. Ashis Nandy, "Reconstructing Childhood: A Critique of the Ideology of Adulthood."

121. Great Britain, "Parliamentary Debates: Kenya Independence Bill," 777.

122. Great Britain, "Parliamentary Debates," 316–17. For a more thorough discussion of these debates, see Joseph R. Slaughter, "Master Plans: Designing (National) Allegories of Urban Space and Metropolitan Subjects for Postcolonial Kenya."

123. Marjorie Oludhe Macgoye, *Coming to Birth*, 36.

124. Ibid., 64, 146.

125. Bakhtin, "Bildungsroman," 24.

126. Ironically, these provisions, which grant economic and cultural rights to colonial states and corporations, give the lie to the misleading argument that civil and political rights have always been primary in the Western-rights tradition or in international law. Of the General Act's thirty-eight articles, only one deals with anything other than trade rights, supplying the rhetorical humanitarian cover for the economic and missionary exploitation of Africa in

the vulgarized language of *Bildung*: "All the Powers exercising sovereign rights or influence in the aforesaid territories bind themselves to watch over the preservation of the native tribes, and to care for the improvement of the conditions of their moral and material well-being" (Article 6). The Act also co-opts the rhetoric of the transatlantic abolitionist movements, construing colonialism as reparation for slavery and the slave trade. On the role of abolition and colonialism in the development of contemporary international human rights law, see Lauren, *Evolution of International Human Rights*, 37–71. We should note here that the "mutual accord" of the General Act incorporates the European nation-states as a right-and-duty bound unit with "a sense of common mission" (Gil Gott, "Imperial Humanitarianism: History of an Arrested Dialectic," 28). In this sense, as much as Africa may have been a discursive and epistemic invention of Europe (as Mudimbe argues), the common European community was itself a geopolitical invention of (or response to) Africa, at least partially the effect of the instrumentalization of discourses of rights and duties toward Africa and Africans (V. Y. Mudimbe, *The Invention of Africa: Gnosis, Philosophy, and the Order of Knowledge*).

127. Chinua Achebe, "Africa's Tarnished Name," 13.

128. Edward W. Said, "Identity, Authority, and Freedom: The Potentate and the Traveler," 16; Frantz Fanon, *The Wretched of the Earth*, 247.

129. Macgoye, *Coming to Birth*, 12.

130. Ibid., 11.

131. Ibid., 29.

132. White et al., *Nairobi*, 77.

133. Ibid., 54. In its repeated use of the word "canalize"—a transitive project and verb usually associated with Apartheid influx-control policy—the plan approximates at the city level the racialized spatial logic of homelands and pass laws that South Africa's National Party would develop to regulate movement between urban and rural areas.

134. Macgoye, *Coming to Birth*, 19, 102.

135. Ibid., 93.

136. Ibid., 73.

137. Ibid., 111.

138. Ibid., 150.

139. Quoted in Anderson, *Imagined Communities*, 25.

140. Macgoye, *Coming to Birth*, 36.

141. Ibid., 73, 90.

142. Ibid., 138, 131.

143. Ibid., 72.

144. Ibid., 93.

145. Edward W. Soja, *The Geography of Modernization in Kenya: A Spatial Analysis of Social, Economic, and Political Change*, 101, 105.

146. Macgoye writes herself into the novel on two occasions: as the assistant to a European woman who cares for Paulina after she is arrested for wandering the streets of Nairobi; and at the Independence day celebrations, where she expresses concern about "how to teach the women the National Anthem . . . and about the new flag" (*Coming to Birth*, 52).

147. Great Britain. House of Lords, *Parliamentary Debates*, 392.

148. Moretti describes this narrow differential as the sociopolitical gap between the ascendant bourgeoisie and the courtly aristocracy, locating the *Bildungsroman* "at the transition point between them" (*Way of the World*, viii). Perhaps it is the slightness of this gap, in which so little now seems at stake, that gives the classical examples both a narrative tedium and an air of inevitability, where the protagonist's struggles seem to consist of little more than insipid bourgeois brooding and self-indulgence. Thomas Carlyle foresaw this response in his 1824 translator's preface to *Wilhelm Meister*: "To the great mass of readers, . . . [the novel] will appear beyond endurance weary, flat, stale, and unprofitable. . . . The hero is a milksop, who, with all his gifts, it takes an effort to avoid despising" (17).

149. Moretti, *Way of the World*, 230.

150. Lukács, *Goethe and His Age*, 64.

151. As Jameson suggests, "Constitutions come into being in order to forestall the revolution" ("The Politics of Utopia," 42). Franco Moretti similarly observes of the social conservatism of the *Bildungsroman* that the possibility of avoiding the revolution needs "not be shown to its victims—but rather to its potential protagonists. . . . It is the bourgeois reader who must be shown the advantages of social reconciliation" (*Way of the World*, 65). In this regard, constitutions and novels appear to work similarly.

152. Bannet, "Rewriting the Social Text," 211.

153. Keenan, *Fables of Responsibility*, 37–42; Lefort, *Political Forms of Modern Society*, 256–57.

154. Keenan, *Fables of Responsibility*, 39, 41.

155. Arendt, *Origins of Totalitarianism*, 296.

156. Cohen, *Sentimental Education of the Novel*, 104.

157. Ibid., 110; Hirsch, "Novel of Formation as Genre," 299.

158. Peter Fitzpatrick, "Terminal Legality? Human Rights and Critical Being," 125.

159. Redfield, *Phantom Formations*, 202.

160. Gayatri Chakravorty Spivak, *Outside in the Teaching Machine*, 45–46.

CHAPTER 3

Normalizing Narrative Forms of Human Rights: The (Dys)Function of the Public Sphere

Epigraph. Weschler credits philosopher and lawyer Thomas Nagel with the succinct formulation of the public work of truth commissions that attempt to turn "knowledge [into] *a*cknowledgment. It's what happens and can only happen to knowledge when it becomes officially sanctioned, when it is made part of the public cognitive scene" (4).

1. Khulumani Support Group, Bobby Rodwell, and Lesego Rampolokeng, "The Story I Am About to Tell," 1.

2. Ibid., 2.

3. Truth and Reconciliation Commission, *Truth and Reconciliation Commission of South Africa Report*, 156.

4. South Africa's truth commission spawned numerous artistic creations exploring the dynamics of reconciliation, including, most famously, *Ubu and the Truth Commission, The Dead Wait*, Antjie Krog's *The Country of My Skull*, and J. M. Coetzee's *Disgrace*. These works joined an informal international canon of truth-commission literature begun in the 1980s by Latin American critics, writers, and artists such as Ariel Dorfman, Marjorie Agosín, Griselda Gámbaro, Alicia Partnoy, Mario Roberto Morales, Diamela Eltit, Luisa Valenzuela, Marta Traba, and many others. On South African literatures, see Shane Graham, "The Truth Commission and Post-Apartheid Literature in South Africa"; William Kentridge, "Director's Note"; and Mark Sanders, "Truth, Telling, Questioning: The Truth and Reconciliation Commission, Antjie Krog's *Country of My Skull*, and Literature after Apartheid."

5. Truth and Reconciliation Commission, *TRC Vol. 6*, 156–57. In the play, "The story I am about to tell" are the first words of the oath by which human rights victims swear to the TRC that what follows "is the truth and nothing but the truth."

6. Truth and Reconciliation Commission, *Truth and Reconciliation Commission of South Africa Report*, 1.

7. Ibid., 112. Cognizant of the socially contingent character of truth, the TRC pragmatically distinguished among four distinct but interrelated genres and contexts of truth: "factual or forensic truth"; "personal or narrative truth"; "social or 'dialogue' truth"; and "healing and restorative truth" (110).

8. Ibid., 110.

9. Ibid., 112.

10. Ibid., 113–14. The TRC sought to naturalize the dialogical form of its hearings by insisting that it derived from "essential norms of social relations between people" in South African communities (114)—the ethical norms of intersubjectivity captured in the Nguni concept of *ubuntu* (humaneness): "People are people through other people" (127). In other words, the commissioners sought to indigenize the habits and practices of modern democracy.

11. Ibid., 112.

12. Edward W. Said, "Permission to Narrate," 34. Said was writing about the Western-dominated international public sphere's foreclosure to the admission (even the formulation) of a Palestinian national narrative.

13. Truth and Reconciliation Commission, *TRC Vol. 1*, 114, 110, 114.

14. Antjie Krog, *Country of My Skull: Guilt, Sorrow, and the Limits of Forgiveness in the New South Africa*, 286–90.

15. Kentridge, "Director's Note," xiii.

16. Truth and Reconciliation Commission, *TRC Vol. 1*, 114.

17. The logic of making known or acknowledging what is already known resembles the plot dynamics of dramatic irony that are sustained on a tension between knowing and not knowing, until they resolve in a recognition scene in which the players in the world of the text are confronted in such a dramatic way with knowledge that the reader–audience already possesses that it must be formally acknowledged. Here too, the story has its own force. The vocabulary of drama provides the favored lexicon for commentary on truth commissions. There is, of course, a generic affinity between the scene and themes of truth commissions and drama. Their intensity and spectacularity appear to be antinovelistic, at least by the evidence of the literary archive where plays abound.

18. Antonio Gramsci, *Selections from the Prison Notebooks*, 348. Gadamer glosses *Bildung* as the human task of "being raised to the universal . . . that requires the sacrifice of particularity for the sake of the universal" (*Truth and Method*, 13). Compare this metaphysical description to Gramsci's sociological analysis of hegemony.

19. Mutua, *Human Rights*, 34, 28.

20. Ibid., 27–28.

21. Habermas, *Structural Transformation of the Public Sphere*, 27.

22. Felski, *Beyond Feminist Aesthetics*, 168.

23. White, *Content of the Form*, x.

24. Habermas, *Structural Transformation of the Public Sphere*, 12–13. Similarly, Felski accounts for the mid-twentieth-century boom in American and European women's *Bildungsromane* "as one indication of the increasing movement of women from the private into the public sphere" (*Beyond Feminist Aesthetics*, 139).

25. Franco Moretti, *Atlas of the European Novel, 1800–1900*, 68.

26. Like the democratic public sphere, official truth commissions undertake the process of acknowledging knowledge with at least the partial consent of the state. Their work of excavating traditionally excluded stories to rewrite state history is done, then, in the service of legitimating the emergent democratic institutions of a revitalized state formation. However, sponsoring governments also tend to perceive them as antagonistic. The first modern example, "The Commission of Inquiry into 'Disappearances' of People in Uganda Since the 25th of January, 1971," was appointed cynically by Idi Amin, and its findings were not only largely ignored, but most of the commissioners were either assassinated or forced to flee Uganda. See Priscilla B. Hayner, "Fifteen Truth Commissions—1974 to 1994: A Comparative Study."

27. As many human rights critics have noted, the valorization of publicness reinforces a historically gendered "public/private bifurcation" that ignores certain "violations of women's rights in the private or cultural sphere" as human rights abuses (Cubilié, *Women Witnessing Terror*, 72; Bunch, "Transforming," 14). To some degree, this is a gendered version of the man–citizen split articulated in eighteenth-century human rights law. Historically, the reification of publicness has meant that woman may become man but not citizen.

28. Nussbaum, *Cultivating Humanity*, 92.

29. Pierre Bourdieu, *The Rules of Art: Genesis and Structure of the Literary Field*, 236.

30. Lukács, *Theory of the Novel*, 88.

31. Jürgen Habermas, "The Public Sphere: An Encyclopedia Article (1964)," 49.

32. The Human Rights Commission established only one other sub-committee: the Sub-Commission on the Status of Women.

33. For an account of the UN debates about the role of freedom of information and expression in counteracting fascism, see Morsink, *Universal Declaration of Human Rights*, 65–69. International law also imposes restrictions on free speech in "respect of the rights or reputations of others" and for "the protection of national security," "public order," or "public health or morals" (ICCPR Article 19). More pointedly, what one has absolutely no right to speak of is violence, at least when it propagandizes for war or advocates "national, racial or religious hatred that constitutes incitement to discrimination, hostility or violence" (Article 20). Georges Sorel's famous defense of proletarian violence dates the modern prohibitions of incitive speech to the consolidation of bourgeois power after the suppression of the 1848 insurrections in France, and he sees these proscriptions as precisely the legal mechanics designed to forestall class warfare and the coming General Strike (*Reflections on Violence*, 65). Class, construed as a historical and not a natural condition of the human, is excluded from the international legal list of identitarian categories (race, ethnicity, nationality, religion) that are vulnerable to hate speech. As such, class has no corporate personality in international human rights law and therefore no legitimate claim to self-determination. For a good introduction to racist and hate speech in international law, see Mari J. Matsuda, "Public Response to Racist Speech: Considering the Victim's Story."

34. Peter Goodrich, *Legal Discourse: Studies in Linguistics, Rhetoric, and Legal Analysis*, 153–54.

35. Seyla Benhabib, *Situating the Self: Gender, Community and Postmodernism in Contemporary Ethics*, 106.

36. Habermas, "Legitimation," 201.

37. Jürgen Habermas, *Communication and the Evolution of Society*. There are, of course, numerous standard Enlightenment assumptions behind the democratic ideology of the public sphere: the possession of a rational faculty; a

capacity for deliberation (which entails both a capacity for personal eloquence—or at least a minimal ability to shape one's opinions in socially acceptable language, in the prevailing argumentative and narrative forms—and
a belief in persons as persuadable subjects); and a sense that something called
the individual will is commensurable with its collective counterpart.

38. Habermas, "Public Sphere," 49.

39. Lyotard, "Other's Rights," 140–41; Habermas, *Structural Transformation of the Public Sphere*, 85.

40. Habermas, *Structural Transformation of the Public Sphere*, 165.

41. Habermas, "Legitimation," 201.

42. Lyotard, "Other's Rights," 138. I suggest that enabling fictions in general tend to misrepresent the positivity of the projects they imagine by describing them as natural—as requiring only negative prohibitions against
discrimination or interference. Isaiah Berlin is usually credited with the current distinction between "negative liberty" and "positive liberty" (*Two Concepts of Liberty*). Negative rights are generally understood as the classic
libertarian civil and political rights whose enjoyment is thought to be guaranteed merely by the prohibition or limitation of certain state activities (e.g.,
torture, slavery, discrimination); social, cultural, and economic rights are generally thought of as positive rights whose enjoyment requires active intervention by the state (e.g., education, social security, due process). The strictness
of the positive–negative distinction has been largely discredited, although the
terms remain common. See Donnelly, *Universal Human Rights in Theory and
Practice*, 33–34; and Henry Shue, "Basic Rights: Subsistence, Affluence, and
U.S."

43. Lyotard, "Other's Rights," 139.

44. Stanley Eugene Fish, "There's No Such Thing as Free Speech, and It's
a Good Thing, Too," 108; Cohen, "Sentimental Communities," 114.

45. Cohen, "Sentimental Communities," 107.

46. Appiah, "Citizens of the World," 197.

47. Fish, "There's No Such Thing," 108.

48. This "cultural" inflection of citizenship can be understood in terms of
T. H. Marshall's history of the category. Marshall, who introduced "citizenship" to the sociological agenda in 1973, argues that in England the "concept
of full membership of a community" expanded from the eighteenth to the
twentieth centuries to include, in chronological order, civil, political, and social rights. The evolution of citizenship necessarily entails certain transformations of socially acceptable narratives as particular human relations become
progressively relevant to public scrutiny and discussion (*Class, Citizenship, and
Social Development: Essays*, 70).

49. Said, *Culture and Imperialism*, 71.

50. Ibid., 79.

51. Felski, *Beyond Feminist Aesthetics*, 137.
52. Lowe, *Immigrant Acts*, 98.
53. Lukács, *Theory of the Novel*, 135. For Lukács, "contemplation" and "action" name the two activities that achieve balance in the fully developed human personality, exemplified for him in Goethe's *Wilhelm Meister's Apprenticeship*. See also Hardin, "Reflection and Action."
54. Arendt, *Origins of Totalitarianism*, 302.
55. Orlando Patterson, *Slavery and Social Death*; Arendt, *Origins of Totalitarianism*, 293. Patterson's description of the slave's "natal alienation" as "social death" aims to correct the standard analytical discourses on slavery that had historically taken the condition to be one of "civil death." He demonstrates that the slave had a restricted civil presence in the courts, and therefore that slavery removed the individual not primarily from the juridical world of rights and responsibilities but from meaningful systems of social relations.
56. Ibid. See also Lyotard, "Other's Rights." It is worth noting the UN's efforts to reduce statelessness. The Convention Relating to the Status of the Stateless Person (1954), for instance, recognizes the individual as a person, despite the lack of a nationality to guarantee such a civil subjectivity, by declaring that "every stateless person has duties to the country in which he finds himself"; the state is to reciprocate by granting the "stateless person" nationality. The Convention on the Reduction of Statelessness (1961) established further protocols for the patriation of the stateless. Such legislative attention suggests that, without the shield of a nation, the stateless expatriate is not only one of the most vulnerable categories of human existence; it represents a threat to a world order that aspires to internationalize the civil subject but can only do so through the logic of nationalism itself.
57. Adeno Addis, "Individualism, Communitarianism, and the Rights of Ethnic Minorities," 1246.
58. The Convention biologizes the mechanics of group perpetuation, and so it identifies women as particularly vulnerable embodiments of group personality based partly on the biology of human reproduction, but also on a patriarchal notion that women are "the repositories, guardians, and transmitters of culture. Women represent the reproduction of the community" (Arati Rao, "The Politics of Gender and Culture in International Human Rights Discourse," 169). Recent calls for rape and forced pregnancy to be included as acts of genocide generally also draw upon this association of women with biocultural reproduction. See Ruth Seifert, *War and Rape: Analytical Approaches*; and Alexandra Stiglmayer, ed., *Mass Rape: The War against Women in Bosnia-Herzegovina*. In Ralph Lemkin's original coinage of the term "genocide"—from which the earliest drafts of the declaration were drawn—cultural genocide was included as half of the twin genocidal crimes of "barbarism" and "vandalism." Acts of cultural vandalism (ethnocide) were ultimately excluded

from the final Convention by the assimilationist-minded delegations from the Americas; see Johannes Morsink, "Cultural Genocide, the Universal Declaration, and Minority Rights," 1009.

59. Crimes against humanity would be those in which the human personality (rather than some identitarian subsection of it) is killed. In this regard, through its synecdochal configuration of the individual as an embodiment of a group, the Genocide Convention figuratively dehumanizes the individual human being in advance of any acts that might constitute genocide.

60. Anderson, *Imagined Communities*, 205.

61. Mercado, *In a State of Memory*, 86.

62. Ibid., 90.

63. Ibid., 86.

64. Appadurai, *Modernity at Large*, 22.

65. Mercado, *In a State of Memory*, 55.

66. Mercado, *En Estado De Memoria*, 44, Mercado, *In a State of Memory*, 48. I cite both the English translation of Mercado's novel and the Spanish original (with my own translations) when the English does not capture fully the richness of Mercado's language.

67. Mercado, *In a State of Memory*, 16.

68. Ibid., 55.

69. Ibid., 56; Jean Franco, "Introduction," xix.

70. Mercado, *In a State of Memory*, 17, 16; Mercado, *En Estado De Memoria*, 18.

71. Mercado, *In a State of Memory*, 100.

72. Ignacio Martín-Baró, *Writings for a Liberation Psychology*, 124. Writing of the "anti-socialization" of Salvadoran children during the 1980s civil war, Martín-Baró emphasized the social "dialectical character" of trauma that affects the process of personalization to correct the dominant individualistic medical model given its scientific imprimatur in the American Psychiatric Association's *DSM-III*.

73. Ralph Freedman, *The Lyrical Novel: Studies in Hermann Hesse, André Gide, and Virginia Woolf*, 1.

74. Ibid., 9.

75. Mercado, *In a State of Memory*, 23.

76. Ibid., 65, 108.

77. Ibid., 92.

78. Ibid., 56; Butler, *The Psychic Life of Power*, 6.

79. CONADEP, *Nunca Más (Never Again)*, 362. The Argentine truth commission notes the particularly concerted assault on public intellectuals and names more than 100 journalists who permanently disappeared and another hundred who were imprisoned for extended periods without trial (362). Timerman's detention was one of the mostly widely denounced crimes of the Argentine dictatorship, and he publicized the experience in his book *Prisoner Without a Name, Cell Without a Number*.

80. Ibid., 363.

81. Ibid., xiii.

82. Ibid., 234.

83. Ibid., 3.

84. Ibid., 234.

85. Ibid., 233. *Nunca Más* attempts to reconstruct the logic behind this aspect of disappearance: "Wiping out the identity of the corpses magnified the shadow hanging over the thousands of disappeared of whom all trace was lost after their arrest or kidnapping . . . giving [families] hope that their loved ones might be alive, in the nebulous category of missing persons . . . which forced the relatives into isolation" (233–34).

86. Martín-Baró, *Writings for a Liberation Psychology*, 125; CONADEP, *Nunca Más*, 10.

87. Cubilié, *Women Witnessing Terror*, 72.

88. Mercado, *In a State of Memory*, 67.

89. Ibid., 69, 71.

90. Ibid., 85. Mercado, *En Estado De Memoria*, 72.

91. Mercado, *In a State of Memory*, 99.

92. Laura Bonaparte and Clara Gertel were both Mothers of the Plaza de Mayo. See the group's website: http://www.madres.org/. For historical accounts of the Mothers movement, see John Simpson and Jana Bennett, *The Disappeared and the Mothers of the Plaza: The Story of the 11,000 Argentinians Who Vanished*; Marguerite Guzman Bouvard, *Revolutionizing Motherhood: The Mothers of the Plaza De Mayo*; and Jo Fisher, *Mothers of the Disappeared*. For a more lyrical treatment, see Marjorie Agosín, *Circles of Madness: Mothers of the Plaza De Mayo*.

93. Mercado, *In a State of Memory*, 99.

94. Harlow, *Barred*, 244; Jean Franco, "Going Public: Reinhabiting the Private," 67.

95. Agosín, *Circles of Madness*.

96. Mercado, *In a State of Memory*, 100.

97. Ibid., 99.

98. Ibid., 100.

99. Ibid., 139.

100. Ibid., 103. Mercado, *En Estado De Memoria*, 87.

101. Mercado, *In a State of Memory*, 92.

102. Ibid., 109.

103. Ibid., 109, 114–15.

104. Ibid., 113. Mercado, *En Estado De Memoria*, 93.

105. Mercado, *In a State of Memory*, 113, 115.

106. Ibid., 102.

107. Ibid., 101.

108. Ibid., 101–2.

109. Ibid., 103.

110. Ibid., 101–2.

111. Ibid.

112. Idelber Avelar, *The Untimely Present: Postdictatorial Latin American Fiction and the Task of Mourning,* 211.

113. Ibid., 228.

114. Bakhtin, *Dialogic Imagination,* 294.

115. Mercado, *In a State of Memory,* 48–49.

116. Ibid., 126–27.

117. Mercado, *En Estado De Memoria,* 102; *In a State of Memory,* 127.

118. Mercado, *In a State of Memory,* 126, 127.

119. Ibid., 135.

120. Franco, "Introduction," xxii.

121. Mercado, *In a State of Memory,* 154–55.

122. Ibid., 109.

123. Lukács, *Theory of the Novel,* 138.

124. Laclau and Mouffe, *Hegemony and Socialist Strategy,* 181.

125. Ibid.

126. Bakhtin, "Bildungsroman," 10.

127. Peter Seitel, "Theorizing Genres—Interpreting Works," 277.

128. Cohen, *Sentimental Education of the Novel,* 18.

129. Moretti, *Way of the World,* 15.

130. Hirsch, "Novel of Formation as Genre," 298.

131. Bakhtin, "Bildungsroman," 23.

132. Gregory Castle, "The Book of Youth: Reading Joyce's Bildungsroman," 22.

133. Todd Curtis Kontje, *Private Lives in the Public Sphere: The German Bildungsroman as Metafiction,* 12.

134. Arendt, *Origins of Totalitarianism,* 300.

135. Hirsch, "Novel of Formation as Genre," 298.

136. Lukács, *Theory of the Novel,* 138.

137. Jacques Rancière, "Who Is the Subject of the Rights of Man?," 304.

138. Judith Butler, "Universality in Culture," 359–60.

139. Mercado, *In a State of Memory,* 103.

140. Ibid., 56.

141. Fraser, "Rethinking the Public Sphere: A Contribution to the Critique of Actually Existing Democracy," 14.

142. Rancière, "Who Is the Subject of the Rights of Man?" 304.

143. There can, of course, be more than one typical (even apparently ideologically contradictory) form in internal and external competition with any

given public sphere, and the degree to which a counterpublic sphere represents a real epistemic alternative to the dominant registers in both the difference between the genres that prevail in the dominant public and the counterpublics and in the transformations that any shared genres undergo.

144. Felski's feminist counterpublic sphere, for example, is at least partially constituted and circumscribed by a predominance of "autobiographical writing" that conditions imperatives different from the *Bildungsroman* (which is also an important genre in her feminist public) for public modes of address and the stories the individual can tell about participation (*Beyond Feminist Aesthetics*, 154).

145. Michael Ondaatje, *Anil's Ghost*, 54.

146. Jost, "La Tradition du 'Bildungsroman,'" 99.

147. Cohen, *Sentimental Education of the Novel*, 18.

148. Jerome Hamilton Buckley, *Season of Youth: The Bildungsroman from Dickens to Golding*, 17.

149. Ibid., 17–18.

150. Appiah, "Citizens of the World," 196.

151. Ondaatje, *Anil's Ghost*, 56.

152. Ibid., 42.

153. Ibid., 153–55.

154. Although the 1982 indemnity initially covered only the month of August 1977, it was later amended in 1988 to extend its effect through a to-be-determined "relevant date." For more detailed information on the Emergency Regulations and their history, see Amnesty International, "Sri Lanka: New Emergency Regulations—Erosion of Human Rights Protection"; Abizer Zanzi, *Sri Lanka's Emergency Laws*; and the Asian Human Rights Commission, *Disappearances—Sri Lanka: Laws That Made Large-Scale Murder Legal*.

155. Stanley Eugene Fish, *Is There a Text in This Class?: The Authority of Interpretive Communities*, 338.

156. Ondaatje, *Anil's Ghost*, 151.

157. Ibid., 184.

158. Ibid., 177.

159. Ibid., 205, 55.

160. For Fish, an "interpretive community" is a socializing body whose communally constructed and contingent norms of interpretation pattern the methods by which its individual readers produce meaning from a text (*Is There a Text in This Class?* 14).

161. Miguel Tamen, *Friends of Interpretable Objects*; Tamen, "Kinds."

162. Ondaatje, *Anil's Ghost*, 269.

163. Ibid., 279.

164. Ibid., 55, 42, 176.

165. Lloyd, *Anomalous States*, 134.

166. Ondaatje, *Anil's Ghost*, 256.

167. Ibid., 200.

168. Palipana's paleoglyphic inscriptions, for instance, provide the opportunity, as Anil says, "to study history as if it were a body" (193), bringing Anil, Sarath, and his brother Gamini together. Palipana himself was expelled from the professional community of anthropologists when he violated its tacit norms for responsible interpretation. Anil and her American friend Leaf are bound together by their forensic analyses of classic Hollywood films and their particular clinical obsession with discovering where Lee Marvin was shot that would still allow him to swim the bay from Alcatraz to San Francisco in *Point Blank* (237).

169. Ondaatje, *Anil's Ghost*, 230.

170. Ibid., 231.

171. Brooks, *Reading for Plot*, 12.

172. Ondaatje, *Anil's Ghost*, 117.

173. Sybil S. Steinber, "Anil's Ghost"; Ron Charles, "An Island Paradise in the Flames of Terror"; David Kipen, "Specter of Civil War in Ondaatje's Ghost."

174. Ondaatje, *Anil's Ghost*, 274.

175. Ibid., 285–86.

176. Ibid., 28.

177. Typologically, *Anil's Ghost* is perhaps most like a twenty-first-century *Don Quixote*—a chivalric romance in which, because of a general lack of understanding of the immediate situation, the "righter of wrongs" (*desfacedor de agravios*) aggravates the very social problems they seek to redress.

178. Ondaatje, *Anil's Ghost*, 98.

179. This structure is not the ordinary chronological rounding of character plotted in the traditional *Bildungsroman* but a process of "personification" modeled on the reconstructive project of forensic science. In *Anil's Ghost*, the information about a particular individual's life that the characters and the novel's readers need to make sense of events typically arrives long after the narration of those events. Although each of the main characters' life stories follows this pattern, Sarath's stands out because we only learn the details of his marriage and his professional biography after his death, too late for the information to have changed either his relationship with Anil or the precipitous conclusion of the novel. Like human rights workers, the reader and the characters never have enough information until it is too late.

180. Ondaatje, *Anil's Ghost*, 29.

181. Ibid., 102.

182. Ibid., 275.

183. Mercado, *In a State of Memory*, 18.

184. Jean Comaroff and John L. Comaroff, *Of Revelation and Revolution: Christianity, Colonialism, and Consciousness in South Africa*, 23.

185. Gramsci, *Selections from the Prison Notebooks*, 348, 417, 348.
186. White, *Content of the Form*, 2.
187. Comaroff and Comaroff, *Of Revelation and Revolution*, 23.
188. Barthes, *Mythologies*, 150, 129, 137.
189. Butler, Laclau, and Žižek, *Contingency, Hegemony, Universality*, 14.
190. Ibid., 50.
191. Somers, "Narrativity, Narrative Identity, and Social Action," 604.
192. Barthes, *Mythologies*, 131.
193. Maritain, *Rights of Man*, 63.
194. Mieke Bal, *Narratology: Introduction to the Theory of Narrative*, 16.
195. The Russian Formalists distinguished between the *fabula*, which represents "the order of events referred to by the narrative,"—"what really happened"—and the *sjuzet*, which designates those events as they are plotted for meaning or effect within the narrative (Brooks, *Reading for the Plot*, 12–13).
196. My understanding of the function of the empty space of the narrator in cultural narratives resembles Ernesto Laclau's description of the "*positive impossibility*" of what he calls the "empty signifier" in the work of hegemony more broadly (*Emancipation(s)*, 40, 43). For Laclau, the empty signifier is the mark of the universal, "a void which can be filled only by the particular"—that in its tendential emptiness maintains "the incommensurability between the universal and particulars" even as it "enables the latter to take up the representation of the former" (Butler, Laclau, and Žižek, *Contingency, Hegemony, Universality*, 58, 57).

CHAPTER 4

Compulsory Development: Narrative Self-Sponsorship and the Right to Self-Determination

1. Epeli Hau'ofa, *Tales of the Tikongs* (Honolulu: University of Hawaii Press, 1994), 67.
2. Ibid., 7, 18.
3. Ibid., 18–20.
4. Ibid., 53, 68.
5. Ibid., 47, 7.
6. Ibid., 68.
7. Ibid., 48.
8. Ibid., 21.
9. Ibid., 53, 48.
10. Arturo Escobar, *Encountering Development: The Making and Unmaking of the Third World* (Princeton: Princeton University Press, 1995), 53–54.
11. Brooks, *Reading for the Plot*, 6.
12. Escobar, *Encountering Development*, 52. Escobar provocatively suggests that "poverty," and its antidote "development," were "problematized" globally only with the World Bank's 1948 definition of "poor countries" (23).

Thus, the same year that the UDHR projected a world based on fundamental equality, the institutionalization of the discourse of development trifurcated the globe into First and Second World developed countries and Third World underdeveloped (or in the language of the time, "retarded") countries that were "the discursive products of the post–World War II climate" (31). For an overview of three worlds theory, see Peter Worsley, *The Three Worlds: Culture and World Development*.

13. Lucian W. Pye, *Politics, Personality, and Nation Building: Burma's Search for Identity*, 10; Escobar, *Encountering Development*, 26.

14. The United States cast its dissenting vote despite the fact that the declaration represented "an attempt to revive the immediate post-war consensus about human rights developed by US President Roosevelt, based on four freedoms—including the freedom from want" (Arjun Sengupta, "On the Theory and Practice of the Right to Development," 840).

15. Pye, *Politics, Personality, and Nation Building*, 10.

16. United Nations Development Programme, *Human Development Report 1990*, 1, 11.

17. The UNDP's annual human development reports commodify the human personality—its characteristics and needs—in the Human Development Index (HDI), which represents an econometricized tabulation of the possibilities for personality development in each nation. The HDI is the information age's analogue to the nineteenth-century *Bildungsroman*—a technology for representing the older humanist vision of *Bildung* in the new paradigmatic SQL-database structures of information science.

18. The late-twentieth-century human-rights focus on general development might seem to mean that the idealist *Bildungsroman* has succumbed to the *realpolitik* of the *Entwicklungsroman*, which is "more general in scope and does not presuppose the more or less conscious attempt on the part of the hero to integrate his powers, to cultivate himself by experience" (Susanne Howe, *Wilhelm Meister and His English Kinsmen: Apprentices to Life*, 6). However, despite its more practical language, human rights law retains the *Bildung* ideal of a harmonious concordance between the individual and society (and between their interdependent developments).

19. Charles Dickens, *Great Expectations*, 489.

20. Jeffers, *Apprenticeships*, 189.

21. Braendlin, "*Bildung* in Ethnic Women Writers," 77.

22. Nyerere, "Freedom and Development," 58, 62.

23. Kwame Nkrumah, *Neo-Colonialism: The Last Stage of Imperialism*, 242.

24. Cassese, *Self-Determination of Peoples*, 33; Vladmir Lenin, "The Socialist Revolution and the Right of Nations to Self-Determination."

25. Carlos P. Romulo, *The Meaning of Bandung*, 35.

26. Ibid., 96.

27. Ibid., 97.

28. See Roland Burke, "'The Compelling Dialogue of Freedom': Human Rights at the Bandung Conference," 959.

29. In a way, this is the same threshold of self-governance that *Robinson Crusoe* surprisingly illustrated for the drafters of the UDHR and that, in a slightly different manner, the Society of the Tower certified for Wilhelm Meister in his articles of apprenticeship.

30. The Trusteeship Council's website is a fascinating digital artifact of legalized colonialism. Containing no historical information or documentation of the council's half-century of work, the site consists of a single webpage declaring its mission to "have been fulfilled" when the "last remaining United Nations trust territory"—Palau—achieved independence on 1 October 1994. Significantly, the official fulfillment of the classic civilizing mission coincides with the dawning of the World Wide Web, and the lack of history at the site might seem to symbolize the end of the paper trail of colonialism (with its enabling technology of double-entry bookkeeping) and its displacement by the electronic technology and structure of (neo)imperialism in the "information age." See http://www.un.org/documents/tc.htm.

31. Achille Mbembe, "African Modes of Self-Writing," 247.

32. Romulo, *The Meaning of Bandung*, 97.

33. Ian Brownlie, ed., *Basic Documents on Human Rights*, 28.

34. Maurice Flory, "Questions Intéressant La France: Négociation ou Dégagement en Algérie," 836. The 1960 Declaration had a fairly rapid and favorable impact on the Algerian cause: five days after its adoption, the UN General Assembly formally recognized "the right of the Algerian people to self-determination and independence" (GA RES 1573[XV]). The "Question of Algeria" offers an instructive case of the new international possibilities for prosecuting a legal claim to self-determination, particularly since France stubbornly insisted that the war in Algeria was a domestic matter and no business of the international community. See Slaughter, "A Question of Narration." For analysis of the relation between the Algerian liberation movements and the 1960 UN Declaration, see generally Mohammed Alwan, *Algeria before the United Nations*; Mohammed Bedjaoui, *Law and the Algerian Revolution*; Maran, *Torture*; and John Talbott, *The War without a Name: France in Algeria, 1954–1962*.

35. Cassese, *Self-Determination of Peoples*, 5.

36. See Charles Habib Malik, *Human Rights in the United Nations*.

37. Antonio Cassese, "The Self-Determination of Peoples," 101.

38. This interpretation remains somewhat controversial despite the findings of an important 1978 UN Special Report on the implementation of the right which concluded that both international law and practice have "conceptualize[d] the right to self-determination as a right of the individual . . . [and]

a people's collective right" (Héctor Gros Espiell, "Implementation of United Nations Resolutions Relating to the Right of People under Colonial Rule and Alien Domination to Self-Determination," 26).

39. This allegorical logic bears out in the provisions for petition in the Optional Protocol to the ICCPR, which established an international committee "to receive and consider . . . communications from individuals claiming to be victims of violations of any of the rights set forth in the Covenant." Although the Human Rights Committee has determined not to hear complaints concerning the right to self-determination and so construes the notion of victimhood rather narrowly, there is nothing in the language of the covenant that precludes such a petition. See Cassese, *Self-Determination of Peoples*, 142–44. Indeed, if we read the law by its letter, then individuals are granted the right to petition on behalf of the intersubjective social relations of which they are a part and an effect. For example, in the case of disappearance, a family member could make a claim based on Article 17 of the ICCPR that "he" has been subjected to "unlawful interference with his privacy, family, home or correspondence."

40. On the relation between the ideology of self-determination and the German-idealist, pedagogical narrative of *Bildung*, see Mücke, *Virtue and the Veil of Illusion*, Redfield, *Phantom Formations*.

41. Nékám, *The Personality Conception of the Legal Entity*, 36.

42. Ibid., 81. Nékám argues that historically in the West, the first "person" to emerge as a legal entity was the group, not the individual: "We can safely say, though it sounds paradoxical, that in the order of evolution it was a so-called artificial person, the family, and not the so-called natural person, the individual, which made its first appearance in law. . . . Even when, finally, the individual truly appears on the scene of the law as a subject of rights, we are still very far removed from the times when it can truly be said that he is taken for such simply because of his being a human individual" (23).

43. Ibid., 29–32.

44. Ibid., 29.

45. George Puttenham, *The Arte of English Poesie, 1589*, 213.

46. Tsitsi Dangarembga, *Nervous Conditions*, 58–59.

47. Ibid., 62, 92–93, 58–59.

48. Ibid., 87.

49. Ibid., 106, 97, 178.

50. Ibid., 1.

51. Susan Z. Andrade, "Tradition, Modernity and the Family as Nation: Reading the *Chimurenga* Struggle into and out of *Nervous Conditions*," 28.

52. Dangarembga, *Nervous Conditions*, 203, 178.

53. Ibid., 58, 107.

54. Ibid., 191, 194.

55. Ibid., 1.
56. Ibid., 204.
57. Wangari wa Nyatetu-Waigwa, *The Liminal Novel: Studies in the Franco-phone-African Novel as Bildungsroman*, 3.
58. My figure of the "implicated reader" is a variant of Wolfgang Iser's "implied reader," which is an effect of the literary text itself. Located somewhere between the fictional world and the realm of real readers, the implicated reader is figured within the dominant social and political structures of both, so that it is not merely a part of the social forces with which the protagonist must contend but also shares what the novel imagines to be characteristic assumptions of an actual reading public. See Joseph R. Slaughter, "One Track Minds: Markets, Madness, Metaphors, and Modernism in Postcolonial Nigerian Fiction."
59. Dangarembga, *Nervous Conditions*, 1.
60. Abel, Hirsch, and Langland, "Introduction," 12. Drawing on the work of Sandra M. Gilbert and Susan Gubar (*The Madwoman in the Attic*), in their introduction to *Voyage In*, Abel, Hirsch, and Langland suggest that this simultaneity of legitimating and rebellious plots may be a generic characteristic of female *Bildungsromane*.
61. Many historians have begun to call the liberation struggle of the 1970s the "second *Chimurenga*" in recognition of the eighteen-month native rebellion against the BSAC in 1896–97. In 2000, attempting to shore up his own authoritarian regime, Mugabe revived the language of liberation, calling for a "Third *Chimurenga*." See Terence Ranger, "Nationalist Historiography, Patriotic History and the History of the Nation: The Struggle over the Past in Zimbabwe."
62. Dangarembga, *Nervous Conditions*, 93.
63. Ibid., 18–19.
64. Ibid., 87.
65. Ibid., 15, 102, 180.
66. Ibid., 138.
67. 1907 Ordinance. The primary documents for some of my information are the official reports of the governmental commissions set up to review native education in 1925 and 1951: Southern Rhodesia. Commission Appointed to Enquire into the Matter of Native Education in all its Bearings in the Colony of Southern Rhodesia., "Report of the Commission Appointed to Enquire into the Matter of Native Education in All Its Bearings in the Colony of Southern Rhodesia"; Southern Rhodesia. Native Education Inquiry Commission, *Report of the Native Education Inquiry Commission, 1951*. For a good historical overview of the social and "scientific" discourses that led to the development of a split between "literary" and "industrial" education in colonial Africa generally, see the first chapter of Gaurav Gajanan Desai, *Subject to*

Colonialism: African Self-Fashioning and the Colonial Library. For histories of educational policy in Rhodesia/Zimbabwe, see Tendayi J. Kumbula, *Education and Social Control in Southern Rhodesia*; Toby Tafirenyika Moyana, *Education, Liberation and the Creative Act*; Marion O'Callaghan, *Southern Rhodesia: The Effects of a Conquest Society on Education, Culture and Information*; and R. J. Zvobgo, *Colonialism and Education in Zimbabwe.*

68. Dangarembga, *Nervous Conditions*, 179.

69. Native Education Inquiry Commission, "Report of the Native Education Inquiry Commission," 9, 31, 9.

70. Dangarembga, *Nervous Conditions*, 115.

71. Ibid., 85, 50.

72. Ibid., 93, 164, 173, 93.

73. Ibid., 16.

74. Jean-Paul Sartre, "Preface," 20.

75. Dangarembga, *Nervous Conditions*, 74, 151, 63, 93.

76. Ibid., 201.

77. Ibid., 53.

78. Ibid., 86.

79. Ibid., 155.

80. Ibid., 178.

81. Ibid., 4.

82. Ibid., 195, 191.Tambu personifies the sociocivil institutions that are to effect her imagined incorporation as a citizen-subject, attributing to them not only the capacity to realize her inner nature but, like the Society of the Tower in *Wilhelm Meister's Apprenticeship*, to speak for nature itself.

83. Ibid., 107, 58.

84. Native Education Inquiry Commission, "Report of the Native Education Inquiry Commission," 6–7.

85. For a general discussion of education for imperial control, see Martin Carnoy, *Education as Cultural Imperialism.*

86. Schwarz, *Misplaced Ideas*, 23.

87. Dangarembga, *Nervous Conditions*, 91.

88. Ibid., 184, 202, 178.

89. Ibid., 93.

90. Ibid., 203.

91. Ibid., 116, 167.

92. Ibid., 115, 121.

93. Ibid., 159, 111.

94. Ibid., 101.

95. Ibid., 62.

96. Andrade, "Tradition, Modernity and the Family as Nation," 37.

97. This is vividly illustrated in a legal subtext of the novel. The combined stipulations of the 1930 Land Apportionment Act (which, among other things,

required Africans to attend only schools in districts where they owned land) and the 1951 Land Husbandry Act (which required Africans to farm their land to maintain possession) mean that Babamukuru's and Tambu's educational success are literally and legally dependent upon her father's continued farming of the homestead. Their development depends, in other words, on the family's continued "squalor."

98. Moretti, *Way of the World*, 27, 7.

99. Theodor W. Adorno, "Theorie Der Halbbildung."

100. Brown, "Suffering," 430.

101. Dangarembga, *Nervous Conditions*, 19.

102. Cited in Heather Zwicker, "The Nervous Collusions of Nation and Gender: Tsitsi Dangarembga's Challenge to Fanon."

103. Ibid., 7, 8.

104. Anderson, *Imagined Communities*, 32.

105. Lloyd, *Anomalous States*, 69.

106. Andrade, "Tradition, Modernity and the Family as Nation," 48.

107. According to Moyana, "simplified versions of [these] British literary classics" were standard in the 1968 Rhodesian curriculum. (*Education, Liberation and the Creative Act*, 53).

108. Cited in Ibid., 54.

109. Zwicker, "Nervous Collusions of Nation and Gender," 5.

110. Susan Fraiman, *Unbecoming Women: British Women Writers and the Novel of Development*, x.

111. Kontje, *Private Lives in the Public Sphere*, 6.

112. Maria Helena Lima, "Decolonizing Genre: Jamaica Kincaid and the *Bildungsroman*," 443.

113. Felski, *Beyond Feminist Aesthetics*, 137.

114. Brooks, *Reading for the Plot*, 19.

115. Ignatieff et al., *Human Rights as Politics and Idolatry*, 5.

116. Williams, *Hegel's Ethics of Recognition*, 70.

117. White, *Content of the Form*, 35.

118. Brooks, *Reading for the Plot*, 13.

119. Ricoeur, *Oneself as Another*, 142.

120. Dangarembga, *Nervous Conditions*, 116.

121. Maria Helena Lima, "Imaginary Homelands in Jamaica Kincaid's Narratives of Development," 859.

122. Booth, "Individualism and the Mystery of the Social Self," 89.

123. Ricoeur, *Oneself as Another*, 143.

124. Williams, *Hegel's Ethics of Recognition*, 135.

125. See Aristotle, *Aristotle's Poetics*, 56.

126. Dangarembga, *Nervous Conditions*, 204.

127. Brooks, *Reading for the Plot*, 23.

128. Ibid., 39.

129. Kermode, *Sense of an Ending*, 46.

130. Brooks, *Reading for the Plot*, 22.

131. Hope, *A Separate Development*, 11, 5, 173.

132. Ibid., 28, 173.

133. Ibid., 5, 107.

134. Ibid., 28.

135. Ibid., 21, 28. As scientific about racial classification as South Africa's National Party aspired to be, the "inherent" distinctions between the races depended upon perpetual discretionary enforcement. Thus, for instance, the Population Registration Act (1950) provides that "if at any time it appears to the Director [of the Registration Office] that the classification of a person . . . is incorrect, he may, . . . [after] affording such person . . . an opportunity of being heard, alter the classification of that person in the register."

136. Ibid., 173, 28.

137. Edgar Harry Brookes, *Apartheid: A Documentary Study of Modern South Africa*, 7.

138. Ibid., 11–12. This abuse of the humanist vision of *Bildung* parallels its use in Nazi Germany, where it "lent itself to first nationalist and then fascist appropriation as the organic theory of the individual became the model for the nation" (Kontje, *German Bildungsroman*, 110).

139. Brookes, *Apartheid*, 14.

140. South Africa. Commission for the Socio-Economic Development of the Bantu Areas and D. Hobart Houghton, *The Tomlinson Report: A Summary of the Findings and Recommendations in the Tomlinson Commission Report*, 4.

141. Chow, *Protestant Ethnic*, 115.

142. Althusser, "Ideology and Ideological State Apparatuses (Notes Towards an Investigation)," 181, 174, 181.

143. Hope, *A Separate Development*, 20, 160.

144. Ibid., 64.

145. Ibid., 17, 83.

146. Ibid., 78, 80.

147. Ibid., 128.

148. Ibid., 20.

149. Ibid., 19, 122.

150. Ibid., 125, 136.

151. Ibid., 173.

152. Ibid., 128, 170, 176.

153. Ibid., 174.

154. Ibid., 177.

155. Ibid., 5.

156. Miles, "Picaro's Journey to the Confessional," 989. Miles identifies the movement from *picaresque* to the confessional as the formal evolutionary trajectory of the European *Bildungsroman* genre itself.

157. Hope, *A Separate Development*, 5.

158. Ibid., 174.

159. Ibid., 170.

160. For analyses of the various historical, legal, and linguistic relations between torture, truth, and speech, see Elaine Scarry, *The Body in Pain: The Making and Unmaking of the World*; Ñacuñán Sáez, "Torture: A Discourse on Practice"; Paige duBois, *Torture and Truth*; and Slaughter, "A Question of Narration." For a study of the history and practice of torture in apartheid South Africa, see Don Foster, Dennis Davis, and Diane Sandler, *Detention and Torture in South Africa: Psychological, Legal, and Historical Studies*.

161. Frank Graziano, *Divine Violence: Spectacle, Psychosexuality & Radical Christianity in the Argentine "Dirty War,"* 102.

162. Sáez, "Torture," 132.

163. Scarry, *Body in Pain*, 51.

164. Duncan Forrest, "The Methods of Torture and Its Effects," 118.

165. Scarry, *Body in Pain*, 49.

166. It is often said that torture requires that the torturers view their victim as something less than human—that it requires "a world view, no matter how crude, that divides man into the torturable and the non-torturable" (Amnesty International, *Report on Torture*, 27). But such a "world view" is itself legitimated by the act of torture—by its process of dehumanization and depersonalization that produces the "torturable" subjects that it posits in its enabling fiction. On torture as a modern mode of production, see Darius M Rejali, *Torture and Modernity: Self, Society, and State in Modern Iran*, 174.

167. Hope, *A Separate Development*, 155.

168. Ibid., 5.

169. Ibid., 20.

170. Ibid., 173.

171. Ibid., 175–76.

172. Ibid., 177.

173. Ibid., 5.

174. Ibid., 174.

175. Ibid., 11, 109.

176. Ibid., 177, 173.

177. Benhabib, *Transformations of Citizenship*, 59.

178. Escobar, *Encountering Development*, 52.

179. Viswanathan, *Masks of Conquest*, 167.

180. Cameroonian Werewere Liking's rewriting of the Malian epic of Sundjata, *L'amour-cent-vies*, offers an excellent literary example of what happens

generically to the story of self-determination when the founding epic act of violence is replaced by a seminal, prosaic "word-action" (Werewere Liking, *It Shall Be of Jasper and Coral; and, Love-across-a-Hundred-Lives: Two Novels*, 201). Liking substitutes the traditional epic rape (in *Sundjata* of Buffalo Woman, in Homer of Helen) with consensual lovemaking. This feminist substitution transforms the story from an epic of violent, virulent empire founding into a collection of intertwined, interdependent, and democratically representative *Bildungsromane*. The once epic hero becomes, as Hegel said of *Wilhelm Meister*, "as good a Philistine as others," taking his place among the national bourgeoisie, marrying, completing an M.A. in philosophy, and opening a sculptor's studio. G. W. F. Hegel, *Aesthetics: Lectures on Fine Art*, 593.

181. This double-voicing is often represented in dissensual *Bildungsromane* by dual protagonists that are, in effect, split personalities (like Tambu and Nyasha); many represent this division in the figure of twins. See Bandele-Thomas, *The Sympathetic Undertaker and Other Dreams*; Diamela Eltit, *El Cuarto Mundo*; Diamela Eltit, *The Fourth World*; and Roy, *The God of Small Things*.

CHAPTER 5

Clefs à Roman: *Reading, Writing, and International Humanitarianism*

1. Calixthe Beyala, *Loukoum: The 'Little Prince' of Belleville*, 30.
2. Escobar, *Encountering Development*, 23–24.
3. Beyala, *Loukoum*, 30.
4. Ibid., 31.
5. Ibid., 3, 31.
6. Calixthe Beyala, *Le Petit Prince de Belleville: Roman*, 53. I am citing from both the English translation of Beyala's novel and the French original, adding my own translations when the English edition differs substantially from the French.
7. Ibid., 54.
8. Harvey J. Graff, ed., *Literacy and Social Development in the West: A Reader*, 3–4.
9. Sérgio Paulo Rouanet, "The End of Culture and the Last Book," 48.
10. H. M. Phillips, *Literacy and Development*, 21–22.
11. The UN declaration on responsibilities is a watered-down response to concerted efforts by a number of groups, most prominently the Tokyo-based NGO InterAction Council, to urge the General Assembly to renew the commitment to a just international order by recognizing human responsibilities as correlatives of rights. The InterAction Council—which includes among its many influential members numerous ex-heads of state as well as ex-U.S. secretary of state Henry Kissinger, ex-World Bank president Robert McNamara,

Egyptian philosophy professor Hasan Hanafi, and philosopher Richard
Rorty—ventriloquized the voice of the UN General Assembly in its 1997 draft
for a "Universal Declaration of Human Responsibilities." The document,
proposed for UN adoption on the fiftieth anniversary of the UDHR, was opposed by most of the Northern (post-)industrialized states, who supported
instead the feeble alternative that I have cited, most of whose articles speak
not to the responsibilities of individuals, groups, or organs of society but to
those of the state. Thus, much of the UN document merely repeats as nonbinding obligations of states what earlier human rights law had already made
the rights of individuals; human responsibility amounts to little more than an
obligation to promote and protect (individualist) human rights. In April 2000,
the Commission on Human Rights studied the question of a declaration of
human responsibilities. Miguel Alfonso Martínez delivered an interim report
in 2002 and the final report, with a predraft declaration on human social responsibilities, in March 2003. Both versions note the historical opposition to
"formal establishment of the correlation between rights and responsibilities"
by what it characterizes as the "countries [and NGOs] of the North" (Miguel
Alfonso Martínez, "Final Report of the Special Rapporteur on Human Rights
and Human Responsibilities," 2). They also describe a unanimous desire on
the part of "Nations of the South" to moderate the individualist bias of the
International Bill of Human Rights by fleshing out the content of the duties
to the community in Article 29 of the UDHR to "afford everyone the possibility of fully developing his or her personality . . . [and] the realization of the
rights and freedoms enshrined in the Universal Declaration" (Martínez, "Interim Report on Human Rights and Human Responsibilities," 10). The interim report cites approvingly the work of the InterAction Council: "There is
at least one non-governmental organization of ample international credibility—and well attested as not being in the service of political or despotic interests, or remotely connected with what have come to be called 'evil empires'
(or 'axes of evil')—that has recently felt the need to take on the task of prepar-
ing a universal declaration of human responsibilities" (22). It is a remarkable
fact of the legacies of global political and discursive bipolarization—and particularly the neoconservative versions after 9/11 and the "War on Terror" that
gave occasion to the Bush administration to perform its own cavalier, Manichean bisection of good and evil in terms of "with us"-ness and "against us"-
ness—that the interim report takes elaborate pains to distinguish (for a Northern audience distrustful of communitarian sentiment and transnational responsibility) the difference between, for example, Richard Rorty and a
terrorist.

   12. For a suggestive analysis of some of the continuities in formal internationalism as it developed over the course of the twentieth century, see Barbara
Harlow, "From the 'Civilizing Mission' to 'Humanitarian Interventionism':

Postmodernism, Writing, and Human Rights." For an excellent history of the origins of contemporary humanitarianism in the Victorian rhetoric that rationalized classical European imperialism, seesee Gott, "Imperial Humanitarianism." On the use and abuse of humanitarianism for the pursuit of "national interests," see David Rieff, *A Bed for the Night: Humanitarianism in Crisis*.

13. Festa, "Sentimental Bonds and Revolutionary Characters," 84.

14. Valéry was describing the work of the International Institute of Intellectual Cooperation, the League of Nations' equivalent of UNESCO. http://www.findarticles.com/p/articles/mi_m1310/is_1993_Sept/ai_14526 9 91.

15. UNESCO, *Books for All: A Programme of Action*, 5.

16. Appadurai, *Modernity at Large*, 36.

17. Baxi, *Future of Human Rights*, 121.

18. Wendy Waring distinguishes between the "market reader," for whom paratextual apparatuses (such as footnotes, glossaries, jacket blurbs and summaries) package a novel, and "the reader inscribed in the narrative," who may not be "identical" with the reader the publisher imagines ("Is This Your Book? Wrapping Postcolonial Fiction for the Global Market," 462). On the general dynamics of "cross-cultural" publishing in "the global late-capitalist system of commodity exchange," see Graham Huggan, *The Postcolonial Exotic: Marketing the Margins*, 6.

19. Casanova, *World Republic of Letters*, 43.

20. Graff, ed., *Literacy and Social Development*, 8.

21. UNESCO, *Fundamental Education: Common Ground for All Peoples: Report of a Special Committee to the Preparatory Commission of the United Nations Educational, Scientific and Cultural Organization, Paris 1946*, vii.

22. Ibid., 1–10. Among the many influential advocates for international "Fundamental Education," the literary critic I. A. Richards contributed to UNESCO's global "war on ignorance" by sharing the results of his attempts in the early 1940s to use the emergent medium of film to teach literacy to children and Chinese sailors *en masse* (259–70). Richards' commitments to literacy and international understanding led to his participation in the project to develop "Basic English," the 850 "essential" words needed to communicate in the language. Richards demonstrated its power with a book defending the need for the UN written entirely in Basic English (*Nations and Peace*).

23. Escobar, *Encountering Development*, 24.

24. Walter Ong, *Orality and Literacy: The Technologizing of the Word*, 178.

25. Ibid., 174.

26. Paul Tiyambe Zeleza, *Rethinking Africa's Globalization*, 368.

27. Jack Goody, *The Domestication of the Savage Mind*, 146–62.

28. Beyala, *Le Petit Prince de Belleville*, 52.

29. Abiola Irele, "In Praise of Alienation," 216–17.

30. On the social distortions proffered in the equation of literacy with modernity, see Harvey J. Graff, *The Literacy Myth: Literacy and Social Structure in the Nineteenth-Century City*; Graff, ed., *Literacy and Social Development*; and E. Verne, "Literacy and Industrialization: The Dispossession of Speech." Recent studies of women and literacy have similarly debunked the developmental policy axiom (that underpinned much of the international programs designed especially to teach women to read and write throughout the decades of development) that regarded "the 'illiterate woman' as the cause, rather than a symptom, of underdevelopment" (Anna Robinson-Pant, " 'The Illiterate Woman': Changing Approaches to Researching Women's Literacy," 18). For an excellent overview of these issues, see Anna Robinson-Pant, ed., *Women, Literacy, and Development: Alternative Perspectives*.

31. Edward W. Said, *Orientalism*, 3.

32. Ray Eldon Hiebert, American University, and United States Agency for International Development, eds., *Books in Human Development: The Final Report*, 11.

33. UNESCO, *Books for All*, 11.

34. Bernth Lindfors, *Long Drums and Canons: Teaching and Researching African Literatures*, 123.

35. Philip G. Altbach, "Literary Colonialism: Books in the Third World," 227.

36. Alan Hill, *In Pursuit of Publishing*, 217, 93. See also Huggan, *Postcolonial Exotic*, 50–56.

37. Gianni Vattimo, "Library, Liberty," 68–70.

38. In the era of decolonization and with the proliferation of electronic media, the ICCPR (1966) tacitly acknowledged the UDHR's chirographic bias, extending the scope of this right to include knowledge transmitted "either orally, in writing or in print, in the form of art, or through any other media" (Article 19).

39. Irele, "In Praise of Alienation," 216.

40. UNESCO, *Books for All*, 5.

41. Ibid; UNESCO, *Fundamental Education*, vii.

42. United Nations, "Third," 660.

43. Ong, *Orality and Literacy*, 175.

44. Verne, "Literacy and Industrialization," 287.

45. Bakhtin, "Bildungsroman," 23. I am making a distinction here between the process of literacy acquisition as training in the use of a technology and the practice of reading more generally, which, as I have discussed in previous chapters, critics have long recognized as a formative activity of the *Bildungsheld*.

46. Martin Swales, *The German Bildungsroman from Wieland to Hesse*, 148.

47. Rouanet, "The End of Culture and the Last Book," 56.

48. R. Mark Hall, "The 'Oprahfication' of Literacy: Reading 'Oprah's Book Club,'" 649, 652, 655. Not incidentally, the staple genre in the first incarnation of Oprah's booklist (1996–2002) was the "life narrative" of an individual (25 of 48), of which a full 75% have been analyzed by critics as *Bildungsromane*. The term *Bildungsroman* appears nowhere in the official materials for the book club; instead they are replete with nonacademic euphemisms: "coming of age," "finding herself," "a journey of self-discovery," etc. (Oprah.com, *Oprah's Book Club Library*). For studies of the operation and impact of Oprah's Book Club in "getting America reading again," as she herself proclaimed, see Robert McHenry, "All Hail Oprah's Book Club"; and Cecilia Konchar Farr, *Reading Oprah: How Oprah's Book Club Changed the Way America Reads*.

49. Although the early, idealist examples of the genre take functional literacy for granted, many of the highly class-conscious novels (particularly the nineteenth-century British variants, such as *Great Expectations*) feature scenes of the struggle for literacy. If the idealist *Bildungsroman* constructs tacit class complicity with its reader, the novels in which the social conditions of literacy acquisition are explicitly addressed implicate their readers within the social relations and formations that make learning to read and write a privilege.

50. Casanova, *World Republic of Letters*, 116, 115.

51. Johan Galtung, "Literacy, Education and Schooling: For What?" 272.

52. Janet Carey Eldred and Peter Mortensen, "Reading Literacy Narratives," 512.

53. Brian V. Street, *Social Literacies: Critical Approaches to Literacy in Development, Ethnography, and Education*, 1. I am not suggesting that these novels are antiliteracy; far from it. Indeed, they insist upon the value of reading and writing even as they refuse to disregard the social implications and personal pitfalls of literacy and its role in stratifying, organizing, and naturalizing modern socioeconomic disparity.

54. Lima, "Decolonizing Genre," 443.

55. Beyala, *Le Petit Prince de Belleville*, 72, Beyala, *Loukoum*, 45. There is a hidden irony here because Mamadou's story is "empowered" by books. Beyala infamously plagiarized much of the French original from, among others, French translations of Howard Buten's *Burt* and Alice Walker's *The Color Purple*. The sometimes major discrepancies between the French and English versions may have something to do with the court judgment finding Beyala guilty of copyright infringement. See Kenneth W. Harrow, *Less Than One and Double: A Feminist Reading of African Women's Writing*, 97–155.

56. Hall, "'Oprahfication' of Literacy," 655.

57. Beyala, *Le Petit Prince de Belleville*, 241; Beyala, *Loukoum*, 164–65.

58. Beyala, *Loukoum*, 165, 173–74, 139.

59. Rancière, "Who Is the Subject of the Rights of Man?" 307.

60. Beyala, *Loukoum*, 13.
61. In the French original, Black and White, as social categories, are always capitalized. I retain that convention here although the English translation does not.
62. Beyala, *Loukoum*, 11.
63. Festa, "Sentimental Bonds and Revolutionary Characters," 76.
64. Beyala, *Loukoum*, 87.
65. Ibid., 79.
66. Ibid., 167.
67. Ibid., 96.
68. Ibid., 137, 144, 138.
69. Ibid., 144.
70. Ibid., 129.
71. Ibid., 2, 22; Beyala, *Le Petit Prince de Belleville*, 39.
72. Beyala, *Loukoum*, 22.
73. Ibid., 11.
74. Ibid., 1.
75. Beyala, *Le Petit Prince de Belleville*, 7. The English translation reads *"Whether they like it or not,"* which has a whole different set of implications in the ambiguity of the notion of "liking culture" (1).
76. Beyala, *Loukoum*, 167.
77. Moretti, *Way of the World*, 21.
78. Pierre Bourdieu and Jean Claude Passeron, *Reproduction in Education, Society and Culture*, 5, 9. For Bourdieu and Passeron, the dominant ideology in a given class or social formation that education reproduces constitutes a "cultural arbitrary" because it "cannot be deduced from any universal principle" that is not "related to the social conditions of [its] emergence and perpetuation" (8).
79. Ibid., 6, 31, x.
80. Beyala, *Loukoum*, 67.
81. Ibid., 57.
82. Ibid., 106; Beyala, *Le Petit Prince de Belleville*, 160–61.
83. Beyala, *Loukoum*, 12; Chow, *Protestant Ethnic*, 107.
84. Chow, *Protestant Ethnic*, 115.
85. Beyala, *Loukoum*, 106.
86. Ibid., 176.
87. Ibid., 175.
88. Ibid., 176.
89. Ibid., 177.
90. Cohen, "Sentimental Communities," 107.
91. Not incidentally, Mamadou also locates himself within an international division of labor, a division that inflects the international dispensation of

rights. At one point in Mamadou's story, he considers the possibility of becoming "a builder one day, but as I think about that more carefully, I don't think I'd like that very much because that's for the Portuguese because of how work is divided internationally" (Beyala, *Loukoum*, 157). Similarly, enthusiasm for the strike of the African street cleaners that Abdou proposes is dampened when someone warns of the "Rumanians[, who] are watching and waiting. . . . to replace you" (74).

92. Manthia Diawara describes this contemporary translation in sharp human rights terms: "As postmodern reality defines historicity and ethics through consumption, those who do not consume are left to die outside of history and without human dignity" ("Toward a Regional Imaginary in Africa," 120–21). The marketization of human rights is the basis of the United Nations Development Programme's reformulation of a human centered approach to development. For instance, the UNDP's first annual "Human Development Report" declares that "people must be free to exercise their choices in properly functioning markets" (*Human Development Report 1990*, 1). For such markets to be more than economic, it is necessary to conceive of the human person (as the UNDP does) as a consumer of "rights" and of human rights as a market system for the distribution of the "goods" of longevity and health, knowledge and skills, freedom, dignity, self-respect, and personality (10). In his own work, Amartya Sen, one of the UNDP's most influential economists, explicitly characterizes all human social relations as market activity: "The contribution of the market mechanism to economic growth is, of course, important, but this comes only after the direct significance of the freedom to interchange—words, goods, gifts—has been acknowledged" (*Development as Freedom*, 6).

93. Butler, "Universality in Culture," 360.

94. Appadurai, *Modernity at Large*, 158.

95. If the twentieth-century history of consecutive French Republics is understood as a series of attempts to avoid repeating the French Revolution, Mamadou's *Bildungsroman* demonstrates how that revolution is forestalled by a social order that keeps its potential protagonists in a liminal state (neither fully enfranchised nor fully disenfranchised) with the perpetual promise of incorporation. On this tendency in Francophone *Bildungsromane*, see Wangari wa Nyatetu-Waigwa, *Liminal Novel*.

96. Beyala, *Loukoum*, 12.

97. Schaffer and Smith, *Human Rights and Narrated Lives*, 3–5.

98. Laclau and Mouffe, *Hegemony and Socialist Strategy*, 159.

99. Cohen and Seu, "Knowing Enough," 189.

100. Beyala, *Loukoum*, 136.

101. Ibid., 22.

102. Ibid., 136.

103. Irène Assiba d'Almeida, *Francophone African Women Writers: Destroying the Emptiness of Silence*, 6.

104. Ibid., 6, 8.

105. Appadurai, *Modernity at Large*, 42.

106. The practical effects of such remediation efforts are unclear and unpredictable; as Laclau and Mouffe remind us, a revolutionary rearticulation of the "egalitarian imaginary" does not "predetermine the *direction* in which this imaginary will operate" (Laclau and Mouffe, *Hegemony and Socialist Strategy*, 168). Indeed, this ambivalence was reconfirmed in the wake of the *banlieue* riots that took place around Paris in Fall 2005, when mainstream news outlets belatedly discovered that "art . . . has long been warning that French-born Arab and black youths felt increasingly alienated from French society and that their communities were ripe for explosion" (Alan Riding, "In France, Artists Have Sounded the Warning Bells for Years").

107. Huggan, *Postcolonial Exotic*, 30.

108. Appadurai, *Modernity at Large*, 21.

109. Festa, "Sentimental Bonds and Revolutionary Characters," 74; Appadurai, *Modernity at Large*, 31.

110. Cohen, "Sentimental Communities," 106.

111. K. Anthony Appiah, "Cosmopolitan Reading," 203.

112. Richard Rorty, "Human Rights, Rationality, and Sentimentality," 123.

113. Elaine Scarry, "The Difficulty of Imagining Other People," 99.

114. Mercado, *In a State of Memory*, 101.

115. Narogin, *Writing from the Fringe*, 149. Mudrooroo explains that his first novel, *Wildcat Falling*, was "heavily edited" to conform with "the Metropolitan tradition. . . . [T]he ending provided the hope that [the unnamed character] might eventually settle down, or be assimilated into the wider Australian society if given the necessary help" (34). Given these widespread editorial practices, Mudrooroo suggests that Aboriginal literature "might be seen as advocating assimilation; or else publishing companies are consciously publishing only those books which advance this ideology" (150). The questions raised about the authenticity of Mudrooroo's Aboriginal identification do not mitigate his insightful structural critiques of the literary industry. See Vincent J. Cheng, Terry Goldie, and Sander L. Gilman, "Forum: Ethnicity."

116. Narogin, *Writing from the Fringe*, 170, 34.

117. Ibid., 149.

118. Slaughter, *Clef À Roman*. Numerous examples could be cited, but Arundhati Roy's story is especially dramatic. Roy's Booker Prize–winning novel, *The God of Small Things* (1997) opened an Arundhati "shaped hole" (to reshape one of the novel's tropes) in the international public sphere, where she gained a *locus standi* ("Locusts Stand I" in the novel's entomological language) as an advocate and activist for social justice and human rights (*The God of Small Things*, 146, 179).

119. Jerome Buckley has rightly noted that *Bildungsromane* tend to be an author's "first or second novel" ("Autobiography in the English *Bildungsroman*," 96–97). Buckley accounts for this phenomenon in terms of authorial biography and professional development—the subjects of the books themselves. I am suggesting that it has perhaps a different historical explanation in the contemporary era of multiculturalism and globalization, where the market for literature by historically marginal authors constructs a systemic, institutional demand for *Bildungsromane*.

120. Jameson, "Third-World Literature," 69.

121. Huggan, *Postcolonial Exotic*, 6.

122. Jameson, "On Literary and Cultural Import-Substitution," 172.

123. Ibid. 173. Since, as Aijaz Ahmad notes, "the vast majority of literary texts from these continents are unavailable in the metropolises," we should note two things: (1) *Bildungsromane* are likely overrepresented in the Western library in proportion to the total literary production of the Third World; (2) "classics" status is conferred to these novels largely on the basis of their improbable existence in the Western archive (*In Theory: Class, Nations, Literatures*, 97). By paying attention to the consumer end of the literary production line, Priya Joshi has revised the traditional picture of the role of the novel in colonialism that sees its dissemination as a one-way dictation from the colonizer to the colonized. Joshi instead finds that "what novels Indians chose to read" affected not only the importation of particular British novels and genres but also influenced the production and publication of "British Literature" (*In Another Country: Colonialism, Culture, and the English Novel in India*, 30).

124. It is important to register Graham Huggan's qualifications about the readership of postcolonial novels; "read by many different people in many different places[,] it would be misleading, not to mention arrogant, to gauge their value only to Western metropolitan response" (*Postcolonial Exotic*, 30). Yet postcolonial novels in English tend to be prepared and packaged for a Western metropolitan audience that still represents the largest potential consumer market. A similar dynamic exists in Francophone writing, and even literature written in many other languages tends to find a larger audience once the text has been translated into one of the major metropolitan languages.

125. Chandra Talpade Mohanty, "Introduction," 34.

126. Jameson, "On Literary and Cultural Import-Substitution," 172–73.

127. King, *Rereading Camara Laye*, 5, 22–25, 53.

128. Ibid., 23, 18, 5.

129. Huggan, *Postcolonial Exotic*, 51.

130. Ngũgĩ wa Thiong'o, *Decolonizing the Mind*, 5.

131. Evelyn Ellerman, "The Literature Bureau: African Influence in Papua New Guinea," 206.

132. SIDA, ed., *Whispering Land: An Anthology of Stories by African Women.*

133. The "new humanitarianism" largely dispenses with the apolitical neutrality of older models of aid in favor of pointed developmental assistance intended to promote social "justice and a political framework which can ensure that human rights are safeguarded" (Fiona Fox, "Conditioning the Right to Humanitarian Aid? Human Rights and the 'New Humanitarianism,'" 26). David Rieff suggests that the new humanitarianism "capture[d] the imagination of idealist peoples in the West" after the "failure of the so-called development decades" and "precisely at the moment when . . . developmentalism beg[a]n to lose [its] authority and prestige" (*Bed for the Night*, 101).

134. Rancière, "Who Is the Subject of the Rights of Man?" 306–7.

135. Abel, Hirsch, and Langland, "Introduction," 13, Lima, "Decolonizing Genre," 435.

136. Baxi, *Future of Human Rights*, 101.

137. Kontje, *German Bildungsroman*, 60. Kontje is elaborating on Jürgen Jacobs' reading of the German genre in his *Wilhelm Meister und seine Brüder* (1972).

138. Bakhtin, *Problems of Dostoevsky's Poetics*, 53, 57.

139. Butler, "Universality in Culture," 359.

CODICIL

Intimations of a Human Rights International: "The Rights of Man; or, What Are We [Reading] For?"

1. The title quotation is an alteration of the title of H. G. Wells's 1939 proposal for an international declaration of rights and his challenge to then–Prime Minister Chamberlain to give an account of British war aims in World War II (Wells, *Rights of Man*).

Alan Cheuse, "*Adama* Tells of a Saudi's Coming of Age" (my transcription).

2. al-Hamad, *Adama*, 245.

3. Joseph Conrad, *Heart of Darkness*, 36.

4. Franco Moretti "conjectures" that a similar dialectic is the ordinary mode of the novel's circulation: "When a culture starts moving towards the modern novel, it's always as a compromise between foreign form and local materials" ("Conjectures on World Literature," 60). While I find the foreign–local dialectic too neat an explanation of the transnationalization, or dissemination, of the genre, the reverse of this structure (local form and foreign content) does seem to facilitate the acceptance, or reception, in the Western literary public sphere of novels written elsewhere.

5. Nandy, "Reconstructing Childhood: A Critique of the Ideology of Adulthood," 65.

6. Buckley, *Season of Youth*, 17–18.

7. al-Hamad, *Adama*, 9.

8. Ibid., 185.

9. Cocalis, "Transformation of Bildung," 405.

10. al-Hamad, *Adama*, 102, 279.

11. Hegel, *Aesthetics*, 593.

12. Khaled Hosseini, *The Kite Runner*, 125.

13. Laura Bush, "Mrs. Bush's Remarks at the 2006 National Book Festival Gala."

14. Scarry, "Difficulty," 105.

15. Casanova, *World Republic of Letters*, 116; Azar Nafisi, *Reading Lolita in Tehran: A Memoir in Books*; Sijie Dai, *Balzac and the Little Chinese Seamstress*.

16. *See* David Damrosch, *What Is World Literature?* 17–18.

17. Appiah, "Cosmopolitan Reading," 204. *See also* A. O. Amoko, "The Problem with English Literature: Canonicity, Citizenship, and the Idea of Africa," 24.

18. Peter Hitchcock, "The Genre of Postcoloniality," 303.

19. Casanova, *World Republic of Letters*, 95.

20. Ibid., 95, 94.

21. Rieff, *Bed for the Night*, 9.

22. Franco Moretti, *Modern Epic: The World-System from Goethe to García Márquez*, 50; Simon Gikandi, "Globalization and the Claims of Postcoloniality," 632.

23. Laura Bush cited in Judy Keen, "First Lady Offers a Few Favorite Books."

24. Gil Gott insightfully concludes that "the cosmopolitan self, the subject of modern international engagement, is fixed through a process of projection in which humanitarianism has played a leading role" ("Imperial Humanitarianism," 34–45).

25. Appiah, "Cosmopolitan Reading," 203.

26. Rorty, "Human Rights," 119, 129, 119. Rorty proposes this "sentimental education" as a way of "putting foundationalism behind us" (122). Rorty implicitly links the cultivation of a human-rights sensibility to *Bildung*, which he translates as "edification" (*Philosophy and the Mirror of Nature*, 360). My reading of human-rights literacy, drawn from the law and *Bildung*, frames an even more radically antifoundationalist vision of the human personality than Rorty's; here, the human person is as "unlike" its human-rights self as it is "unlike" Rorty's "other people."

27. Bruce Robbins, "Sad Stories in the International Public Sphere: Richard Rorty on Culture and Human Rights," 216; Rorty, "Human Rights," 129; Festa, "Sentimental Bonds and Revolutionary Characters," 91.

28. Rorty, "Human Rights," 128. To be fair, Rorty's lecture was delivered a year before the Rwandan genocide, at the heady beginning of what appeared

to be the fulfillment of the new humanitarianism's promise in the Balkans. It was also before it had become absolutely clear that those efforts in the former Yugoslavia actually helped round up Bosnian refugees seeking UN protection, making their massacre by Serbian forces easier.

29. Ibid., 133–34.

30. Scarry, "Difficulty," 98, 102.

31. Casanova, *World Republic of Letters*, 13; Baxi, *Future of Human Rights*, 131.

32. Casanova, *World Republic of Letters*, 21.

33. Djelal Kadir, "To World, to Globalize—Comparative Literature's Crossroads," 8.

34. Rorty, "Human Rights," 134.

35. Rieff, *Bed for the Night*, 68.

36. Lauren, *Evolution of International Human Rights*, 51–53.

37. Scarry, "Difficulty," 104–5.

38. Rieff, *Bed for the Night*, 69.

Abel, Elizabeth, Marianne Hirsch, and Elizabeth Langland. "Introduction." In *The Voyage In: Fictions of Female Development*, edited by Elizabeth Abel, Marianne Hirsch, and Elizabeth Langland, 3–19. Hanover, N.H.: University Press of New England, 1983.

Abraham, Nicolas, and Maria Torok. *The Wolf Man's Magic Word: A Cryptonymy*. Vol. 37, *Theory and History of Literature*. Minneapolis: University of Minnesota Press, 1986.

Achebe, Chinua. "Africa's Tarnished Name." In *Multiculturalism and Hybridity in African Literatures*, edited by Hal Wylie and Bernth Lindfors. Trenton, N.J.: Africa World Press, 2000.

Addis, Adeno. "Individualism, Communitarianism, and the Rights of Ethnic Minorities." *Notre Dame Law Review* 67 (1992): 1233–61.

Adorno, Theodor W. "Theorie Der Halbbildung." In *Gesammelte Schriften*, 93–121. Frankfurt am Main: Suhrkamp, 1972.

Aeschylus. *Oresteia: Agamemnon, the Libation Bearers, the Eumenides*. Translated by Richmond Alexander Lattimore. Chicago: University of Chicago Press, 1958.

Agamben, Giorgio. *Homo Sacer: Sovereign Power and Bare Life*. Translated by Daniel Heller-Roazen. Edited by Werner Hamacher and David E. Wellbery, *Meridian: Crossing Aesthetics*. Stanford: Stanford University Press, 1998.

———. *Remnants of Auschwitz: The Witness and the Archive*. Translated by Daniel Heller-Roazen. New York: Zone Books, 1999.

Agosín, Marjorie. *Circles of Madness: Mothers of the Plaza De Mayo*. New York: White Pine Press, 1992.

Ahmad, Aijaz. *In Theory: Class, Nations, Literatures*. London: Verso, 1992.

al-Hamad, Turki. *Adama*. Translated by Robin Bray. Saint Paul, Minn.: Ruminator Books, 2003.

Alfonso Martínez, Miguel. "Final Report of the Special Rapporteur on Human Rights and Human Responsibilities." New York: United Nations. Commission on Human Rights, 2003.

———. "Interim Report on Human Rights and Human Responsibilities." New York: United Nations. Commission on Human Rights, 2002.

Allport, Gordon W. *Personality: A Psychological Interpretation*. New York: H. Holt, 1937.

Altbach, Philip G. "Literary Colonialism: Books in the Third World." *Harvard Educational Review* 45, no. 2 (1975): 226–36.

Althusser, Louis. "Ideology and Ideological State Apparatuses (Notes Towards an Investigation)." In *Lenin and Philosophy, and Other Essays*, 127–86. London: Monthly Review Press, 1971.

Alwan, Mohammed. *Algeria before the United Nations*. New York: Robert Speller and Sons, 1959.

Amato, Joseph Anthony. *Mounier and Maritain: A French Catholic Understanding of the Modern World*. Tuscaloosa: University of Alabama Press, 1975.

Amnesty International. *Report on Torture*. London: Gerald Duckworth, 1973.

———. "Sri Lanka: New Emergency Regulations—Erosion of Human Rights Protection." 18: Amnesty International, 2000.

Amoko, A. O. "The Problem with English Literature: Canonicity, Citizenship, and the Idea of Africa." *Research in African Literatures* 32, no. 4 (2001): 19–43.

An-Na'im, Abdullahi Ahmed, ed. *Human Rights in Cross-Cultural Perspectives: A Quest for Consensus*. Edited by Bert Lockwood Jr, *Pennsylvania Studies in Human Rights*. Philadelphia: University of Pennsylvania Press, 1992.

Anderson, Benedict. *Imagined Communities: Reflections on the Origin and Spread of Nationalism*. Revised ed. London: Verso, 1991.

Andrade, Susan Z. "Tradition, Modernity and the Family as Nation: Reading the *Chimurenga* Struggle into and out of *Nervous Conditions*." In *Negotiating the Postcolonial: Emerging Perspectives on Tsitsi Dangarembga*, edited by Ann Elizabeth Willey and Jeanette Treiber, 25–60. Trenton, N.J.: Africa World Press, 2002.

Appadurai, Arjun. *Modernity at Large: Cultural Dimensions of Globalization, Public Worlds*. Minneapolis: University of Minnesota Press, 1996.

———. "Plenary Address." *American Comparative Literature Association Annual Conference*. Ann Arbor, 2004.

Appiah, K. Anthony. "Citizens of the World." In *Globalizing Rights: The Oxford Amnesty Lectures 1999*, edited by Matthew J. Gibney, 189–232. Oxford: Oxford University Press, 2003.

———. "Cosmopolitan Reading." In *Cosmopolitan Geographies: New Locations in Literature and Culture*, edited by Vinay Dharwadker, 197–227. New York: Routledge, 2000.

Arendt, Hannah. *The Human Condition, Charles R. Walgreen Foundation Lectures*. Chicago: University of Chicago Press, 1958.

———. *The Origins of Totalitarianism*. New with added prefaces ed. New York: Harcourt Brace, 1973.

Arias, Arturo. *After the Bombs*. Translated by Asa Zatz. Willimantic, Ct.: Curbstone Press, 1990.

Aristotle. *Aristotle's Poetics*. Translated by James Hutton. New York: Norton, 1982.

Asad, Talal. *Formations of the Secular: Christianity, Islam, Modernity, Cultural Memory in the Present.* Stanford: Stanford University Press, 2003.

Asian Human Rights Commission. 2001. Disappearances—Sri Lanka: Laws That Made Large-Scale Murder Legal. In, http://www.ahrchk.net/hrsolid/mainfile.php/1998vol08no12/1859/. (accessed July, 2005).

Auerbach, Erich. *Mimesis: The Representation of Reality in Western Literature.* Translated by Willard Trask. Garden City, N.Y.: Doubleday, 1957.

Austin, J. L. *How to Do Things with Words, William James Lectures, 1955.* Cambridge, Mass.: Harvard University Press, 1962.

Austin, John. *Lectures on Jurisprudence; or, the Philosophy of Positive Law.* Edited by Robert Campbell. 5th ed. London: J. Murray, 1911.

Avelar, Idelber. *The Untimely Present: Postdictatorial Latin American Fiction and the Task of Mourning.* Edited by Stanley Fish and Fredric Jameson, *Post-Contemporary Interventions.* Durham: Duke University Press, 1999.

Bakan, Joel. *The Corporation: The Pathological Pursuit of Profit and Power.* New York: Free Press, 2004.

Bakhtin, M. M. *Problems of Dostoevsky's Poetics.* Translated by Caryl Emerson, *Theory and History of Literature.* Minneapolis: University of Minnesota Press, 1984.

———. "The *Bildungsroman* and Its Significance in the History of Realism (toward a Historical Typology of the Novel)." In *Speech Genres and Other Late Essays,* edited by Caryl Emerson and Michael Holquist, 10–59. Austin: University of Texas Press, 1986.

———. *The Dialogic Imagination: Four Essays.* Translated by Caryl Emerson and Michael Holquist. Edited by Michael Holquist, *University of Texas Press Slavic Series.* Austin: University of Texas Press, 1981.

Bal, Mieke. *Narratology: Introduction to the Theory of Narrative.* Translated by Christine Van Boheemen. 2nd ed. Toronto: University of Toronto Press, 1997.

Balen, Malcolm. *The Secret History of the South Sea Bubble: The World's First Great Financial Scandal.* 1st ed. London: Fourth Estate, 2003.

Balibar, Étienne. "Citizen Subject." In *Who Comes after the Subject?* edited by Eduardo Cadava, Peter Connor, and Jean-Luc Nancy, 33–57. New York: Routledge, 1991.

Bandele-Thomas, 'Biyi. *The Sympathetic Undertaker and Other Dreams.* Oxford: Heinemann, 1993.

Bannet, Eve Tavor. "Rewriting the Social Text: The Female Bildungsroman in Eighteenth-Century England." In *Reflection and Action: Essays on the Bildungsroman,* edited by James Hardin, 195–227. Columbia: University of South Carolina Press, 1991.

Barnes, Sandra T. "Global Flows: Terror, Oil, and Strategic Philanthropy." *African Studies Review* 48, no. 1 (2005): 1–22.

Barney, Richard A. *Plots of Enlightenment: Education and the Novel in Eighteenth-Century England*. Stanford: Stanford University Press, 1999.

Barthes, Roland. *Mythologies*. Translated by Annette Lavers. New York: Noonday Press, 1972.

Baxi, Upendra. *Mambrino's Helmet?: Human Rights for a Changing World*. New Delhi: Har-Anand Publications, 1994.

———. *The Future of Human Rights*. New Delhi: Oxford University Press, 2002.

Bedjaoui, Mohammed. *Law and the Algerian Revolution*. Brussels: International Association of Democratic Lawyers, 1961.

Bénabou, Marcel. *To Write on Tamara?* Translated by Steven Randall. Lincoln: University of Nebraska Press, 2004.

Benhabib, Seyla. *Situating the Self: Gender, Community and Postmodernism in Contemporary Ethics*. New York: Routledge, 1992.

———. *Transformations of Citizenship: Dilemmas of the Nation State in the Era of Globalization: Two Lectures*. Assen: Koninklijke Van Gorcum, 2001.

Benjamin, Lewis Saul. *The South Sea Bubble*. London: D. O'Connor, 1921.

Berlin, Isaiah. *Two Concepts of Liberty*. Oxford: Oxford University Press, 1958.

Beti, Mongo. *Mission to Kala*. Translated by Peter Green. London: Heinemann Educational Books, 1964.

Beverley, John. *Against Literature*. Minneapolis: University of Minnesota Press, 1993.

———. *Subalternity and Representation: Arguments in Cultural Theory, Post-Contemporary Interventions*. Durham, N.C.: Duke University Press, 1999.

———. *Testimonio: On the Politics of Truth*. Minneapolis: University of Minnesota Press, 2004.

Beverley, John, and Marc Zimmerman. *Literature and Politics in the Central American Revolutions, New Interpretations of Latin America Series*. Austin: University of Texas Press, 1990.

Beyala, Calixthe. *Le Petit Prince de Belleville: Roman*. Paris: A. Michel, 1992.

———. *Loukoum: The 'Little Prince' of Belleville*. Translated by Marjolijn De Jager. Oxford: Heinemann, 1995.

Bloch, Ernst. *Natural Law and Human Dignity*. Translated by Dennis J. Schmidt. Edited by Thomas McCarthy, *Studies in Contemporary German Social Thought*. Cambridge, Mass.: MIT Press, 1986.

Booth, Wayne. "Individualism and the Mystery of the Social Self; or, Does Amnesty Have a Leg to Stand On?" In *Freedom and Interpretation: The Oxford Amnesty Lectures, 1992*, edited by Barbara Johnson, 69–102. New York: Basic Books, 1993.

Bourdieu, Pierre. *The Rules of Art: Genesis and Structure of the Literary Field*. Translated by Susan Emanuel. Stanford: Stanford University Press, 1996.

Bourdieu, Pierre, and Jean Claude Passeron. *Reproduction in Education, Society and Culture*. London: Sage Publications, 1977.

Bouvard, Marguerite Guzman. *Revolutionizing Motherhood: The Mothers of the Plaza De Mayo, Latin American Silhouettes*. Wilmington, Del.: Scholarly Resources, 1994.

Bowne, Borden Parker. *Personalism, N. W. Harris Lectures, 1907*. Boston: Houghton Mifflin, 1908.

Bradol, Jean-Hervé. "Introduction: The Sacrificial International Order and Humanitarian Action." In *In the Shadow of 'Just Wars': Violence, Politics, and Humanitarian Action*, edited by Fabrice Weissman and Médecins sans frontières (Association), 1–22. Ithaca: Cornell University Press, 2004.

Braendlin, Bonnie Hoover. "*Bildung* in Ethnic Women Writers." *Denver Quarterly* 17, no. 4 (1983): 75–87.

Brontë, Emily. *Wuthering Heights: An Authoritative Text, with Essays in Criticism*. Edited by William M. Sale Jr. 2nd ed. New York: Norton, 1972.

Brookes, Edgar Harry. *Apartheid: A Documentary Study of Modern South Africa*. London: Routledge and K. Paul, 1968.

Brooks, Peter. *Reading for the Plot: Design and Intention in Narrative*. Cambridge, Mass.: Harvard University Press, 1984.

Brown, Wendy. "Suffering the Paradoxes of Rights." In *Left Legalism/Left Critique*, edited by Wendy Brown and Janet E. Halley, 420–34. Durham, N.C.: Duke University Press, 2002.

———. " 'The Most We Can Hope For . . .': Human Rights and the Politics of Fatalism." *South Atlantic Quarterly* 103, no. 2/3 (2004): 451–63.

Brownlie, Ian, ed. *Basic Documents on Human Rights*. 3rd ed. Oxford: Clarendon Press, 1992.

Bruford, Walter Horace. *The German Tradition of Self-Cultivation: Bildung from Humboldt to Thomas Mann*. London: Cambridge University Press, 1975.

Brugger, Winfried. "The Image of the Person in the Human Rights Concept." *Human Rights Quarterly* 18, no. 3 (1996): 594–611.

Buckley, Jerome. "Autobiography in the English *Bildungsroman*." In *The Interpretation of Narrative: Theory and Practice*, edited by Morton W. Bloomfield, 93–104. Cambridge, Mass.: Harvard University Press, 1970.

Buckley, Jerome Hamilton. *Season of Youth: The Bildungsroman from Dickens to Golding*. Cambridge, Mass.: Harvard University Press, 1974.

Bunch, Charlotte. "Transforming Human Rights from a Feminist Perspective." In *Women's Rights, Human Rights: International Feminist Perspectives*, edited by Julie Stone Peters and Andrea Wolper, 11–17. New York: Routledge, 1995.

———. "Women's Rights as Human Rights: Toward a Re-Vision of Human Rights." *Human Rights Quarterly* 12 (1990): 486–98.

Burke, Kenneth. "Literature as Equipment for Living." In *The Philosophy of Literary Form*, 253–62. New York: Vintage, 1957.

Burke, Roland. "'The Compelling Dialogue of Freedom': Human Rights at the Bandung Conference." *Human Rights Quarterly* 28, no. 4 (2006): 947–65.

Bush, George. "Speech." Kabul, Afghanistan, 1 March 2006.

Bush, Laura. 2006. Mrs. Bush's Remarks at the 2006 National Book Festival Gala. In Office of the First Lady, *http://www.whitehouse.gov/news/releases/2006/09/20060929–16.html.* (accessed 15 November 2006).

Butler, Judith. "Universality in Culture." In *Comparative Political Culture in the Age of Globalization: An Introductory Anthology,* edited by Hwa Yol Jung, 357–62. Lanham, Md.: Lexington Books, 2002.

———. *The Psychic Life of Power: Theories in Subjection.* Stanford: Stanford University Press, 1997.

Butler, Judith P., Ernesto Laclau, and Slavoj Žižek. *Contingency, Hegemony, Universality: Contemporary Dialogues on the Left.* Edited by Ernesto Laclau and Chantal Mouffe, *Phronesis.* London: Verso, 2000.

Cain, Kenneth, Heidi Postlewait, and Andrew Thomson. *Emergency Sex and Other Desperate Measures: A True Story from Hell on Earth.* New York: Miramax Books, 2004.

Carlyle, Thomas. "Translator's Preface." In *Wilhelm Meister's Apprenticeship,* 15–21. New York: Collier Books, 1962.

Carnoy, Martin. *Education as Cultural Imperialism.* New York: D. McKay, 1974.

Casanova, Pascale. *The World Republic of Letters.* Translated by M. B. DeBevoise. Edited by Edward W. Said, *Convergences: Inventories of the Present.* Cambridge, Mass.: Harvard University Press, 2004.

Cassese, Antonio. *Self-Determination of Peoples: A Legal Reappraisal.* Cambridge: Cambridge University Press, 1995.

———. "The Self-Determination of Peoples." In *The International Bill of Rights: The Covenant on Civil and Political Rights,* edited by Louis Henkin, 92–113. New York: Columbia University Press, 1981.

Cassin, René. "Historique de la Declaration Universelle de 1948." In *La Pensée et L'action,* 103–18. Paris: Editions F. Lalou, 1972.

Castle, Gregory. "The Book of Youth: Reading Joyce's Bildungsroman." *Genre* 22, no. 1 (1989): 21–40.

Chakrabarty, Dipesh. *Provincializing Europe: Postcolonial Thought and Historical Difference, Princeton Studies in Culture/Power/History.* Princeton: Princeton University Press, 2000.

Chandler, David. "The Limits of Human Rights and Cosmopolitan Citizenship." In *Rethinking Human Rights: Critical Approaches to International Politics,* edited by David Chandler, 115–35. New York: Palgrave Macmillan, 2002.

Charles, Ron. "An Island Paradise in the Flames of Terror." *Christian Science Monitor,* May 4 2000, 17.

Cheah, Pheng. *Spectral Nationality: Passages of Freedom from Kant to Postcolonial Literatures of Liberation.* New York: Columbia University Press, 2003.

Cheng, Vincent J., Terry Goldie, and Sander L. Gilman. "Forum: Ethnicity." *PMLA* 113, no. 3 (1998): 449–52.

Cheuse, Alan. "*Adama* Tells of a Saudi's Coming of Age." In *News Hour*: National Public Radio, 2003.

Chow, Rey. *The Protestant Ethnic and the Spirit of Capitalism.* New York: Columbia University Press, 2002.

Clastres, Pierre. *Archeology of Violence.* Translated by Jeanine Herman. New York: Semiotext(e), 1994.

Cocalis, Susan L. "The Transformation of Bildung from an Image to an Ideal." *Monatshefte: Fur Deutschen Unterricht, Deutsche Sprache und Literatur* 70, no. 4 (1978): 399–414.

Cohen, Margaret. "Sentimental Communities." In *The Literary Channel: The Inter-National Invention of the Novel*, edited by Margaret Cohen and Carolyn Dever, 106–32. Princeton: Princeton University Press, 2002.

———. *The Sentimental Education of the Novel.* Princeton: Princeton University Press, 1999.

Cohen, Margaret, and Carolyn Dever. "Introduction." In *The Literary Channel: The Inter-National Invention of the Novel*, edited by Margaret Cohen and Carolyn Dever, 1–34. Princeton: Princeton University Press, 2002.

Cohen, Stanley. *Denial and Acknowledgement: The Impact of Information About Human Rights Violations.* Jerusalem: Center for Human Rights, 1995.

———. *States of Denial: Knowing About Atrocities and Suffering.* Cambridge, UK: Blackwell, 2001.

Cohen, Stanley, and Bruna Seu. "Knowing Enough Not to Feel Too Much: Emotional Thinking About Human Rights Appeals." In *Truth Claims: Representation and Human Rights*, edited by Mark Philip Bradley and Patrice Petro, 187–201. New Brunswick: Rutgers University Press, 2002.

Comaroff, Jean, and John L. Comaroff. *Of Revelation and Revolution: Christianity, Colonialism, and Consciousness in South Africa.* Chicago: University of Chicago Press, 1991.

Comaroff, John. "The Discourse of Rights in Colonial South Africa: Subjectivity, Sovereignty, Modernity." In *Identities, Politics, and Rights*, edited by Austin Sarat and Thomas R. Kearns, 193–236. Ann Arbor: University of Michigan Press, 1995.

CONADEP. *Nunca Más (Never Again).* London: Faber and Faber in association with *Index on Censorship*, 1986.

Conrad, Joseph. *Heart of Darkness.* Edited by Paul B. Armstrong. Fourth ed., *Norton Critical Edition*. New York: Norton, 2006.

Cornell, Drucilla. "Bodily Integrity and the Right to Abortion." In *Identities, Politics, and Rights*, edited by Austin Sarat and Thomas R. Kearns, 21–84. Ann Arbor: University of Michigan Press, 1995.

———. *Just Cause: Freedom, Identity, and Rights*. Lanham, Md.: Rowman and Littlefield, 2000.

Cot, Pierre. "Preface." In *Law and the Algerian Revolution*. Brussels: International Association of Democratic Lawyers, 1961.

Crenshaw, Kimberlé, ed. *Critical Race Theory: The Key Writings that Formed the Movement*. New York: New Press, 1995.

Cubilié, Anne. *Women Witnessing Terror: Testimony and the Cultural Politics of Human Rights*. 1st ed. New York: Fordham University Press, 2005.

d'Almeida, Irène Assiba. *Francophone African Women Writers: Destroying the Emptiness of Silence*. Gainesville: University Press of Florida, 1994.

Dahl, P. "The '*Bildungsroman*.'" In *History of European Literature*, edited by Annick Benoit-Dusausoy and Guy Fontaine, 422–26. London: Routledge, 2000.

Dai, Sijie. *Balzac and the Little Chinese Seamstress*. Translated by Ina Rilke. London: Chatto and Windus, 2001.

Damrosch, David. *What Is World Literature?* Edited by Emily Apter, *Translation/Transnation*. Princeton: Princeton University Press, 2003.

Dangarembga, Tsitsi. *Nervous Conditions*. London: Women's Press, 1988.

Defoe, Daniel. *Robinson Crusoe*. New York: Signet, 1980.

de la Parra, Teresa. *Mama Blanca's Memoirs*. Translated by Harriet D. Onís and revised by Frederick H. Fornoff. Edited by Doris Sommer. Critical ed., *Pittsburgh Editions of Latin American Literature*. Pittsburgh: University of Pittsburgh Press, 1993.

Delgado, Richard, and Jean Stefancic. *Critical Race Theory: An Introduction*, *Critical America*. New York: New York University Press, 2001.

de Man, Paul. *The Resistance to Theory*, *Theory and History of Literature, Volume 33*. Minneapolis: University of Minnesota Press, 1986.

Derrida, Jacques. "Declarations of Independence." In *Negotiations: Interventions and Interviews, 1971–2001*, edited by Elizabeth Rottenberg, 46–54. Stanford: Stanford University Press, 2002.

———. "Force Du Loi: Le 'Fondement Mystique De L'autorité.'" *Cardozo Law Review* 11, no. 5/6 (1990): 919–1046.

Desai, Gaurav Gajanan. *Subject to Colonialism: African Self-Fashioning and the Colonial Library*. Durham: Duke University Press, 2001.

Dewey, John. "Personality." In *A Cyclopedia of Education*, edited by Paul Monroe. New York: Macmillan, 1911.

———. "The Historic Background of Corporate Legal Personality." *Yale Law Review* 35, no. 6 (1926): 655–73.

Diawara, Manthia. "Toward a Regional Imaginary in Africa." In *The Cultures of Globalization*, edited by Fredric Jameson and Masao Miyoshi, 103–24. Durham, N.C.: Duke University Press, 1998.

Dickens, Charles. *Great Expectations*. Edited by Angus Calder, *Penguin Classics*. New York: Penguin Books, 1965.

Dilthey, Wilhelm, Rudolf A. Makkreel, and Frithjof Rodi. *Selected Works (V.5): Poetry and Experience*. Princeton: Princeton University Press, 1985.

Donnelly, Jack. *Universal Human Rights in Theory and Practice*. Ithaca: Cornell University Press, 1989.

Douzinas, Costas. *The End of Human Rights: Critical Legal Thought at the Turn of the Century*. Oxford: Hart Pub., 2000.

Dow, Unity. *Juggling Truths*. North Melbourne: Sinifex Press, 2003.

Drinan, Robert F. *The Mobilization of Shame: A World View of Human Rights*. New Haven: Yale University Press, 2001.

duBois, Paige. *Torture and Truth*. New York: Routledge, 1991.

Edgell, Zee. *Beka Lamb, Caribbean Writers Series. 26*. London: Heinemann, 1982.

Eldred, Janet Carey, and Peter Mortensen. "Reading Literacy Narratives." *College English* 54, no. 5 (1992): 512–39.

Ellerman, Evelyn. "The Literature Bureau: African Influence in Papua New Guinea." *Research in African Literatures* 26, no. 4 (1995): 206–15.

Elliott, Robert C. *The Literary Persona*. Chicago: University of Chicago Press, 1982.

Eltit, Diamela. *El Cuarto Mundo*. Santiago: Planeta, 1988.

———. *The Fourth World*. Translated by Dick Gerdes. Lincoln: University of Nebraska Press, 1995.

Escobar, Arturo. *Encountering Development: The Making and Unmaking of the Third World, Princeton Studies in Culture/Power/History*. Princeton: Princeton University Press, 1995.

Espiell, Héctor Gros. "Implementation of United Nations Resolutions Relating to the Right of People under Colonial Rule and Alien Domination to Self-Determination." New York: United Nations. Commission on Human Rights. Sub-Commission on Prevention of Discrimination and Protection of Minorities, 1978.

Falk, Richard A. "Reframing the Legal Agenda of World Order in the Course of a Turbulent Century." In *Reframing the International: Law, Culture, Politics*, edited by Richard A. Falk, Lester Edwin J. Ruiz, and R. B. J. Walker, 46–69. New York: Routledge, 2002.

Fanon, Frantz. *The Wretched of the Earth*. Translated by Constance Farrington. New York: Grove Weidenfeld, 1963.

Farr, Cecilia Konchar. *Reading Oprah: How Oprah's Book Club Changed the Way America Reads*. Albany: SUNY Press, 2004.

Felski, Rita. *Beyond Feminist Aesthetics: Feminist Literature and Social Change*. Cambridge, Mass.: Harvard University Press, 1989.

Festa, Lynn. "Sentimental Bonds and Revolutionary Characters: Richardson's *Pamela* in England and France." In *The Literary Channel: The Inter-National Invention of the Novel*, edited by Margaret Cohen and Carolyn Dever, 73–105. Princeton: Princeton University Press, 2002.

Fish, Stanley Eugene. *Is There a Text in This Class?: The Authority of Interpretive Communities*. Cambridge, Mass.: Harvard University Press, 1980.
———. "There's No Such Thing as Free Speech, and It's a Good Thing, Too." In *There's No Such Thing as Free Speech: . . . And It's a Good Thing, Too*, 102–19. New York: Oxford University Press, 1994.
Fisher, Jo. *Mothers of the Disappeared*. Boston: South End Press, 1989.
Fitzpatrick, Peter. "Terminal Legality? Human Rights and Critical Being." In *Critical Beings: Law, Nation and the Global Subject*, edited by Peter Fitzpatrick and Patricia Tuitt, 119–36. Aldershot, England: Ashgate, 2004.
Flew, Antony. *A Dictionary of Philosophy*. Revised 2nd ed. New York: St. Martin's Press, 1984.
Flory, Maurice. "Questions Intéressant La France: Négociation ou Dégagement en Algérie." *Annuaire Français de droit international* 7 (1961): 836–855.
Forrest, Duncan. "The Methods of Torture and Its Effects." In *A Glimpse of Hell: Reports on Torture Worldwide*, edited by Duncan Forrest. New York: New York University Press; Amnesty International, 1996.
Forster, E. M. *Aspects of the Novel*. New York: Harcourt Brace, 1955.
Foster, Don, Dennis Davis, and Diane Sandler. *Detention and Torture in South Africa: Psychological, Legal, and Historical Studies*. New York: St. Martin's, 1987.
Foucault, Michel. *The Archaeology of Knowledge and the Discourse on Language*. Translated by A. M. Sheridan Smith. New York: Pantheon, 1972.
———. "Two Lectures." In *Power/Knowledge: Selected Interviews and Other Writings, 1972–1977*, edited by Colin Gordon, 78–108. Brighton, Sussex: Harvester Press, 1980.
Fox, Fiona. "Conditioning the Right to Humanitarian Aid? Human Rights and the 'New Humanitarianism.'" In *Rethinking Human Rights: Critical Approaches to International Politics*, edited by David Chandler, 19–37. New York: Palgrave Macmillan, 2002.
Fraiman, Susan. *Unbecoming Women: British Women Writers and the Novel of Development, Gender and Culture*. New York: Columbia University Press, 1993.
Franco, Jean. "Going Public: Reinhabiting the Private." In *On Edge: The Crisis of Contemporary Latin American Culture*, edited by George Yúdice, Jean Franco, and Juan Flores, 65–83. Minneapolis: University of Minnesota Press, 1992.
———. "Introduction." In *In a State of Memory*, xiii–xxiv. Lincoln: University of Nebraska Press, 2001.
Fraser, Nancy. "Rethinking the Public Sphere: A Contribution to the Critique of Actually Existing Democracy." In *The Phantom Public Sphere*, edited by Bruce Robbins, 1–32. Minneapolis: University of Minnesota Press, 1993.
Freedman, Ralph. *The Lyrical Novel: Studies in Hermann Hesse, André Gide, and Virginia Woolf*. Princeton: Princeton University Press, 1963.

Frye, Northrop. *Anatomy of Criticism*. Princeton: Princeton University Press, 1957.

Gadamer, Hans-Georg. "Education Is Self-Education." *Journal of Philosophy of Education* 35, no. 4 (2001): 529–538.

———. *Truth and Method*. Translated by Garrett Barden and John Cumming. New York: Seabury Press, 1975.

Galtung, Johan. "Literacy, Education and Schooling: For What?" In *Literacy and Social Development in the West: A Reader*, edited by Harvey J. Graff, 271–85. Cambridge: Cambridge University Press, 1981.

Gandhi, Leela. "'Learning Me Your Language': England in the Postcolonial *Bildungsroman*." In *England through Colonial Eyes in Twentieth-Century Fiction*, edited by Ann Blake, Leela Gandhi, and Sue Thomas, 56–75. New York: Palgrave, 2001.

Gikandi, Simon. "Globalization and the Claims of Postcoloniality." *South Atlantic Quarterly* 100, no. 3 (2001): 627–58.

Gilmore, Leigh. *The Limits of Autobiography: Trauma and Testimony*. Ithaca, N.Y.: Cornell University Press, 2001.

Goethe, Johann Wolfgang von. *Wilhelm Meister's Apprenticeship*. Translated by Eric A. Blackall and Victor Lange. Edited by Victor Lange, Erick Blackall, and Cyrus Hamlin. 12 vols. Vol. 9, *Goethe's Collected Works*. Princeton: Princeton University Press, 1989.

———. *Wilhelm Meister's Apprenticeship and Travels*. Translated by Thomas Carlyle. 2 vols. London: Chapman and Hill, 1894.

———. *Wilhelm Meisters Lehrjahre*. München: Wilhelm Goldmann Verlag, 1964.

Goldstein, Leslie Friedman, ed. *Feminist Jurisprudence: The Difference Debate*. Lanham, Md.: Rowman and Littlefield, 1992.

Goodrich, Peter. *Legal Discourse: Studies in Linguistics, Rhetoric, and Legal Analysis*. Edited by Stephen Heath, Colin MacCabe, and Denise Riley, *Language, Discourse, Society*. London: MacMillan Press, 1987.

Goody, Jack. *The Domestication of the Savage Mind*. Edited by Jack Goody and Geoffrey Hawthorn, *Themes in the Social Sciences*. Cambridge: Cambridge University Press, 1977.

Gott, Gil. "Imperial Humanitarianism: History of an Arrested Dialectic." In *Moral Imperialism: A Critical Anthology*, edited by Berta Esperanza Hernández-Truyol, 19–38. New York: New York University Press, 2002.

Gourevitch, Philip. *We Wish to Inform You that Tomorrow We Will Be Killed with Our Families: Stories from Rwanda*. New York: Farrar, Straus and Giroux, 1998.

Graff, Harvey J. *The Literacy Myth: Literacy and Social Structure in the Nineteenth-Century City, Studies in Social Discontinuity*. New York: Academic Press, 1979.

————, ed. *Literacy and Social Development in the West: A Reader.* Edited by Peter Burke and Ruth Finnegan, *Cambridge Studies in Oral and Literate Culture.* Cambridge: Cambridge University Press, 1981.

Graham, Shane. "The Truth Commission and Post-Apartheid Literature in South Africa." *Research in African Literatures* 34, no. 1 (2003): 11–30.

Gramsci, Antonio. *Selections from the Prison Notebooks.* Translated by Quintin Hoare and Geoffrey Nowell Smith. Edited by Quintin Hoare and Geoffrey Nowell Smith. New York: International, 1971.

Graziano, Frank. *Divine Violence: Spectacle, Psychosexuality and Radical Christianity in the Argentine "Dirty War."* Boulder: Westview Press, 1992.

Gready, Paul. "Introduction." In *Political Transition: Politics and Cultures,* edited by Paul Gready, 1–26. London: Pluto Press, 2003.

Great Britain. "Parliamentary Debates." Edited by House of Lords. London: H. M. Stationery Office, 28 March 1960.

————. "Parliamentary Debates: Kenya Independence Bill." Edited by House of Lords. London: H. M. Stationery Office, 28 November 1963.

Gunesekera, Romesh. *Reef.* London: Granta Books, 1994.

Habermas, Jürgen. *Communication and the Evolution of Society.* Translated by Thomas McCarthy. Boston: Beacon Press, 1979.

————. "On Legitimation through Human Rights." In *Global Justice and Transnational Politics: Essays on the Moral and Political Challenges of Globalization,* edited by Pablo De Greiff and Ciaran Cronin, 197–214. Cambridge, Mass.: MIT Press, 2002.

————. "The Public Sphere: An Encyclopedia Article (1964)." *New German Critique* 1, no. 3 (1974): 49–55.

————. *The Structural Transformation of the Public Sphere: An Inquiry into a Category of Bourgeois Society.* Translated by Thomas Burger and Frederick Lawrence, *Studies in Contemporary German Social Thought.* Cambridge, Mass.: MIT Press, 1989. Reprint, 1991.

Hall, R. Mark. "The 'Oprahfication' of Literacy: Reading 'Oprah's Book Club.'" *College English* 65, no. 6 (2003): 646–67.

Hardin, James N. "Reflection and Action: Essays on the Bildungsroman: An Introduction." In *Reflection and Action: Essays on the Bildungsroman,* edited by James N. Hardin, ix–xxvii. Columbia: University of South Carolina Press, 1991.

Harlow, Barbara. *Barred: Women, Writing, and Political Detention.* Hanover, N.H.: University Press of New England, 1992.

————. "From the 'Civilizing Mission' to 'Humanitarian Interventionism': Postmodernism, Writing, and Human Rights." In *Text and Nation: Cross-Disciplinary Essays on Cultural and National Identities,* edited by Laura García-Moreno and Peter C. Pfeiffer, 31–47. Columbia, S.C.: Camden House, 1996.

Harrow, Kenneth W. *Less Than One and Double: A Feminist Reading of African Women's Writing, Studies in African Literature*. Portsmouth, N.H.: Heinemann, 2002.

Hartman, Saidiya V. *Scenes of Subjection: Terror, Slavery, and Self-Making in Nineteenth-Century America*. Edited by Arnold Rampersad and Shelley Fisher Fishkin, *Race and American Culture*. New York: Oxford University Press, 1997.

Harvey, W. J. *Character and the Novel*. Ithaca: Cornell University Press, 1965.

Hau'ofa, Epeli. *Tales of the Tikongs*. Edited by Vilsoni Hereniko, *Talanoa: Contemporary Pacific Literature*. Honolulu: University of Hawaii Press, 1994.

Hayner, Priscilla B. "Fifteen Truth Commissions—1974 to 1994: A Comparative Study." *Human Rights Quarterly* 16 (1994): 597–655.

Hegel, G. W. F. *Aesthetics: Lectures on Fine Art*. Translated by T. M. Knox. Vol. I. Oxford: Clarendon Press, 1975.

———. *Hegel's Philosophy of Right*. Translated by T. M. Knox. London: Oxford University Press, 1967.

Hickey, James E. "The Source of International Legal Personality in the 21st Century." *Hofstra Law and Policy Symposium* 2, no. 1 (1997): 1–18.

Hiebert, Ray Eldon, American University, and United States Agency for International Development, eds. *Books in Human Development: The Final Report*. Washington: Department of Journalism, American University, 1964.

Hill, Alan. *In Pursuit of Publishing*. London: J. Murray in association with Heinemann Educational Books, 1988.

Hirsch, Marianne. "The Novel of Formation as Genre: Between Great Expectations and Lost Illusions." *Genre* 12, no. 3 (1979): 293–311.

Hitchcock, Peter. "The Genre of Postcoloniality." *New Literary History* 34, no. 2 (2003): 299–330.

Hope, Christopher. *A Separate Development*. Johannesburg: Ravan Press, 1980.

Hosseini, Khaled. *The Kite Runner*. New York: Riverhead Books, 2003.

Howe, Susanne. *Wilhelm Meister and His English Kinsmen: Apprentices to Life*. New York: Columbia University Press, 1930.

Huggan, Graham. *The Postcolonial Exotic: Marketing the Margins*. London: Routledge, 2001.

Humboldt, Wilhelm von. *Humanist without Portfolio: An Anthology of the Writings of Wilhelm Von Humboldt*. Translated by Marianne Cowan. Detroit: Wayne State University Press, 1963.

———. *Linguistic Variability and Intellectual Development*. Translated by George C. Buck and Frithjof A. Raven. Philadelphia: University of Pennsylvania Press, 1971.

———. *The Limits of State Action*. Translated by J. W. Burrow. London: Cambridge University Press, 1969.

———. "Theory of Bildung." In *Teaching as a Reflective Practice : The German Didaktik Tradition*, edited by Stefan Hopmann Ian Westbury, and Kurt Riquarts, 57–62. Mahwah, N.J.: L. Erlbaum Associates, 2000.

———. *Über Die Verschiedenheit Des Menschlichen Sprachbaues Und Ihren Einfluß Auf Die Geistige Entwicklung Des Menschengeschlechts*. Darmstadt: Claassen and Roether, 1949.

Humphrey, John P. *Human Rights and the United Nations: A Great Adventure*. Dobbs Ferry, N.Y.: Transnational Pub., 1984.

———. "The Magna Carta of Mankind." In *Human Rights*, edited by Peter Davies. New York: Routledge, 1988.

Ignatieff, Michael, K. Anthony Appiah, David A. Hollinger, Thomas W. Laqueur, and Diane F. Orentlicher. *Human Rights as Politics and Idolatry*. Edited by Amy Gutmann. Princeton: Princeton University Press, 2001.

Irele, Abiola. "In Praise of Alienation." In *The Surreptitious Speech: Présence Africaine and the Politics of Otherness, 1947–1987*, edited by V. Y. Mudimbe, 201–224. Chicago: University of Chicago Press, 1992.

Jameson, Fredric. "On Literary and Cultural Import-Substitution in the Third World: The Case of the Testimonio." *Margins* 1 (1993): 11–34.

———. *The Political Unconscious: Narrative as a Socially Symbolic Act*. Ithaca: Cornell University Press, 1981.

———. "The Politics of Utopia." *New Left Review* 25 (2004): 35–54.

———. "Third-World Literature in the Era of Multinational Capitalism." *Social Text* 15, no. 3 (1986): 65–88.

Jeffers, Thomas L. *Apprenticeships: The Bildungsroman from Goethe to Santayana*. New York: Palgrave Macmillan, 2005.

Johnson, Barbara. "Anthropomorphism in Lyric and Law." *Yale Journal of Law and the Humanities* 10 (1998): 549–574.

Johnson, M. Glen. "A Magna Carta for Mankind: Writing the Universal Declaration of Human Rights." In *The Universal Declaration of Human Rights: A History of Its Creation and Implementation, 1948–1998*, edited by M. Glen Johnson, Janusz Symonides, and UNESCO, 19–75. Paris: UNESCO, 1998.

Joshi, Priya. *In Another Country: Colonialism, Culture, and the English Novel in India*. New York: Columbia University Press, 2002.

Jost, François. "La Tradition du 'Bildungsroman.'" *Comparative Literature* 21 (1969): 97–115.

Jouvenel, Bertrand de. *Sovereignty: An Inquiry into the Political Good*. Translated by J. F. Huntington. Indianapolis: Liberty Fund, 1997.

Kadir, Djelal. "To World, to Globalize—Comparative Literature's Crossroads." *Comparative Literature Studies* 41, no. 1 (2004): 1–9.

Kant, Immanuel. "An Answer to the Question: What Is Enlightenment?" In *What Is Enlightenment?: Eighteenth-Century Answers and Twentieth-Century*

Questions, edited by James Schmidt, 58–64. Berkeley: University of California Press, 1996.

———. *Groundwork on the Metaphysics of Morals*. Translated by Mary J. Gregor. Edited by Karl Ameriks and Desmond M. Clarke, *Cambridge Texts in the History of Philosophy*. Cambridge: Cambridge University Press, 1998.

Keen, Judy. "First Lady Offers a Few Favorite Books." *USA Today*, January 13, 2005.

Keenan, Thomas. *Fables of Responsibility: Aberrations and Predicaments in Ethics and Politics*. Stanford: Stanford University Press, 1997.

———. "Mobilizing Shame." *South Atlantic Quarterly* 103, no. 2/3 (2004): 435–49.

Kelman, Mark. *A Guide to Critical Legal Studies*. Cambridge, Mass.: Harvard University Press, 1987.

Kennedy, David. *The Dark Sides of Virtue: Reassessing International Humanitarianism*. Princeton: Princeton University Press, 2004.

Kennedy, Duncan. "The Critique of Rights in Critical Legal Studies." In *Left Legalism/Left Critique*, edited by Wendy Brown and Janet E. Halley, 178–228. Durham: Duke University Press, 2002.

Kentridge, William. "Director's Note." In *Ubu and the Truth Commission*, viii–xv. Cape Town: University of Cape Town Press, 1998.

Kermode, Frank. *The Sense of an Ending*. New York: Oxford University Press, 1966.

Khouri, Norma. *Honor Lost: Love and Death in Modern-Day Jordan*. New York: Atria Books, 2003.

Khulumani Support Group, Bobby Rodwell, and Lesego Rampolokeng. "The Story I Am About to Tell." Unpublished manuscript.

King, Adele. *Rereading Camara Laye*. Lincoln: University of Nebraska Press, 2002.

Kipen, David. "Specter of Civil War in Ondaatje's Ghost." *San Francisco Chronicle*, April 27, 2000, B1.

Koepke, Wulf. "Quest, Illusion, Creativity, Maturity, and Resignation: The Questionable Journey of the Protagonist of the *Bildungsroman*." *Helios* 17, no. 1 (1990): 129–44.

Kontje, Todd Curtis. *Private Lives in the Public Sphere: The German Bildungsroman as Metafiction*. University Park: Pennsylvania State University Press, 1992.

———. *The German Bildungsroman: History of a National Genre*. Columbia, S.C.: Camden House, 1993.

Krog, Antjie. *Country of My Skull: Guilt, Sorrow, and the Limits of Forgiveness in the New South Africa*. New York: Times Books, 1998.

Kumbula, Tendayi J. *Education and Social Control in Southern Rhodesia*. Palo Alto: R. and E. Research Associates, 1979.

Laclau, Ernesto. *Emancipation(S)*. Edited by Ernesto Laclau and Chantal
  Mouffe, *Phronesis*. London: Verso, 1996.
Laclau, Ernesto, and Chantal Mouffe. *Hegemony and Socialist Strategy: Towards
  a Radical Democratic Politics*. London: Verso, 1985.
Laferrière, Dany. *Dining with the Dictator*. Toronto: Coach House Press, 1994.
Lauren, Paul Gordon. *The Evolution of International Human Rights: Visions
  Seen, Pennsylvania Studies in Human Rights*. Philadelphia: University of
  Pennsylvania Press, 1998.
Lauterpacht, Hersch. *An International Bill of the Rights of Man*. New York:
  Columbia University Press, 1945.
Lefort, Claude. *The Political Forms of Modern Society: Bureaucracy, Democracy,
  Totalitarianism*. Translated by Alan Sheridan. Edited by John B. Thompson.
  Cambridge, Mass.: MIT Press, 1986.
Legal Storytelling. Spec. Issue of *Michigan Law Review*, 87, no. 8 (1989).
Lenin, Vladmir. "The Socialist Revolution and the Right of Nations to Self-
  Determination." In *Collected Works*, 143–56. Moscow: Progress Publishers,
  1964.
Levinas, Emmanuel. "The Rights of Man and the Rights of the Other." In
  Outside the Subject, 116–25. Stanford: Stanford University Press, 1994.
Liking, Werewere. *It Shall Be of Jasper and Coral; and, Love-across-a-Hundred-
  Lives: Two Novels*. Translated by Marjolijn de Jager. Charlottesville: Univer-
  sity Press of Virginia, 2000.
Lima, Maria Helena. "Decolonizing Genre: Jamaica Kincaid and the *Bildungs-
  roman*." *Genre* 26, no. 4 (1993): 431–60.
———. "Imaginary Homelands in Jamaica Kincaid's Narratives of Develop-
  ment." *Callaloo* 25, no. 3 (2002): 857–867.
Lindfors, Bernth. *Long Drums and Canons: Teaching and Researching African
  Literatures*. Trenton, N.J.: Africa World Press, 1995.
Lloyd, David. *Anomalous States: Irish Writing and the Post-Colonial Moment*.
  Dublin: The Lilliput Press, 1993.
———. "Arnold, Ferguson, Schiller: Aesthetic Culture and the Politics of
  Aesthetics." *Cultural Critique* 2 (Winter 1985–86): 137–69.
Lloyd, David, and Paul Thomas. *Culture and the State*. New York: Routledge,
  1998.
Lowe, Lisa. *Immigrant Acts: On Asian American Cultural Politics*. Durham,
  N.C.: Duke University Press, 1996.
Lukács, Georg. *Goethe and His Age*. Translated by Robert Anchor. London:
  Merlin Press, 1968.
———. *Goethe und Seine Zeit*. Bern: A. Francke, 1947.
———. *The Theory of the Novel: A Historico-Philosophical Essay on the Forms of
  Great Epic Literature*. Translated by Anna Bostock. Cambridge, Mass.: MIT
  Press, 1971.

Lyotard, Jean-François. "The Other's Rights." In *On Human Rights: The Oxford Amnesty Lectures 1993*, edited by Stephen Shute and Susan Hurley, 135–47. New York: Basic Books, 1993.

———. *The Postmodern Condition: A Report on Knowledge*. Translated by Geoff Bennington and Brian Massumi. Edited by Wlad Godzich and Jochen Schulte-Sasse. Vol. 10, *Theory and History of Literature*. Minneapolis: University of Minnesota Press, 1984.

Macgoye, Marjorie Oludhe. *Coming to Birth*. New York: Feminist Press, 2000.

Mahoney, Dennis F. "The Apprenticeship of the Reader: The Bildungsroman of the 'Age of Goethe.'" In *Reflection and Action: Essays on the Bildungsroman*, edited by James Hardin, 97–117. Columbia: University of South Carolina Press, 1991.

Malik, Charles Habib. *Human Rights in the United Nations, United Nations at Work No. 1*. New York: UN Department of Public Information, 1952.

———. *Man in the Struggle for Peace*. New York: Harper and Row, 1963.

Mamdani, Mahmood. *When Victims Become Killers: Colonialism, Nativism, and the Genocide in Rwanda*. Princeton, N.J.: Princeton University Press, 2001.

Manguel, Alberto. "The Library of Robinson Crusoe." In *The Book: A World Transformed*, edited by Eduardo Portella, 79–91. Paris: UNESCO Pub., 2001.

Maran, Rita. *Torture: The Role of Ideology in the French-Algerian War*. New York: Praeger, 1989.

Maritain, Jacques. "Introduction." In *Human Rights: Comments and Interpretations*, edited by UNESCO, 9–17. New York: Columbia University Press, 1949.

———. *The Rights of Man and Natural Law*. Translated by Doris C. Anson. New York: Scribner's Sons, 1943.

Mark, Gregory A. "The Personification of the Business Corporation in American Law." *The University of Chicago Law Review* 54, no. 4 (1987): 1441–83.

Markandaya, Kamala. *Nectar in a Sieve*. New York: J. Day, 1954.

Marks, Stephen P. "From the 'Single Confused Page' to the 'Decalogue for Six Billion Persons': The Roots of the Universal Declaration of Human Rights in the French Revolution." *Human Rights Quarterly* 20, no. 3 (1998): 456–514.

Marshall, T. H. *Class, Citizenship, and Social Development: Essays*. Westport, Ct.: Greenwood Press, 1973.

Martín-Baró, Ignacio. *Writings for a Liberation Psychology*. Edited by Adrianne Aron and Shawn Corne. Cambridge, Mass.: Harvard University Press, 1994.

Martini, Fritz. "Bildungsroman—Term and Theory." In *Reflection and Action: Essays on the Bildungsroman*, edited by James Hardin, 1–25. Columbia: University of South Carolina Press, 1991.

Marx, Karl. *Capital: A Critique of Political Economy.* Translated by Ben Fowkes. Vol. I. New York: Vintage, 1977.

———. "On the Jewish Question." In *Karl Marx, Frederick Engels: Collected Works,* 146–74. London: Lawrence and Wishart, 1975.

Maslan, Susan. "The Anti-Human: Man and Citizen before the Declaration of the Rights of Man and of the Citizen." *South Atlantic Quarterly* 103, no. 2/3 (2004): 357–74.

Matsuda, Mari J. "Public Response to Racist Speech: Considering the Victim's Story." In *Words That Wound: Critical Race Theory, Assaultive Speech, and the First Amendment,* edited by Mari J. Matsuda, Charles R. Lawrence III, Richard Delgado, and Kimberlè Williams Crenshaw, 17–51. Boulder: Westview Press, 1993.

Matsuda, Mari J., Charles R. Lawrence III, Richard Delgado, and Kimberlè Williams Crenshaw, eds. *Words That Wound: Critical Race Theory, Assaultive Speech, and the First Amendment, New Perspectives on Law, Culture, and Society.* Boulder: Westview Press, 1993.

Mbembe, Achille. "African Modes of Self-Writing." *Public Culture* 14, no. 1 (2002): 239–273.

McHenry, Robert. "All Hail Oprah's Book Club." *The Chronicle of Higher Education* 48, no. 35 (2002): B.17.

Mercado, Tununa. *En Estado De Memoria.* Córdoba, Argentina: Alción Editora, 1990.

———. *In a State of Memory.* Translated by Peter Kahn, *Latin American Women Writers.* Lincoln: University of Nebraska Press, 2001.

Merriam, Charles. "The Assumptions of Democracy." *Political Science Quarterly* 53, no. 3 (Sep. 1938): 328–49.

———. "The Ends of Government." *The American Political Science Review* 38, no. 1 (Feb. 1944): 21–40.

———. "The Meaning of Democracy." *The Journal of Negro Education* 10, no. 3 (Jul. 1941): 309–17.

Miles, David. "The Picaro's Journey to the Confessional: The Changing Image of the Hero in the German *Bildungsroman.*" *PMLA: Publications of the Modern Language Association of America* 89 (1974): 980–92.

Mill, John Stuart. *On Liberty.* Edited by David Spitz. Norton Critical ed. New York: Norton, 1975.

Miller, J. Hillis. *Versions of Pygmalion.* Cambridge, Mass.: Harvard University Press, 1990.

Minden, Michael. *The German Bildungsroman: Incest and Inheritance, Cambridge Studies in German.* Cambridge: Cambridge University Press, 1997.

———. "The Place of Inheritance in the Bildungsroman: Agathon, Wilhelm Meister's Lehrjahre, and Der Nachsommer." In *Reflection and Action: Essays on the Bildungsroman,* edited by James Hardin, 254–92. Columbia, S.C.: University of South Carolina Press, 1991.

Mohanty, Chandra Talpade. "Introduction." In *Third World Women and the Politics of Feminism*, edited by Chandra Talpade Mohanty, Ann Russo, and Lourdes Torres, 1–47. Bloomington: Indiana University Press, 1991.

Morales, Mario Roberto. *Face of the Earth, Heart of the Sky*. Translated by Edward Waters Hood. Tempe, AZ: Bilingual Press/Editorial Bilingüe, 2000.

Moretti, Franco. "'A Useless Longing for Myself': The Crisis of the European Bildungsroman, 1898–1914." In *Studies in Historical Change*, edited by Ralph Cohen, 43–59. Charlottesville: University Press of Virginia, 1992.

———. *Atlas of the European Novel, 1800–1900*. London: Verso, 1998.

———. "Conjectures on World Literature." *New Left Review* 1 (2000): 54–68.

———. *Modern Epic: The World-System from Goethe to García Márquez*. London: Verso, 1996.

———. *The Way of the World: The Bildungsroman in European Culture*. Translated by Albert Sbragia. New ed. London: Verso, 2000.

Morgan, Ellen. "Humanbecoming: Form and Focus in the Neo-Feminist Novel." In *Images of Women in Fiction: Feminist Perspectives*, edited by Susan Koppelman Cornillon, 183–205. Bowling Green: Bowling Green University Popular Press, 1972.

Morsink, Johannes. "Cultural Genocide, the Universal Declaration, and Minority Rights." *Human Rights Quarterly* 21, no. 4 (1999): 1009–1060.

———. *The Universal Declaration of Human Rights: Origins, Drafting, and Intent, Pennsylvania Studies in Human Rights*. Philadelphia: University of Pennsylvania Press, 1999.

———. "World War Two and the Universal Declaration." *Human Rights Quarterly* 15 (1993): 357–405.

Moyana, Toby Tafirenyika. *Education, Liberation and the Creative Act*. Harare, Zimbabwe: Zimbabwe Publishing House, 1989.

Muchnick, Irvin. 3 May 2006. Kite Bummer: Why Literary Fiction Needs Steroid Testing. In *BeyondChron*, http://www.beyondchron.org/news/index.php?itemid=3234. (accessed 29 May 2006).

Mücke, Dorothea E. von. *Virtue and the Veil of Illusion: Generic Innovation and the Pedagogical Project in Eighteenth-Century Literature*. Stanford: Stanford University Press, 1991.

Mudimbe, V. Y. *The Invention of Africa: Gnosis, Philosophy, and the Order of Knowledge, African Systems of Thought*. Bloomington: Indiana University Press, 1988.

Mugo, M. M. G. *African Orature and Human Rights, Human and Peoples' Rights Monograph Series*. Lesotho: Institute of Southern African Studies, 1991.

Murry, John Middleton. "The Isolation of Russia: And the Way Out." *The Adelphi* 3, no. 4 (1932): 195–205.

Mutua, Makau. *Human Rights: A Political and Cultural Critique, Pennsylvania Studies in Human Rights.* Philadelphia: University of Pennsylvania Press, 2002.

Nafisi, Azar. *Reading Lolita in Tehran: A Memoir in Books.* New York: Random House, 2003.

Nandy, Ashis. "Reconstructing Childhood: A Critique of the Ideology of Adulthood." In *Traditions, Tyranny, and Utopias,* 56–76. Delhi: Oxford University Press, 1987.

Narogin, Mudrooroo. *Writing from the Fringe: A Study of Modern Aboriginal Literature.* South Yarra, Melbourne: Hyland House, 1990.

Native Education Inquiry Commission. "Report of the Native Education Inquiry Commission." Salisbury, Southern Rhodesia, 1951.

Nékám, Alexander. *The Personality Conception of the Legal Entity, Harvard Studies in the Conflict of Laws.* Cambridge, Mass.: Harvard University Press, 1938.

Ngũgĩ wa Thiong'o. *Decolonizing the Mind: The Politics of Language in African Literature.* Portsmouth N.H.: James Currey/Heinemann, 1986.

Nkrumah, Kwame. *Neo-Colonialism: The Last Stage of Imperialism.* New York: International, 1966.

Nordenbo, Sven Erik. "*Bildung* and the Thinking of *Bildung.*" In *Educating Humanity: Bildung in Postmodernity,* edited by Klaus Peter Mortensen, Lars Løvlie, and Sven Nordenbo, 25–36. Oxford: Blackwell, 2003.

Noyes, John K. "Goethe on Cosmopolitanism and Colonialism: *Bildung* and the Dialectic of Critical Mobility." *Eighteenth-Century Studies* 39, no. 4 (2006): 443–62.

Nussbaum, Martha Craven. "Capabilities and Human Rights." In *Global Justice and Transnational Politics: Essays on the Moral and Political Challenges of Globalization,* edited by Pablo De Greiff and Ciaran Cronin, 117–49. Cambridge, Mass.: MIT Press, 2002.

———. *Cultivating Humanity: A Classical Defense of Reform in Liberal Education.* Cambridge, Mass.: Harvard University Press, 1997.

———. *Women and Human Development: The Capabilities Approach.* Cambridge: Cambridge University Press, 2000.

Nyerere, Julius K. "Freedom and Development." In *Freedom and Development | Uhuru Na Maendeleo,* 58–71. Oxford: Oxford University Press, 1973.

O'Callaghan, Marion. *Southern Rhodesia: The Effects of a Conquest Society on Education, Culture and Information.* England: UNESCO, 1977.

Ondaatje, Michael. *Anil's Ghost.* New York: Knopf, 2000.

Ong, Walter. *Orality and Literacy: The Technologizing of the Word.* Edited by Terence Hawkes, *New Accents.* London: Methuen, 1982.

Oprah.com. 2004. Oprah's Book Club Library. In http://www.oprah.com/obc/pastbooks/obc_pastdate.jhtml. (accessed July, 2004).

Patterson, Orlando. "Freedom, Slavery, and the Modern Construction of Rights." In *Historical Change and Human Rights: The Oxford Amnesty Lectures, 1994,* edited by Olwen Hufton, 131–78. New York: Basic Books, 1995.

———. *Slavery and Social Death: A Comparative Study.* Cambridge, Mass.: Harvard University Press, 1982.

Peri Rossi, Cristina. *The Ship of Fools: A Novel.* Translated by Psiche Hughes. Reprint ed. London: Readers International, 2000.

Pestalozzi, Johann Heinrich. *How Gertrude Teaches Her Children: Pestalozzi's Educational Writings.* Edited by Ebenezer Cooke, John Alfred Green, and Daniel N. Robinson, *Significant Contributions to the History of Psychology 1750–1920.* Washington: University Publications of America, 1977.

Peters, Julie Stone. "Law, Literature, and the Vanishing Real: On the Future of an Interdisciplinary Illusion." *PMLA* 120, no. 2 (2005): 442–53.

Phelps, Teresa Godwin. *Shattered Voices: Language, Violence, and the Work of Truth Commissions.* Edited by Bert B. Lockwood Jr., *Pennsylvania Studies in Human Rights.* Philadelphia: University of Pennsylvania Press, 2004.

Phillips, H. M. *Literacy and Development.* Switzerland: UNESCO, 1970.

Piaget, Jean. "The Right to Education in the Modern World." In *Freedom and Culture,* edited by UNESCO, 69–118. London: Wingate, 1951.

Pollis, Adamantia, and Peter Schwab. "Human Rights: A Western Construct with Limited Applicability." In *Human Rights: Cultural and Ideological Perspectives,* edited by Adamantia Pollis and Peter Schwab, 1–18. New York: Praeger, 1979.

———. "Introduction." In *Human Rights: New Perspectives, New Realities,* edited by Adamantia Pollis and Peter Schwab, 1–8. Boulder, Colo.: Lynne Rienner, 2000.

Pratt, Mary Louise. *Toward a Speech Act Theory of Literary Discourse.* Bloomington: Indiana University Press, 1977.

Puttenham, George. *The Arte of English Poesie, 1589.* Edited by R. C. Alston, *English Linguistics, 1500–1800—A Collection of Facsimile Reprints.* Menston, England: Scolar Press, 1968.

Pye, Lucian W. *Politics, Personality, and Nation Building: Burma's Search for Identity.* New Haven: Yale University Press, 1962.

Rancière, Jacques. "Who Is the Subject of the Rights of Man?" *South Atlantic Quarterly* 103, no. 2/3 (2004): 297–310.

Ranger, Terence. "Nationalist Historiography, Patriotic History and the History of the Nation: The Struggle over the Past in Zimbabwe." *Journal of Southern African Studies* 30, no. 2 (2004): 215–34.

Rao, Arati. "The Politics of Gender and Culture in International Human Rights Discourse." In *Women's Rights, Human Rights: Internatinal Feminist Perspectives,* edited by Julie Peters and Andrea Wolper, 167–75. New York: Routledge, 1995.

Redfield, Marc. *Phantom Formations: Aesthetic Ideology and the Bildungsroman.* Ithaca, N.Y.: Cornell University Press, 1996.

———. "The Bildungsroman." In *Oxford Encyclopedia of British Literature,* edited by David Scott Kastan, 191–94. Oxford: Oxford University Press, 2006.

Rejali, Darius M. *Torture and Modernity: Self, Society, and State in Modern Iran.* Boulder: Westview Press, 1994.

Richards, I. A. *Nations and Peace.* New York: Simon and Schuster, 1947.

Ricoeur, Paul. *Oneself as Another.* Translated by Kathleen Blamey. Chicago: University of Chicago Press, 1992.

———. "Self as *Ipse.*" In *Freedom and Interpretation: The Oxford Amnesty Lectures, 1992,* edited by Barbara Johnson, 103–19. New York: Basic Books, 1993.

Riding, Alan. "In France, Artists Have Sounded the Warning Bells for Years." *New York Times,* November 24, 2005, 1.

Rieff, David. *A Bed for the Night: Humanitarianism in Crisis.* New York: Simon and Schuster, 2002.

Rivabella, Omar. *Requiem for a Woman's Soul.* Translated by Paul Riviera and Omar Rivabella. New York: Random House, 1986.

Robbins, Bruce. *Feeling Global: Internationalism in Distress.* New York: New York University Press, 1999.

———. "Sad Stories in the International Public Sphere: Richard Rorty on Culture and Human Rights." *Public Culture* 9 (1997): 209–32.

Robert, Rudolph. *Chartered Companies and Their Role in the Development of Overseas Trade.* London: Bell, 1969.

Robinson, Mary. "Realising Human Rights: 'Take Hold of It Boldly and Duly . . .'" Paper presented at the Romanes Lectures, Oxford University, 11 November 1997.

Robinson-Pant, Anna. " 'The Illiterate Woman': Changing Approaches to Researching Women's Literacy." In *Women, Literacy, and Development: Alternative Perspectives,* edited by Anna Robinson-Pant, 15–34. London: Routledge, 2004.

———, ed. *Women, Literacy, and Development: Alternative Perspectives.* Edited by David Barton, *Routledge Studies in Literacy; 1.* London: Routledge, 2004.

Romulo, Carlos P. *The Meaning of Bandung.* Chapel Hill: University of North Carolina Press, 1956.

Roosevelt, Eleanor. *Christmas 1940.* New York: St. Martin's Press, 1986.

———. *Eleanor Roosevelt's My Day: The Post-War Years, 1945–1952.* Edited by David Emblidge. New York: Pharos Books, 1990.

———. *Human Rights: A Documentary on the United Nations Declaration of Human Rights.* New York: Folkway Records, 1958. Record Album.

———. "The Promise of Human Rights." *Foreign Affairs* 26 (1948): 470–477.

Rorty, Amélie Oksenberg. "Characters, Persons, Selves, Individuals." In *Theory of the Novel: A Historical Approach*, edited by Michael McKeon, 537–553. Baltimore: Johns Hopkins University Press, 2000.

Rorty, Richard. "Human Rights, Rationality, and Sentimentality." In *On Human Rights: The Oxford Amnesty Lectures 1993*, edited by Stephen Shute and Susan Hurley, 111–34. New York: Basic Books, 1993.

———. *Philosophy and the Mirror of Nature*. Princeton: Princeton University Press, 1979.

Rouanet, Sérgio Paulo. "The End of Culture and the Last Book." In *The Book: A World Transformed*, edited by Eduardo Portella and Rafael Argullol, 43–58. Paris: UNESCO Pub., 2001.

Rousseau, Jean Jacques. *The Social Contract, or, Principles of Political Right*, 1762.

Roy, Arundhati. *The God of Small Things*. New York: Random House, 1997.

Sáez, Ñacuñán. "Torture: A Discourse on Practice." In *Tattoo, Torture, Mutilation and Adornment: The Denaturalization of the Body in Culture and Text*, edited by Frances Mascia-Lees and Patricia Sharp, 126–44. Albany: SUNY Press, 1992.

Said, Edward W. *Culture and Imperialism*. New York: Knopf, 1993.

———. "Identity, Authority, and Freedom: The Potentate and the Traveler." *boundary 2* (1994): 1–18.

———. *Orientalism*. New York: Vintage Books, 1979.

———. *Out of Place: A Memoir*. New York: Knopf, 1999.

———. "Permission to Narrate." *Journal of Palestine Studies* 13, no. 3 (1984): 27–48.

———. *The World, the Text, and the Critic*. Cambridge, Mass.: Harvard University Press, 1983.

Saleilles, Raymond. *De la Personnalité Juridique: Histoire et Théories: Vingt-Cinq Leçons d'Introduction á un Cours de Droit Civil Comparé sur les Personnes Juridiques*. Paris: A. Rousseau, 1910.

Sammons, Jeffrey L. "The Mystery of the Missing *Bildungsroman*; or, What Happened to Wilhelm Meister's Legacy?" *Genre: Forms of Discourse and Culture* 14, no. 2 (1981): 229–246.

Sanders, Mark. "Truth, Telling, Questioning: The Truth and Reconciliation Commission, Antjie Krog's *Country of My Skull*, and Literature after Apartheid." *MFS: Modern Fiction Studies* 46, no. 1 (2000): 13–41.

Sarat, Austin, and Thomas R. Kearns. "Editorial Introduction." In *Identities, Politics, and Rights*, edited by Austin Sarat and Thomas R. Kearns, 1–17. Ann Arbor: University of Michigan Press, 1997.

Sartre, Jean-Paul. "Preface." In *The Wretched of the Earth*, 7–31. New York: Grove Weidenfeld, 1963.

Scarry, Elaine. *The Body in Pain: The Making and Unmaking of the World*. New York: Oxford University Press, 1985.

———. "The Difficulty of Imagining Other People." In *For Love of Country?*
edited by Martha Craven Nussbaum and Joshua Cohen, 98–110. Boston:
Beacon Press, 2002.

Schaffer, Kay, and Sidonie Smith. *Human Rights and Narrated Lives: The Ethics
of Recognition.* New York: Palgrave, 2004.

Schane, Sanford A. "The Corporation Is a Person: The Language of a Legal
Fiction." *Tulane Law Review* 61 (1987): 563–609.

Scheler, Max. *Formalism in Ethics and Non-Formal Ethics of Values: A New Attempt toward the Foundation of an Ethical Personalism.* 5th revised ed., *Northwestern University Studies in Phenomenology and Existential Philosophy.*
Evanston: Northwestern University Press, 1973.

Schiller, Friedrich. *On the Aesthetic Education of Man, in a Series of Letters.*
Translated by Elizabeth M. Wilkinson and L. A. Willoughby. Oxford:
Clarendon, 1967.

Scholes, Robert E., and Robert Kellogg. *The Nature of Narrative.* New York:
Oxford University Press, 1966.

Schwarz, Roberto. *Misplaced Ideas: Essays on Brazilian Culture.* Translated by
John Gledson. Edited by James Dunkerley, Jean Franco, and John King,
Critical Studies in Latin American Culture. London: Verso, 1992.

Scott, Joan Wallach. *Only Paradoxes to Offer: French Feminists and the Rights of
Man.* Cambridge, Mass.: Harvard University Press, 1996.

Searle, John R. *Speech Acts: An Essay in the Philosophy of Language.* Cambridge:
Cambridge University Press, 1972.

Seidel, Michael. *Robinson Crusoe: Island Myths and the Novel, Twayne's Master-
work Studies.* Boston: Twayne, 1991.

Seifert, Ruth. *War and Rape: Analytical Approaches.* Geneva: Women's International League for Peace and Freedom, 1993.

Seitel, Peter. "Theorizing Genres—Interpreting Works." *New Literary History* 34, no. 2 (2003): 275–97.

Sen, Amartya. *Development as Freedom.* New York: Oxford University Press,
1999.

Sengupta, Arjun. "On the Theory and Practice of the Right to Development."
Human Rights Quarterly 24 (2002): 837–889.

Shaffner, Randolph P. *The Apprenticeship Novel: A Study of The "Bildungsro-
man" as a Regulative Type in Western Literature with a Focus on Three Classic
Representatives by Goethe, Maugham, and Mann, Germanic Studies in America.
No. 48.* New York: P. Lang, 1984.

Shue, Henry. "Basic Rights: Subsistence, Affluence, and U.S." *Foreign Policy* 5
(1980).

SIDA, ed. *Whispering Land: An Anthology of Stories by African Women.* Stock-
holm: Swedish International Development Authority, 1985.

Simpson, John and Jana Bennett. *The Disappeared and the Mothers of the Plaza: The Story of the 11,000 Argentinians Who Vanished.* New York: St. Martin's Press, 1985.

Slaughter, Joseph R. "'A Mouth with Which to Tell the Story': Silence, Violence, and Speech in the Narrative of *Things Fall Apart.*" In *Emerging Perspectives on Chinua Achebe*, edited by Ernest N. Emenyonu, 121–49. Trenton, N.J.: Africa World Press, 2004.

———. "A Question of Narration: The Voice in International Human Rights Law." *Human Rights Quarterly* 19, no. 2 (1997): 406–30.

———. 2003. *Clef À Roman*: Some Uses of Human Rights and the *Bildungsroman*. In *Politics and Culture*, http://aspen.conncoll.edu/politicsandculture/page.cfm?key=244. (accessed May 29, 2006).

———. "Master Plans: Designing (National) Allegories of Urban Space and Metropolitan Subjects for Postcolonial Kenya." *Research in African Literatures* 35, no. 1 (2004): 30–51.

———. "One Track Minds: Markets, Madness, Metaphors, and Modernism in Postcolonial Nigerian Fiction." In *African Writers and Their Readers: Essays in Honor of Bernth Lindfors*, edited by Toyin Falola and Barbara Harlow, 55–89. Trenton, N.J.: Africa World Press, 2002.

———. 2004. The Textuality of Human Rights: Founding Narratives of Human Personality. In *2004 Interdisciplinary Law and Humanities Junior Scholar Workshop Papers*, SSRN, http://ssrn.com/abstract=582021 or DOI: 10.2139/ssrn.582021. (accessed May 29, 2006).

Slaughter, Joseph, and Jennifer Wenzel. "Letters of the Law: Women, Human Rights, and Epistolary Literature." In *Women, Gender, and Human Rights: A Global Perspective*, edited by Marjorie Agosín, 289–311. New Brunswick: Rutgers University Press, 2001.

Smith, John H. *The Spirit and Its Letter: Traces of Rhetoric in Hegel's Philosophy of Bildung.* Ithaca: Cornell University Press, 1988.

Smith, Patricia, ed. *Feminist Jurisprudence.* New York: Oxford University Press, 1993.

Soja, Edward W. *The Geography of Modernization in Kenya: A Spatial Analysis of Social, Economic, and Political Change, Syracuse Geographical Series.* Syracuse: Syracuse University Press, 1968.

Somers, Margaret R. "Narrativity, Narrative Identity, and Social Action: Rethinking English Working-Class Formation." *Social Science History* 16, no. 4 (1992): 591–630.

Sorel, Georges. *Reflections on Violence.* Translated by T. E. Hulme. New York: Collier Books, 1950.

South Africa. Commission for the Socio-Economic Development of the Bantu Areas, and D. Hobart Houghton. *The Tomlinson Report: A Summary of the Findings and Recommendations in the Tomlinson Commission Report.* Johannesburg: South African Institute of Race Relations, 1956.

Southern Rhodesia. Commission Appointed to Enquire into the Matter of
    Native Education in All its Bearings in the Colony of Southern Rhodesia.
    "Report of the Commission Appointed to Enquire into the Matter of Na-
    tive Education in All Its Bearings in the Colony of Southern Rhodesia."
    142. Salisbury: Government Printer, 1925.
Southern Rhodesia. Native Education Inquiry Commission. *Report of the Na-
    tive Education Inquiry Commission, 1951*. Bulawayo: Printed for the Govern-
    ment Printing and Stationery Dept. by the Rhodesian Printing and
    Publishing Co., 1952.
Soyinka, Wole. "Foreword." In *Universal Declaration of Human Rights*, v–vi.
    Ibadan: Institut Français de Recherche en Afrique, 1994.
Spivak, Gayatri Chakravorty. *Outside in the Teaching Machine*. New York:
    Routledge, 1993.
————. "Righting Wrongs." In *Human Rights, Human Wrongs: Oxford Am-
    nesty Lectures 2001*, edited by Nicholas Owen, 168–227. Oxford: Oxford
    University Press, 2003.
Staves, Susan. "'The Liberty of a She-Subject of England': Rights Rhetoric
    and the Female Thucydides." *Cardozo Studies in Law and Literature* 1, no. 2
    (1989): 161–183.
Stein, Peter. "Nineteenth Century English Company Law and Theories of
    Legal Personality." *Quaderni Fiorentini* 11/12, no. 1 (1982–83): 503–19.
Steinber, Sybil S. "Anil's Ghost." *Publishers Weekly* 247, no. 12 (2000): 70.
Stiglmayer, Alexandra, ed. *Mass Rape: The War against Women in Bosnia-Her-
    zegovina*. Lincoln: University of Nebraska Press, 1994.
Street, Brian V. *Social Literacies: Critical Approaches to Literacy in Development,
    Ethnography, and Education, Real Language Series*. London: Longman, 1995.
Swales, Martin. *The German Bildungsroman from Wieland to Hesse*. Princeton:
    Princeton University Press, 1978.
Talbott, John. *The War without a Name: France in Algeria, 1954–1962*. New
    York: Knopf, 1980.
Tamen, Miguel. *Friends of Interpretable Objects*. Cambridge, Mass.: Harvard
    University Press, 2001.
————. "Kinds of Persons, Kinds of Rights, Kinds of Bodies." *Cardozo Studies
    in Law and Literature* 10, no. 1 (1998): 1–32.
Taylor, Charles. *The Ethics of Authenticity*. Cambridge, Mass.: Harvard Univer-
    sity Press, 1992.
Tihanov, Galin. "The Ideology of *Bildung*: Lukács and Bakhtin as Readers of
    Goethe." *Oxford German Studies* 27 (1998): 102–40.
Tönnies, Ferdinand. *Community and Society (Gemeinschaft Und Gesellschaft)*.
    Translated by Charles P. Loomis. East Lansing: Michigan State University
    Press, 1957.

Trotsky, Leon. "On Lenin's Testament." In *The Suppressed Testament of Lenin; the Complete Original Text, with Two Explanatory Articles*, 8–41. New York: Pioneer, 1935.

Truth and Reconciliation Commission. *Truth and Reconciliation Commission of South Africa Report*. 7 vols. Vol. 1. New York: Macmillan, 1999.

———. *Truth and Reconciliation Commission of South Africa Report*. 7 vols. Vol. 6. Cape Town: Truth and Reconciliation Commission, 2003.

UNESCO. *Books for All: A Programme of Action*. Paris: UNESCO, 1974.

———. *Fundamental Education: Common Ground for All Peoples: Report of a Special Committee to the Preparatory Commission of the United Nations Educational, Scientific and Cultural Organization, Paris 1946*. New York: Macmillan, 1947.

———, ed. *Human Rights: Comments and Interpretations*. New York: Columbia University Press, 1949.

Unger, Roberto Mangabeira. *The Critical Legal Studies Movement*. Cambridge, Mass.: Harvard University Press, 1986.

United Nations. "Plenary Meetings of the General Assembly: Summary Records of Meetings 21 September–12 December." Paris: General Assembly, 1948.

———. "Third Session, Proceedings of the Third Social and Humanitarian Committee." Lake Success: Third Committee, 1948.

———. *Yearbook of the United Nations 1948*. New York: Office of Public Information, 1949.

United Nations Development Programme. *Human Development Report 1990*. New York: Oxford University Press, 1990.

United States. Dept. of State. Library. *International Relations Dictionary*. 2nd ed. Washington, D.C.: U. S. Government Printing Office, 1980.

Vargas Llosa, Mario. *The Storyteller*. Translated by Helen Lane. New York: Farrar, Straus and Giroux, 1989.

Vasak, Karel. "Pour une Troisième Génération des Droits de l'Homme." In *Essays on International Humanitarian Law and Red Cross Principles in Honour of Jean Pictet*, edited by C. Swinarski. The Hague: Martinus Nijhoff, 1984.

Vattimo, Gianni. "Library, Liberty." In *The Book: A World Transformed*, edited by Eduardo Portella and Rafael Argullol, 67–72. Paris: UNESCO Pub., 2001.

Verne, E. "Literacy and Industrialization: The Dispossession of Speech." In *Literacy and Social Development in the West: A Reader*, edited by Harvey J. Graff, 286–303. Cambridge: Cambridge University Press, 1981.

Viswanathan, Gauri. "An Introduction: Uncommon Genealogies." *Ariel: A Review of International English Literature* 31, no. 1/2 (2000): 13–31.

———. *Masks of Conquest: Literary Study and British Rule in India*. New York: Columbia University Press, 1989.

Volio, Fernando. "Legal Personality, Privacy, and the Family." In *The International Bill of Human Rights: The Covenant on Civil and Political Rights*, edited by Louis Henkin, 185–208. New York: Columbia University Press, 1981.

Vondung, Klaus. "Unity through *Bildung*: A German Dream of Perfection." *Independent Journal of Philosophy* 5/6 (1988): 47–55.

Wallerstein, Immanuel Maurice. *The Modern World-System: Capitalist Agriculture and the Origins of the European World-Economy in the Sixteenth Century, Studies in Social Discontinuity.* New York: Academic Press, 1974.

Wangari wa Nyatetū-Waigwa. *The Liminal Novel: Studies in the Francophone-African Novel as Bildungsroman, American University Studies. Series XVIII. African Literature 6.* New York: Peter Lang, 1996.

Waring, Wendy. "Is This Your Book? Wrapping Postcolonial Fiction for the Global Market." *Canadian Review of Comparative Literature/Revue Canadienne de Littérature Comparée* 22, no. 3/4 (1995): 455–65.

Warren, Samuel D., and Louis D. Brandeis. "The Right to Privacy." *Harvard Law Review* 4, no. 5 (1890).

Watt, Ian P. *The Rise of the Novel: Studies in Defoe, Richardson, and Fielding.* Berkeley: University of California Press, 1957.

Wells, H. G. *The Rights of Man; or, What Are We Fighting For?* Harmondsworth: Penguin Books, 1940.

Weschler, Lawrence. *A Miracle, a Universe: Settling Accounts with Torturers.* New York: Pantheon Books, 1990.

Weston, Burns H. "Human Rights." In *Human Rights in the World Community: Issues and Action*, edited by Richard Claude and Burns Weston. Philadelphia: University of Pennsylvania Press, 1992.

Weyrauch, Walter O. "On Definitions, Tautologies, and Ethnocentrism in Regard to Universal Human Rights." In *Human Rights*, edited by Ervin H. Pollack, 198–201. Buffalo: Jay Stewart Publications, 1971.

White, Hayden. *The Content of the Form: Narrative Discourse and Historical Representation.* Baltimore: John Hopkins University Press, 1987.

White, Leonard, William Thornton, L. Silberman, P. R. Anderson, and Nairobi (Kenya) City Council. *Nairobi: Master Plan for a Colonial Capital.* London: H. M. Stationery Office, 1948.

Williams, Raymond. *The Sociology of Culture.* New York: Schocken Books, 1982.

Williams, Robert R. *Hegel's Ethics of Recognition.* Berkeley: University of California Press, 1997.

Witte, W. "Alien Corn—the 'Bildungsroman': Not for Export?" *German Life and Letters* 33, no. 1 (1979): 87–96.

Wormser, I. Maurice. *Frankenstein, Incorporated.* New York: Whittlesey House McGraw-Hill, 1931.

Worsley, Peter. *The Three Worlds: Culture and World Development.* Chicago: University of Chicago Press, 1984.

Wyatt, Edward. "Wrenching Tale by an Afghan Immigrant Strikes a Chord." *Times*, December 15, 2004, 1+.

Zanzi, Abizer. 2002. Sri Lanka's Emergency Laws. In, India Seminar, http://www.india-seminar.com/2002/512/512%20abizer%20zanzi.htm. (accessed July, 2005).

Zeleza, Paul Tiyambe. *Rethinking Africa's Globalization*. Trenton, N.J.: Africa World Press, 2003.

Zobel, Joseph. *Black Shack Alley*. Translated by Keith Q. Warner. Washington, D.C.: Three Continents Press, 1980.

Zvobgo, R. J. *Colonialism and Education in Zimbabwe*. Harare: SAPES Books, 1994.

Zwicker, Heather. "The Nervous Collusions of Nation and Gender: Tsitsi Dangarembga's Challenge to Fanon." In *Negotiating the Postcolonial: Emerging Perspectives on Tsitsi Dangarembga*, edited by Ann Elizabeth Willey and Jeanette Treiber, 3–24. Trenton, N.J.: Africa World Press, 2002.